D1551797

The Cherokees and Christianity, 1794–1870

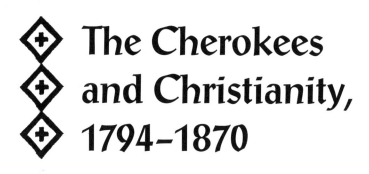

The Cherokees
and Christianity,
1794–1870

Essays on Acculturation
and Cultural Persistence

William G. McLoughlin

Edited by Walter H. Conser, Jr.

The University of Georgia Press

Athens and London

© 1994 by the University of Georgia Press
Athens, Georgia 30602
All rights reserved
Designed by Erin Kirk New
Set in Palatino by Tseng Information Systems, Inc.
Printed and bound by Thomson-Shore, Inc.
The paper in this book meets the guidelines for
permanence and durability of the Committee on
Production Guidelines for Book Longevity of the
Council on Library Resources.

Printed in the United States of America

98 97 96 95 94   C   5 4 3 2 1

Library of Congress Cataloging in Publication Data

McLoughlin, William Gerald.
The Cherokees and Christianity, 1794–1870 : essays on
acculturation and cultural persistence / William G. McLoughlin ;
edited by Walter H. Conser.
p.   cm.
Includes bibliographical references and index.
ISBN 0-8203-1639-3 (alk. paper)
1. Cherokee Indians—Missions.   2. Cherokee Indians—Religion and
mythology.   3. Cherokee Indians—Cultural assimilation.
4. Christianity—Southern States.   I. Conser, Walter H.   II. Title.
E99.C5M43   1994
299'.785—dc20   93-38460

British Library Cataloging in Publication Data available

*To all of Bill's students through the years,
graduate and undergraduate, those whom he
knew in courses and those whom he knew
in causes.*

—Virginia McLoughlin

Contents

Preface

With the publication of this volume, William G. Mc-Loughlin's scholarly analysis of the southeastern Indians extends over four major books and thirty articles. In his academic career as one of his generation's most distinguished historians of American religion, McLoughlin explored in prizewinning monographs such topics as modern revivalism, religious reform, and the separation of church and state in the United States. For the last twenty years of his career he focused on the Cherokee Indians and examined such themes as Christian missionary activity with the Cherokees, controversies over slaveholding among the Cherokees, and other aspects of the turbulent history of the Cherokee Nation. In these books on the Cherokees, as with his earlier works, McLoughlin was concerned to describe in rich detail the role of religion in these contexts and to assess its meaning and significance for an understanding of the larger American culture and society.

The essays that compose this volume explore the important theme of acculturation and cultural persistence within the Cherokee Nation. They demonstrate McLoughlin's continuing awareness of the complexity of that process, his comprehension of the multivalent functions of religion, and his sensitivity to the persistent challenges that Native American societies have faced in their engagement with the United States government. At the time of his death on December 28, 1992, William McLoughlin's manuscript for this volume was close to completion. With the agreement of his widow, Virginia McLoughlin, I undertook the final editing and preparation of the manuscript for publication. This editorial work consisted of clarifying minor discrepancies, eliminating repetitions among the essays, and incorporating Professor McLoughlin's most recent revisions into the text of various chapters. The result is a book that is a fine example of the scholarship and imagination of one who was an excellent historian, a respected teacher, and an outstanding human being.

Walter H. Conser, Jr.

Acknowledgments

Some of these essays were published under slightly different titles.

"The Missionaries' Dilemma," *Canadian Review of American Studies* 16 (4), Winter 1985: 395–409.

"Two Boston Missionaries," in *Massachusetts and the New Nation*, Conrad Edick Wright, ed. (Boston: Massachusetts Historical Society, 1992): 152–201.

"The Reverend Evan Jones and the Cherokee Trail of Tears, 1838–1839," *Georgia Historical Quarterly* 73 (3), Fall 1989: 559–83.

"Missionaries as Cultural Brokers," in *Between Indian and White Worlds: The Cultural Broker*, Margaret C. Szasz, ed. © 1994 by the University of Oklahoma Press.

"Christianity and Racism: Cherokee Responses to the Debate over Indian Origins, 1760–1860" (with Walter H. Conser, Jr.), *American Quarterly* 41, June 1989: 243–64. © 1989 by the American Studies Association.

"Fighting against Civilization: Ghost Dance Movements in Cherokee History," *Ethnohistory* 37 (1). © 1990 by Duke University Press.

The Cherokees and Christianity, 1794–1870

Introduction

But if the President of the white people should cease to protect us and our rights and rob us of our rights, then I say to you . . . bear like Job. Like Job may you be rewarded.—Chief John Ross to the Cherokees on the eve of Indian removal

This book is part of the long and complex concern of historians with the interaction between Christianity and culture. The people of the United States believed themselves to be "a Christian nation" in the nineteenth century, and even though they had constitutionally mandated a separation of church and state, they sought to impose their own form of evangelical Protestantism upon all who lived here. For them it was the one true religion; for Native Americans it was "the white man's religion" and had little, if any, concern for them. Yet over the years, as the two cultures interacted, the Indians came to find much that was useful and attractive in Christianity just as they did in many of the tools and functions of white society. How this process of acculturation worked is the theme of these essays.

The Cherokees stopped warring against the United States in 1794. By 1825 they were known as "the most civilized tribe in America." Despite the trauma of their removal to the West on the Trail of Tears in 1838, they managed to rebuild their social and political order, to prosper, and to become once again a showpiece of Indian acculturation. They had a constitution modeled on that of the United States; they elected a chief, vice-chief, and bicameral legislature; they had an effective judiciary with trial by jury; they had a free public school system with more than sixty schools whose teachers were trained in two Cherokee academies (all schools were by law conducted in English); they published a bilingual newspaper, the *Cherokee Advocate*, which kept them abreast of congressional affairs as well as of the efforts of their annual delegation to Washington, D.C.; and they had a prosperous economy based upon farming corn, wheat, cotton, and large herds of cattle and horses. Most Cherokees were farmers, but many were merchants, mill owners, salt manufacturers, hotel owners, storekeepers, blacksmiths, and skilled artisans.

Increasingly they practiced a form of Christianity that they had adapted to many of their own values and beliefs. God and the Great Spirit were one, and they believed that Adam, the first man, was red. Because God protected the weak against oppression, they claimed him as their savior against the whites who were trying to destroy their nation. They were also slaveholders, and during the Civil War the Nation divided between the Union and Confederacy. For many of the war years Cherokees fought against Cherokees and destroyed all they had so painfully rebuilt since their forced removal to the West.

These essays are more concerned with their "Christianization" than their "civilization." They examine the various stages of the Cherokees' cultural confrontation with Christian imperialism, which they saw at first as an effort to subvert their own true religion. Between 1794 and 1861, missionaries from six different denominations were welcomed into the Nation primarily because they promised to start schools for its children. The first five essays in this collection examine the reactions of the Cherokees (and to some extent, other southeastern tribes) to the inevitable clash between the missionaries and their own religious leaders. Because the people of the United States considered themselves "a Christian nation," the decision of Congress to remove the Indians from their ancient homelands led to a very negative reaction toward Christianity even though several of the missionaries to the Cherokees took great risks to help them in resisting it.

Because the Cherokees had adopted farming in the manner of their white neighbors, they adopted also the "peculiar institution" of black slave labor. They were surprised to find that not only were Christians split into a wide variety of Christian beliefs and practices but they also differed strongly over whether God ordained, condemned, or tolerated slavery of Africans. Several of the essays in part 1 address the Cherokee reactions to this dilemma. It is a measure of how acculturated the Cherokees had become by 1850 that they took sides on this issue, just as white people did, and fought against each other in the Civil War. They tried in vain to maintain neutrality in what they liked to call "the white man's civil war."

The essays in part 2 start by examining the crucial problem of racism that divided the southern part of North America into red, white, and black long before 1776. But the main thrust of this section of the book concerns the ways in which the Cherokees either adapted Christianity to their own needs or rejected it as inimical to their identity. As in the United States, it proved impossible from 1830 to 1860 to separate religion from politics.

A short epilogue contains the Fast Day Proclamation by the full-blood chief of the Cherokees in 1870, a document that clearly indicates how far the "Christianization" of the Nation had come by that time.

It is my hope that the combined effect of these essays will provide new and constructive insights into the continuing reexamination of the place of Native Americans (and African Americans) in the United States, for we have, since 1776, been a multiracial country—even when we spoke of it as "a white man's country." Because each of the essays stands alone, they can be read separately; because each is concerned with different facets of the same issue ("Christianization"), their impact is cumulative. The reader will soon come to see why it is so important to put the term "Christianization" in quotation marks.

There is no easy way to sum up the complexity of the Cherokees' experiences with what they at first called "the white man's religion," in the days when they thought it had nothing to teach them. Their story, like that of other Native American people, is ongoing. As Christianity changes its emphasis from one century to another, so do the people who claim it as their own, and vice versa.

Part I
The Missionaries

Chapter 1
Native American Reactions to Christian Missions

Because there were more than three hundred Native American tribes, each with its own culture and religion, it is impossible to generalize about how "the" Indian reacted to Christianity. Historians have therefore tended to choose specific tribes as examples of different kinds of reactions. Although this essay starts with a brief overview of some of the different ways in which different tribes have reacted since 1492 (some putting missionaries to death, others seeming to embrace them), it concentrates on the Cherokees. The Cherokees are of particular importance because they were called "the most civilized tribe in America" and many whites considered them exemplary of the successful "Christianization" and "civilization" that all tribes ought to follow.

As this essay indicates, the Cherokees were far from united in their reactions to the missionaries. They soon learned to discriminate among the many varieties of Protestantism that prevailed in the United States. Some Cherokees rejected Christianity entirely (generally the full-bloods); others (generally those of mixed Indian-white ancestry) were inclined to adopt it as they adopted farming in place of hunting. But there was no single or simple reason for adopting or rejecting Christianity. This essay indicates which missionary styles were most successful and why "Christianization" may have been more successful with the Cherokees than with other tribes.

By 1861 some missionaries believed that the Cherokee Nation was as "Christian" as the white frontier communities around them (perhaps more so, considering how violent and lawless many frontier settlements were). Yet, underneath an outward Christian veneer, the Cherokees retained a great deal of their traditional religious outlook.

If the Indians had tried to make the whites live like them, the whites would have resisted, and it was the same way with many Indians.—Big Elk of the Santee Sioux

Native American reactions to Christian missionaries were as varied as the number of Indian tribes and usually differed even within the same tribe. Some tribes rose up and murdered the missionaries among them; some Indians embraced them and their religion. Most tribes were initially tolerant, curious, and bemused by the strange ideas the missionaries preached. After more familiarity with Christianity, some were drawn to aspects of it that seemed helpful and compatible but rejected those aspects that were strange or disturbing. Eventually, as Robert K. Berkhofer has noted, almost every tribe became divided into a Christian and a pagan faction.[1] Some tribes were able to adapt Christianity to their needs and even to create a new, syncretic religion that combined some traditional ways with new Christian beliefs.[2] Other tribes who followed ghost dance prophets simply appropriated God and Jesus to themselves and looked for a premillennial apocalypse that would eliminate the ruthless white man and enable "God's favorite people" to return to their former way of life.[3]

The most violent reactions against the spiritual invasion of the Europeans were taken against those who utilized military power to impose a totally new religious system overnight. This pattern predominated in the Spanish invasions of what is now Arizona and New Mexico. On several occasions the conquered Pueblo Indians rebelled and after bloody battles drove the Spanish and their missionaries out. This happened in 1598, in 1680, and again in 1695. In each of these uprisings, Catholic missionaries were killed along with royal governors, administrators, soldiers, and civilians. In the great Pueblo rebellion of 1680, twenty-one out of thirty-three missionaries in the area were killed; then the Indians burned the mission churches along with the soldiers' presidio and the governor's hacienda. Pueblo anticlericalism was generated by the close link between the church and the state; Catholic missionaries utilized the soldiers to whip and torture those who refused to accept the new official religion.[4]

Death also came to Jesuit missionaries of the French empire in

America when they went to live among the Hurons, identified with their culture and chiefs, and then were captured by the traditional enemies of the Hurons in the 1630s. The Iroquois, after defeating the Hurons, tortured to death four Jesuits; that ended the French efforts to Christianize the Hurons.[5]

The only Protestant missionaries known to have been murdered in what is now the United States were killed in 1847. A group of Congregationalists led by the Reverend Marcus Whitman founded the Waiilatpu mission in the Walla Walla Valley in Oregon. It included a school that was attended by children of the Cayuse tribe. The Cayuses, like other tribes in Oregon, had suffered greatly from the influx of thousands of whites invading along the Oregon Trail—especially from the ravages of the new diseases that the whites brought with them. In most Native American cultures diseases were considered the product of malevolent spirits, particularly witches. When a number of Cayuse children caught measles at the Waiilatpu mission school and brought the disease back into the tribe, the medicine men concluded that the missionaries were using witchcraft to decimate them. Cayuse warriors attacked the missions, killing Whitman, his wife, and twelve others. The United States government used this incident to launch an all-out war against all the tribes in Oregon and clear the area for white settlement.[6]

The absence of missionary deaths in the English colonies in the United States is attributable chiefly to the general lack of concern over Christianization of the Indians in the colonial era. The most famous colonial mission effort was the Reverend John Eliot's establishment of a series of communities (called "praying towns") in Massachusetts after 1651. The inhabitants of these towns were the remnants of the conquered Nipmuc, Pennacook, and Massachusetts tribes who voluntarily committed themselves to becoming civilized and Christianized. Eliot's experiment ended badly in 1675 with the outbreak of King Philip's War in New England. The Puritan population feared that even Christian Indians could not be trusted. Some of them did run off to join King Philip, but most were herded into stockades on an island in Boston Harbor. The praying towns never reopened.[7]

Warfare was the common relationship of the Indians to the English in the colonial era when the eastern coast was our first frontier. By 1794, after the Battle of Fallen Timbers, the Mississippi Valley seemed safe for settlement on our second frontier. As thousands of white settlers poured into the valley, the first concerted missionary movement began to civilize both the frontiersmen and the Indians, now called "the children of the forest," part of the romantic mode of nineteenth-century American thought.

Indian religions, as James Axtell has noted, were generally inclusivist and not exclusivist.[8] That is, they were always willing to add new religious experiences or visions (including the sacred stories and prophecies of other tribes) to their religion. By 1800 many aspects of African and Christian religious ideology were appearing in Indian oral tradition. Native Americans were generally willing to listen to the first missionaries to see what they could learn from them. After all, these white shamans represented a culture that had made tremendous discoveries in technology, and they seemed to have access to great spiritual power on behalf of their people. Many Indians believed that all the wisdom of white civilization was included in its "Great Book," the Bible, which the missionaries always held up as the source of all the important wisdom of their culture. When part of the Great Book was first translated to a Cherokee chief named Yonaguska, he said, "It seems to be a good book; strange that the white people are not better after having had it so long."[9] But the more they heard about the confusing doctrines of Calvinism and Anglicanism, the less interested the Indians became. For example, after hearing a Calvinist minister preach on the fall of Adam and Eve and the innate depravity of all human beings ever since, a Cherokee woman said, "What a pity that all men were not made good from the beginning."[10] And when told of the crucifixion of Christ, the Indians asked, "Why did you kill your God?" Or, as another Cherokee said, "Why did God not make man holy? . . . Why did he let Satan tempt Eve?" After a Presbyterian minister had visited them many times and harangued them about the famous five points of Calvinism, a group of Cherokee chiefs told their British agent that they were tired of listening to him: tell him to go away and stop bothering us, they said, "he has too long plagued us with what we cannot understand."[11]

Another common reaction to Christianity was typified by a woman who, having listened for some time to a missionary explaining the proper form of behavior for all human beings, said it seemed bizarre and alien to her. "It was her belief," she told the missionary, "that the Cherokees were an entirely different race of people from whites and that a religion for the whites was not intended for the Cherokees."[12]

Another woman told a missionary "that there was nothing in [the Christian] religion, at least, that Indians would get to heaven without it and that Christianity was necessary for white people only."[13] The Indians had their own view of an afterlife, but it did not include whites. When a Cherokee priest slipped into a mission school dormitory at night, he told the students that he had recently died and gone to heaven, where he saw many old friends, relatives, and chiefs "but had met no white people there."[14]

Faced with increasing pressure to become like the white man in thought and behavior, the Indian tribes became cultural relativists, while the missionaries remained convinced that there was only one true ideology and lifestyle for all human beings. The Indians' position was clearly stated by the famous Seneca chief Red Jacket in 1805, after listening to a Presbyterian preacher:

> Brother, you say there is but one way to worship and serve the Great Spirit. If there is but one Religion, why do you white people differ so much about it? Why not all agree, as you can all view the [same] book? Brother, we do not understand these things. We are told your Religion was given to your forefathers and has been handed down from father to son. We also have a Religion that was given us and we worship accordingly. It teaches us to be thankful for all the favors we receive, to love each other and be united. We never quarrel about religion as you whites do. The Great Spirit has made us all, but he has made a difference between his red and white children. He has given us different complexions and different customs. To you he has discovered the [mechanical] arts; to us they have been kept out of sight . . . and since he has made us different in other respects, why may we not conclude that he has given us a different religion according to our understanding. The Great Spirit does right. He knows what is best for [each of] his [different] children.[15]

Cultural pluralism, as the Indians defined it, also included polygenesis—the idea, considered heresy by Christians, that God created more original human beings than Adam and Eve. Many tribes developed what they said were ancient myths describing how the Great Spirit had originally made three different kinds of men, one red, one black, and one white. The red man was his favorite, so he placed him on the American continent; the white one he placed in Europe; the black man, in Africa. To the white man he gave the Great Book, which he used to learn technology; to the red man he gave bows and arrows with which to hunt; to the African he gave hoes and axes to be used for agriculture. Trouble and disorder came into the world when the white man left the place God intended for him, went first to Africa in big ships and captured black men, and then brought them into the Indians' continent, enslaving the blacks and trying to steal the Indians' lands.[16]

But polygenesis played into the hands of white racists, who soon developed a theory of racial hierarchy with the white man at the top and the black man at the bottom. To protect at least their intermediate status, the southeastern American Indians had to differentiate themselves from Africans, as their white conquerors did, or else fall into the category of "colored" people.[17] Initially the Indians were not racist. If anything, they thought that blacks would be valuable friends who knew things they did not know—agricultural skills, military skills, and, above all, English language and attitudes. Consequently they welcomed runaway slaves, adopted them, intermarried with them, and gave them positions of influence. This was especially true among the Seminoles in Florida. But it soon became evident that befriending runaway slaves caused friction with the white slaveholders around them. Gradually the southeastern Indians slipped into the practice of chattel slavery themselves as part of their acculturation to southern white civilization. The combination of polygenesis, Christian theology, and racism that emerged among slaveholding Indians is evident in the following "ancient" myth of creation told to a missionary by a Shawnee:

In the beginning the Great Spirit created three men and placed them in a state of trial, forbidding them to eat of the fruit of a certain tree. But in the absence of their Creator, they made an examination and concluded that the fruit was good. Accordingly they took, each of them, an apple. But one of them put his into his pocket untasted. Another did the same after eating [only] a piece of his. The third devoured his entire[ly]. When the Great Spirit came back, he perceived that the apples were gone and became displeased. "Did I not tell you," says he, "not to eat of that fruit?" Whereupon the [first] one took his apple from his pocket [uneaten]. Unto him the Great Spirit said, "I give you the bible and knowledge of letters to guide you in the troubles you will fall into." Then the other took out his [apple] partly eaten. For his disobedience the Great Spirit changed the color of his skin [to red] and gave him His law in his heart only. The third, because of his having devoured the whole of his [apple], was blacked all over and left without moral obligation [or moral understanding].[18]

At the outset of missionary activity, when Europeans first met the Native Americans, they were astonished to discover that the Indians considered their way of life far superior to that of the whites. James Axtell, in his fine study of seventeenth-century Christian missions, *The Invasion Within*, writes that a major obstacle to missions "was the disconcerting belief of the natives in their own superiority" and that of their culture. "The Indians could not imagine a better life than their own. Like their Christian adversaries, they too believed that the supreme being had made them 'the best people in the world' and given them 'the best country' for their inheritance."[19] It was not easy to dissuade them of this, for the religious system of every tribe was the sophisticated product of centuries of experience during which the Native Americans had worked out a comprehensive, satisfying, and effective understanding of the proper relationship of man, nature, and the supernatural. Their religions suited their environment and their way of life perfectly and explained all that needed to be explained. Their religious rites and ceremonies also gave them some control over any forces of nature that threatened to disrupt their lives. They knew that the spirit world was basically benevolent, that the earth provided them with vegetables, the animals sacrificed themselves for their meat, the flowers and herbs provided cures for their illnesses or wounds. If they thanked the gods for their harvest; if they kept themselves in a proper frame of cooperation, communal responsibility, and friend-ship through their annual purification rites and forgiveness of hard feelings; and if they performed proper dances or ceremonies to bring rain or avert pestilence, then the world would remain orderly and its people would be in harmony with one another and with the natural and supernatural spirits of the universe. From birth, Indian children learned these sacred myths, histories, and dances and participated in the tribal ceremonies that kept the evil spirits of the underworld at bay. Harmony was the highest ideal, for it was necessary in all spheres of life. Indian religions were corporate religions; everyone was responsible for participating in all aspects of them for the good of the whole.[20]

The three great stumbling blocks in accepting Christianity were its failure to address the basic issues of corporate harmony, bountiful harvests, and sacred healing. Christianity was an individual effort to get right with a strict God who would hold each individual respon-sible for his own soul and would help that individual who had faith in him to compete successfully in making his own fortune against the competition of his fellow beings. Christianity, in its American form, was based on a competitive, materialistic, aggressive ethic completely at odds with everything in the corporate, communal religion of the Indians. Christianity also held that native medicine was evil and must not be utilized to cure the sick because it invoked pagan spirits. However, missionaries were seldom doctors and provided no other source of medical care. American Christians had made healing a secular aspect of their lives, separating it from its spiritual component. Christianity was dualistic—dividing body and soul, heaven and earth, sacred and secular. Indian religion was transcendental, mystical, monistic. Christianity provided no control over harvests except "scientific" farming, a system that required not only special knowledge but also heavy financial investment and constant labor. Natural disasters were accepted as "God's will." Most important, the Christian way of life totally disrupted the familial structure and the prescribed roles of male and female in Indian life. Christians scorned the communal farms in which women and children cultivated the fields while the men were hunters and warriors. Nor did they think women should have a voice in tribal councils. Women were to work in the house while men tilled the field, and communal property was to be abandoned for private ownership of property. Under Christianity the tribal granaries that provided public relief when harvests failed would cease to exist; the hospitality ethic would be abandoned; every family would be on its own to thrive or starve. Furthermore, the exogamous marriages based upon clan affiliation, the matrilineal control of the home and children, and the reliance upon maternal uncles to care for the children would all have to be given up, and the husband would be the sole authority and provider. In short, into every aspect of Indian spiritual and daily life the missionaries brought disorder and disharmony.

It is not surprising, therefore, that Christianity made virtually no impact in tribes that were sufficiently strong, autonomous, and healthy to pursue their own way of life. Every scholar of Indian missions has confirmed the view that Christianity succeeded only when a tribe had lost its autonomous ability to control its affairs either through military conquest, or by losing its hunting grounds to white settlers, or by removal from its homeland to some barren reserve, or by the ravages of epidemics for which it had no immunity. But once a tribe reached this state of cultural disorientation and dysfunction, Christianity did have something important to offer. Christianity is a religion of hope, of miracles, of divine support for the weak and oppressed. When a tribe had reached the point of despair, Christianity provided a way out. It offered spiritual power for personal and tribal revitalization on new principles. It made God's power available to Indians, not only to the white man.

But the first missionaries to the slowly disintegrating tribes had to prove that they had this power and that their system of religion could really improve the life of, and restore harmony to, these outcasts. The Indians proved astute in the questions they asked about Christianity, and sometimes they were derisive in taunting the power claimed by the missionaries. "Can any white man catch thunder?" they asked. "Can any white man catch lightning? Can any white man catch the wind?" Or in theology they asked, "Who made the Savior?" "Why didn't God make all men good?"[21] They wanted to know why God had allowed evil to enter the world. "If you had an orchard, and you told your children they might go into it and eat of the fruit of every tree but one, you would be very careful no wicked man should go and tell your children they might disobey you."[22] Yet God was unable to keep Satan out of the Garden of Eden.

Was the medicine of Christians more effective than their own medicine? This had to be demonstrated. Was their explanation of the role of the sun and the moon in controlling human life verifiable? As one missionary noted, "The Cherokees are peculiarly inquisitive, and although they discover much grandeur in the work of God, yet the book of nature is to them in many respects sealed. And a minister not well versed in Geography, Natural Philosophy, Astronomy, and mathematics generally labours under many great disadvantages among them. . . . [A] complete knowledge of these subjects is necessary in order to explain them to the understanding of the Indians."[23] The Indians knew that religion was more than simply the saving of individual souls. They were aware of the superior knowledge of the Euro-Americans in technology. But they were not so sure about their superior knowledge of nature and the supernatural. How could the white man prove that the world was round and the earth went around the sun when human experience seemed to prove the opposite?

Many tribes at first welcomed the white missionaries because they wanted them to teach all of the secrets contained in the Great Book, for once the Indians knew these, they could compete with white men on equal terms and perhaps restore and strengthen their own way of life. As one old Cherokee chief said when he welcomed the first missionary to the Nation in 1799, "I believe you have been inspired by the Great Spirit to come here . . . [in order to share] the Great Book from which [the Cherokees] can learn all things."[24] It took some time before the Indians realized that the Bible was only a spiritual and not a scientific guide to the white man's power over the universe.

Historians differ as to whether the white man's (especially the missionaries') prejudices against the Indians were basically racist or ethnocentric—did white people feel that Indians were by nature inferior or only that, though they were far behind the Euro-Americans in the march of human progress, they were capable of catching up? The first Indian policy adopted by the United States in 1789 accepted the view that all men are created biologically equal (or as Jefferson put it, "I believe the Indian is the equal of the European in mind and body").[25] President Washington adopted the policy that held that, with Christianization and education, the Indians would within half a century be able to catch up with other Americans and become equal citizens of the new republic. Professor Michael Coleman has defended the claim that the missionaries as a whole were never racists.[26] Others, like George Fredrickson, have noted that not until the 1830s did Western scientists move from the environmental theory of the geographical or climatic (but superficial) causes of racial differentiation to the view that there was a clear and ineradicable hierarchy of human races with the African and the Indian close to the bottom and the Anglo-Saxon Caucasian at the top.[27] Because most Protestant missionaries relied on revelation for their view of anthropology, and because the Bible says that all human beings are descendants of the same parents and "God has made of one blood all nations," Coleman argues that the missionaries never adopted the theory of racial hierarchy. Nonetheless, it is certain that many missionaries to the southern Indians owned black slaves and said that God had cursed Ham and ordained the institution of slavery; and certainly most frontier whites believed that "you can't civilize an Indian," "once an Indian, always an Indian." But even if we choose to call it ethnocentrism, it seems clear that many missionaries took a very dim view of the potential of the Indian to overcome his inveterate bad habits and customs.

A detailed discussion of Native American reactions to missionaries for more than five hundred years and among more than three hundred tribes would take a large volume. However, the variations within one tribe during the period from 1800 to 1860 may serve as a useful case study. The records of the Cherokee people provide examples of many reactions typical of the eastern woodland tribes in that period. However, the Cherokees were in some respects atypical; first, by 1830, 25 percent of them were descendants of mixed white-Indian ancestry, which meant that they had a decided edge over other tribes in leaning toward acculturation after their final defeat in 1794. Second, because they adopted the institution of black chattel slavery (as did other southeastern tribes), they were a multiracial mirror of white society (Indian, white, and black). Third, their rapid acculturation between 1794 and 1830 won them, correctly enough, the title of "the most civilized tribe in America." Nonetheless, three-quarters of the Cherokee people were full-bloods and traditionalists; their resistance to missionaries was as strong and persistent as that in any tribe. Furthermore, with five different missionary societies at work in a tribe of more than fifteen thousand, a wide variety of missionary styles was practiced within their twelve-thousand-mile tract. All the missionaries to the Cherokees were evangelical Protestants, but in a predominantly Protestant country that claimed to be at that time "a Christian nation," they were probably representative of the missionary enterprise in the United States throughout the nineteenth century.

Although the Cherokees never murdered a missionary, they did threaten to do so; they also intimidated them and occasionally stoned both missionaries and their converts. At the other end of the spectrum, however, many Cherokees came to admire and respect the missionaries, and by 1860 about 12 percent of the Nation claimed membership in one or another of the five Protestant denominations among them. In between intimidating and joining the Christians were a variety of other reactions from ghost dance movements to antimissionary rebellions, from joining and then apostatizing to practicing both the old and the new ways at the same time. Consequently, this case study can produce a fairly accurate portrait of Native American reactions to the missionaries.

In 1805 when the missionary effort was just starting, the bulk of the Cherokees had little interest in Christianity or education. As the federal agent, Return J. Meigs, wrote to the secretary of war in 1805, "Many Cherokees think that they are not derived from the same stock as the white, that they are the favorites of the great spirit, and that he never intended they should live the laborious life of the whites." [28] However, by 1819 many Cherokees had discovered much that was beneficial in the missionary enterprise. An aged chief named Path-killer, a full-blood who neither spoke nor read English and who never became a convert, told some missionaries in 1819, "I cannot keep from weeping when I see what [you] good people are doing for us." One missionary reported, "[This chief] is telling his people wherever he goes that schools are very good for them, and they must keep their children in school until their teachers say they have learned enough." [29] Another chief, who came to a mission school to speak to the students at about the same time, told them, "Remember, the whites are near to us. With them we have constant intercourse, and you must be sensible that unless you can speak their language, read, and write, as they do, they will be able to cheat you and trample on your rights." [30]

But although schools were popular, most Cherokees strongly objected to missionary preaching, for it was obviously a spiritual assault upon their most sacred beliefs and practices. When the Moravians, the first missionary group to enter the Nation, arrived in 1799 and asked for land on which to build a permanent mission station, they told the assembled chiefs that they wished to bring them the good news of the gospel. The chiefs flatly rejected their request, saying, "We have no ears to hear it." [31] It took much lobbying by the federal agent before the tribe relented and agreed to give the Moravians a trial for three years on the promise that by that time they would have started a free boarding school for any children who wished to attend. The chiefs considered it "an experiment" only. [32] However, the Moravians expected to make some converts immediately, who would then settle with them at the mission enclave, and their children would be the ones who would enter the school. When at the end of three years they had made no converts and therefore had opened no school, the chiefs concluded that the experiment was a failure and ordered the Moravians to pack up and leave. The federal agent had no choice but to enforce their decision, but he had already told the Moravians that they were mistaken to put Christianization before education. [33]

At the very time that the council voted to expel the Moravians, a Presbyterian minister from Tennessee, Gideon Blackburn, came before the chiefs and offered to start four schools. He said he would not do any preaching. The council approved his offer. He did start two schools but never got up to four for lack of funds. His schools were located in that part of the Nation within Tennessee that contained a very high proportion of Cherokees of mixed ancestry—some with white fathers, many with white grandfathers. When white men married Cherokees, they brought their children up to speak English, and they wanted them to behave like white men and women. It did not bother the mixed-blood parents that Blackburn ran his schools as Presbyterian parochial schools—requiring prayers morning and night and grace at all meals; teaching students the Presbyterian catechism and having them memorize Bible verses; making them sing gospel hymns and attend religious services on Sundays; teaching them to pray and consider conversion. He also taught them table manners, gave them an American diet, dressed them as whites, and forbade them to participate in any native sports or religious activities. This regimen did not sit well with full-blood parents, however, and because Blackburn's schools were taught in English, few full-bloods remained long in them.[34]

Blackburn, however, came to a bad end. He meddled in politics, and it was his undoing. First of all he urged the Cherokee mixed-bloods to push laws through the council that would Christianize the Nation—laws to outlaw polygamy, birth control, and matrilineal inheritance, and laws to enforce Christian marriage, paternalism in the home, and the observance of the Sabbath. He boasted in some of his appeals for funds that he was single-handedly turning the Cherokees into a Christian tribe.[35] However, his real downfall came in 1809 when he undertook a secret mission for the federal government from which he sought to profit in two ways: first, he would sell whiskey (which he made in his own distillery in Maryland, Tennessee), and second, he would persuade the government to give him a large tract of Cherokee land for his own use. Through conversations with the secretary of war, Blackburn learned that the government was eager to explore the navigable waterways between Tennessee and the Gulf of Mexico, and he agreed to undertake this. He hired a boat, put his brother in charge, loaded twenty-two hundred gallons of whiskey on board, and told everyone he was undertaking a business venture to sell whiskey in Mobile. The boat left Maryville, sailed down the Connesauga and Coosa Rivers through the Cherokee Nation, and then entered the Creek Nation heading for the Alabama River, which emptied into the Gulf of Mexico. His boat had no sooner entered the Creek Nation than its chief, Big Warrior, stopped the vessel and confiscated its cargo for breaking the federal law prohibiting the sale of spirituous liquor to the Indians. Blackburn's crew had evidently been peddling whiskey as they went along, figuring they would have plenty left when they got to Mobile. The more people investigated Blackburn's whiskey trip, the more they discovered about his secret mission for the government. None of the tribes wanted white bargemen going back and forth through their countries causing trouble and coveting their well-cultivated land along the riverbanks. Soon the whole story was out and Blackburn's reputation ruined. As another missionary wrote, "Even in this land where, in truth, very little Gospel light has appeared, the opponents [of the Gospel] have received a reason for slander. In fact, Mr. Blackburn undertook a journey through the land principally to reconnoiter the waterways here as far as the Bay of Mobile. . . . [He] purchased a large quantity of whiskey in order to trade with . . . on their journey. . . . [T]he disgrace of this venture falls in large part on religion."[36] Even the desire to educate their children could not lead mixed-bloods to tolerate missionary efforts to undermine the sovereignty of their nation. They withdrew their children from Blackburn's schools, and they soon closed.

The most prestigious and well-financed missionary agency to seek entry into the Cherokee Nation was the American Board of Commissioners for Foreign Missions. Though ostensibly interdenominational, it was essentially a Congregational organization run from Boston. In 1816 this agency sent the Reverend Cyrus Kingsbury to speak to the Cherokee council about starting mission stations and schools. Having lost Blackburn's schools, the Nation was ready to entertain the American Board's offer. In 1818 the first Congregational mission was started at Chickamauga, Tennessee. The American Board believed that civilization and Christianization should proceed together, so it combined its school with a model farm. In the morning the students learned the three Rs; in the afternoon the boys worked in the fields and barns, the girls in the households of the women missionaries. The object was to train the boys to be farmers and the girls to be farmers' wives. As in Blackburn's schools, the Christian religion (of a Calvinist variety) was deeply embedded in the curriculum and daily life.[37] Classes were taught in English, and the majority of the students were of mixed ancestry. By 1830 the Congregationalists had established ten mission stations, most of them with schools and mission churches.

The Congregationalists also meddled in politics, but they had the good sense to do so on behalf of the Cherokees. In 1819 the federal government was desperately trying to force the Cherokees to move west of the Mississippi. Secretary of War John C. Calhoun told the Cherokees they had only two choices, move west or lose their tribal status and be incorporated as individual citizens in the various states in which they lived. Partly out of self-interest (having invested large sums in their Cherokee activities), the Congregationalists sent a delegate from Boston to Washington to lobby with Calhoun on behalf of allowing the Cherokees to retain their land as a tribe. Calhoun finally agreed, but only after exacting the sale of fifty-five hundred square miles of Cherokee land from the tribe. The Cherokee chiefs expressed tremendous gratitude to "their friends at the north" for this timely assistance.[38] Seldom had a prominent white organization come to the defense of any tribe against the will of the federal government.

But while this created good feelings toward the Congregationalists, it did not prevent considerable friction among the full-bloods as the Congregationalists expanded their operation and began to send itinerant preachers around the Nation to challenge the traditionalists in its local communities. This itinerant evangelism produced a series of internal conflicts as zealous missionaries set out to destroy the influence of the native priests and medicine men (called *adonisgi* by the Cherokees). By 1825 the whole Nation was divided into bitterly opposing factions, the Christian and the traditionalist. Furthermore, while some Cherokees joined the Congregational mission churches, they were dismayed to find that more than the salvation of their own souls was at stake. Their missionary pastors adamantly refused to permit them to participate in any tribal ceremony—not their harvest thanksgiving, not their rainmaking ceremonies, not their traditional sports contest, and not even their medical practices. The missionary letters are filled with stories of these conflicts.

In 1824, in the missionary station called Carmel, a poor Cherokee named Pritchett came to the door of the Congregational missionary, the Reverend Moody Hall, and asked for food, lodging, and clothing. According to the hospitality ethic of the Cherokees, it was a fundamental social obligation to give help to the needy or to any traveler passing through. But Parson Hall unceremoniously turned Pritchett away, calling him a lazy beggar (as one might do in Massachusetts). Pritchett, who had heard Hall preach about Christ's command to feed the hungry, house the homeless, and clothe the naked, returned to

Hall's home a few days later; this time he appeared at the door without a stitch of clothing. When the missionary tried to force him out of the house, Pritchett denounced him as a hypocrite, pulled a knife from behind his back, and swung the knife at Hall and his wife. Others managed to disarm Pritchett, but Hall and his wife fled from the mission the next day and never returned. He lost the respect of his converts, whom he had repeatedly told to be brave in the face of opposition when taking their stand for Christianity.[39]

In another incident, eight local chiefs in the town of Etowah demanded that the Congregational missionary, the Reverend Isaac Proctor, be removed from their town because he was dividing the people. Proctor had told his followers they could not participate in the town council meetings because this required participation in various rituals. In addition, he preached that Christians were superior to pagans, and, because some black slaves, owned by the chiefs, were members of his congregation, these slaves had become unruly, refusing to serve their pagan masters because as Christians they were now superior to them in the eyes of God. Furthermore, the Christian converts at Proctor's church sang songs that taunted the traditionalists, songs with such refrains as "You will die, you will die." They meant that the pagans would roast in eternal hellfire, but some of them took it as a death threat. The tribal chief, Charles Hicks, himself a mixed-blood convert to Christianity, tried to smooth over these difficulties in Etowah, but in the end, the traditionalists made life so miserable for Proctor that he left.[40]

A third, and more serious, conflict arose in the town of Taloney in 1827. The Congregational missionary had aroused the righteous zeal of some of his converts by his denunciation of the ungodly rituals and ceremonies that took place at the town council house. A few of the more zealous converts decided to take action and proceeded to burn the council house to the ground. The traditionalists threatened to respond by burning down the mission school that was used for Sunday services. Again, the tribal chiefs calmed the traditionalists down, but the two factions were by no means reconciled.[41] Christians would not participate in the annual purification ceremony in which old quarrels and bad feelings were forgiven and forgotten.

The most difficult conflicts between missionaries and Cherokees who were trying to come to terms with Christianity involved the debate over medical care. The missionaries commonly referred to the

Cherokee medicine men as "conjurers" or "sorceresses" who engaged in charlatanism and trickery. As noted above, the Cherokees did not separate their spiritual and medical beliefs any more than they separated their political life and their religious ceremonies. But the missionaries insisted on this. As one missionary advised an *adonisgi*, "I told her it was very good for her to administer medicine to the sick, but it was not good to use the art of conjuring [to invoke spiritual aid in the process]."[42] However, no medical healing could take place without the invocation of the spiritual beings whose power controlled healing. Many converts tried secretly to resort to traditional medicine, but if they were found out, the missionary called them publicly before the church and the other members to censure or expel them for their heathen practices. This form of public humiliation rankled deeply among a people for whom community respect was essential. In one case a Cherokee told his missionary pastor that his son was extremely sick and he wanted to take him to an *adonisgi* for treatment. The missionary sternly forbade it. At the next church meeting, the father brought his son with him. "He held out to me the arm of his little boy," the missionary wrote later; "[it was] almost covered with sores." The father said angrily, "There, those may be there till he dies. I shall not doctor them." When the church members saw this, they were outraged at the missionary, who reported to his board, "The whole church forsook me."[43]

One missionary reported that when he forbade his converts to attend a rainmaking ceremony during a severe drought, his church members "concluded to leave the service of God and turn back to their old ways." The missionary could offer no way to save their crops. One departing church member shouted at the pastor that in his opinion "the service of Satan [was] as sweet as the service of God."[44] Mission statistics show that as many as 50 percent of those converted were either expelled or voluntarily abandoned Christianity.

As tensions in the Cherokee Nation heightened in the 1820s, the local chiefs and *adonisgi* did all they could to promote resistance to the invasion of itinerant missionaries, especially after the Methodists and Baptists joined the missionary work in the Nation. One missionary reported, "They threatened to whip me if I returned [and] throw me in the river."[45] A native convert, licensed to exhort, was told by a local chief that he would put out his eyes if he returned. Stones were thrown at the homes of those who invited an itinerant evangelist to preach. One missionary who had distributed tracts and hymn books on a previous visit returned to find that the local chief had confiscated and publicly burned them all. In some cases husbands beat their wives and their slaves for trying to attend preaching services.[46] Truly the missionary movement brought not peace but a sword to the Cherokees.

These localized resistance efforts sometimes swelled into large-scale national resistance. The first such nationwide effort to throw off the white man's endeavor to Christianize and civilize them occurred in 1811–12 when a number of Cherokees had visions and heard voices from the Great Spirit urging them to give up their new ways and return to their old ones.[47] The federal agent reported in 1812,

> [The Cherokees] are at this time in a remarkable manner . . . endeavoring to appease the Anger of the Great Spirit. . . . They have revived their religious dances of ancient origin with as much apparent solemnity as ever was seen in worship in our churches. . . . Among them are some fanatics [and prophets] who tell them that the Great Spirit is angry with them for adopting the manners, customs and habits of the white people who, they think, are very wicked.[48]

This movement died out in 1813 when the Creek War began and soon merged with the War of 1812, which took the minds of the Cherokees off religion. The Cherokees, however, refused to fight with Tecumseh and the British.

The most serious anti-mission and anticivilization movement occurred between 1824 and 1827 and is known to historians as White Path's Rebellion. White Path led a great number of traditional chiefs in opposing the rapid acculturation that was picking up speed at this time. Scores of laws were being passed by the council that encouraged trade and a market economy and at the same time catered to the wishes of the missionaries by outlawing traditional ways and promoting Christian practices. The traditionalists believed that the mixed-bloods were going too far and too fast. They elected an illegal council of their own. Representatives came to this council at the town of Ellijay (a traditionalist stronghold) from every town in the Nation. Thousands of people gathered there to support the rebellion and to engage in traditional dances and ceremonies. This council proceeded to act as though it were the legitimate representative of the people. It repealed the laws it did not like and passed new ones that reinstated the old customs.[49] The missionaries reported that the council expressed strong anti-mission sentiment. "It appears that some of the Cherokees have become hostile to the Presbyterians [and Congregational] missionaries and want to drive them out," one missionary reported.[50]

This movement peaked in 1827 just as the official chiefs, led by John Ross, were perfecting a national constitution modeled on that of the United States. They recognized that Andrew Jackson would probably be elected in 1828 and that he was certain to support the frontier demand to remove all Indians from the eastern half of the Mississippi Valley. Ross and the mixed-bloods believed that if the Cherokees could show that they were now a Christianized and civilized people, operating under the same kinds of laws and institutions as white Americans, they might be permitted to remain in the East. In the summer of 1827 Ross arranged a conference with White Path and the rebel chiefs. The two sides agreed to put aside their differences for the time being in order to unite against the overwhelming threat of losing their homeland forever. Jackson was elected the following year, and he did succeed in removing the Indians. At first the missionaries opposed the Indian removal program, but when they backed off from opposition after 1832, there was a third upwelling of traditionalism throughout the Nation, and the missionaries as a whole never regained support after that. One of the Moravian missionaries reported the resurgence of Cherokee traditionalism in 1835–37: "For three nights the Indians held a Medicine Dance at old Julstaya's, and this was the fourth and last principal one of revelry. After dark we heard the quick beating of drums and the savage whooping of the dances . . . [and] at day-break it appeared as if the vaults of hell had let loose the raving furies; the woods resounded with whooping and yelling."[51] Thus the tyranny of the white majority in Jacksonian democracy overwhelmed the good intentions of both the missionaries and the Cherokees.

The negative responses of Native Americans to missionaries are far easier to document than the positive ones; this is as true for the Cherokees (especially the full-bloods) as for any other tribe. But there were some missionaries who managed to gain the respect, admiration, and even the warm friendship of the Cherokees. The two qualities that appealed most to the Cherokees were the willingness to treat them as equals—or as they said, "brothers"—and the missionaries' openly and unequivocally taking their side in disputes with the federal government. Such missionaries were few. Inveterate ethnocentrism led most missionaries to adopt at best a patronizing paternalism toward "the children of the forest," and involvement in politics by a missionary was forbidden by all mission boards as well as by the government (which subsidized the mission schools). Nevertheless, some missionaries were ready to take such stances.

The Reverend Daniel S. Butrick of the American Board made a lifelong effort to treat the Cherokees as equals. As soon as he arrived in the Cherokee Nation in 1818, he went to live with a Cherokee-speaking family in order to learn their language; he spent most of his long career traveling among them, visiting in their homes—especially those of the full-bloods. He publicly opposed removal and remained in the East with those Cherokees who refused to accept the fraudulent removal treaty of 1835 even though the majority of his colleagues on the American Board not only left for the new homeland in the West in 1836 but urged the Cherokees to give up and come with them. Butrick stuck it out during the difficult years of Cherokee resistance from 1835 to 1838, and on the eve of the Cherokees' forced removal at bayonet point, he gathered his mission church members together and led them in voting to excommunicate from the church those who had signed the fraudulent treaty. In effect, Butrick declared that no Christian could condone betrayal of the Nation and no Christian church should have fellowship with such traitors.

Butrick did not, like most of his colleagues, think it best to concentrate mission efforts among the mixed-blood, English-speaking Cherokees and their children. Nor did he consider it hopeless to try to civilize and Christianize full-blood adults. "The Indians are a quick-sighted, discerning people," he said; "they knew who is wise and who is not." And they also know who respected them and who looked down on them.[52] The full-bloods believed that most missionaries were "haughty" because they refused to learn to speak Cherokee and devoted all their time to the English-speaking members of the tribe.[53] Butrick won the respect of the full-blood majority not only by learning their language but by praising its beauty and dexterity when most missionaries considered it too crude to express the glories of God and the complexities of Christian theology. "In many respects," he said, "their language is far superior to ours; theological concepts of every kind and degree may be communicated to this people in their own language with as clearness and accuracy as in ours."[54]

Butrick found it shocking that his colleagues devoted most of their time to the mixed-bloods, especially to those who were prosperous and acculturated. "This is the case . . . with many, if not most missionaries" he wrote; "they will not come down far enough [to the poorer Cherokees] to take hold even of their blankets to lift them out. . . . They think they must equal [in their lifestyle], if not surpass, the first class of Cherokees, and thus fix their marks [for Christian behavior and refinement] entirely beyond the reach of all common Indians." [55] Butrick believed that most missionaries were full of "pride and superiority" and said that the Indians, seeing this, returned the contempt. His own respect for the Cherokees brought their respect in return.

The Methodist circuit riders, most of them young and themselves of little education, proved popular among the Cherokees when they came into the Nation after 1823. Three of them married Cherokees and began raising Cherokee families as they preached. [56] (Missionary marriage to an Indian was frowned upon in most denominations.) Once married to a Cherokee, a white man became a member of the tribe and was treated as such. The Methodists never established permanent mission stations; they lived with the Cherokees as they traveled around the circuits. In addition, their Arminian theology, their exhilarating, spirited camp meetings, and their willingness to tolerate and give encouragement to "backsliders" who fell into spiritual error made them seem more friendly in their evangelism than the stern authoritarians in the Calvinist denominations.

The Methodist missionaries were also admired for their public attacks on Jackson's removal policy in 1830. One American Board missionary heard a Methodist say at a revival meeting that there was "a council held in Hell—which extended to some of the [Georgia] state legislature and also included the President of the United States—all for the purpose of robbing the Cherokees of their country." [57] Late in 1830, all eight of the circuit riders among the Cherokees signed and published a protest against the removal policy. Several of them were arrested when they refused to take an oath to obey the state of Georgia. However, when the Methodist mission board rebuked them for this and repudiated their involvement in politics, the circuit riders felt they had to desist. Methodism thereafter lost Cherokee support. One of the circuit riders, James J. Trott, became so disgusted with his denomination's refusal to support the Cherokee Nation against removal that he left the Methodists to join another denomination. [58]

The most heroic missionaries in defense of Cherokee rights were Samuel A. Worcester and Elizur Butler of the American Board. They too refused to sign Georgia's oath of allegiance and went to jail in protest. When they were sentenced to four years at hard labor in the Georgia penitentiary, the Cherokees rallied to support them. The missionaries brought a test case before the United States Supreme Court that John Marshall decided in 1832 in favor of Cherokee treaty rights.[59] But the jubilation was short lived. When Jackson refused to enforce Marshall's decision, Worcester and Butler gave up the fight. In January 1833, they asked for a pardon from the governor of Georgia and urged the Cherokees to accept removal, and three years later Worcester moved west with members of his mission church. For several years after removal the Cherokee council did its best to get Worcester expelled from the Nation for this turnabout.

By far the most successful missionary—not only in winning the respect of the Cherokees but in making more converts for his denomination than any other—was the Reverend Evan Jones. Jones served as a missionary for the northern Baptists to the Cherokees from 1821 until his death in 1872. He worked chiefly with the full-bloods, sided with the great majority of the Cherokees against Andrew Jackson, walked with them on the Trail of Tears, served as a chaplain in one of their regiments during the Civil War, and had the unique honor of being officially admitted as a full member of the tribe with a pension from the Cherokee treasury for his long and faithful service to the Cherokee Nation.[60]

When he started his work, Jones was as ethnocentric and aggressive as any other missionary, but he soon discovered that this was the wrong way to go about winning the Cherokees to Christianity. He was one of the few who took the trouble to learn Cherokee so that he could preach to and converse with them in their own language; he translated the Bible into Cherokee using the Sequoyan syllabary. He realized that the best persons to preach Christianity were Cherokees who themselves had found it helpful. Unlike most other missionaries, he ordained and then trained the most articulate Cherokee converts (whether they knew English or not) to become itinerant evangelists, to form churches, and to become Cherokee Christian ministers. He spent much of his time living with the Cherokees in their log cabins, eating their food, getting to know their problems, and providing all possible assistance to them.

At one time in his career, when Jones was censured by his board for meddling too much in politics, his friend Daniel Butrick wrote in astonishment to admonish that board:

> Has not your board been acquainted with Mr. Jones near thirty years? Have they not seen the [Baptist] church growing and flourishing under his care when he stood alone? Do they not know that he has still the entire confidence of the Cherokees? . . . Do they not know that the Baptist church, having grown up principally under his care, number[s] about one thousand and embraces several [Cherokee] preachers of sound judgment and unexceptionable character . . . together with many other[s] who are considered among the best men in the Nation? Do they not know that this church has done probably five times as much for religious purposes [as any other]? . . . Do they not know that Mr. Jones possesses the entire confidence of . . . the Principal chief and National Council?[61]

Jones also received warm support from the Cherokee full-bloods at this crisis in his career. Five of the Cherokee preachers he had ordained wrote to the board denouncing what they called "the false accusations" made to the board against their "beloved brother." They reminded the board that Jones had accompanied them "all the way through [their] long journey to this country" and shared in all their suffering. "[His] whole family are esteemed by us and the whole country." These Cherokee preachers especially commended Jones for having produced such a remarkable translation of the Bible into Sequoyan: "[Formerly] we had no word of God in our own language, and now [that] we have so much of it that we can read ourselves, we find all his teaching to agree with it." They concluded by asking the board, "What missionary has done more than he has, or as much?"[62]

Jones got into trouble with his board for his vigorous and persistent opposition to Jackson's removal policy and his determination to serve the Cherokee cause of resistance to it in any way that he could. He became such a thorn in the side of the federal officials that in 1836 they summarily banished him from the Nation. Still he continued to itinerate secretly through the Nation and assisted the resistance until the United States Army drove the Cherokees westward in September 1838.

Jones was opposed to the institution of slavery, and he taught his preachers to oppose it. Eventually the Cherokee Nation split over this institution into northern and southern factions. During the Civil War the Cherokees formed regiments that fought on both sides, and Jones aided the Union Cherokees. After the war he returned to the ravaged Nation and helped to reconcile the two parties.

Perhaps the most remarkable achievement of Evan Jones was his work in creating the Cherokee Keetoowah Society in 1857.[63] It was formed to counter a secret proslavery society called the Knights of the Golden Circle led by the mixed-bloods. The knights tried to disrupt Jones's religious services and threatened to horsewhip him and drive him from the Nation. But his Baptist converts rallied around him, and the organization provided resistance to the effort of the slaveholders to bring the Nation into the war on the side of the Confederacy.

The Keetoowah Society was remarkable for three reasons. First, its ultimate goal was not simply to end slavery but to return control of the Cherokee government to the full-blood majority (which it did in 1867). Second, the members of this society formed a Cherokee Home Guard regiment that was ordered in 1861 to fight against a neighboring Creek faction that was pro-Union; on the eve of the battle, this regiment mutinied, crossed the lines, and fought with the Union Creeks against the Confederate Creeks, Texans, and Cherokees. They later went to Kansas and formed two Union regiments that fought throughout the war. Third, the Keetoowah Society was syncretic in its union of Cherokee traditionalists and Christians. Meetings were opened with Christian prayer, and many of its leaders were Cherokee Baptist preachers; at the same time, the meetings were conducted on traditional lines with the smoking of tobacco and traditional rituals and dances, and the *adonisgi* were as prominent in it as the Baptist ministers.

The long and successful career of Evan Jones (who made the northern Baptists the largest religious group in the Cherokee Nation) demonstrates the essential features of successful missionary work: first show respect and equality, not ethnocentric paternalism; learn their language and their customs in order to understand their feelings and their needs, and find ways to bridge the gap between the best of the old ways and values and the best of the new; then create a native ministry and let it take the leadership. Successful missionary work also included meddling in politics on the side of the Indians when they were right even if it put the mission in jeopardy. Finally, a good missionary was to live by his own religion's principles as an example of its inherent values and let the Indians see that its ideals of brotherhood and sisterhood transcend ethnic and racial lines just as the principles of social justice do. He had to enable the Indians to see that the Christians' God was not culture bound but that his power was available to all people, that in fact, God was chiefly the friend of the oppressed, not the oppressor.

Professor Margaret Szasz has coined the term "cultural broker" or "cultural mediator" for those who tried to bridge the gap between white Americans and Native Americans.[64] The great failure of most nineteenth-century Christian missionaries was their aggressive spiritual pride and their overemphasis on the individualistic aspects of their faith. They were more concerned to save souls one by one than to save the corporate soul of the tribes to which they ministered. The Native American reaction to this could scarcely help being one of rejection. This behavior lies at the heart of Robert K. Berkhofer's judgment on "the inevitable failure of the missionary enterprise" in the era.[65]

◈ Chapter 2
The Missionaries' Dilemma

Christianity took many forms in nineteenth-century America. In some tribes as many as six different forms of evangelical Protestantism sometimes competed for converts. In a few tribes only Roman Catholicism was present. The United States had separated church and state, leaving every individual free to choose his or her own form of religion. The Native American found it difficult to conceive how any order or harmony could be sustained in a nation with so many competing religious groups.

White Americans overcame their divisiveness by insisting that the United States was in fact an evangelical Protestant nation (though tolerant of deviants). Protestant evangelicalism became in the nineteenth century what historians have called the "second establishment." The form of evangelicalism that most denominations adopted shared a primary concern for individual repentance and a belief in faith and salvation by grace in a personal confrontation with the Holy Spirit. Native Americans were expected to have the same kind of conversion experience. Missionaries also believed that they could remain aloof from social and political problems within the Indian nations or between them and the United States. A prime directive for missionary work was "never meddle in politics." Simply by converting Indians, one by one, missionaries would transform heathen communities into sober, enlightened, hardworking, pious individuals fit to become citizens of the United States.

Experience soon taught that this was not so easy. Too many social, political, and even economic issues (such as black chattel slavery) had moral ramifications. It was one thing to tell Indians that they must give up alcohol or polygamy but quite another to tell them to accept Andrew Jackson's policy of removal from their homeland. This essay examines some of the dilemmas with which the missionaries found it excruciatingly difficult to cope between 1794 and 1870.

The dilemma of the missionary is not unlike that which Edmund S. Morgan defined as the "Puritan dilemma." Moreover, "the central problem of Puritanism is the problem of every age," as Morgan also noted.

> It was the question of what responsibility a righteous man owes to society. If society follows a course that he considers morally wrong, should he withdraw and keep his principles intact, or should he stay? . . . Henry Thoreau did not hesitate to reject a society that made war with Mexico. William Lloyd Garrison called on the North to leave the Union in order to escape complicity with the sin of slaveholding. John Winthrop had another answer.[1]

Winthrop's answer to the dilemma was to struggle to the best of his ability to live as a responsible citizen in a world full of sin, corruption, and confusion. For Morgan, Winthrop was a model of responsible Christian citizenship.

In one sense the missionary dilemma in early-nineteenth-century America was easier and, in another sense, harder than Winthrop's. It was easier because American missionaries lived in a freer country and most were confident that their country was already on the true path to the millennium; it was harder because they were not, as Winthrop was in Massachusetts Bay, actively directing the policies of their countries, but rather they were the passive recipients of national policies. American missionaries, especially if they lived in foreign countries that were within the sphere of U.S. economic and political power, always ran the risk of becoming accessories of that power. They have frequently been accused of being agents of U.S. foreign policy. The United States' political imperialism and its Christian imperialism are seen by some to go hand in hand. The missionaries' dilemma was, and in many respects still is, how to react to national policies that may be detrimental to the Christian goals of their mission.

What choice should a missionary make when he (or she) conscientiously believes his government to be wrong in its foreign policy? Should he stand up and protest in the name of a higher law, or should he somehow separate his mission of saving souls from his mission to "reform the world in the image of God's holy kingdom" (as Morgan says Puritanism commanded John Winthrop to do [p. 8])? There used to be a very specific statement of this point in the Methodist Christian Discipline: "As far as it respects civil affairs, we believe it the duty of Christians, and especially all Christian ministers, to be subject to the supreme authority of the country where they may reside, and to use all laudable means to enjoin obedience to the powers that be; and therefore, it is expected that all our preachers and people, who may be under any foreign government, will behave themselves as peaceable and orderly subjects."[2] Consider that statement today in terms of a missionary to the former Soviet Union or to El Salvador, Guatemala, Chile, Nicaragua, or the Philippines. Or consider it in terms of a missionary in one of the southern states about to secede from the Union in 1861, and one understands the dilemma that this essay discusses. In short, is it possible or proper for a missionary to say, as one missionary said back in 1832: "As a missionary to the heathen, I feel that I have a right to be dead to the political world. That I have no call from the example of the Blessed Redeemer or his apostles to engage in political controversies or to speak evil of dignitaries"?[3]

Although this is a perennial problem for missionaries, this essay describes it in terms of nineteenth-century foreign missionaries. To give the dilemma a further turn of the screw, my examples are drawn from the evangelical missionaries to the five major tribes of the southeastern Indians in the United States between 1789 and 1860. The Indian nations were considered a foreign mission field in those years because they had totally different cultures, they spoke foreign languages, and they dealt with the United States through treaties. To be a missionary to the Indians in the early nineteenth century was to enter a foreign land. The southeastern Indian nations (Cherokee, Creek, Choctaw, Chickasaw, and Seminole) had the power under treaties to admit or refuse missionaries and the power to expel them. "The powers that be" in an Indian nation were the tribal chiefs and council, or at least so the Indians thought.

The dilemma of political protest for the missionaries to the southeastern Indians began in 1828 when the United States decided to change its original Indian policy. The problem became acute three years later when the state of Georgia jailed several missionaries. Georgia claimed that, as a sovereign state, it had jurisdiction over all land within its boundaries regardless of federal treaties with Indian nations that had fixed tribal boundaries within Georgia (and other southern states). The Indians claimed to be subject only to the federal government; and the missionaries within the Indian nations agreed with them. Georgia, believing that the missionaries would encourage Indian resistance to its jurisdiction, placed them in a dilemma. The Bible said the Christians must "obey the powers that be," but after 1828 it was not clear whether Georgia or the federal government was the legal authority in such a situation. Where did federal authority end and states' rights begin? Looking back now, one can understand why these early-nineteenth-century missionaries felt betrayed by their government when Jackson sided with Georgia and other southeastern states followed Georgia's example. Yet, in another sense, the missionaries were betrayed by their own overfacile commitment to the belief that the United States of America was ordained by God to be the redeemer nation of the world. They learned from sad experience in 1832 that they could not trust their government to express God's will or their postmillennial expectations. It was a sobering experience. They had made promises to the Indians in the name of their government that they could not keep. The United States made it clear after 1832 that it was not going to treat the Indians as equals nor to help them to become citizens on the land of their forefathers. It was not going to honor its treaty commitments, nor the pledges of its first five presidents, nor the words of its Constitution, nor even the decisions of its Supreme Court in regard to Indian rights.

When the missionaries in the Southeast first became aware of what their government was doing, they had two "choices." They could stand up in opposition to the government and urge the Indians to do the same, or they could acquiesce in the decisions of the powers that were, urging ultimate reliance upon God's Providence. Some chose one path, some the other. Neither was successful. Neither those who tried in vain to oppose the government's actions nor those who acquiesced in them were able to sustain the respect of the Indians. After 1832 most southeastern Indians lost faith both in the United States and in the missionaries.

Briefly, when the first missionaries arrived to establish permanent stations among the southeastern tribes in 1800, the situation was this: these five nations, comprising roughly fifty thousand persons, inhabited most of the area west of the original thirteen states to the Mississippi River and south of Tennessee (the area destined to become the "Cotton Kingdom"). Because these tribes had honored their treaties with the king in 1776, they fought on the losing side in the Revolutionary War. They had lost a great deal of their original land in the treaties following the defeat. The British stopped fighting in 1783, but their Indian allies continued to wage guerrilla warfare against the frontier settlers until 1794.

After 1794, a general peace prevailed west of the Appalachians until 1812. George Washington's administration formulated an Indian policy that called for congressional control over Indian territories and congressional funding to civilize the Indians. By treaties with the various Indian nations, the federal government guaranteed their boundaries and their right to manage their own internal affairs. The program of "civilizing the Indians" was designed to persuade them to become farmers by giving them horses, plows, axes, and hoes, to teach them English, and to encourage them to become Christians. The ultimate goal was to admit the Indians as equal citizens of the new nation once they had become civilized and Christianized. As they became individual farmers, it was assumed that they would willingly cede what was left of their old hunting land in order to accommodate the influx of white settlers in the West. Washington expected that within fifty years all the Indians east of the Mississippi would be able to support themselves by their crops, that the tribes would cease to exist as independent nations, and that Native Americans and white Americans would live happily together as equal citizens in the new republic.

The missionary's role was to provide the schooling and the moral training to "wean" the Indians from their savage customs so that they, or their children, would blend easily into the cultural institutions of Euro-American society. In short, the melting pot idea of assimilation was to be promoted by mission schools for the Native Americans in the same way that public schools would assimilate incoming aliens from the non-English nations of Europe. To Christianize was to Americanize.

The first missionaries to establish permanent stations among the southeastern Indians were the Moravians. They were followed by the Presbyterians, Baptists, Congregationalists, and Methodists. Generally speaking, all five denominations shared an evangelical approach to Christian theology. The Presbyterians, Baptists, and Congregationalists were more Calvinistic, and the Moravians and Methodists more Arminian; but the theological shift associated with the Second Great Awakening tended to blur denominational and theological differences. In general, an Indian who was acceptable as a member of one mission church could as easily have become a member of another. The missionaries gladly entered into the government's program to "uplift" the heathen Indians to the level of white Americans. Their ethnocentricity may shock one today, but they undertook the policy of civilizing and Christianizing the Indians in a wholly different light. What is most striking about the Indian missionary enterprise was its extremely divisive impact upon the Indian communities. The missionaries came not to bring peace but a sword. It did not trouble them that they turned pro-mission Indians against anti-mission Indians, mixed-bloods against full-bloods, "progressives" against "traditionalists," mission students against their parents, Christian wives against traditionalist husbands. There was no thought of cultural pluralism. The mission enterprise was a battle against the forces of darkness by the forces of light, and the evangelical concept of conversion required a total commitment not only to the theology and doctrines of Christianity but also to the norms of personal and social behavior that prevailed in middle-class white communities (considered to be the God-given norms of any civilized people).

But to give these nineteenth-century missionaries their due, most of them came to see in 1828 that Andrew Jackson's new Indian policy would not help the Indians but harm them. When that happened, they openly criticized their own government for its injustices. The circumstances of this confrontation are well known. One of the major reasons that many on the frontier voted for Jackson in 1828 was that he was determined to put an end to George Washington's original Indian policy of civilization and assimilation. Instead, Jackson wanted to force all the Indians east of the Mississippi to move to what is now Oklahoma and Kansas in order to facilitate expansion of the whites to the West. The state of Georgia provided the catalyst for this when it passed its law in 1828 bringing all of the Cherokee and Creek land within its boundaries under the jurisdiction of the state, thereby abrogating the treaties that had placed the Indian nations under the protection of the federal government. Because the Georgians rightly suspected that the northern missionaries opposed Jackson's Indian removal policy, they passed another law in 1830 requiring all missionaries to take an oath of allegiance to the state of Georgia or to leave that part of the Indian nations within its borders. For refusing to sign this oath many missionaries were arrested, and ultimately two Congregational missionaries of the American Board of Commissioners for Foreign Missions (whose headquarters was in Boston) were tried, convicted, and placed in the Georgia state penitentiary for four years at hard labor.[4]

Most of the missionaries felt that Georgia's actions were both unjust and unconstitutional; they would force the Indians to leave their homeland because as citizens of Georgia they would face extreme oppression.[5] Although most missionaries tried to be circumspect about voicing their opinions of Georgia's actions and did not use their mission pulpits to preach against these laws, they felt free to express their dislike for them when asked by the Indians. The Methodist circuit riders among the Cherokees went even further. They met together in September 1830 and unanimously passed a resolution calling upon all Methodists to express their opposition to the policies of Georgia and of President Jackson.[6] In December 1830, the missionary leaders of the other three denominations among the Cherokees (the Moravians, Congregationalists, and Baptists) met and signed a similar statement. In these statements the missionaries said that they did not wish to be considered as entering into the political controversy nor to seem to side with the Whig Party against Jackson and the Democrats, but they did feel that the public should know two important facts that had bearing on the case: first, that the removal of the Indians would be totally demoralizing and would undermine all of the work that the government and missionaries combined had done to educate them and to convert them to a farming economy and a republican government; second, that the Jacksonians were misrepresenting the Indians, particularly the majority of full-bloods, by claiming that they were in favor of removal. The missionaries knew for a fact that the full-bloods were even more adamantly opposed to removal than were the mixed-bloods.[7]

Because these public manifestos did not enter into the constitutional or political aspects of the problem, the missionaries believed that they were being apolitical—that they were only supplying information for the public and not meddling in politics. The Georgians thought differently and planned to arrest those who did not swear their loyalty to Georgia.

At this point the mission boards entered the picture. Should they come to the defense of their missionaries, tell them not to sign the oath, supply them with lawyers, insist that they were only preaching the gospel and not meddling in politics? Or should they urge them to sign the oath and get on with the business of saving souls? The first mission board to react was the Methodist. The Tennessee Conference of Methodists met at Nashville in November 1830 and, citing that article of the Methodist Discipline quoted above, censured their missionary circuit riders for meddling in politics; they were told to remain silent on the removal issue and to devote themselves to saving souls. Only one of the Methodist missionaries was residing in Georgia and was therefore obliged to sign the oath (he was married to a Cherokee). Acting on his conscience, this Methodist, the Reverend James J. Trott, refused to sign the oath and was sentenced to four years imprisonment. He received no aid whatsoever from his mission board, and a year later, in disgust, he left the Methodists and became a missionary for the Disciples.[8]

The Moravian board of Salem, North Carolina, was the next to act. It told its missionaries that they should neither sign the oath nor remain in the Cherokee Nation to challenge it. The Moravians closed their missions in Georgia and moved to that part of the Cherokee Nation that lay within the borders of Tennessee. Here they tried to carry on their work by itinerancy.[9]

The major controversy took place among the Congregationalists. Their Boston-based mission board was made up predominantly of Whigs, and it told its missionaries that although the decision to obey or to challenge the oath law was up to each individual, nonetheless it would provide financial and legal support to any missionary who chose to challenge it. The board was convinced that the Georgia law was unconstitutional; it wanted a test case brought before the Supreme Court. At first, the five Congregational missionaries whose stations were located within Georgia were united in refusing to sign the oath. But when Jackson said that he would support Georgia's right as a sovereign state to assert jurisdiction over the Indians within its borders, three of the five changed their mind and decided to leave Georgia and, like the Moravians, continue their mission work from bases within the Cherokee Nation but outside the bounds of Georgia. The Reverend Samuel A. Worcester and Dr. Elizur Butler, however, became the heroes of the Cherokee people and of the northern Whigs by carrying their case to the Supreme Court and winning it. Jackson refused to enforce John Marshall's decision, and the missionaries remained in jail until they asked for a pardon.[10]

More important for this discussion, however, are the arguments used by the Reverend Daniel S. Butrick, speaking for those Congregational missionaries who declined to join Worcester and Butler. Butrick's defense of his position is a classic statement of the view that a missionary's sole purpose is to save souls and that he has neither the duty nor the right to enter into any political activity whatsoever:

> The sole business of a missionary is to promote the religion of Jesus. Whatever may be the duties of a settled pastor in his own country . . . it is certain that a missionary who is an alien in a foreign land has nothing to do with civil affairs and his only business is to propagate religion. . . . Some may be ready to say that as citizens of the United States we are bound to bear our part in the political struggle of the day and do all in our power to put down those rulers who do not act according to our views of justice. . . . [But] as a missionary to the heathen, I feel that I have a right to be dead to the political world. That I have no call from the example of the Blessed Redeemer or his apostles to engage in political controversies or to speak evil of dignitaries.[11]

There are three points in Butrick's defense of missionary political neutrality that merit examination: (1) how is one to define his concept of "propagating religion"? (2) did Jesus and the apostles advocate political neutrality? (3) who were "the powers that be" whose authority was to be respected in this instance?

To take the last point first, Butrick held the view that Georgia was the rightful sovereign in this case. It might as easily be argued that the Cherokee Nation still had power over its own internal affairs by its treaties, or that Jackson as upholder of the Constitution was the sovereign power, or that the Supreme Court as final arbiter of the meaning of a treaty clause was the chief power to be obeyed. Butrick's acceptance of Georgia as the power he chose to obey is questionable and certainly could be taken as a political decision on his part.

Second, whether Jesus and the apostles ever engaged in political action can be left to theologians; however, a historical case can be made that Jesus was certainly considered a political threat to the Roman rule and to that of the Jewish Sanhedrin. Whether or not Jesus was himself trying to arouse the Jews to reassert their sovereignty or religious freedom at the time of his trial, the potential for such an insurrection was always possible, and any imperial authority might agree with Pontius Pilate that he was a charismatic figure around whom revolt might ultimately center, even if his challenge was indirect.[12]

Finally, of course, there is the question about what it means to "propagate religion." Butrick spoke for the individualistic approach to soul saving that prevailed among evangelicals of his day, but whether that was part of the cultural captivity of the American churches in 1832 or whether it is always the basis of Christian evangelism is a question one can leave for the moment.

Butrick did score some points against Worcester and Butler when he noted that they seemed more concerned with their popularity among the Cherokees than with the teachings of the Redeemer and the apostles. Worcester's maneuver, Butrick said, made the missionaries appear to be "Cherokee patriots" rather than ministers of God. "When we came into their country," Butrick noted, "we swore that we would not engage in any political activities or interfere in any aspect of their tribal life. . . . [I]t is no more our duty to enter the list of combatants to defend their political rights than it would be in case of war to enter their ranks and fight their battles." Here again, however, one might ask how Butrick defined "political activities" and "interference in tribal life."

The religious press in the North certainly saw Worcester and Butler as heroes in a political struggle against Jacksonian tyranny and Georgia's states' rights theory. Butrick also noted that the law of Georgia, while it might cause him some inconvenience by forcing him to another spot in the Nation, did not actually prohibit him from missionary work. Therefore, it was not a question of "obeying God rather than man." He could still engage in itinerant preaching while living in Tennessee. To this Worcester responded, "True—but everyone must perceive that the prohibition of the residence of missionaries within a given territory is a great restraint upon the preaching of the gospel there."

Whatever the debater's points scored by each side in this controversy, it is difficult to believe that either escaped the missionary's dilemma. Both were claiming to be apolitical when the world perceived them both—and the Cherokees perceived them both—to be very much engaged in politics. They were simply on different sides. Neither was truly neutral. After 1832 the missionaries ceased to criticize either Jackson or Georgia, although for six more years the Cherokees struggled to persuade Congress to reverse Jackson's decision.

The reaction of the Native Americans to the missionaries' decision after 1832 to acquiesce in Jackson's removal policy and to preach salvation without social justice was predictable. Most Indians concluded that all of the missionaries' professions of friendship toward them had been insincere. If the missionaries would not come to their defense either as Christian brethren or as oppressed human beings, then it seemed that the religion of the missionaries was itself unworthy. There was not only a tremendous falling off in conversions and mission church membership but a concomitant revival of the traditional religion. The Indians could only conclude after 1832 that Christians spoke with forked tongues. The southeastern Indians had made more progress in acculturation than any other Indian nations. Most of them by 1832 were independent yeoman farmers living in their own log cabins, dressing and behaving pretty much as the white frontier farmers did. They were praised by the missionaries as "the five civilized tribes." Yet the tremendous effort they had made to accomplish this transition was all for nought. Instead of being admitted as equal citizens, they were to be forcibly removed to the farthest extreme of the republic and placed on reservations. As a result, some Indians blamed Christianity itself for their predicament. One Cherokee chief, formerly a convert to Christianity, told a missionary in 1835 that all those who oppressed his people were Christians. "I observed," the missionary said, "that he ought not to suppose all the white people christians. All did not approve what had been done." But the chief replied, "O, yes, all christians. The government of the United States is a christian government and is upheld by christians. All alike. The government does it and the people uphold the government. All are christians."[13] The missionary found himself unable to explain why a Christian nation would support a president who behaved so unjustly toward the Indians. Political neutrality, far from saving the missionaries from Indian criticism, only led some Indians to reject all Christians.

Perhaps the most poignant aspect of the whole missionary dilemma was the problem of black slavery, an institution that all of the five civilized tribes quite logically adopted when they tried to imitate the southern white man's system of civilization. By 1830 some Cherokees were so wealthy as to own more than fifty slaves and to cultivate hundreds of acres of cotton; these Cherokee slaveholders lived lavishly from the income of their plantations and in their commodious houses precisely as white slaveholders did.

Prior to the removal of the five southeastern Indian nations on their respective "Trails of Tears" between 1832 and 1839, the issue of slavery was not particularly troublesome to the missionaries. Once the abolition movement caught fire in the North, however, the stand that a missionary agency took on the question of slavery was bound to have political ramifications. Before 1845 the Baptists and Methodists were national denominations, and their missionaries drew support from North and South. The Presbyterians remained a national organization until the Civil War broke out. The Moravians were also a national denomination with missionary centers in Salem, North Carolina, and Bethlehem, Pennsylvania. Even the American Board, though dominated by New England Congregationalists, claimed to be a national and not a sectional society.

There were three stances a missionary agency could take toward slavery: (1) it could hold that slavery was the law of the land and hence a political question in which the church could not, or should not, meddle; (2) it could take a proslavery position and argue that since it was the law of the land and since the Redeemer and his apostles never openly condemned the institution, it was not only justifiable by Old Testament example but also beneficial to the slaves and to the nation and a blessing to be supported and expanded; or (3) it could advocate opposition to slavery as a sin against the injunction to love one's neighbor as oneself.

The denominations that carried on missionary work among the slaveholding tribes of the South were badly divided over this issue. When the Baptist Foreign Mission Society ordained a slaveholding Cherokee as a minister and employed him as a missionary to his people, it precipitated a debate that led to the division of that denomination in 1845.[14] Thereafter, northern Baptists among the Cherokees opposed slavery whereas the southern Baptists supported it. The same division occurred among the Methodists. The Congregationalists on the American Board tried to persuade their missionaries quietly to oppose slavery among the southern Indians and to refuse to admit Indian slaveholders into their churches. In this they failed. In 1859 the American Board decided to give up all of its missions to the slaveholding Indians rather than continue to support missionaries who would not actively oppose slavery. Their missionaries thereupon joined the foreign mission board of the old-school wing of the Presbyterian Church, which was dominated by its southern members. The Moravians refused to discuss the matter, but, like the old-school Presbyterians, they employed slave labor at their mission stations and made no effort to oppose slavery in any way.

Only the northern Baptists went so far as to exclude from their mission churches all Indians who held slaves. They did not take his step until 1852, however, and as a result of their antislavery agitation, one of their missionaries was expelled from the Cherokee Nation and another was threatened with mob violence. After their removal to the Indian Territory with their black slaves, all of the southeastern Indian nations passed laws prohibiting any missionary from preaching against, or in any way opposing, slavery. They also passed laws prohibiting missionaries from teaching slaves to read and write; consequently slaves were excluded from mission schools.

Between 1840 and 1861 there were many aspects of this mission problem in that part of the Indian Territory that is now Oklahoma. One was the practice some mission stations adopted of purchasing slaves with the aim of having them work their way to freedom by paying them a salary. Most of these mission slaves were paid so little, however, that they died before they could pay off the eight hundred to one thousand dollars that the missions had paid for their purchase. The missionaries claimed that by such acts they were striking a blow to liberate slaves. Nevertheless, to the slaveholding Indians it appeared that these missionaries were as much a part of the slaveholding system as anyone else.

Another irony was that sometimes an Indian slaveholder and his black slave were both members of the same mission church; some of the slaves purchased by the missionaries were their own church members. In one particularly horrific case among the Choctaws, the wife of a slave owner burned one of her female slaves alive for allegedly having incited her husband to kill their master. Both the wife of the murdered Indian slave owner (who supervised the burning) and the black slave woman (a mother of eight children) who was burned to death were members of the mission church. The missionary pastor of the church felt that he could take no action against the slave owner because she had acted out of grief for the murder of her husband. She was admitted to the next communion with the other mission church members, Indian, white, and black.[15]

The Presbyterian Foreign Mission Board claimed to follow a policy of complete neutrality on the slavery question among the southern

Indians. Yet it proved impossible to sustain that position. The Indians were suspicious of any missionary who did not own a slave or positively support the system. As one Presbyterian missionary reported to his board from the Creek Nation in 1856: "The [Creek] Council meets soon. It is said great things are to be done. . . . All the white men who are suspected of being abolitionists are to be sent off they say, myself among the rest." [16] Presbyterian missionaries in the Choctaw Nation who expressed some doubts about the virtues of slavery as an institution were immediately discharged by their boards lest they give the mission a bad reputation. Neutrality seemed a simple enough position in theory, but by the 1850s there was no practical room in the South for neutrality over slavery. It often happens that way in politics. Yet the claim continues to be made that missionaries neither can nor should take any stand on political affairs.

To those who argued that obeying "the powers that be" required neutrality on slavery, the antislavery people answered, just as convincingly, that there were other interpretations of the Constitution and that there was a higher law than the Constitution to which Christians owed obedience.

To those missionaries who said that there could be no mission work among the slaveholding Indians unless missionaries were neutral on that issue, there were those who pointed out that the great majority of the full-blood Indians were antislavery; to take a neutral or proslavery position in the Cherokee Nation was to side with the wealthy, mixed-blood minority against the poor, full-blood majority. It was among the full-bloods that the northern Baptists worked, and this had enabled them to exclude slaveholders from their mission churches. In fact, the northern Baptist missionaries even organized a secret abolitionist society among their full-blood converts.[17]

Finally, what happened to the Christian missionary cause when the Civil War began? The proslavery Presbyterian missionaries joined the Confederate States and urged the Indians to do likewise. The Indians became divided among themselves and proceeded to wage their own bloody civil war. What, then, did the missionary cause or the Indians gain by neutrality? Virtually all mission stations in all the southern tribes closed during the war.

It is hardly surprising that missionaries such as Cyrus Kingsbury, who had left the antislavery American Board in 1859 to join the Presbyterian Foreign Mission Board in the Choctaw Nation, blamed Lincoln for causing the Civil War: "What could have induced the Lincoln administration," Kingsbury asked after Fort Sumter was fired upon, "so suddenly to change its policy and to plunge the country into such a horrible war? How easily all matters might have been settled if there had been a mind for it." Presumably Kingsbury thought the easy way to have settled the sectional tension would have been for the Lincoln administration to follow the position of the Presbyterian Foreign Mission Board and proclaim a policy of neutrality toward the institution of slavery.[18]

It is often said that in difficult matters such as these the missionary must leave the outcome to God's Providence. Man proposes and God disposes. God works in mysterious ways beyond the ability of man to fathom. There are some revealing statements by missionaries to the southern Indians on this point. Daniel Butrick used the providential discovery of gold in the Cherokee Nation in 1828 as an argument to defend his refusal to oppose Indian removal. With gold in their land the Cherokees might have become the wealthiest of the Indian nations and developed a power base that their lack of votes denied. Butrick, however, felt that the discovery of gold might be a snare and a delusion leading the Cherokees from godliness to materialism: "Suppose by suffering we [missionaries] could procure for the Cherokees the continued possession of this country, who knows but that very possession might prove their ruin and ban them from the Kingdom of heaven? Their gold mines might prove a greater snare than all the dangers of the west. . . . Who knows but these very afflictions are designed to take them to a far distant region and render them a light to all the [Indian] nations west of the Rocky Mountains?"[19] In the West it turned out that the Cherokees and other southeastern nations were placed on reservations that became the sources of tremendous riches in gas and oil, but few of them ever benefited from these discoveries.

A more shocking use of the Providence doctrine to defend the missionaries' neutrality with regard to removal after 1832 was made by the Reverend John Thompson, a missionary of the American Board: "It may be part of God's plan in promoting the interests of His church to destroy the majority of the Cherokees. . . . The Redeemer's cause may, for aught I know, be promoted in the end by such an event."[20] What were the Indians to think of a missionary who said that his God might promote his cause by destroying them? What incentive did that offer for them to become Christians?

The missionary's dilemma, like that of the Puritan, required him to be in the world but not of the world. This was not the same thing as being dead to the political world. Or, to put it another way, neutrality was not a real option.

Chapter 3
Two Bostonian Missionaries

Boston considered itself the "hub of the universe" in nineteenth-century America. It hoped to make the western areas of the United States models of Boston society. In this effort, not only did Bostonians compete with missionaries from the South, who hoped to model the West and the Indians on the Cotton Kingdom, but even among Boston missionaries there arose striking differences over how to convert the Indians.

The Bostonians were badly divided at the start of the nineteenth century between Federalists and Jeffersonians, between supporters of an established, tax-supported religious system and opponents of it, between Calvinists and Unitarians, and of course between a growing mercantile upper class (which sent its sons to Harvard) and a growing middle class (which sent its sons to smaller colleges if at all). Among the most intense denominational conflicts was that between evangelical Baptists (ardent supporters of Jefferson) and evangelical Congregationalists (ardent Federalists). Both denominations were opposed to the Unitarianism of Harvard College, but each disagreed with the other's style of "Christianizing" the Indians.

This essay concentrates on the competition within the Cherokee Nation between the American Board of Commissioners for Foreign Missions and the Baptist Board of Foreign Missions. The former represented a conservative and strict evangelicalism (inherited from Puritanism); it was led by the Reverend Samuel A. Worcester. The latter adopted a much looser, democratic approach and was led by the Reverend Evan Jones. Both men were Calvinists, and both made immense personal sacrifices to help the Cherokees. Yet in the end they could not agree either on the nature of conversion, on organizing Cherokee churches, on Cherokee slavery, or on translating the Bible into Cherokee. It is not surprising that the Cherokees found it necessary to choose between them. What is significant is that the vast majority chose the Baptists, who remain to this day the most popular denomination among the Cherokees.

I should have fancied myself in New England.—A visitor to a
mission station of the American Board of Commissioners for
Foreign Missions

Although Boston was undergoing many changes in the
first half of the nineteenth century, there was still general agreement that the hub of New England provided the nation with a model
of social order, enterprise, piety, and patriotism. The divisions that
wracked the politics, economic affairs, and religious structure of Boston still seemed capable of producing a transcendent drive to make the
rising republic model itself on New England. In no area was the ideal-
ism of Boston more evident than in the efforts of hundreds of missionaries to provide the heathen nations of the world with a blueprint for
their future. But what seemed a goal common to all denominations—
to civilize and Christianize the world—proved more frustrating and
divisive than Boston's Christians imagined. Even among the Indian
nations of America, pluralism, competition, and division could not be
overcome any more easily than in Boston itself. The two Boston-based
denominational mission agencies that put the most effort, time, and
money into this work—the Congregationalists' and the Baptists'—not
only could not remake the Indians in the New England image, they
could not even agree what that image should be. In the end, though,
they had a closer fit than those missionaries who came to the Indian
nations from the southern part of the United States.

Clifton J. Phillips observed some years ago that the foreign mission
movement of the early nineteenth century "made Boston a representative name for the New World in Smyrna, Canton, Honolulu, or
Bombay."[1] As he put it, "The first and a large part of the continuing American religious contacts with distant lands . . . were made by
New Englanders, supported by a New England constituency." Phillips
also correctly observed that, despite the continued influence of deistic
thought and the rise of Unitarianism around Boston, "the theological currents that fed American evangelicalism" were chiefly Calvinistic—the theology of the Puritans.[2] There were other currents, of
course, working to promote the foreign mission movement that had
its beginning in Boston in 1810. A more evangelical version of Calvin-

ism, tending toward free will (rather than predestination) and general atonement (rather than limited atonement), modified the harsher elements in Puritanism and the doctrines of Jonathan Edwards and his followers. The freedom to choose salvation sparked the revivalism that spread westward with the frontier, and as it gained force, those who had organized to bring Christianity to the farthest outposts of heathendom around the world became concerned to save the souls of the heathen in their own backyard—the Native Americans. Because Indian nations were considered a foreign culture, a pagan society, peoples with totally different customs and languages, and peoples who dealt with the United States through the diplomatic process of treaty making, missions to the Native Americans were placed under the foreign mission boards of that era. Two of the largest foreign mission boards in the young republic, both based in Boston, chose to make a major effort among the Cherokees.

This essay compares the efforts of the American Board of Commissioners for Foreign Missions (ABCFM) and the Baptist Board of Foreign Missions (BBFM) in order to discover why the former was a relative failure among the Cherokees whereas the latter was the outstanding success among Native American missions. The answer lies deep in New England history. Henry Knox, a Bostonian, had formulated the new nation's Indian policy of "civilizing and Christianizing the Indians" to prepare them for full and equal citizenship when he was George Washington's secretary of war in 1789.[3] Prior to the formation of these two large missionary institutions and the appointment of their first missionaries to the southeastern Indians in 1817, little had been done to carry out Knox's plan.

Comparison of the ABCFM and the BBFM sheds light not only on the nature of foreign missions in general but also on the role of New Englanders, and Bostonians in particular, in the cultural development of the new nation. Boston was soon to be called the "hub of the universe," and its rising commerce and industry made it in these years the wealthiest, most sophisticated, and most influential part of the nation. It is generally assumed that the Unitarians and the Congregationalists spoke for Boston, but though both descended from the Puritans, they were hardly unified. A growing religious pluralism was emerging in New England, as the rise of the Jeffersonian party and the effort to separate church and state indicated. In some respects the Trinitarian, or "orthodox," Congregationalists had more in common with the Baptists than with the Unitarians: both considered themselves Calvinists, and both supported revivalism and missions. The Universalists, however, another rising sect, had more in common with the Unitarians. As the Baptists and the Methodists rose in numbers and influence, they joined other sects in fighting the final battle against the Puritan system of religious taxes and found support from the Democratic Party. The Baptists were split into Calvinists and Freewill denominations just as the old Puritans were split into Trinitarian and Unitarian wings. Though the Baptists shared the Methodists' enthusiasm for revivalism, most, being Calvinist, abhorred the Methodists' Arminianism. They differed bitterly with the Congregationalists over pedobaptism and religious taxes but shared their dislike for Unitarianism. Both Congregationalists and Baptists had the majority of their constituents in rural areas and among the middle class, but the Baptists were socially parvenu, still struggling for respectability against two centuries of prejudice. The Congregationalists, having recently lost control of Harvard College, were struggling to found a new divinity school at Andover, while the Baptists were forming their first divinity school in Massachusetts at Newton Centre. As the Congregationalists struggled to maintain influence against the rising tide of Unitarianism, the Baptists struggled to break into the respectable ranks hitherto confined to Congregationalists. Missionary activity offered advantages to both groups.

The foreign mission movement grew out of the religious revitalization produced during the Second Great Awakening. Perry Miller argued that the Awakening is best understood as a nationalistic movement. The evangelical preachers and revivalists "were not simply preaching nationalism, they were enacting it."[4] So, too, was the missionary movement, especially among the Indians. Not only was the United States to be a Christian nation, but, ultimately, the whole world was to be brought to live in the image of America. The postmillennial optimism of the era was evident in the *Annual Report* of the ABCFM in 1827. The goal of foreign missions, it stated, was "no less than the moral renovation of the world."[5] Years later, on the one hundredth anniversary of the board's founding, the president of the ABCFM declared that "so far as America [was] concerned," the nation's "trusteeship for the world was born here."[6] He was speaking at Andover, Massachusetts.

Not only would the foreign mission movement Christianize and civilize the world, it would reconstitute other nations on the model of New England. As Francis Wayland, the pastor of the First Baptist Church in Boston, put it in 1824, "one object" of foreign missions was to "render" every heathen village into "as happy and as gladsome a place as the loveliest village that smile[d] upon . . . the New England landscape."[7] Missions to the Native Americans were intended to produce the same effect. "When missionaries went from the Missionary rooms to the heathen, the salvation they took with them was inseparably bound up with that definite New England culture of which they were a product," wrote the biographer of the superintendent of the ABCFM's mission to the Cherokees. "The spread of the Gospel had resolved itself . . . into a . . . way of living according to New England standards." Among the Cherokees, missionaries "managed to maintain a standard of proper dress and appearance. There was something absolute about this standard of proper appearance; it was part of what the Lord expected of them."[8] The reason for this was obvious; more than ninety percent of the missionaries of the ABCFM and the BBFM came from New England.[9]

Yet there were significant differences between the Congregationalists of the ABCFM and the Baptists of the BBFM—differences that prevented their merging into one mighty evangelical Calvinist mission agency and that, in fact, put them at odds in as many ways as they brought them together. In the end, it was the Baptist version of New England that took root among the Cherokees as it did throughout the white communities of the West.

One way to distinguish between the two agencies is to compare the personalities, styles, and work of the superintendents of each. The Reverend Samuel A. Worcester was superintendent of the ABCFM mission to the Cherokees from 1825 till his death in 1859. The Reverend Evan Jones came to the Cherokee Nation in 1821 and was superintendent of the BBFM mission from 1824 until his superannuation in 1866, though he continued to be active among the Cherokees until his death in 1872. During the long tenures of these two servants of their New England boards, the name Boston became as representative of the United States in the Cherokee Nation as it did in Smyrna, Canton, Honolulu, and Bombay.

In Evan Jones the Cherokees found a champion who marched with them across the Trail of Tears and later served as a chaplain in a Cherokee regiment during the Civil War; he assisted them in several treaty negotiations and was formally adopted into the tribe. Samuel A. Worcester became a martyr to Cherokee treaty rights by spending fifteen months at hard labor in a Georgia penitentiary to bring a successful case before the United States Supreme Court in opposition to Georgia's effort to assert jurisdiction over the Cherokees' homeland. Both men brought schools to Cherokee children to help them cope with a changing way of life, and both gave honest advice and the benefit of their influence to Cherokee leaders in their difficult diplomatic relations with the United States. Politically, Worcester was of more help prior to 1832; thereafter, Jones was the more useful. Both sacrificed much (and so did their wives and children) to help the Cherokees overcome hardship and despair with spiritual and moral counsel and example. Bostonians could have found no better men to advance their cause. Both men deplored the fact that the Cherokees had adopted the southern institution of black slavery and, in their different ways, did what they could to oppose it.

Yet the image of New England that came to reside with the Cherokees was closer to that of the Baptists, perhaps because the marginal status of the Baptists in New England gave them more insight into the ambiguous status of the Indians in America. Today more Cherokees belong to Baptist churches than to those of any other denomination; there are no Congregationalists and few Presbyterians among them. Something in the respective styles of the two boards and their superintendents created very different reactions to them. They had different visions of the future of Native Americans in the new republic.

Clifton Phillips noted that to understand missionary work, it is necessary to "understand the intellectual backgrounds of the missionary enterprise as well as to appreciate the type of personality which" foreign missions and commerce "made Boston representative of in the New World."[10] During the first flush of missionary zeal, evangelical unity seemed to prevail. Baptists throughout the United States contributed to the ABCFM prior to forming their own board.[11] Worcester and Jones were good friends and collaborators in the 1820s. The two boards, working within a few blocks of each other in Boston, shared information and advice. But with the passage of time, major differences in policy and style developed between the two boards, as well as a certain amount of rivalry for preeminence. After the Cherokees went west, Worcester and Jones became estranged.

Part of the difficulty arose from the fact that the ABCFM's missionaries and the BBFM's agents adopted different strategies for Christianizing and civilizing the Indians. The ABCFM's representatives decided to work first and foremost with those they considered the leaders of the Nation. They believed these leaders to be those of mixed white-Indian ancestry. The mixed-bloods usually spoke English and were interested in raising their children to be as much like whites as possible. They therefore welcomed the missionaries and led them to establish their missions in those parts of the Nation in which English-speaking Cherokees were more numerous. The missionaries of the BBFM, who came later, were assigned those areas in which the full-blood, Cherokee-speaking families were more numerous. Although three-fourths of the Cherokees were full-bloods, the mixed-bloods and English-speakers had a disproportionate amount of influence and wealth. The early Puritans too had courted the chiefs and their assistants. It seemed only sensible when seeking cooperation with foreign nations to win the approval first of the leaders. The Baptists were not averse to this strategy, but they were ready to accept the task of reaching those who needed the most help. In later years they found that the full-blood majority was quite able to assert its own kind of political power. Though the difference may not have been wholly apparent to the missionaries, a historian might find significant the fact that the Baptists in New England tended to support the Jeffersonian Democrats while the Congregationalists supported the Federalists.

This same tendency was evident in the preference of the ABCFM for "a settled ministry," or fixed mission establishments, whereas the BBFM, after a brief trial of this system, concluded after 1827 that an itinerant ministry was more effective. The Baptists reached out to the Cherokees; the Congregationalists sought to draw them in. Likewise, the Baptists soon developed a large cadre of "native preachers" to assist them in their work—Cherokees who preached in the Cherokee language; the Congregationalists very seldom found Cherokees worthy of licensing or ordination. In the decade preceding the Civil War, the Baptists became actively engaged in promoting antislavery agitation among the Cherokees; the ABCFM, though opposed to the institution, refrained from such agitation. Both mission agencies were interested in translating the Bible into Cherokee, but after 1840 they offered competing translations, not only because of the Baptist opposition to pedobaptism but as a result of different standards in presenting the gospel.

To many of the Cherokee Nation, the differences between these two New England agencies seemed slight. The resident federal agent to the Cherokees spoke of Jones and Worcester as mere instruments of their boards in Boston. In reality, the missionaries in the field were often at odds not only with each other but also with those who hired and paid them. Worcester and Jones were men of strong will, fervent piety, deep dedication, and great courage. But they differed in their personalities, their mission styles, and their relationship with their boards. In the process of supporting these mission superintendents the ABCFM and the BBFM revealed important differences of their own.

Samuel A. Worcester was born in 1798 in Worcester, Massachusetts.[12] His father became the parish minister in Peacham, Vermont, where young Samuel grew up. For six generations back his ancestors had been ministers in New England, and he knew he was destined for the same calling. From childhood he was steeped in Calvinist theology and Federalist politics. When he finished grade school, he attended Peacham Academy to prepare for college. One of his teachers was young Jeremiah Evarts, a recent Yale graduate and early treasurer of the ABCFM. At seventeen, Worcester walked seventy-one miles to Burlington, Vermont, to enroll in Vermont University; the uncle after whom he was named, Samuel Austin, was then its president. Harvard, by then, was no place for a Calvinist to train for the ministry, so after college Worcester enrolled at the Andover Theological Seminary, from which more than two hundred graduates entered the foreign mission service in the nineteenth century. He underwent the usual conversion experience, which entitled him to believe that he was one of the predestined elect. Upon graduation in 1825 he volunteered to work for the ABCFM. Another uncle, the Reverend Dr. Samuel Worcester, had been pastor of a leading Congregational church in Salem and, while corresponding secretary of the Prudential Committee of the ABCFM from 1812 to 1821, had conducted its work from his church. Dr. Worcester died in 1821 while visiting the board's Cherokee mission; he was buried in the Nation. Because young Samuel had a reputation as a linguist, the board (now led by Jeremiah Evarts) chose him in 1825 to head its mission to the Cherokees. He was ordained for this work in Park Street Church in Boston by his father; he took up residence in the Cherokee Nation with his young wife that same year.

Evan Jones was born in Brecknockshire, Wales, in 1788.[13] His native language was Welsh. Apprenticed to a linen draper as a boy, he went to London to practice this trade and found work in a small dry-goods store. After attaining some training in Latin, Greek, and Hebrew, he taught school for a time. He married a young woman who was a sales clerk in the draper's shop where he had first worked. About 1814, he opened his own dry-goods store at Ludgate in London. That business failed in 1821, and he immigrated with his family to Philadelphia, where he evidently had relatives. The Joneses settled in Berwyn and, although they had been Methodists in London, joined the Great Valley Baptist Church soon after arriving in the United States. In the summer of 1821, when the BBFM issued a call for volunteers to join their mission to the Cherokees, Jones agreed to go as a teacher; his wife and five children went with him. The mission station was in Valley Towns in western North Carolina. Three years later he felt a call to preach. Baptists then required no theological training for their ministers, and he was ordained by a denominational association in Tennessee. That same year, the BBFM appointed him superintendent of its Cherokee mission. From his arrival among the Cherokees, Jones was determined to translate the Bible into their language. A son, born in 1824, John Buttrick Jones, grew up speaking Cherokee as his native tongue, and later, after receiving college and divinity school degrees, he returned to join his father as a missionary and translator. Both Jones and Worcester lost their first wives soon after becoming missionaries; Worcester remarried to another missionary from New England, and Jones married a young woman from Tennessee.

The missionary boards for which these two men worked were composed of the leading ministers and lay leaders of their respective denominations. The ABCFM was formally organized in 1810 and incorporated in 1812.[14] The BBFM originated in 1813 in Boston when two of the five Williams College graduates at Andover who had been instrumental in the founding of the ABCFM, by now missionaries in India, abandoned the ordinance of infant baptism, were rebaptized by immersion, and left the service of the ABCFM. They applied to a group of prominent Baptist clergymen in Boston and Salem requesting their help in continuing their work abroad. The Reverend Thomas Baldwin of Boston and the Reverend Lucius Bolles of Salem formed a Baptist society in February 1813 for "Propagating the Gospel in India and other Foreign Parts." The Reverend Daniel Sharp of Boston became its first corresponding secretary—in effect, the head of the executive committee of the board. A year later, these Boston

Baptists called a national denominational convention in Philadelphia in order to expand the base of support. Baptists from the mid-Atlantic states, the South, and the West joined New Englanders to create the General Missionary Convention of the Baptist Denomination in the United States for Foreign Missions.[15] A historian of Baptist missions, Robert G. Torbet, notes that "while the leading spirit in this plan for national organization was Boston, deference was paid to Philadelphia as the center of the oldest Baptist association."[16] The official organ of the BBFM was the *American Baptist Magazine,* edited in Boston by Baldwin and Francis Wayland. In 1825 the headquarters of the BBFM was moved from Philadelphia to Boston; its executive committee thereafter remained in the hands of Baptists in the Boston-Salem area. As with the ABCFM, most of the missionaries of this board came from New England.[17]

When incorporated, the ABCFM consisted entirely of Trinitarian Congregationalists from Massachusetts and Connecticut. Its first board was elected in 1810 by the General Associations of the two states, five from Massachusetts, four from Connecticut. Two years later, however, the board expanded to include Presbyterians (and in 1816 Dutch Reformed Calvinists) from the mid-Atlantic states. Eight Presbyterian members were added to the board in 1812, but the New Englanders always constituted the majority.[18] The board met annually to set policies but delegated the day-to-day operations to a staff in Boston headed by a corresponding secretary and known as the Prudential Committee.

The men who constituted these two national mission societies included a high percentage of the most prominent lay and clerical leaders of the United States; college presidents, governors, congressmen, and industrialists worked together with the ministers, who were also prominent in the leading national reform agencies of the day. The interlocking directorate of religious benevolence played a major role in shaping American culture in the pre–Civil War era. The mission societies raised millions of dollars to uplift and mold the Christian republic and to spread its evangelical beliefs and republican institutions around the world. By the 1840s the ABCFM was raising $250,000 a year and the BBFM more than $80,000.[19]

The ABCFM did not enter the field of Native American mission work until 1816; the BBFM did so in 1817. At this time there were more than 120,000 Native Americans in more than eighty tribes living between the Appalachians and the Mississippi. They occupied much of the best land in the region. When the War of 1812 ended the threat of British military support for these tribes, white settlers surged into the area. Suddenly the problem of "civilizing and Christianizing" these "pagans" loomed as a pressing need if the Knox-Washington policy of incorporating the Indians as equal citizens was to succeed. In 1819 Congress passed the so-called Civilization Act to provide money for mission schools among these tribes. Missionary societies were prime lobbyists for this legislation.

New England mission societies concentrated their activities in the Southeast among the Cherokees, Choctaws, Creeks, Chickasaws, and Seminoles. These tribes totaled sixty thousand members living on prime cotton land. As soon as the war ended, the ABCFM sent the Reverend Cyrus Kingsbury to canvass them to petition President Madison to grant the board the sole and exclusive right to provide them missionaries—a request Madison denied because the Moravians and some local Baptists and Presbyterians were already active there.[20] In 1817 the BBFM commissioned the Reverend Humphrey Posey of North Carolina to negotiate with the Cherokees to start a Baptist mission station.[21] Because the federal government was trying to persuade the Cherokees to move west of the Mississippi, Posey did not receive permission from the tribal council to start a mission until 1819, when the Cherokees had sold enough land to the federal government to ward off this removal effort. The council designated Valley Towns, lying along the Hiwassee River in the Great Smoky Mountains, for the Baptist mission station because the full-bloods who inhabited that area had no school. Kingsbury had been allowed to start his first mission two years earlier at Chickamauga (later called Brainerd mission) on the Tennessee River, where the mixed-bloods were more numerous.

The Baptists expanded their mission into two stations in North Carolina and two in northwestern Georgia. The ABCFM established nine mission stations in the Tennessee, Alabama, and Georgia areas of the Cherokee Nation. Between 1817 and 1838 the ABCFM sent more than thirty-five ministers, school teachers, and artisans to these stations, providing a budget for them of more than ten thousand dollars a year in addition to the funds provided for their schools by the federal government. The BBFM sent a total of nine missionaries, teachers, and artisans to the Cherokee Nation with an annual budget of two thousand dollars exclusive of federal support. At the same time the Moravians had two mission stations in the Georgia area. The Methodists entered the Nation in 1821 and by 1831 had eight circuit-riding missionaries but no permanent mission stations or schools in the Nation. Because the public measured missionary success in terms of conversion statistics, competition was inevitable. The Cherokees soon came to recognize a difference between those who brought them "civilization" from the South (the Moravian mission board was located in North Carolina; the Methodists were sent by the Methodist conference of Tennessee) and those who brought them a somewhat different version of it from New England. Because the Congregationalists established the most numerous and efficient schools, they were at first looked upon with the most favor by the Nation's leaders.

By the time the New England missionaries arrived in the Cherokee Nation, the Cherokees had made great strides toward adapting to the white man's way of life. Their territory included about twelve million acres, and their population was close to twenty thousand, not counting another three to five thousand who had moved west and lived in western Arkansas Territory. Their people were rapidly accommodating to a market economy, living in log cabins, farming small tracts with a horse or a mule. That quarter of the Cherokees who were descendants of traders, former soldiers, and Tory loyalists who had come to live among them between 1700 and 1800 were living by white standards. Some were quite wealthy and owned as many as ten to twenty black slaves.[22] Surrounded by white settlers, the Cherokees had to centralize and strengthen their old governmental structure both to resist white intruders and to cope with federal efforts to acquire their land by purchase. By the 1820s they had established a system of laws and a political structure that resembled those of the white communities around them. They were eager to have schools for their children so they could interact more effectively with whites. On the other hand, the three-quarters of the Cherokees who were full-bloods, speaking only Cherokee, continued to hold on to as many of their old ways as they could; they lived outside the main centers of commerce and kept to themselves. They were not entirely happy at the rate of acculturation pressed upon them by the mixed-bloods who dominated the bicameral legislature, the supreme court and local courts, and the centralized police system; nor did they welcome the constitution, adopted in 1827, modeled on that of the United States. Closely knit together by seven interlocking exogamous clans, intensely patriotic, and hardworking, the Cherokees were far from the simple "savage" the missionaries expected. They were soon being called "the most civilized tribe in America."

When the Cherokees were forced to remove from their ancient homeland in 1838 and had to start life over again in what is now northwestern Oklahoma, all four mission agencies formed new mission stations there. The ABCFM established five stations; the BBFM, one. The Baptist Mission station was started at Breadtown close to the Arkansas border; later the settlement was called Baptist Mission. Branch churches of the Baptist mission spread out to the north and west; most of them were in the eastern part of the Nation. Worcester established his station at Park Hill, twenty miles southwest of Baptist Mission and three miles from the Cherokee capital at Tahlequah; Park Hill was a suburb of the capital where the chief and mixed-bloods built their homes, stores, and farms. The other four American Board stations were in the central part of the Nation. Although the inauguration of a Cherokee public school system in 1841, supported by tribal funds and taught by Cherokee teachers, decreased the importance of mission schools, the effort of the missionaries to start native churches under native preachers continued. Jones continued to work among the scattered full-bloods.

Worcester and Jones met often over the years. They shared a common interest in learning the Cherokee language and translating the Bible into it through the use of the syllabary devised in 1821 by Sequoyah. But their differences in personality, style, and approach to mission work caused them to drift apart after 1832. They came to disagree in five particular areas: (1) evangelism; (2) Cherokee removal from the East; (3) translating; (4) how to react to slavery among the Cherokees; and (5) the development of a native ministry. Their differences reflected their boards' disagreements and ultimately the margin between success and failure in Indian missions. While the differences in some of these areas may seem more of style than of substance, together they add up to distinctions that were reshaping Boston and the future of the United States.

Evangelism and Schools

From the outset, the American Board adopted a highly
paternalistic approach to mission work. Its missionaries strove to
make their stations model enclaves of civilized society—Christian
communities as similar as possible to those of New England. They believed that Cherokee children must be required to live apart from their
parents and from the pagan, backward ways of their communities.
Their missions consisted of a boarding school (which functioned as
part of a model farm) and a mission church surrounded by the houses
of the missionary families and their children. As Cyrus Kingsbury
wrote to Dr. Samuel A. Worcester at the outset of the board's work
among the southeastern Indians, "The children should be removed
as much as possible from the society of the natives and placed where
they would have the influence of example as well as precept. This can
be done only by forming the school into one great missionary family
where they would be boarded by the missionaries and teacher and
be entirely under their direction and have their pious, orderly and
industrious example constantly before them."[23] The board used the
mission farm to teach Indian boys how to become farmers; missionary
wives educated young Cherokee girls to become farmer's wives. The
girls learned the household skills of making butter, cheese, soap, and
candles as well as cooking, spinning, weaving, sewing, and mend-
ing. Brainerd mission also built its own gristmill and sawmill. The
mission church provided the spiritual center of the community, and
regular attendance was required. The schools not only taught reading,
writing, and arithmetic but obliged all pupils to memorize a Calvinist catechism, to recite Bible verses, and to engage in daily prayer,
hymn singing, and spiritual self-examination. The missionary families
lived in clapboard houses like those of any New England town and
maintained a high standard of manners, dress, and morality to set an
example for "the children of the forest."

The Baptists, after a short period in which they imitated the enclave system of the ABCFM, concluded in 1827 that it was far more
important for their missionaries to itinerate on horseback through
the Cherokee Nation along fixed circuits, preaching wherever Cherokees might be gathered together, spending their nights in the homes
of the Cherokees, spreading the Word of God. Taking note of the
success of Methodist circuit riders, the Baptists adopted the system

of "protracted meetings," or camp meetings, announced in advance and lasting three or four days in the woods or clearings. Protracted meetings, being social as well as religious gatherings and encouraging direct participation in spontaneous singing, shouting, and prayer, were in some respects similar to the various ceremonial gatherings the Cherokees had long practiced. The Baptists, though less emotional in their preaching than Methodists, were ready to employ the "anxious bench" and to form preparatory "societies" under native leaders in which those "awakening" to the principles of Christianity could reinforce one another in prayer and Bible study between protracted meetings. The Baptists were also much quicker than the Congregationalists to baptize and admit to church membership any earnest Cherokee who, though ignorant of doctrinal details, seemed ready to make a genuine commitment to give up the old religion for the new. As one critical American Board missionary said of the Baptist and Methodist converts, "Persons can scarcely be convinced of sin or begin to think seriously on eternal things before they are dragged into the bosom of some church." The danger of this, he went on, was that "having joined a church, the work [was] done in their estimation"—the Cherokee believed himself to be a full-fledged Christian and ceased to strive to purify himself; "all their convictions [of sin were] stifled . . . and their case rendered almost hopeless." [24]

The Congregationalists of the ABCFM were far more rigid. They disliked revival meetings and the emotional pressure of the "anxious bench." They seldom itinerated. They held the Cherokee to the same standards of doctrinal knowledge, faith, and practice as the people of New England. As Worcester's biographer wrote, "Salvation was so complex and the way to its accomplishments so slow and devious that the end might . . . be lost in the pursuit of the means." [25] A long period of probation preceded baptism and a longer one preceded admission to communion; in between, the "awakened" sinner was required to study the catechism, examine his or her own conscience, engage in regular prayer and worship, and live without sin in order to demonstrate proof of "election." Church membership was held up as a high privilege; it marked the end of the road to conversion, not the beginning, and Cherokees found it extremely trying. Those who did meet the standard tended to feel quite superior to those who did not.

In addition, the Congregationalists were unlike the Baptists in their determination to concentrate their evangelistic efforts upon the more enlightened and influential Cherokees. As Cyrus Kingsbury said in 1816, "Those who will be the first educated will be the children of the half-breeds and the leading men of the nation. . . . [O]n their education and influence the character of the nation will very much depend."[26] Jeremiah Evarts, the corresponding secretary of the ABCFM, reiterated this view in 1827: "It is of great consequence to have the females in the principle [*sic*] families instructed. In this way only will education become popular and fashionable."[27] Their plan to Christianize and civilize the Cherokees from the top down was precisely the opposite of the Baptists'; it was as paternalistic as the Federalists' view of politics. The Baptists, however, shared the view of the Jacksonian Democrats that the heart of the nation rested with the common man, that the voice of the people is more likely than that of the "aristocrats" to be the voice of God.

Many statements by Congregationalist missionaries reveal their disdain for the "low standards" and cheap tactics of both the Baptists and the Methodists. Their attitude was similar to their Puritan forefathers' disdain for the "superficial" conversion tactics of "Papist" missionaries to the heathen. As one American Board missionary put it, "Their means of receiving members is directly calculated to lead souls to hell." "No more than one out of twenty of their members was a real christian."[28] Another wrote specifically of Evan Jones, "Last Sabbath Mr. Jones was in the neighborhood. . . . It was said that five were baptized, some of them, if not all, I have reason to think, as ignorant of the cause of their baptism as the infants we baptize."[29] Such remarks were meant to explain why Congregational missions were adding only three or four members a year after 1839, while "the Baptist and Methodist churches [were] greatly enlarged." Butrick reported, "They take such measures, however, as none of your missionaries, I presume, would adopt to enlarge the number of their followers."[30]

Furthermore, the Congregationalists charged, after Cherokees were admitted to church membership, the Baptists failed to keep close "watch and care" over them and to censure or excommunicate them for lapses in Christian conduct. "Our Baptist brethren do not believe, as we do, with regard to the covenant obligations of parents nor do they instruct their members so fully respecting the sacredness of the holy Sabbath."[31] They cited examples of parents who neglected to bring their children to church and church members who were seen working their farms on Sunday. Baptists tended to be tolerant of such lapses; Congregationalists were not.

This is not to say that the Congregationalists took no interest in the full-bloods. When the first of the missionaries discovered that their required payment of a dollar per week for room and board at the Brainerd school meant that few full-bloods could attend, they abandoned the fee. This immediately resulted in doubling the number of full-bloods in the student body for a short time. On the other hand, the American Board missionaries seemed unaware of the damaging ethnocentrism embodied in their determination to teach only in English. Their missionaries made little effort to learn Cherokee. It quickly became apparent that children of mixed-blood parents who spoke English in their homes were able to learn much faster than those from Cherokee-speaking homes. Soon the ratio of mixed-bloods to full-bloods in American Board schools was three to one, the exact opposite of their proportion among the Cherokees.[32]

When new students were admitted to the American Board schools, the teachers noted opposite their names whether they were "half Cherokee," or "one eighth," or "five eighths." They also noted which were "lower class," which were "middle class," and which had "influential parents."[33] This may only have represented their concern to reach those of the "leading families," and it may only have been a statement of perceived "fact" that the mixed-blood and middle-class children performed much better than the full-blood and lower-class children. But none of the teachers thought it necessary to employ interpreters or try bilingual education. Inadvertently, these schools hardened or exacerbated a growing distinction within the Cherokee Nation between mixed-bloods and full-bloods, or what the whites called "the enlightened and intelligent class" and "the ignorant and backward class." By 1851, Worcester's mission school at Park Hill had not a single full-blood student; they were all, he said, "one-half to one-quarter white."[34] The Congregationalists were shocked, however, when one mixed-blood parent complained because his son was forced to work in the fields of the mission farm as part of his education. Only black slaves did field work in his opinion, and so he offered to lend the mission one of his slaves if they would free his son from this degrading work.[35]

Cherokee students quickly absorbed the missionary bias against full-bloods. In writing of their school experience at Brainerd the mixed-blood children revealed their own embarrassment regarding backward Cherokees: "The unenlightened parts of this nation," wrote one twelve-year-old mixed-blood, "assemble for dances around a fire. . . . They dance all night and torture themselves by scratching their bodies with snakes' teeth. . . . Their dishes are made by themselves from Clay." However, this student continued, "Many [Cherokees] about this [mission] station are more civilized . . . and appear as well as white people."[36] Another wrote, "The missionaries do a great deal of good; they teach us to behave as Christian people do and how to study as white children do."[37] When a parent took an advanced pupil out of the school to live at home, one missionary wrote, "We are very sorry to part with this child and have her taken back to the region of darkness."[38]

Baptist missionaries were not immune to this ethnocentrism, but on the whole it affected them much less. Evan Jones hardly ever mentioned in his reports whether his schoolchildren or converts were of full-blood or mixed ancestry and never tried to gauge their social class. "The Cherokee children learn as fast as any Children I ever saw," said the Reverend Thomas Roberts, Jones's colleague at Valley Towns; "[their] mental powers appear to be in no respect inferior to those of whites."[39] Jones expressed his opposition to his board's rule that all schools must be taught only in English. "I think it would be a great improvement in our system if those who don't understand English were taught to read first in Cherokee. To condemn them to the hard fate of acquiring every idea of God and his salvation, as well as the arts of civilization, through the medium of an unknown tongue, and that too without a Grammar or vocabulary to assist them, appears to be at variance with reason."[40] In part, language was a problem because Valley Towns was in the heart of the full-blood region. More than 90 percent of the six thousand Cherokees in this mountain region were Cherokee-speaking full-bloods. Yet Jones never suggested as a solution that his denomination should concentrate more on reaching the mixed-bloods, nor did his board make such a suggestion. Jones identified his work with the poorer Cherokees out of his own experience as a Welshman in London, as a foreigner in America. From his first day in Valley Towns he bent all his efforts toward learning to speak and write Cherokee. It was one of the most difficult Native American languages, but by 1830 Jones was preaching in it and had learned to write in the Sequoyan syllabary. Most Congregationalists agreed with Dr. Worcester, the first corresponding secretary of the ABCFM, who opposed any use of the Cherokee language; he said it "would perpetuate the dying Indian tongue."[41] Although the board later relented and encouraged Dr. Worcester's nephew to translate the Bible and other religious works into Sequoyan, it always considered this only a temporary expedient. "Assimilated in language," said the board in its annual report in 1827, "they will more readily become assimilated in habits and manners to their white neighbors."[42]

The Baptist approach to acculturation favored syncretism rather than assimilation. The Baptists did not demand total conformity to white standards. As they traveled among the Cherokees, shared their cabins and food, understood their customs, appreciated their way of life, they ceased to make sharp distinctions between Christian and pagan, civilized and unenlightened. Evan Jones dropped his initial hostility toward their dances, ball plays (an early form of lacrosse played with web-ended sticks), and medical practices. He always spoke of their medicine men as "adoniskee," not as "conjurers." Some Congregationalist missionaries accused Jones of admitting "adoniskee" to his mission churches and permitting them to continue their traditional practice of medicine. He told his board in 1830 that he had spoken with a female doctor: "She said our way was very different from theirs. . . . She wished to know if the word of God condemned the practice of medicine altogether. I told her all medical substances were free to be used with thankfulness to God."[43] He later admitted this woman to the mission church, although she continued to practice her medicine in what she considered the secular fashion of Christian doctors. Similarly, Baptists took advantage of the traditional "purification ritual" of the Cherokees. Designed to free people from the resentments of petty quarrels and to restore harmony to the community, this ritual required entering a running stream and dipping oneself under the water while an *adonisgi* recited a sacred formula. The Baptists called attention to the similarity of this to their practice of total immersion as a symbol of purification from sin.

One of the American Board's missionaries, Daniel S. Butrick, became friendly with Evan Jones and adopted both his itinerant preaching strategy and his concern to reach the full-blood majority. He tried to learn Cherokee and informed his board that if it did not reach out more wholeheartedly toward the full-bloods, the Baptists and Methodists would reap the largest harvest of souls:

There is a very great difference between the social classes within the Cherokee Nation. . . . [T]he most enlightened scarcely know the depths of ignorance in which the great body of these people lie nor how to get down to them so as to raise them up. . . . This is the case also with many, if not most, missionaries: They will not come down far enough to take hold even of their blankets to lift them out of this horrible pit. They think they must be equal [in comfort], if not surpass, the first class of Cherokees, and thus fix their marks entirely beyond the reach of all the common Indians.[44]

Butrick concluded, "If we will not condescend to the poorest class of Cherokees . . . they will either go to the Baptist or Methodist meetings where they can find someone who does not feel above them. . . ." Butrick was not alone in noting this. Dr. Marcus Palmer, sent by the ABCFM to examine why its Cherokee mission churches were not increasing in membership, reported in 1855 that the board's missionaries tended to neglect "the most ignorant, depraved, poor and filthy Indians" and "visit[ed] only the better families who [could] furnish good entertainment [hospitality]." Not only did they fail to evangelize among the poor, but they "especially treat[ed] such with apparent coldness when they call[ed] at the station."[45] Such disdain went strongly against the hospitality ethic that was deeply engrained in Cherokee tradition; no Cherokee ever refused food and lodging to a traveler or turned away a poor person needing help. Congregationalists tended to view Cherokee visitors of low status as beggars, persons too lazy to work. Their refusal to give anything to such "visitors" aroused considerable anger and hostility over the years. At least one Congregationalist missionary was driven from his station for such behavior. Whereas the Baptist missionaries were seen as kind and generous, the Congregationalists were considered harsh skinflints.[46] The prediction of Daniel Butrick came true. In 1860 the Reverend Charles Torrey reported to the ABCFM from the Cherokee Nation, "The Methodists and Baptists have full possession of this field."[47]

Removal of the Cherokees

If the Baptists seemed more sympathetic toward the mass of Cherokees with regard to evangelism and bilingual education, the Congregationalists appeared at first to offer them more assistance in their political relations with officials in Washington, D.C. To some extent, this resulted from the fact that prior to removal the Baptist effort was chiefly in North Carolina and, as such, was insulated from the crisis fomented by the Georgians when they asserted jurisdiction over the Cherokee land within their borders. As early as 1819 the American Board had used its connections in Washington to help the Cherokees stave off an effort to remove them to western Arkansas Territory. After 1828, when Andrew Jackson came to the assistance of Georgia's efforts to remove the Cherokees, Samuel A. Worcester, situated at the Nation's capital of New Echota, within Georgia's boundaries, felt compelled to protest. He did not have to convince Jeremiah Evarts that Jackson's removal program would be extremely detrimental to all of the board's work among the southeastern tribes.

The BBFM, on the other hand, endorsed the removal plan in the 1820s, largely because two-thirds of the members of its denomination lived in the South and West, where Jackson's program had overwhelming support.[48] Even though the executive committee of the BBFM in Boston was hesitant about Indian removal, its policies were controlled by the triennial missionary convention attended by denominational representation from all over the United States. The ABCFM, having no significant representation from the South except among conservative Presbyterians, and being represented in the Northwest chiefly by transplanted New Englanders, had strong support in opposing removal.

Furthermore, the Reverend Isaac McCoy, a highly popular Baptist missionary to the Pottawatomis, Weas, Ottawas, and other small tribes in Michigan, Indiana, and Illinois from 1816 to 1826, was convinced that removal would be beneficial to the majority of tribes east of the Mississippi. In 1827 he wrote a book (which Andrew Jackson later endorsed) calling for "collocation" of the eastern tribes west of the Mississippi River away from the baneful influences of the advancing frontier.[49] His plan won enthusiastic support from Wilson Lumpkin and other leading politicians in Georgia. Through their influence among southern Baptists, the triennial convention voted in 1823 to instruct the BBFM to petition Congress in support of Indian removal. This lobbying by the board continued in subsequent years, much to the discomfort of the executive committee and Evan Jones. Jones was constantly confronted by angry Cherokees asking why the Baptists had taken sides with their enemies: "I have been challenged on the subject repeatedly," he wrote to the board.[50]

The ABCFM had won Cherokee approval on this issue as early as 1819, when it sent Dr. Samuel A. Worcester to Washington to work with a delegation of Cherokees against an earlier effort to make them move westward. Worcester met with the secretary of war and helped the Cherokees to make a treaty that he, and they, thought would guarantee their right to remain in their homeland forever. One of the leaders of the Cherokees, John Ross, wrote to the board after the treaty to thank the board for its help: "I cannot express my feelings of gratitude on behalf of the Cherokee Nation."[51] Although all missionary agencies insisted that representatives in the field should never meddle in politics, neither the ABCFM nor the BBFM had any qualms about this.

By 1828 Jeremiah Evarts had become corresponding secretary of the Prudential Committee. Born in Vermont, a graduate of Yale in 1802, a lawyer, and the editor of the official organ of the ABCFM, the *Missionary Herald*, Evarts served as treasurer of the board from 1811 to 1821. Dr. Worcester had conducted the Prudential Committee's business from Salem; in 1821 Evarts moved its headquarters to Pemberton Square in Boston.[52] Evarts made several trips to Washington to lobby against Jackson's removal program. In 1818 he launched a national protest campaign against it in a series of articles published in the *National Intelligencer* in Washington, pointing out the unconstitutionality and immorality of the policy. When the removal bill finally passed in May 1830, despite strong opposition from congressmen from New England, Evarts persuaded the ABCFM to petition Jackson in opposition to another aspect of the removal campaign—the effort of Georgia to detribalize the Cherokees and seize their land. Realizing that New England missionaries opposed this, Georgia passed a law requiring all white men in the Cherokee area of Georgia to swear an oath of allegiance to Georgia upon penalty of four years at hard labor.

When the Reverend Samuel A. Worcester and a colleague, Dr. Elizur Butler, told the Prudential Committee that they could not conscientiously sign this oath, the committee unanimously voted to support them in a test case before the United States Supreme Court. In 1831 Worcester and Butler were convicted in Georgia and sent to the state penitentiary. Chief Justice John Marshall sustained their appeal to the Supreme Court in *Worcester* v. *Georgia*. Worcester and Butler became, momentarily, heroes of the Cherokee Nation, and the ABCFM was hailed as its savior.

Meanwhile, one of the Baptist missionaries to the Cherokees, the Reverend Duncan O'Briant, who had been supported in his work by the Sarepta Missionary Society of Georgia, signed the oath and then further angered the Cherokees by leading his congregation across the Mississippi in 1832 to start a new mission in the area designated for the Cherokees under the removal program.[53] The BBFM approved of O'Briant's decision, but some members of the executive committee in Boston had second thoughts (which McCoy attributed to the influence of Evarts and the ABCFM upon them).[54] Lucius Bolles, corresponding secretary of the committee, wrote to Evan Jones to ask his opinion. Jones, on his own initiative, had attended a meeting of missionaries at Worcester's home in December 1830 and had signed a manifesto opposing removal. He now urged the board to reconsider its position and to withdraw its support for removal. Opposition to this measure, he wrote, was "the decided, constant, unvarying voice of the whole body of the people . . . they have no disposition to remove," and any suggestion that they should do so given "to a Christian or Pagan Cherokee from a Missionary would be regarded with indignation and his influence and usefulness would be utterly destroyed."[55] The support that the board had already given to O'Briant "had the effect to bring into question . . . the friendly feelings of [the] denomination towards the Indians."[56]

When it became clear that Jackson would not carry out Marshall's decision, Worcester and Butler gave up their opposition. They petitioned Governor Lumpkin of Georgia for a pardon in January 1833 and were released. The ABCFM wrote to Chief John Ross, advising him of the reversal of its position and suggesting that he face the inevitable and acquiesce in removal. Ross was shocked beyond measure at this betrayal. The Cherokees, who had hailed Worcester and Butler as heroes, now denounced them as traitors. The warm feelings of the Cherokees toward the ABCFM were permanently undermined. Worcester added to their anger when he urged his translator, Elias Boudinot, a leading figure among the mixed-bloods, to organize a party to support a removal treaty. As a result, the Cherokees became divided into two bitterly hostile factions, one led by Boudinot, his cousin, and his uncle, favoring removal, and a much larger one, led by John Ross, determined to oppose it to the bitter end. When Evan Jones threw his wholehearted support behind Ross, the Baptists gained new respect, and the BBFM in Boston expressed the hope that its missionaries would soon replace the Congregationalists as the most prominent Christian force among the Cherokees. In 1835, Worcester moved to the new western area, leaving the Cherokees to look after their own struggle. Later that year, Boudinot and a small group of Cherokees, most of them mixed-bloods, signed a removal treaty without the consent of the Cherokee council. Cherokee law imposed the death penalty for anyone who sold tribal land without approval of the council and chiefs. But the United States Senate ratified the fraudulent treaty of New Echota. Boudinot, his cousin, and uncle were later executed by the Cherokees for treason in 1839. The mass of Cherokees refused to consider the treaty valid and stood their ground for three more years.

Evan Jones and his full-blood converts, led by the Reverend Jesse Bushyhead, an ordained Baptist Cherokee, concentrated all their energies on helping Chief Ross persuade Congress to rescind the treaty. Jones became so deeply involved in this Cherokee resistance movement that when General John Wool was sent to disarm the Cherokees in 1836—for fear that they might resort to armed rebellion— Jones refused to help him. Wool thereupon expelled Jones from the Nation. Jones simply moved a few miles across the Cherokee border into Tennessee. From there he continued to itinerate through the Nation, preaching with his native ministers and rallying support for the antiremoval party. Finally, in June 1838, President Martin Van Buren sent the United States Army to remove the Cherokees by force. Chief Ross appointed Jones to assist in the removal process, which the United States government allowed the Cherokees to manage themselves. Jones marched with them on the Trail of Tears eight hundred miles to their new home. Just prior to leaving, he called together his four hundred Cherokee church members and persuaded them to vote to refuse Christian fellowship with any Cherokee who had signed the false removal treaty. Signing that treaty had been a sin against God.[57]

Competition over Translating

From the outset of their work among the Cherokees, Evan Jones and Samuel A. Worcester had given a high priority to translating the Bible into Cherokee. For some years they assisted each other in this process, and after 1841 they agreed to publish on their own presses the different books of the Bible that each translated without duplicating the works the other printed. Thus, working in tandem and binding together the books translated and published separately by each, they jointly labored to give the Cherokees the whole Bible in their own tongue. The enterprise was in the best tradition of inter-denominational Christian mission work, but it fell afoul of the inevitable differences between the two denominations over the ordinance of baptism. Furthermore, as the partnership turned into rivalry, the Baptists proved more adept at producing a translation that appealed to the Cherokees. The parvenu Baptists once again gained upon the descendants of the Puritans who had persecuted them.

Samuel A. Worcester had persuaded his board to send a printing press to his station in New Echota with fonts of type in the Sequoyan syllabary. It arrived in 1827, and, with the assistance of Elias Boudinot, Worcester began publishing parts of the Bible, gospel hymns, and religious tracts in 1828. Evan Jones in Valley Towns had begun his efforts to translate the Bible and prepare a Cherokee grammar and spelling book in 1822. However, he had no college education, and his board did not trust him with such a serious scholarly undertaking. It ordered him to make itinerant preaching his chief occupation and declined to send him a printing press. Once the ABCFM began publishing, the BBFM told Jones to utilize Worcester's translations. Of necessity Jones learned to speak and write Cherokee, for he found interpreters both inadequate and expensive. He continued to make his own translations of the parts of the Bible that Worcester had not printed, and during the 1820s he traveled often to New Echota to consult with Worcester and Boudinot about the Cherokee language. Worcester never learned to speak Cherokee, and after 1833 Jones found in Jesse Bushyhead a translator every bit as good as Boudinot.

After Worcester and Boudinot deserted the Cherokee antiremoval cause and went west, Jones finally persuaded his board, in 1838, to send him a printing press with Sequoyan type fonts. By this time removal was inevitable, so the BBFM sent the press to Baptist Mission in the West. It did not arrive until 1841. Worcester now had a new press in operation at Park Hill, and the BBFM instructed Jones to publish only those parts of the Bible that Worcester had not yet printed. Jones reported that the antiremoval Cherokees were still so angry with Worcester that they were reluctant to read anything from his press. But when the two men began binding together the books of the Scriptures each published separately, the Cherokees accepted them.

Fortunately, Worcester and Boudinot had chosen a Cherokee word for "baptize" that meant "to wash in water." Because the Cherokees often washed by dipping themselves totally in a stream or river, Jones at first had no qualms about using Worcester's translations. Worcester told his board, "The verb which we translate 'baptize' signifies 'to wash' whatever the mode of washing. Its prevailing use, it is true, relates to washing by immersion, but by no means its exclusive use. . . . The truth is, there is no ground of controversy between us and our Baptist brethren [on this point]."[58] The native preachers or interpreters of each denomination put their own gloss upon the term.

Shortly after Jones obtained his press, his converts built a cabin to house it, and the board sent a printer from Boston to set type and print and bind the publications as they appeared. Jones at first received help from Bushyhead, but when the native translator died in 1844, he turned to his own son, John Buttrick Jones, who was now twenty and fluently bilingual. However, John had little education, having lived all his life in the Cherokee Nation. Not until 1855, after John had gone east and obtained college and divinity school degrees, did Jones have the kind of learned support for his work that enabled him to compete on equal terms with Worcester. Until then, however proud the BBFM was over Jones's success in saving souls, it was always dubious about his competence as a translator—part of the inferiority feeling the denomination had long had about itself in Puritan New England.

Evan Jones first aroused Worcester's criticism when he broke his pledge and began printing copies of books of the Bible that Worcester had already translated and published. Then Jones and his son annoyed Worcester when they used different words to describe the process of baptism; they put it in a context that meant "to go all the way into the water" and not simply "to wash." Worcester first voiced this concern in 1846 when he was putting together a new compilation of all the books of the Bible he and Jones had published. Noticing that Jones was using different words to describe baptism, he wrote to the Prudential Committee asking whether it would be proper for his books to go out with one translation of this word while Jones's book, bound within the same cover, used a different one. "A practical question arises in regard to the circulation of the Baptist translation of the part of the New Testament together with our translation of other parts. . . . [T]hey have translated thus in Luke, 'I indeed baptize you in water. . . .' We have 'with water.' "[59] Worcester thought that if he failed to include a preface to the volume pointing out his disagreement, "the poison [would be] diffused" and confusion would arise between "sprinkling" and "dipping." But if he did publish such a disclaimer, then he would accentuate the denominational differences that missionaries wished to hide. It was always embarrassing to explain to the heathen why there were so many different forms of Christianity.

Worcester complained again in 1852 that Jones and his son were publishing their material too hastily and with too little reliance on the original Hebrew and Greek. "They are also going on with the translation of scripture at a rate altogether too rapid to be correct." "Mr. Jones has translations made by those who know nothing of Hebrew and then revises them himself . . . without either superior knowledge of the Hebrew or greater care in the comparison than I use." [60] Worcester expressed doubts about Jones's knowledge of Hebrew, and finally, in 1851, he angrily told a friend that he considered Jones's translations "worthless." [61]

When the Baptist board learned of this, it ordered Jones to stop printing and to sell the press. The board did not want to foment discord in the New England missionary camp, and it still worried that Jones lacked the learning to compete with Worcester. Jones and his printer, Hervey Upham, fought back. They went to the best interpreters and bilingual Cherokees in the Nation and solicited endorsements of Jones's translations. These men said freely that Jones's translations were, from the Cherokees' point of view, far superior to the pedantic translations of Worcester. Hervey Upham relayed to the board what John Foster, one of the bilingual Cherokees, said: "He has conversed with those capable of discriminating between the two translations. He says our translation is admitted to be the most correct, that it is better Cherokee, more readily understood and more gladly received by full Cherokees than the Park Hill translation." [62]

Worcester, of course, had his own supporters, especially among the ABCFM missionaries. "Mr. Jones' translations," said one of them, "have taken unwarrantable liberties in favor of his peculiar views"; "his mode of translation, in many parts [is] a sort of running commentary." [63] Nevertheless, the Cherokees preferred Jones's translations, which seemed to them to capture the idioms of their speech better and to be more easily comprehensible. As in so many other aspects of its mission work, the ABCFM cared more for the letter than the spirit of the gospel. The Puritan heritage was not so compatible with the frontier as the common touch of the Baptists.

After discovering the Cherokees' preference and support for Jones, the BBFM relented; it allowed him to keep his press and continue his translating. With the return of John B. Jones from divinity school in 1855, the BBFM at last felt confident that it had a scholar equal to Worcester. It asked him to make any revisions necessary in his father's translations. John wrote to the board in 1856, "Matthew has been translated under the direction of the Rev. S. A. Worcester, missionary of the American Board, yet it is susceptible of a much better rendering. There are but few passages in which our views of baptism would make a difference in the rendering; e.g., 3:11. Mr. Worcester puts 'I baptize with water.' . . . I have chosen the radical conjugation of the same verb. The expression is equal to the English expression, 'I baptize in water.' . . . To express the act of baptism, we use the same word, Go-ha-wo-ah, 'I dip thee.' "[64] John went on to explain very learnedly the various Greek words and their Cherokee correlates on this topic, demonstrating such a thorough mastery of both languages that the board was prepared to defend his translations before any competent body. The BBFM and the ABCFM were never reconciled on this issue. In the end, the Cherokees made the choice.

The Problem of Slavery among the Cherokees

Although the board and missionaries of the ABCFM agreed with the board and missionaries of the BBFM on the immorality of black chattel slavery, the ABCFM could never persuade its agents that slavery was a sin that could not be tolerated in Christian churches. To slaveholding Cherokees both Worcester and Jones were rank abolitionists, but the latter was far more offensive because he did something about it.

Bostonians became increasingly antislavery in the 1840s and 1850s, but during the early years of Congregational and Baptist missions among the slaveholding Indians, both were strangely indifferent to the problem. In fact, both mission boards and missionaries had utilized slave labor in building and sustaining their mission stations. After 1840, however, local pressures from northern church members required both boards to look more closely into the matter. Humphrey Posey, when he established the Baptist mission at Valley Towns, appears to have used slave labor and may have owned slaves himself.

Evan Jones noted in the 1840s that some of the Baptist missionaries to the Cherokees had hired slaves as domestic servants and for hard labor. But he maintained that personally he had always opposed the institution.[65] In 1850 he told Solomon Peck, the corresponding secretary of the BBFM, that as early as 1832 he had persuaded two of his converts to free their slaves.[66] Still, slavery had hardly been a problem among the full-bloods with whom Jones worked because most of them were too poor to own any.

Because the missionaries of the ABCFM catered chiefly to the more well-to-do mixed-bloods who owned most of the slaves in the Nation, their mission churches were much more entangled with the institution. A much higher proportion of their converts were slaveholders. The missionaries of the ABCFM not only hired slaves regularly but sometimes purchased them and let them work to earn their freedom at an agreed-upon rate of pay per month.

The slavery question came to a head for the BBFM in the early 1840s when there were about fifteen hundred black slaves among the Cherokees—almost 10 percent of the population. In 1844, when a group of antislavery Baptists in the northern states broke off from the BBFM and founded the Baptist Free Mission Society, they claimed that the BBFM condoned the sin of slavery.[67] The official newspaper of this group stated that the Reverend Jesse Bushyhead, who was in the employ of the board as an assistant missionary and translator, was a slaveholder. Solomon Peck wrote in confidence to Jones to inquire about the truth of this charge. Jones delayed answering. Providentially, Jesse Bushyhead died soon after. Then Jones admitted that Bushyhead had indeed owned slaves, but he noted that Bushyhead had treated them as though they were free. One of them was, in fact, a Baptist convert who had been doing exceptional evangelistic work for the Baptist cause among Cherokee slaves.[68]

Once the issue became controversial in mission work, the white Baptists in the South and Southwest displayed concern that the BBFM seemed to be dominated by Bostonians, who might refuse to appoint slaveholders as missionaries. In December 1844, the Alabama Baptist convention specifically asked the board this question; the executive committee of the board replied that it would never appoint as a missionary anyone who owned slaves.[69] In 1845, the Baptist denomination split into southern and northern branches that have never reunited. Each, therefore, sponsored its own foreign mission board, publishing house, and tract society. Asked by the board in Boston whether they would like to shift their employment to a southern board, the Baptists' missionaries to the Cherokees (all New Englanders) unanimously said no. The Baptist Free Mission Society continued to press the question of the board's collusion with slavery among the Cherokees. It particularly pressed to know whether the board's missionaries employed slaves or whether any Cherokee converts owned slaves. The board in turn pressed Evan Jones for an answer in 1848, but he declined to respond for almost a year.

The ABCFM faced a similar antislavery schism in its ranks. In 1846 the antislavery Congregationalists formed the American Missionary Association. Its trustees pressed the same kinds of inquiries upon the American Board. The executive committees of the ABCFM and the BBFM, perhaps after some formal discussion between them, decided to investigate. Letters were sent asking Worcester and Jones to list the number of slave owners in their mission churches, whether slaves were employed at the mission stations, and whether any preaching was done to mission churches to explain the sin of slavery and root it out. Both Worcester and Jones, speaking for the missionaries under their charge, replied that they had occasionally hired slaves and that they did not preach publicly against the sin of slavery. They both pointed out that since slavery was the law of the land in the Cherokee Nation, it would cause no end of trouble to oppose it. Furthermore, they believed that the resident federal agent of the United States, George M. Butler, himself a slaveholder from South Carolina, would accuse them of meddling in politics. Worcester reported that fifteen out of his two hundred church members owned slaves; Jones reported that four out of about a thousand of his church members did. Both missionaries saw no way to resolve this question without jeopardizing their work. According to their mutual commitment to congregational autonomy, the ABCFM and the BBFM had to leave the expulsion of members of a church for sinful behavior to the vote of the members. But to raise a debate on this issue in all the mission churches could totally disrupt them. Jones admitted that slaveholding was a sin deserving expulsion of members involved in the institution; Worcester insisted that no "apostolic example" made slaveholding a ground for denying church membership.[70]

Neither board could accept the status quo. Both said that if mission churches continued to condone slavery, the board had the right to cease providing any financial support for them and thus to withdraw their missionaries. The northern Baptist triennial convention in 1848 actually passed a vote declaring its intention to do this. The ABCFM, while stating the right in the abstract, never voted to carry it out. Worcester therefore continued to debate with his board, but Jones had to act. After talking with each of its slaveholding members, Jones persuaded them to take a letter of dismission, signed by him or their native pastor. This entitled them to join any other Baptist church without prejudice, although at that time there were no southern Baptist churches in the Cherokee Nation.[71]

Worcester, speaking for his colleagues, told his board, "While the strongest language of reprobation is not too strong to be applied to the system of slavery, truth and justice require this Board to say that the relations of a Master to one whom the constitution of society has made a slave is not to be regarded as in all cases such a sin as to require the exclusion of the Master . . . from Christian ordinances."[72] He and his colleagues, however, refused to preach on this matter from the pulpit. They went even further and said they would not give up hiring slaves when they needed their labor: "Either stations must be abandoned or slaves must be hired," Worcester told his board.[73]

When Jones finally reported in 1852 that there was no longer any connection between the institution of slavery and the Baptist mission among the Cherokees, he became a hero to his board and to the northern antislavery Baptists. However, he aroused the ire of southern Baptists. They concluded that they must now send missionaries to help those Cherokees dismissed by Jones as well as other Cherokee slaveholders who believed in Baptist principles.[74] Jones and his board also aroused the anger of the slaveholding interests in the Cherokee Nation and the more ardent proslavery officials in the Bureau of Indian Affairs.

The ABCFM became embarrassed by the fact that whereas the Baptists in Boston had solved this problem, they could not. The Prudential Committee specifically asked Worcester why he could not accomplish what the Baptists had. Jones's churches were still thriving. Worcester's were not. In his defense, Worcester said that Jones had broken the rule of strict congregational autonomy: "Jones has assumed prerogatives which did not belong to him." He had no right to give a Cherokee church member an honorable dismission to another church if he or she had sinned; nor had he any right to usurp the powers of local churches and their pastors to discipline their own church members or not, as they chose.[75]

When word got back to the Baptist board that Worcester disapproved of Jones's actions and of the pressure the BBFM had placed upon him to act contrary to established ecclesiastical rules, Solomon Peck wrote to Worcester for an explanation. It embarrassed the BBFM that its colleagues on the Prudential Committee of the ABCFM believed that it had placed improper pressure upon a missionary in the field. The Prudential Committee believed that the BBFM should not have capitulated to popular clamor on this issue. Worcester, who had been a classmate of Peck's at Andover Theological Seminary, replied: "I believe there are many truly pious persons who hold slaves and whom therefore my Lord accepts as members of His Church; and because I believe that He accepts them, I dare not reject them."[76] Moreover, "If our Board should instruct me to inform my church that it must refuse fellowship to all slaveholders or lose their patronage . . . I could not do it. I would sooner lose my right arm. If the Board insisted, I must resign my commission [as a missionary]. To tell the church that they must free themselves from such members or lose patronage . . . compels them to do wrong, [and] Mr. Jones, according to my judgment, should have met it with manly resistance." Acting under his board's wrongful orders, Jones infringed the principle of congregational autonomy and then pretended that those he dismissed were still in good standing. Peck had put his superintendent in an untenable position and Jones had caved in. "It seems to me that Mr. Jones's undertaking was only preposterous." This cleared both Worcester and his board of embarrassment by sticking to the rules. To him it was characteristic of the Baptists' work throughout that they cared more for results than for principles.

Peck was not impressed by these punctilious and self-serving remarks. "The independency of churches is a doctrine held and guarded by Baptists with utmost scrupulousness," he said, but Worcester had forgotten that missions among the heathen were not on the same footing as the churches in a Christian society. It was perfectly right and proper, Peck went on, for a missionary superintendent "among churches recently gathered from the heathen," to assume some prerogative in exceptional circumstances, and this was clearly one of them.[77] Worcester sent copies of the exchange to his board. The Congregationalists, unwilling to force the resignation of a man who had done so much for their cause, did not push him any further. They doubtless preferred his high standards to the pragmatism of the Baptists.

When the federal agent, George Butler, learned what Jones had done, he solicited depositions from the dismissed Baptists, who were angry about their forced withdrawals. He sent these to the commissioner of Indian Affairs with a request that Jones be expelled from the Cherokee Nation. He also included a complaint against Worcester for being an "abolitionist." Jones and Worcester, he said, were merely "instruments" in the hands of their board in Boston.[78] The commissioner took no action on this complaint, but when Jones and his son expanded their opposition to slavery, the government responded.

In 1856 Evan and John B. Jones helped to organize a secret antislavery society among the Cherokee full-bloods, led by Baptist converts, in opposition to a secret proslavery society that the Cherokee slaveholders had formed.[79] The purpose of the slaveholders' organization was to drive all abolitionists from the Nation by vigilante action; it also hoped to elect more proslavery candidates to the Cherokee council. The full-bloods named their organization the Keetoowah Society. Its members pledged themselves to elect antislavery candidates to the council and to keep the Cherokee Nation neutral if war should break out in the United States between the slaveholding and non-slaveholding states. Membership in this society was limited to non-English-speaking Cherokees, and its ultimate goal was to assure that the full-blood majority controlled the Nation's destiny. Its meetings were held in the woods around a council fire with dancers and debates according to ancient forms, but they opened with prayers by native Baptist preachers. These Cherokees thus combined traditionalism with Christian moral reform and American political activism in a syncretic movement of major significance.

As soon as Agent Butler became aware of the Keetoowah Society, he informed the commissioner of Indian Affairs, Alfred B. Greenwood.[80] Greenwood issued orders to break up the organization and arrest its leaders. Neither Butler nor the agent who followed him succeeded in this, but in 1860 John B. Jones was expelled from the Nation "for propagating abolition or antislavery sentiments among the Cherokees." [81] A year later, Evan Jones fled in fear of his life from proslavery vigilantes.

Samuel Worcester, who, like Jones, had at times risked his own position in order to help freed slaves who were in danger of being sold back into bondage among the Cherokees, was not expelled. He died peacefully in his bed at Park Hill in 1859. A year later the ABCFM voted to close its mission to the Cherokees. The leaders of the American Missionary Association asserted that it did so because the board was unable to stamp out collusion with slavery by its missionaries (and after 1861 some former missionaries of the ABCFM did support the southern cause). The board asserted that the mission was closed because it had accomplished its goals: "We are at the time when the [Cherokee] nation may be regarded as so far Christianized that we may transfer our funds to other fields," wrote Rufus Anderson, the board's corresponding secretary, in March 1860.[82] Anderson noted that the board had spent a total of $374,137 on the Cherokee mission since 1816; it had sent 18 clerical missionaries, 29 lay missionaries, and 60 female assistants, for a total of 107 persons to Christianize and civilize that nation. He did not mention that for the preceding fifteen years the mission had made no gain in its number of total Cherokee converts. In 1860, the Congregationalists had fewer than two hundred members, the northern Baptists fifteen hundred, and the southern Methodists almost as many as the Baptists.

When the Civil War began, most of the one-third of the Cherokees who were of mixed ancestry, including the bulk of the slaveholders, fought with the Confederacy; most of the full-bloods fought with the Union. The Joneses served as chaplains in the Cherokee Union regiments.

Creating a Native Ministry and Self-Supporting Churches

The ultimate goals of all foreign missionary agencies were to awaken the heathen to the truth of Christianity, to train a native ministry, and to establish self-supporting churches. After forty-five years among the Cherokees, neither the ABCFM nor the BBFM had achieved the last of these goals, and the Congregationalists had done little toward creating a native ministry. Among the many reasons for the failure to establish self-supporting native churches were the scattered and migratory population, the general poverty of the mass of Cherokees, and the lack of any Cherokee tradition of voluntary financial support for denominational institutions. The missionaries had disorganized the traditional tribal religion but could not replace it with an exact replica of their own system. Some of the mixed-blood communities at Park Hill and Tahlequah did have the money and stability to support a church or two, but they were not especially pious, particularly the males. Two-thirds of the mission church members were females.

Insofar as the Baptists came close to achieving the ultimate goals of mission work, the cause lay in their greater emphasis upon establishing a native ministry and their willingness to license, ordain, and train it. Because the Congregationalists insisted on a well-trained, learned, professional ministry, their standards for ordaining native ministers were unrealistically high. Between 1817 and 1860, the ABCFM missionaries ordained only two of their Cherokee converts and encouraged only three native lay exhorters—all of these prior to removal. From 1834 to 1860 they found no Cherokee able to meet their standards or even worthy of being sent east for ministerial training. The two they did ordain, John Huss in 1831 and Stephen Foreman in 1834, were very different. Huss was a full-blood who neither spoke nor wrote English; his zeal and piety were considered sufficient to allow him to preach to the full-bloods, and he was originally ordained as an itinerant evangelist. After 1839 he became pastor of a small, full-blood congregation at Honey Creek in the West. But Huss proved to be an embarrassment to Worcester because he could not control the morals of his family; his oldest daughter was promiscuous, and Huss could not reform her. What was worse, he continued to let her live in his home despite her sinful disobedience to parental authority.[83] A minister who could not regulate his own family affairs was a poor example for the Cherokees, and Huss's failure in this respect contributed much to Worcester's decision as superintendent to ordain no more full-bloods. Huss did preach solid, orthodox Calvinism, but his church had fewer than a dozen members, several of whom were black slaves.

Stephen Foreman, on the other hand, was of mixed ancestry and bilingual and had received considerable theological training at Union Seminary in Virginia and at Princeton Theological Seminary in New Jersey. Because he knew Greek, Latin, and Hebrew, he was invaluable to Worcester as a translator at Park Hill. Yet Foreman never wanted to be pastor of a church, although he did sometimes preach in Worcester's church when Worcester was ill or absent. He devoted himself to trade and farming, for which he utilized black slaves; his slave owning proved an embarrassment. "Mr. Foreman," Worcester wrote in 1851, "is too much involved in secular cares and too little devoted to the spiritual welfare of his people." [84]

The best exhorter of the ABCFM was Samuel J. Mills, a mixed-blood, but after being encouraged to preach, he died before he could be licensed. Two Cherokee full-bloods, Jesse Barrow and Epenetus, were hired by the board to exhort and teach Sequoyan schools for a few years in the early 1830s, but when David Greene, the corresponding secretary, asked Worcester in 1842 why he did not ordain these or other native converts as the Baptist were doing, Worcester replied that neither was capable: "Although if we took for ourselves no higher standard than those have done who license Baptist preachers . . . I think we should have made ministers of them much before now. . . . The reason they [the Baptists] get them so cheap, is that they are cheap men." [85]

A few pious Cherokees were elevated to the rank of deacon or lay elder in the ABCFM's mission churches. These posts required them to oversee the moral standards of church members, raise funds, and otherwise assist their white pastors. But as Daniel Butrick observed to the board, the Cherokees made poor deacons because they did not like to press their brethren to live up to high Christian standards.[86] It was not the Cherokee way to use spiritual authority to enforce moral standards on relatives, friends, and neighbors.

The most compelling reason for not ordaining more native ministers was the singular failure of the American Board's Cornwall mission school to accomplish this end. During its ten-year existence, from 1817 to 1827, this academy in Connecticut enrolled eleven of the most promising young Cherokee converts (among others from overseas foreign missions of the board). Most of the Cherokees spent two or three years there preparing for college or ministerial training, but not a single one became a preacher. Most became merchants, lawyers, political leaders, or farmers. For Worcester and his colleagues, the fault for this lay with the Cherokees themselves. Somehow they seemed unable to measure up to the high calling required of a Congregational minister to the heathen.

The Baptists, by tradition, inclination, and circumstances found it easier to develop a native ministry, although they never succeeded in making their native churches self-sustaining. Prior to 1838 Jones had licensed or ordained thirteen Cherokees, most of them full-bloods. Some of these took charge of local congregations or branches of the Valley Towns mission; some of them were circuit-riding evangelists. Only one, Jesse Bushyhead, was pastor of a self-sustaining church, at Amohee, Tennessee. Bushyhead was bilingual, of mixed ancestry, a wealthy man, and a political leader, but he had no formal religious training other than attendance at a Presbyterian mission school. Baptists believed a man filled with the Holy Spirit, called by God, ardent in the work, and gifted at saving souls was sufficiently qualified for ordination. Jones, of course, did test the men he ordained or licensed through careful inquiry into their conversion experience, their understanding of basic Calvinist doctrines, their ability to preach, and their moral conduct. But earnestness, sincerity, and dedication were the chief requirements.

Many of those ordained prior to removal went west and continued their work. By 1860, there were twenty native Baptist preachers and evangelists, nine of them pastors of branch churches of the mission. Their congregations consisted almost wholly of full-bloods and sometimes contained a few black slaves. At first some of the ordained pastors were given new names by Jones (Onanaya became Peter; Kaneeda became John Wickliffe), but after 1839 most of them retained their original names: Tannenole, Dsulawee, Beaver Carrier, David Foreman, John Foster, Moses Potts, Smith Christie, Lewis Downing. Only one native preacher licensed by Jones was ever dropped from the ministry; his failing was alcoholism. Two became southern Baptists in the late 1850s, but on the whole they were remarkably faithful and constant; many of them remained active after the Civil War.

The executive committee of the BBFM was seldom willing to budget more than three or four hundred dollars to pay native preachers. Most of them had to support themselves and their families by farming or other work. Jones and his colleagues constantly urged the board to provide more funds for these men, pointing out that the success of their mission was due largely to them: "Nearly all our success with the Cherokees," said Hervey Upham in 1848, "is through the Native Assistants, and if it was not for them, we could hope to accomplish but little."[87] Willard Upham said the same: "The secret of our success is no doubt to be found in the great employ of Native Agency, without which I think nothing extensive can be expected."[88] And four years later he reported, "Native Agency is here found to succeed better than any other means. As a denomination, we have encouraged it more than all others put together, and as a result our prosperity has been in the same ratio. The American Board have a large corps of [white] missionaries (compared with ourselves) stationed at different points in the nation, and yet they accomplish but little." [89]

When the Baptist board insisted that the Cherokees must learn to support their own ministers, Jones patiently explained why this was so difficult: "In order to judge the ability of the Cherokees to support their Native Preachers," he wrote in 1857,

> it should be borne in mind that there are among them [the Cherokees] two distinct classes in very different circumstances with regard to property [wealth] and the means of acquiring it. One is that of the mixed blood, who speak English and are considered the intelligent [knowledgeable] and wealthy class. . . . The other class, which constitutes the body of the Nation and to which our labors have been chiefly devoted, is the full Cherokees. . . . They live by agriculture . . . they have met with many [natural] disasters . . . they were greatly impoverished [by removal] and are not yet recovered. [90]

He also explained that within their limited means, the full-bloods donated a great deal to support mission work. In 1849 he made a list of fourteen churches built entirely by the labor and donated supplies of his Cherokee congregations. He estimated the value of these buildings at $3,360.[91] He also pointed out that they contributed large amounts of food and did the cooking for dozens of protracted meetings year after year where hundreds gathered for several days. He estimated the cash value of these donations of food and forage for 1849 alone at more than $1,529.[92] The corresponding secretary, Edward Bright, responded that if they could provide these services, they could pay salaries as well; he suggested that Jones should cut back on camp meetings and use the money spent on them to pay native pastors.[93]

Recognizing that his native preachers often found it difficult to explicate some of the texts in the Bible (they preached from the translations of Jones and Worcester), Jones spent considerable time trying to improve their knowledge. At least once a month he gathered all his native preachers and deacons together at his home and spent two or three days helping them to understand the Bible and counseling them on pastoral duties. After 1855, his son John assisted in this. "Our last meeting for instructing the preachers was attended by many," John wrote in 1856. "We spent several days solving their difficulties, answering their questions and commenting on the various passages of scripture they wished explained. The labors of the day were sometimes protracted to eleven at night." [94] Daniel Butrick of the American Board attended one of these meetings and reported that there were six ordained Cherokee pastors and twenty-six licentiates present; Jones, he said, went through the Bible's book of Hebrews, which had just been printed and which was new to most of the native assistants. [95]

Nonetheless, the Congregationalists were extremely critical of these Baptist native ministers. "The preachers are apparently as ignorant as those of the Methodists," wrote Elizur Butler in 1851. [96] And even Jones's colleague Willard Upham reported that the Cherokee pastor Keneeda was so woefully ignorant of theology that he misinterpreted the texts he preached from and made almost no effort to discipline or excommunicate those of his flock who were known drunkards, those who failed to attend church regularly, or those who were immoral women. Speaking of the native ministers as a whole, Upham said, "I was greatly pained to find them so deficient in biblical knowledge, especially in regard to the great and precious doctrines of the Bible." [97] Like Samuel Worcester, Upham seemed to believe that native ministers should preach as though their listeners were New England Christians steeped in two centuries of Calvinist doctrines.

Robert Berkhofer argues that the whole missionary movement among the Native Americans was not only a failure but an "inevitable failure." [98] He makes no distinction between the work of the BBFM and that of the ABCFM among the Cherokees or other tribes because, in his view, they both suffered from the same fundamental mistakes and misconceptions. They both thought "the only good Indian was a carbon copy of a good white man." [99] They both believed that the goal of mission churches was "to supplant the indigenous rituals and religious societies as the new religious and social gathering place and entertainment center" of any Native American people. [100] Berkhofer's judgment is too sweeping. The traditional Indian religions were no longer capable of being sustained or of sustaining any of the tribes in their pristine forms. In many respects Christianity provided a means of revitalization. More detailed examination of the syncretic aspects of missionary work may provide a somewhat more positive assessment. The differences in the success of these two Boston-based mission agencies to the Cherokees seem to provide one way to evaluate this.

From 1817 to 1832, the ABCFM missionaries provided new hope and vital assistance to the Cherokees as they reconstructed their social and political order. They provided schools to help the Cherokee young adjust to new circumstances; they provided political assistance to native chiefs; they encouraged the Cherokees to feel they were capable of doing everything a white man could. From 1832 to 1860, the BBFM took the lead in sustaining hope among a large proportion of the full-bloods demoralized by removal and lacking the means to profit from the new market economy. It is some measure of the accomplishments of the Joneses that through the Keetoowah Society and their antislavery principles they saved the Nation from total defeat resulting from an unfortunate, but temporary, Cherokee alliance with the slaveholders. After the Civil War the Joneses returned as agents of the northern Baptist Home Mission Society and once again helped the common people restructure their nation. In 1867 they helped to create a new political party that elected Lewis Downing, a native Baptist pastor and colonel of a Cherokee Union regiment, as chief, thereby establishing full-blood control over the Nation as it faced Reconstruction.

Unlike the aloof, paternalistic, and high-toned Congregationalists of the ABCFM, the more pragmatic and democratic Baptists gave a social and political meaning to mission work and a participatory egalitarianism to church activities. In this form (shared with the Methodists) Christianity became a live option and a lively force in Cherokee culture. It seems plausible to argue that the success of the BBFM relative to that of the ABCFM derived both from the long history of the Baptist denomination as a popular movement among the poorer members of society and from its sense of inferiority and marginality in New England. In the early years of the republic, the Jeffersonian party assisted the Baptists in ending the last vestiges of the tax-supported favoritism the old Puritan churches had enjoyed in New England. The divisions within Congregationalism itself enabled a new sense of pluralism to develop in Boston, and new economic opportunities raised many Baptists to positions of wealth and respectability. The Second Great Awakening, the upsurge of nationalistic expansion, and the reform spirit that took such strong root in Boston provided opportunities for Christian cooperation—and competition—in spreading the political and social ideals of the Christian republic far and wide. Baptists profited from the missionary, temperance, and antislavery movements by demonstrating their commitment to the same ideals as the once dominant Congregationalists. A new definition of *e pluribus unum* emerged in America, and in their efforts to bring Christianity and republicanism to the Cherokees, the Baptists and Congregationalists carried westward the pluralism that was changing the face of Boston. The Baptists' comparative success among the Cherokees may well have derived from their embodiment of the new democratic spirit of the age, which encouraged rule from the bottom up rather than the top down. The Congregationalists' failure seems to have derived from the persistence of a certain puritanical rigidity in religion and an elitist paternalism in social attitudes that was out of step with the times. They lacked the common touch that came naturally to the Baptists.

Chapter 4
The Reverend Evan Jones and the
Cherokee Trail of Tears, 1838-1839

The forced removal of the Cherokees from their ancestral home-
lands to territory in the West is popularly known as the Trail of Tears. One of
the best-known episodes in Cherokee political history, it also had tremendous
significance for Cherokee spiritual life. Bonds to revered landscapes of moun-
tains, valleys, and springs and sacred connections to specific flora, fauna,
and wider ecologies were sundered, and traditional Cherokee religious life was
damaged.

Cherokee ties to Christianity were also strained, sometimes beyond repair.
How Christian missionaries responded to the demands on the Cherokees made
by federal and state governments was closely monitored by all parties. This
essay illustrates the challenges and hardships that the Cherokees faced during
the removal and the resourceful fortitude that they displayed in meeting these
difficulties. It also shows the manner in which politics and Christianity became
inseparable in the crucible of the removal controversy.

The Valley Towns mission was the first Baptist station
among the Cherokees of North Carolina, although Moravians, Presbyterians, Methodists, and Congregationalists were already active in
those parts of the Cherokee Nation lying within Georgia, Alabama,
and Tennessee.[1] Evan Jones and his family arrived at the Valley Towns
mission in 1821. In 1824 Jones felt a spiritual call to become a minister
and was ordained as pastor of the Valley Towns mission church by
some ministers from Georgia and Tennessee.[2] From 1824 to 1838, he
worked faithfully among the Cherokees in western North Carolina as
superintendent of the mission, while his wife and daughters taught
the mission school. In 1831 his wife died, and he married Pauline Cun-
ningham, a Tennessean employed at the mission who had also cared

for Elizabeth during her final illness. In 1833 Jones and his new wife were accused of murdering a missionary assistant and her newborn child; the woman was unmarried and the scandal nearly ended his career, although he and Pauline were acquitted.[3]

Jones proved to be a highly successful missionary. By 1838 his preaching and that of several Cherokee assistants and exhorters had led more than five hundred Cherokees to join the Valley Towns church and various branch churches in the region. Among the most successful of Jones's Cherokee colleagues in this evangelistic work was the Reverend Jesse Bushyhead of Amohee. Bushyhead, who later became chief justice of the Cherokee supreme court, was a man of considerable ability. The two devoted much time and effort to translating the Bible into Cherokee, using the syllabary devised by Sequoyah (George Guess) in 1821. For this effort, and in order to preach directly to non-English-speaking Cherokees, Jones learned to speak, read, and write Cherokee—an achievement few other missionaries accomplished.

In 1830, Congress, at President Andrew Jackson's urging, passed the Indian Removal Act, authorizing the exchange of lands in the West for the lands still occupied by tribes living east of the Mississippi River,[4] but the Cherokees vehemently opposed removal and refused to agree to such an exchange. However, President Thomas Jefferson had made a pact with the state of Georgia in 1802 in which the federal government agreed to remove the Indians from Georgia's boundaries as soon as possible. In 1828, Georgia assumed control over all Cherokee land within its borders, dissolved the Cherokee legislature and laws, and declared the Cherokees citizens of Georgia (though without the right to testify in court against whites or to hold civil office). The Cherokee chief, John Ross, argued that Georgia had no right to do this. A lawsuit before the United States Supreme Court upheld Ross's claim, but Jackson refused to enforce it. The Cherokees still refused to sign a treaty of removal and exchange of land. Then, in December 1835, they were betrayed by a small group of chiefs who made a treaty with Jackson's commissioner, the Reverend John F. Schermerhorn, at New Echota.[5] The treaty was fraudulent by Cherokee law because it was never ratified by the Cherokee council. Nevertheless, the United States Senate ratified the Treaty of New Echota in May 1836. Under its terms, the Cherokees were given five million dollars for their homeland and allowed two years to pack up and move to a new home in what is now northeastern Oklahoma (about four thousand Cherokees had voluntarily moved west between 1796 and 1833).

The strongest resistance to removal came from the Cherokee full-bloods who lived in the Great Smoky Mountains, and Evan Jones shared their determination not to be cheated out of their homeland. When General John E. Wool was sent with three thousand soldiers to Valley Towns in August 1836 to disarm the Indians (because whites feared they might take up arms to defend their land), Jones refused to cooperate with him. Wool thereupon expelled him from the Cherokee Nation. Jones took refuge with his family in New Columbus, Tennessee; from there he continued to itinerate and preach through the northern part of the Cherokee Nation, assisted by Jesse Bushyhead and other Christian Cherokee preachers. While itinerating, he did all he could to strengthen the antiremoval cause, working with Chief John Ross to thwart the removal plan of Jackson's handpicked successor, President Martin Van Buren. That resistance met with no sympathy from Congress or the president. Two years after the ratification of the fraudulent treaty, Cherokee resistance ceased.

On May 24, 1838, the Cherokee people came under the military rule of the United States Army. The secretary of war considered them to be in defiance of the laws of the United States by continuing to live on land that now belonged to the white citizens of Georgia, Alabama, Tennessee, and North Carolina—land on which the Cherokees had been living long before the whites came to America. Evan Jones did what he could to help, but the problems were overwhelming.

From May 24 to July 1, General Winfield Scott's soldiers rounded up sixteen thousand Cherokees (two thousand pro-removal Cherokees had left voluntarily between January 1836 and May 1838). The prisoners were driven from their homes to three separate embarkation points or to large stockaded "forts." The embarkation points were along the Tennessee River: one at the federal agency at Calhoun, Tennessee, one at Ross's Landing near present-day Chattanooga, and one at Gunter's Landing, near Guntersville, Alabama. The stockades were called Fort Hetzel (near Cleveland, Tennessee) and Fort Butler (near Columbus, Tennessee). The federal government had hired steamboats to take the Cherokees down the Tennessee River to the Ohio, down the Ohio to the Mississippi, down the Mississippi to the Arkansas River, and up the Arkansas to Fort Gibson, in what is now northeastern Oklahoma. By boat, the trip was more than nine hundred miles.

The first detachments of Cherokee men, women, and children—twenty-eight hundred of them—were forced onto the boats on June 6, 13, and 17. Another detachment of one thousand went overland, eight hundred miles under military guard. All refused to accept government clothing on the ground that this would constitute acquiescence in the justice of the removal. The thirteen thousand Cherokees still in camps pleaded not to be forced west until autumn. Because of the prolonged drought that began early that spring and lasted through September, there was fear of serious epidemics breaking out along the way as a result of bad drinking water. Summertime was called the "sickly season" by western travelers, the worst possible time to go west. Cholera, smallpox, malaria, and dysentery were common in large convoys of travelers.[6] In the summer, rivers were low and boats had great difficulty navigating; travelers often had to stop for weeks, hoping that rain would raise the water level so that they could proceed. Meanwhile, the passengers remained crowded together without adequate food or water. Much of the fear and panic that Jones described among the first Cherokees removed in June 1838 sprang from their belief that they faced certain death on the boats. The Reverend Daniel Butrick, who, like Jones, chose to march along the Trail of Tears with the Cherokees, spoke in his journal of the loading of the first Cherokee contingents into "filthy boats" that planned to "land them at Little Rock, a most sickly place." He believed that "to remain anywhere on that sickly river [was] only a most expensive and painful method of putting the poor people to death."[7] Those who went overland also faced problems in finding good water for themselves, their horses, and their oxen. They too believed that sickness would take many lives along the way.

After the first three thousand Cherokees were deported, George Lowrey (who was acting chief until John Ross returned from Washington on July 13) sent a petition to General Scott pleading with him to allow the remaining Cherokees to wait until September 1 before making their long, hazardous journey. Aware of the hysteria that prevailed, Scott acceded to the request on June 19. But the momentary relief from this concession soon turned to horror as the Cherokees discovered that the overcrowded stockades and embarkation depots were totally inadequate to house thousands of people through the long, hot summer. The army had given little thought to their construction because it expected the Cherokees to inhabit them for only a few weeks; the forts lacked adequate shelter, water, and sanitary facilities. Within a month all of the camps were swept by epidemics that took hundreds of lives. Few doctors were available in the camps, though the army tried to hire more. Many of the Cherokees preferred the services of their own medicine men and believed that the white doctors who "went from the tent of the dead to the tent of the sick" brought death with them. "Their doctors generally allowed no one to visit their patients but those whom they needed to wait upon them. They believe that unclean persons will prevent the favorable operation of [Cherokee] medicine."[8] The two systems of medicine worked against each other and compounded the difficulties. As a result, the stockades and embarkation depots became worse death traps than the boats.

Estimates vary on the total who died, but it is generally believed that two thousand to twenty-five hundred died in the camps before starting on their journey, one thousand to fifteen hundred died on the trip, and another thousand died within a year after their arrival. The primary victims were the children and the aged; no family escaped without some loss. Even John Ross, who traveled under better conditions than most, lost his wife, Quatie. The delay in departure granted by General Scott meant that most of the emigrants were on the road when winter came and had to travel through snow, sleet, and ice. Roughly one-fourth of the Nation died. A soldier who was present said later, "I fought through the Civil War and have seen men shot to pieces and slaughtered by thousands, but the Cherokee removal was the cruelest work I ever knew."[9]

There is no better way to visualize this process than through the eyes of Evan Jones. His letters and journals provide a vivid account of his own experience in the camps and along the journey:

June 4, 1838: Cherokee Agency. I write to you on this occasion under the pressure of great anxiety. The troops of the United States have actually commenced taking the Cherokees in Georgia and carrying them to the forts. I have just learned that about six hundred who have been brought from the Georgia part of the Nation into [the camp at] Ross's Landing are to be hurried off in the morning by Steam boat. Their fields and growing crops, furniture, except a few light articles, cattle, horses, hogs, sheep, farming implements, etc. left to the mercy of plunderers. It is said, indeed, that collectors will be appointed to gather up and take care of the property, but allowing these collectors to be men of the strictest probity, the neighbouring plunderers will take care that [they] shall have little to collect. In many places fierce contests have arisen between rival claimants of the poor Indian's field.

Great anxiety pervades the community. News has arrived that the

Delegation [in Washington] has failed to effect an arrangement with the Gov't. notwithstanding the basis of a treaty of final settlement has been agreed upon.

Tomorrow was the day appointed for taking all the Cherokees within the Chartered limits of Tennessee and today for taking those of North Carolina, but for some cause this business has been postponed till the 12th Inst. on which day, unless some countermanding orders should arrive, all the Indians in North Carolina, Tennessee, and Alabama are to be collected and transported to Arkansas.

The Indians are perfectly still, peacefully working in their fields and gardens, awaiting the arrival of the appointed day, but resolutely refusing to recognize the unjust and unauthorized instrument of New Echota. . . . It is hoped that the people of God will hear the poor afflicted Cherokees in faith before the throne of mercy.

P.S. A rumor has just reached this place that the President has laid the Cherokee business before Congress.

June 16, 1838: Camp Hetzel. The Cherokees are nearly all prisoners. They have been dragged from their houses and camped at the forts and military posts all over the Nation. In Georgia, especially, the most unfeeling and insulting treatment has been experienced by them, in a general way. Multitudes were not allowed time to take anything with them but the clothes they had on. Well-furnished houses were left a prey to plunderers who like hungry wolves, follow the progress of the captors and in many cases accompany them. These wretches rifle the houses and strip the helpless, unoffending owners of all they have on earth. Females who have been habituated to comforts and comparative affluence are driven on foot before the bayonets of brutal men. Their feelings are mortified by the blasphemous vociferations of these heartless creatures.

It is a painful sight. The property of many has been taken and sold before their eyes for almost nothing; the sellers and buyers being in many cases combined to cheat the poor Indian. Private purchases, or at least the sham of purchases, have in many instances been made at the instant of arrest and consternation: the soldiers standing with guns and bayonets, impatient to go on with their work, could give but little time to transact business. The poor captive in a state of distressing agitation, his weeping wife almost frantic with terror, surrounded by a group of crying, terrified children, without a friend to speak one consoling word, is in a very unfavourable condition to make advantageous disposition of his property even were suitable and honest purchasers on the spot, but more especially so when the only purchasers present are harpies, not second in deeds of villainy to the wretches who plunder the shipwrecks of voyagers on the seacoast. The truth is the Cherokees are deprived of their liberty and stripped of their entire property at one blow. Many who a few days ago were in comfortable circumstances are now the victims of abject poverty. Many who have been allowed to return to their homes under passport to inquire after their property, have found their houses, cattle, hogs, ploughs, hoes, harness, tables, chairs, earthen ware, all gone. And this is not a description of extreme cases. It is altogether a faint and feeble representation of the work of barbarity which has been perpetrated on the unoffending, unarmed, and unresisting Cherokees. I say nothing yet of several cold-blooded murders and other personal cruelties, for I would most conscientiously avoid making the slightest erroneous impression on any persons, being not in possession of precise and authentic information concerning all the facts in these cases of barbarity.

Our brother, Bushyhead, and his family, Rev. Stephen Foreman, native missionary of the American Board, the Speaker of the National Council, and several men of character and respectability are here, prisoners with their families.

It is due to justice to say that at this station (and I learn the same is true of some others) the officer in command treats his prisoners with great respect and indulgence. But fault rests somewhere. They are prisoners and their families are prisoners without a crime to justify the fact.

These savages, prisoners of the christians, are all hands busy, some cutting and some carrying posts and plates and rafters, some digging holes for posts, and some preparing seats for a temporary place of preaching tomorrow. . . .

We have not heard from our brethren in the mountains since their capture. . . . I have no doubt, however, but the grace of God will be sufficient for them, and that their confidence is reposed in the God of their salvation.

My last account from them was truly cheering. In a few days they expected the victorious army to sweep them into their forts, but they were going on steadily with their labor of love to dying sinners. Bro. Oganaya wrote me, May 27th, which I only read a few days ago, that seven males and three females were baptized at Taquohee on that day. He says . . . "We are in great trouble. . . . On Monday next it is said that we are to be taken, and I suppose it is true. Many are greatly terrified." Their fears are realized before this time.

The principal Cherokees have sent a petition to General Scott begging most earnestly that they may not be sent off to the West till the sickly season is over. They have not received any answer yet. The Agent is shipping them off by multitudes from Ross's Landing. It will be a miracle of mercy if one-fourth escape the exposure to that sickly climate at this most unfavourable season. A most piteous petition was presented by the prisoners at Ross's Landing to the Commanding officer at that place, but to no purpose. Nine hundred in one detachment and seven hundred in another were driven into the boats like culprits to the place of execution. They were exceedingly depressed, almost in the agonies of despair. Most of their faces, I fear, we shall not see again till the great day when the oppressor and the oppressed shall appear before the tribunal of the righteous judge. I have no language to express the emotions which rend our hearts to witness their season of cruel and unnecessary oppression. For if it be determined to take their land and reduce them to absolute poverty, it would seem to be mere wanton cruelty to take their lives also.

July 10, 1838: The overthrow of the Cherokee Nation is completed. The whole population are made prisoners. The work of war in time of peace was commended in the Georgia part of the Nation and was executed in most cases in unfeeling and brutal manner, no regard being paid to the orders of the commanding General in regard to humane treatment of the Indians and abstaining from insulting conduct. In that state, in many cases, the Indians were not allowed to gather up their clothes, not even to take away a little money they might have. All was left to the spoiler. I have only heard of one officer in Georgia (I hope there were more) who manifested any thing like humanity in the treatment of the persecuted people. They were driven before the soldiers, through mud and water, with whooping and hallowing like droves of cattle. No regard was paid to the condition of helpless females. Several infants were born on the open road under the most revolting circumstances. This of course was in direct violation of the Commanding General's orders, but was no less afflictive to the poor sufferers on that account.

At Ross's Landing, the place to which most of the Georgia Indians were brought, the scenes of distress defy all description. In many instances they were dragged from their homes without change of clothing and marched one hundred and twenty or thirty miles through heat and dust and rain and mud, in many cases bare-footed, lodged on the hard ground, destitute of shelter from dews and rains. They had of course become very dirty and on that account they have been reproached as degraded wretches. On arriving at the Depot, they were required to give up their horses and ponies, which they had brought along. Refusing to do so, men, women, and children and horse were driven promiscuously into one large pen made for the purpose. The horses were there taken by force and cried off to the highest bidder and sold for almost nothing. They were then urged to take money from the commissioners of the Treaty, but they, with one consent refused.

At the time for sailing, an effort was made to get their consent to go into the boats, but not an individual would agree. The agent then struck a line through the camp, the soldiers rushed in and drove the devoted victims into those loathesome receptables of disease and death. It is said by eye witnesses that the scene of this distress was agonizing in the extreme.

The dread which pervaded the community of being sent off at this season was intense. Several memorials to Gen'l. Scott were prepared and signed, praying for some relaxation in the course of capturing the Nation and of delay in transporting them to the West on the ground of the moral certainty that the great body of those sent off at this season would die. (The two principal ones were sent to him at Valley Towns by express.) Before an answer to these memorials was received, the whole Nation was in captivity, the property of the Indians, either stolen by plunderers or sold by commissioners appointed for that purpose. Those Commissioners often took the property before the eyes of the owners and against their consent and protestations. In some cases the Indians drove their cattle into the possession of some friend to save them from being sacrificed by these men who are said to act under a system of responsibility. The responsibility, however, is of little advantage to the poor Indian who is beggared by their protection.

The work of capture being completed, and about three thousand of the captives sent off, the general agreed to suspend the further transportation of the captives till the lst of September. This arrangement, though but a small favor, diffused universal joy through the camps of the prisoners.

Just at this moment, the Agent started off one thousand and forty in a company to go part of the way by land and part by water. The Cherokees supposed that this company was included in the arrangement and that they were to be stopped to participate in the indulgence (if such it can be called) granted to the rest of the nation. But on inquiry, was found that he had no intention to delay their transportation a moment. A petition on their behalf couched in the most earnest and respectful and submissive terms was presented to him, but to no purpose. This refusal was viewed and felt by the Cherokees to be a cruel and wanton disregard not only of the feelings and comfort, but also of the lives, of their people.

The expulsion of the Indians is about to be dispatched in such haste as to allow no time for deliberation. My intention to write on the subject of the Mission, as intimated in a late letter, is entirely frustrated by the suddenness of the military movement. . . . So important a crisis and so many new aspects in the condition of this people can never be expected to be witnessed by us again.[10]

Although the army had succeeded by July 10 in rounding up most of the Cherokees, several hundred had managed to escape the dragnet either by running into the hills before capture or on their way to the stockades. A large proportion of these escapees were from the mountain region. Fearing that these people would starve or perhaps be hunted down and shot by frontier whites, John Ross urged all refugees to turn themselves in. In a letter written on July 11, Jones reported the effort that he and Jesse Bushyhead made to find the refugees from the Valley Towns area.

> *July 11, 1838:* I have omitted till now to say that as soon as General Scott agreed to suspend the transportation of the prisoners till autumn, I accompanied brother Bushyhead who, by permission of the General, carried a message from the chiefs to those Cherokees who had evaded the troops by flight to the mountains. We had no difficulty in finding them. They all agreed to come in on our advice and surrender themselves to the forces of the United States though, with the whole nation, they are still as strenuously opposed to the treaty as ever. Their submission therefore is not viewed as an acquiescence in the principles of the terms of the treaty, but merely as yielding to the physical force of the United States.
>
> On our way we met a detachment of 1300 prisoners. As I took some of them by the hand, the tears gushed from their eyes. Their hearts, however, were cheered to see and hear the word of consolation. Many members of the church were among them. At Fort Butler we found a company of 300 just arrived from the mountains on their way to the general depot at the Agency.[11]

Jones, and the handful of missionaries from the other denominations who agreed to stay with the Cherokees at the camps, were particularly concerned to locate the members of their mission churches who were scattered among the various stockades and depots. In this they were greatly assisted by their native preachers. Once found, they were organized for religious services and mutual assistance. During the summer months there was a constant effort to maintain church services and to win more converts. In mid-July Jones wrote,

> I believe that the Christians, the salt of the earth, are pretty generally distributed among the several detachments of prisoners, and these Christians maintain among themselves the stated worship of God in the sight of their pagan brethren and of the white heathens who guard them. Brethren Wickliffe [Kaneeda] and Oganaya and a great number of the

members of the church at Valley Towns fell into Fort Butler, seven miles from the mission [at New Columbus]. They never relaxed their evangelical labors, but preached constantly at the fort. They held church meetings, received ten [new] members and on Sabbath [day], by permission of the officer in command, went down to the river and baptized them. They were guarded to the river and back. Some whites present affirmed it to have been the most solemn and impressive religious service they ever witnessed.[12]

Jones's reports to the mission board during the summer of 1838 speak of an almost constant round of religious meetings and scores of baptismal ceremonies. By his count, more than 175 new members were added to the Baptist denomination alone during the encampment.[13] In June the *American Baptist Magazine* reported, "Mr. Jones and Mr. Bushyhead, as a result of a sudden outpouring of the Spirit, baptized 55 in one day."[14] The mood of those who sought consolation in the Christian faith was essentially one of stoic martyrdom. Though despised and rejected on earth, they expected to find a better world after death where friends and families would be reunited and they would suffer no more. Many also were saddened by the deaths of children or parents; few escaped illness. Jones himself was so ill in July that he thought he was going to die.[15] On August 27, he wrote to the board:

> In the midst of much anxiety and urgent haste in the preparation for removal, it is a matter of sincere and humble gratitude that the gospel is making advances altogether unprecedented in the christian history of the Cherokees. The pressure of their political troubles appears to be overruled to the spiritual advantage of the people. The sentiment of the poet appears to be happily realized in them. Behind a frowning providence, he hides a smiling face. . . . Yesterday . . . Bro. Bushyhead and myself baptized fifty-six hopeful believers in the Lord Jesus Christ in the presence of an immense concourse of serious and attentive spectators.[16]

Jones also had to report that Astooeestes, one of the native preachers from Dseyohee, had died that month. He did not speak of the revival of the old religion in the camps, where ancient ceremonies and dances led by the *adonisgi* were as popular as the Christian services of the missionaries. What was remarkable was the lack of friction between the two religious groups. Each allowed the other the consolations of the religion of his or her choice.

The full-bloods, regardless of their religious outlook, were united in blaming the loss of their homeland upon those who had signed the Treaty of New Echota. As sickness and despair mounted during the summer of 1838, so did the resentment against those who had betrayed the Nation. Evan Jones shared the anger of the Cherokees against the traitors, and so did the Reverend Daniel S. Butrick of the American Board. At some time in the early fall, just before the Cherokees were to depart for the West, Butrick gathered the members of the Haweis and Brainerd mission churches of which he was pastor, and Evan Jones gathered all of the Baptist Cherokees under his care, and each addressed in his own way the question of the sinfulness of the behavior of the Treaty party. Butrick's church members voted that it was not only a political crime but a Christian sin for which those signers of the treaty who were Christian should ask forgiveness of their brethren. In effect, this placed the treaty signers under church censure and denied them the right to take communion. His church members, Butrick told the Prudential Committee of his board, "considered their conduct a crime for which they ought to repent." He cited Romans 13:2 and I Samuel 15:23 as the biblical basis for this censure.[17] Butrick's board told him that he should not have permitted such a vote of the churches because it mixed politics and religion. Butrick, the board said, was "fomenting discord" by abetting this action.[18]

Evan Jones realized that his board would take an equally critical view if he were to encourage such action, but he did it anyway. He never wrote to his board about it, but Butrick took note of it: "The Baptist church, consisting of three or four hundred members, were [*sic*] unanimous, I believe . . . in the opinion that those who made and executed the treaty had committed a sin against God and their brethren for which the church ought to call them to account." The sin in this case was "usurpation and rebellion against the just [Cherokee] authorities."[19] Nothing marks more clearly the politicization of religion in this crisis. It also indicates how closely missionaries such as Butrick and Jones had come to view politics and Christianity from the Cherokees' perspective. The full-bloods of the old religion planned a different sort of punishment for the traitors.

Throughout the summer and early fall of 1838, Jones not only worked among his converts but continued to assist the patriot leaders in the difficult task of organization and preparation for the exodus. Through the foresight of John Ross, the secretary of war had been persuaded that it would be cheaper and more humane if the planning and management of removal were taken over by the Cherokees themselves. The army was happy to be relieved of that task, but many merchants and their political friends (who had hoped to enrich themselves from profitable contracts) were upset. Congress had appropriated more than one million dollars to pay for the expense of the journey and for provisions during the Cherokees' first year after arrival until they could build cabins, plant crops, and obtain their first harvest. Ross and his chiefs spent the summer deciding how to plan the journey and distribute the wagons, horses, blankets, and food supplies among the thirteen thousand Cherokees who would make the trip. Evan Jones played a significant role in all of this, acting as a secretary for Ross; his handwriting appears in many of the letters signed by Ross and other chiefs in the piles of correspondence with the War Department, the suppliers, and those appointed to lead the march.

The chiefs decided it best to send the remaining Cherokees by an overland route rather than by boat. Ross divided them into thirteen contingents of roughly equal size, trying to arrange for whole towns to travel under their local headmen. Assuming that the journey would be about eight hundred miles in length, traveling an average of ten miles per day, the trip could be completed in eighty days. He allocated $65.88 per person. Other estimates covered transportation, clothing, livestock, wagonmasters, physicians, and the costs of ferry and turnpike tolls. Ross's brother, Lewis, acted as quartermaster, buying all the provisions and seeing that they were available at specific points along the route. All of this had to be cleared through the War Department, and there were constant disputes over the estimates and the costs, particularly when it was decided that the journey could not start on September 1 as planned. The first contingent did not leave until October 1.

Evan Jones never had any doubt that he would march along the Trail of Tears with the Cherokees. He decided that his family should remain in Columbus, Tennessee, until he had scouted out the land in the West and found a suitable place for the reestablishment of the Baptist mission station. Only his oldest son, Samuel, went with him on the journey; Samuel was in his late twenties and took a job as assistant wagonmaster in his father's detachment. Two detachments, number three and four, contained the bulk of the mountain Cherokees from North Carolina; they were headed by Jesse Bushyhead and Situagi.

Because Situagi could neither read nor write English, Evan Jones was appointed as his assistant and performed most of the planning and paperwork for that detachment. Jones informed his board of this appointment but emphasized his religious duties: "We hope that by a combination of effort between the Presbyterians and Baptists in the nation, nearly, if not quite all [the detachments] can be moderately supplied with religious aid." [20] Only two Presbyterian (really Congregational) missionaries would make the trip: Daniel S. Butrick and Dr. Elizur Butler; three of their native ministers, John Huss, Epenetus, and Stephen Foreman, would share in the religious duties for that denomination. Two Moravian missionaries stayed with the Cherokees in the camps, but they departed in their own wagons in September and did not accompany any detachment. One Methodist preacher, David Cumming, was later reported to have accompanied the Cherokees, but he is never mentioned by Jones. Jones and Bushyhead were assisted by Oganaya, Kaneeda, Dsusulawe, Beaver Carrier, John Foster, and Tanenole.

By the end of September, all was in readiness for the long, overland journey. The first contingent under John Benge left the old Nation on October 1; Jesse Bushyhead's contingent left on October 5, and Situagi and Jones left with their contingent on October 16. Both these contingents followed the same route, crossing the Tennessee River at Blythe's Ferry where the Hiwassee River flowed into it and then traveling to Pikesville, McMinnville, Murfreesboro, and Nashville. At Nashville, Lewis Ross waited to supply them with shoes, clothing, blankets, and their first batch of provisions. Other provisions were to be gathered at carefully spaced intervals along the route. Situagi's contingent contained 1,250 persons; the aged and children went in 62 wagons; some went on the 560 horses; and many traveled on foot. The records list Situagi as "Conductor"; Evan Jones, "Assistant Conductor"; Peter Oganaya, "Manager"; Kaneeda (Kaneta), "Assistant Manager"; John Foster, "Interpreter"; Jesse Watkins (one of the witnesses at Jones's trial), "Wagon Master"; and Samuel Jones, "Assistant Wagon Master." Two white physicians went with them, Dr. John Murry and a Dr. Isaacs. They did not realize it, but they would be three and one-half months on the road through the most bitter part of the winter. [21]

Jones wrote to John Ross from McMinnville, Tennessee, on October 27, reporting that the detachment reached Sequechie Valley on the first night, overtook Bushyhead's detachment on Cumberland Mountain, and then camped at a place called "Meadows." On October 26 they went sixteen miles, but "people were somewhat fatigued with passing so rapidly over the board roads," and they concluded to rest there that day and the next.

> Mr. Bushyhead's Detachment detained by their Oxen being poisoned from eating Ivey. . . . They purpose[ly] start[ed] on Monday and keeping a day behind us on the road. He has had a distressing time with the discontents. . . . We paid Forty Dollars at the Walden's Ridge gate. . . . On the Cumberland mountain they fleeced us 75 cents a wagon and 12½ cents a horse. . . . I shall be glad to hear from you at Nashville to know about the Tents and blankets, if we are to receive the latter at that place. Mr. Coody has written to Mr. Bushyhead today that Blankets, shoes, etc. are ready for them there.[22]

Detachments three and four reached Nashville on November 4, and the *Baptist*, a newspaper in that city, published a long article about Jones and Bushyhead:

> Four detachments of the emigrating Cherokees have, within a few days, passed through our city and seven others are behind and are expected to pass in a day or two. They average about a thousand each. Of the third party, our brother, Evan Jones, who has been eighteen years a missionary in the nation is conductor, and the fourth is under the direction of the celebrated Dtsakagedhee, known among us as Bushyhead. In the two parties they direct we learn there are upwards of 500 Baptists.
>
> During two or three days that their business detained them in the vicinity of the city, we have had the pleasure of some intercourse with these and others of our Cherokee brethren; and more lovely and excellent Christians we have never seen. On Monday evening last, the 5th of November, several of them were with us at the monthly concert of prayer for missions. It was expected that the meeting would have been addressed by Oganiah (Peter), Ganetuh (John Wickliffe) [Kaneeda], and the Chief, Suttuagee, all in Cherokee, and interpreted by Dsagee (John Foster). Some of these brethren, however, were sick. . . . The services were commenced by singing a song in Cherokee by Brother Jones (who, by the way, is called by the Indians Gawoheeloosekeh), [by] Dtsake- gedehee in English, and by Ahtzhtee in Cherokee interpreted by Brother Bushyhead. . . . Last night, the 7th, Brother Jones and Brother Bushyhead were again with us. . . . Brother Bushyhead addressed us in English. . . . He told us he could very well remember when his nation knew nothing of Jesus Christ; he detailed to us some particulars in relation to their

[former] religious opinions . . . their habits, domestic manners, and contrasted them with the present condition and character of his people and thus illustrated the happy effects already produced among them by the gospel. . . . He adverted to the opposition to missions waged by some Tennessee [anti-mission or Hardshell] Baptists and presented himself and hundreds of his brethren as living instances of the blessing of God upon missionary labors.

Brother Jones followed in a very eloquent address on the same subject, adding some interesting observations about the translation of the Bible into Cherokee in the letters invented by Seequayah (G. Guess) at present in progress by himself and Brother Bushyhead. The services closed at a late hour and $14.62 more [in addition to $15.18 the first night] were handed in aid to the mission when our brothers left us to pursue their march to the west.[23]

Neither Jones, Bushyhead, nor the editor of the newspaper made any reference to the removal policy that had caused this forced exodus. The editor concluded by saying, "We trust that a recollection of the numerous instances recited of God's goodness and mercy to our red brethren will add fervor to many a prayer and zeal to many an effort for the salvation of the noble-hearted Indian."

From Nashville the two detachments crossed the Cumberland River and continued northwest toward Hopkinsville, Kentucky, then marched to Marion, Kentucky, where they turned due west and crossed the Ohio River at Golconda, Illinois. From there they moved across southern Illinois and crossed the Mississippi at Cape Girardeau, Missouri. By then it was December; there was considerable ice on the Mississippi, and this held up many detachments. Once across, they continued southwest across Missouri to Farmington, Rolla, and Lebanon. After entering the state of Arkansas, they turned due west again near Fayetteville and continued into what was then called western Arkansas Territory (later "Indian Territory" and finally Oklahoma). The only extant letter from Jones describing this part of the trip was written from Little Prairie, Missouri, on December 30, 1838:

December 30, 1838: Camp of the 4th Detachment of Emigrating Cherokees, Little Prairie, Mo. We have now been on our road to Arkansas seventy-five days and have travelled five hundred and twenty-nine miles. We have been greatly favored by the kind hand of providence of our heavenly father. We have met with no serious accident and have been detained only two days by bad weather. It has however been exceedingly cold for some time past which renders the condition of those who are but thinly clad very uncomfortable. . . . [E]very morning [we] make fires along the road at short intervals. This we have found a great alleviation to the sufferings of the people.

At the Mississippi River we were stopped from crossing by the ice running so that the boats could not pass for several days. Here Bro. Bushyhead's detachment came up with us and we had the pleasure of having our tents in the same encampment, and before our detachment got all over, Rev. Stephen Foreman's detachment came up. . . . Our native preachers are very assiduous in their labors. . . . Their influence is very salutary. . . . [T]here will be an immense amount of suffering and loss of life attending the removal. Great numbers of the old, the young, and the infirm will inevitably be sacrificed. And the fact that the removal is effected by coercion makes it the more galling to the feelings of the survivors.[24]

The last three hundred miles of the journey took the contingents four weeks. They finally reached their destination on February 2, 1839. They had started the trip with 1,250 persons and arrived with 1,033. Jones reported 71 deaths and 5 births, so part of the loss must have resulted from persons who either sneaked off to return to their old homes or joined another detachment somewhere along the road.[25] Bushyhead, whose detachment arrived on February 23, reported 82 deaths on the trip.

For the Cherokees, the Trail of Tears ended when the last of the thirteen contingents reached their new home in March 1839, and they were in desperate condition. The federal government had promised to provide rations for them to live on until they could grow their first crop, but the private contractors, greedy for profits, provided rotten meat, moldy corn and wheat, and generally much less than they were required to furnish of all three.[26] Along the Arkansas frontier, white entrepreneurs brought barrels of whiskey into the Nation (against federal and Cherokee law) to wring from the Cherokees their last few dollars. Sickness and death from exhaustion, disease, overexposure, and malnutrition continued to wrack them for another year. On top of that, intense political factionalism broke out between the "Old Settlers" (those already in the West) and the recent immigrants. The Old Settlers refused to give up their own leaders and laws, expecting that the recent immigrants (who outnumbered them three to one) would yield to their government.

In the midst of this crisis, Evan Jones was once more expelled from the Cherokee Nation in October 1839. Members of the Treaty party, friendly with the federal government, dug up the old scandal about the murder trial, and the federal government held that Jones was not morally fit to be a missionary. He had to return to Tennessee. It took him two years (and the Whig Party victory in 1840) before he could persuade the authorities in Washington to allow him to return with his family to rebuild his scattered and discouraged mission churches.

◈ Chapter 5
Missionaries as Cultural Brokers

Successful missionaries have been described as "cultural brokers." They preached Christianity and promoted "civilization" successfully because they presented these alternatives to the Indians in ways that elicited a positive rather than a negative response.

With regard to the Cherokees, there is no doubt that the Reverend Evan Jones was the most successful of all missionaries. He worked among the Cherokees from 1821 to 1872, and his son joined him and continued his work. Evan Jones was criticized for his success by his zealous missionary rivals because they believed he compromised too much in theology, he meddled too much in politics, he ordained too many Cherokees to preach who lacked adequate training, he translated the Bible in the vernacular language of the Cherokees, and he allowed the Cherokees to accept Christianity in their own terms. In short, he "let down the bars" of strict adherence to evangelical belief and practice.

Yet, in the long run, was this not the only (as well as the best) way to transform a non-Christian people into a Christian people? White Americans could hardly boast of strictness of belief and practice in their own communities. And ordained Cherokee preachers were certainly the best equipped to tell their brothers and sisters what Christianity could mean to them.

Many twentieth-century historians have criticized the missionaries for their ethnocentrism and portrayed their soul saving as an effort to stamp out Indian pride, dignity, and culture. Moreover, the claim most missionaries made, that they did not want to get involved in politics, seemed hollow when they insisted on transforming Indian laws, traditions, customs, and behavior to fit white American mores. Like the politicians in Washington who set Indian policy, they were convinced that they knew what was best for the Indians and that they need not consult them or seek their cooperation.

It is easy to condemn missionaries for lacking the relativistic twentieth-century perspective on politics and cultural pluralism. To be fair to the missionary movement, however, historians must show that alternative approaches were practiced at the time and that these practices were not only viable but also more consistent with fundamental Christian and American values. The two missionaries described in this chapter were not typical, but they did provide such an alternative. Throughout their careers, they questioned whether God was the patron of white expansionism; they sought the views and cooperation of the people they came to serve; they tolerated a syncretic adaptation of Christian faith and practice to the perspectives of Native Americans. Moreover, they frankly and openly meddled in politics when they thought morality and justice were on the side of the Indians and not of federal policy or frontier intrusion. What makes these missionaries (and the board that supported them for more than half a century) important for the current reassessment of Indian missions is that by using this alternative approach, these two men became the most successful Protestant missionaries of their day. They are still remembered with honor and respect, even by Cherokees who did not become Christians.

The careers of Evan Jones and his son, John B. Jones, from 1821 to 1876 are significant because, unlike most of their fellow missionaries, their sincere dedication to Christianizing the Cherokees did not weaken their ability to transcend ethnocentrism. For them, Christianity became a source for sustaining and revitalizing Cherokee culture against the juggernaut (or, as Charles Royce called it, "the giant anaconda") of white civilization. The Joneses saw no contradiction between preserving and evangelizing the Cherokee Nation. God was not white. Nor was he red.

In becoming the most successful missionaries of their day, the Joneses found the key to good relations with the Cherokees in establishing close personal ties with the full-blood majority and with those leaders, such as Chief John Ross, who supported the majority in defense of national unity and autonomy (Ross called it "Cherokee sovereignty"). They identified their goals with those of the Cherokees; they had come to help the Cherokees, not to transmogrify them. To do so, they convinced the Cherokees that the God of Christians was a source of power, hope, consolation, and justice to all who believed in him regardless of race or nationality. Though they might differ with traditionalists regarding the true way to define, worship, and commune with the Great Spirit, the Giver of Breath, this in no way hindered or lessened their respect for the Cherokee people and their concern for Cherokee treaty rights and tribal structure. If God wanted peace, harmony, and love on earth, he did not want it at the expense of the Indians. The Joneses taught that the best of the traditionalist worldview could be combined with the best of Christianity to restructure and strengthen their fragmented culture. Cherokee revitalization and not assimilation was their goal, as it was of those they came to assist.

For these reasons, they supported bilingual education for all Cherokees; they established a native ministry to lead Cherokee converts and trained those they ordained to be supporters of their people in politics as well as in religion. Between Cherokee national survival and the prosperity of the United States they saw no necessary contradiction. Emerson, Whitman, and Thoreau saw this as "a nation of nations," and the Joneses agreed. The Joneses believed the Cherokees would find more strength, unity, vision, and spiritual assistance from the God of Christianity than from their traditional worship, but that did not mean they had the right to deride or disdain those Cherokees who clung to the old ways. To divide the Nation between a Christian party and a pagan party, the Joneses insisted, would be self-defeating. Over time, Christianity would prove itself more helpful; they labored to make it a live option.

At bottom, the great weakness in evangelical theology from the Native Americans' point of view was its insistence on helping individuals while neglecting the well-being of the community. The Joneses realized that a religious system that placed private salvation above community solidarity threatened destruction to the Cherokees. They resisted the constant pressure of their mission board to measure success in terms of conversion statistics. Instead, they worked to build a new sense of Cherokee community in terms of the evangelical concept of brotherhood and sisterhood rather than to exalt the Protestant ethic of self-reliance. Similarly, they defended the traditional belief in the communal ownership of the land and opposed the views of contemporary reformers who insisted that only the division of Indian land into privately owned tracts could save the Indians from "disappearing."

To demonstrate their confidence in the justice and mercy of God, the Joneses spoke out against federal policies that they considered contrary to the best interests of the Cherokees. In so doing, they were rebuked by their mission board, the federal authorities, and their fellow missionaries for "meddling in politics" instead of simply saving souls. But the Joneses and their converts emphasized those biblical texts that said that God was on the side of the oppressed; he was no respecter of persons or nations but only of righteousness. Too many other missionaries placed worship of the flag on the same par as worship of the Cross or else shrugged off injustice as "God's will."

When Evan Jones, at the age of thirty-three, entered the Cherokee Nation with his wife and four children (under the aegis of the Baptist Board of Foreign Missions in Philadelphia), the Cherokees were already badly divided.[1] Almost 25 percent of the tribe of twenty thousand were of mixed ancestry, chiefly white men who had married Cherokee women and raised their children by white standards. Many of these whites came to live among the Cherokees as Tories who, after 1776, had expected that the Cherokees (loyal allies to King George III) would help defeat the Revolutionists. After 1783, these whites and their Cherokee families did not feel comfortable about returning to white society; and having been adopted into the Nation through their marriages, they stayed on to wage guerrilla warfare on white American frontiersmen until 1794. Thereafter, they played important roles in making peace with the United States and in the economic transformation of the Cherokee Nation from a self-subsistent communal farming and hunting society to a market economy with intensive cotton growing, cattle grazing, and trading. Many of these mixed-bloods and intermarried whites brought black slaves into the Nation to do their hard labor. Because those of mixed ancestry spoke English, they proved very useful to their adopted nation by jealously guarding the treaty rights and tribal sovereignty that protected them and their enterprises. Most considered themselves nominally Christian.

Three-fourths of the Cherokees remained traditionalists. Evan Jones came to live among this Cherokee-speaking portion of the Nation that was chiefly located in the Great Smoky Mountains in the region of western North Carolina and northwestern Georgia. This group took much longer to adapt to a system of horse-and-plow farming. The chiefs, recognizing that the tribe must adapt to a new way of life now that they were surrounded by whites, sold off the hunting grounds and used the invested income to encourage nuclear families to move out of their communal villages, build log cabins, and start tilling the soil to grow their own food. At the same time, they organized a more centralized form of government and encouraged road building, trade with whites, and the admission of missionaries to start schools. However, as acculturation proceeded more rapidly among the mixed-bloods, and as a new national police force began to enforce laws promoting a market economy and patrilineal inheritance (and laws prohibiting polygamy, witchcraft, infanticide, Sabbath breaking, and gambling—at the insistence of missionaries), a cultural gap developed between the mixed-bloods and full-bloods. By the mid-1820s, the full-bloods, believing that acculturation was moving too fast and too far, tried to overthrow the elected government in what historians describe as "White Path's Rebellion."[2] Many of them advocated total rejection of the white man's ways and expulsion of the meddling missionaries. Most of the missionaries had shown more deference to the mixed-blood, English-speaking faction than to the full-bloods. As one missionary put it in 1816, "Those who will be the first educated will be the children of the halfbreeds and the leading men of the nation. . . . On their education and influence the character of the nation will very much depend."[3] Evan Jones rejected this elitist view of acculturation from the top down, preferring to work from the bottom up.

The most critical intratribal division developed after 1832 over the question of Indian removal. When it became clear that Andrew Jackson and the Democrats would support any state's right to expropriate Indian land, the Cherokees, like many other tribes, split over whether to move at once across the Mississippi or to remain on their ancestral land and insist on their treaty rights. In 1835, a handful of mixed-blood leaders signed a fraudulent treaty at New Echota yielding their homeland and agreeing to remove. About two thousand Cherokees (mostly mixed-bloods) soon left for new land in what is now northeastern Oklahoma. They were known as the "Removal party" or the "Ridge-Boudinot party." However, the overwhelming majority, fifteen thousand Cherokees, called the "Patriot party," led by Chief John Ross, refused to acknowledge the validity of the treaty and stood fast.

At the same time that the division grew between mixed-bloods and full-bloods (and parallel to it), there arose a division of rich and poor. Although all land was tribally owned, wealth and status accrued more rapidly to those who owned slaves. Between 1810 and 1860, the number of black slaves in the Cherokee Nation grew from 583 to more than 3,000. The same pattern of social and class distinctions developed among the Cherokees as had developed between the slaveholding plantation owners in the surrounding white slave states and the poor white non-slaveholders. This division was exacerbated by the tendency of missionaries to show preference toward the "progressive" mixed-bloods and disdain toward the "backward" full-bloods. It was further increased by the fact that missionaries from the slaveholding states preached that black slavery was perfectly compatible with Christianity, whereas missionaries from the North (especially after 1831) preached that slaveholding was a sin.

All of these internal divisions (full-blood vs. mixed-blood, slaveholding vs. non-slaveholding, Cherokee-speaking vs. English-speaking, rich vs. poor, Christian vs. traditionalist, proremoval vs. antiremoval) greatly influenced the behavior of the missionaries. Mission agencies received regular financial support from the federal government for their work and until 1832 had supported the United States' Indian policy. The War Department, which controlled the Bureau of Indian Affairs until 1849, considered missionaries to be the paid agents of the government and thus bound to support all official policies. The four mission agencies active among the Cherokees (Moravian, Congregational, Baptist, and Methodist) either supported removal or accepted it as an unfortunate necessity.

From the Cherokee point of view, there could be no neutrality on the issue. The Patriot party believed the missionaries should support resistance because removal was unconstitutional and unjust. Cherokees of the Removal party believed that the missionaries should support them because removal was unavoidable. The Reverend Samuel A. Worcester of the American Board of Commissioners for Foreign Missions agreed that the policy was unjust but, having suffered eighteen months in the Georgia penitentiary in an unsuccessful effort to force Jackson to uphold Cherokee treaty rights, accepted removal as inevitable in 1832. With his interpreter, Elias Boudinot (a leader of the Removal party), Worcester moved west in 1835. For this he was severely criticized by the Ross party, especially the full-bloods. He never again enjoyed the popularity that was his prior to 1832. All of the Methodist missionaries opposed removal, but for this they were censured by their mission board in Tennessee. The Moravians, though opposed to removal in principle, gave up their mission stations in 1832 rather than oppose the government.

The Baptist board (which had moved from Philadelphia to Boston in 1825) at first favored removal but modified its stance in 1832 largely because Evan Jones persuaded its members that their mission would lose support if they did not take the side of the Cherokees in their struggle. The full-bloods, among whom Jones worked, were among the staunchest supporters of the Patriot party. Sympathizing with them, Jones supported their cause, but because his board preferred not to oppose removal openly (owing to the large proportion of southern and frontier people in the Baptist denomination), he gave his support secretly. He did not tell his board how actively he worked with Chief John Ross and Ross's full-blood supporters in sustaining Cherokee resistance to removal. Yet this work included writing (anonymously) several antiremoval petitions to Congress signed by the Cherokees in his part of the Nation, writing a tract opposing the argument of the Removal party (which was signed by the Patriot chiefs), and openly speaking to the full-bloods in their own language at councils called to oppose removal.

In May 1838, the federal government ordered General Winfield Scott to invade the Cherokee Nation, forcibly round up all Cherokees, and ship them to the West on riverboats or overland on foot, in wagons, or on horseback. When Chief Ross persuaded the general to let the Cherokees manage the removal process themselves, Ross chose Evan Jones to lead one of thirteen contingents of Cherokee emigrants along the eight-hundred-mile journey through the winter of 1838–39. Jones reported that he made more converts during the removal crisis than he had in the preceding fifteen years. Following removal, the Baptists had the largest number of Christian preachers and converts of any missionary agency. Although most traditionalists did not become Christians, they came to respect Jones for his stand; over the next thirty years, more and more traditionalists eventually became Baptists.

After Jones brought his contingent of twelve hundred Cherokees safely to their new home over the Trail of Tears, he so annoyed the federal government and the Removal party by aiding the Ross party to gain dominance in their new home that complaints were lodged against him by Ross's Cherokee opponents. The War Department agreed that Jones should not be allowed to remain in the Nation, but his mission board refused to appoint another missionary and protested to the secretary of war on his behalf. So did Chief Ross and the council. But not until the Jacksonians were thrown out of office and new secretary of war was appointed in March 1841 did the federal government allow him to return to missionary work.

John B. Jones was born in the North Carolina area of the Cherokee Nation in 1824. His mother taught at the mission school, while his father, having been ordained that same year, itinerated through the Nation. John (as did several of his brothers and sisters) grew up with Cherokee as his native language. By the age of twenty, he had determined to become a missionary to the Cherokees. He underwent a crisis conversion at a revival meeting conducted by a Cherokee Baptist preacher whom his father had converted and ordained. His first great contribution to the Cherokees was to help his father translate the Bible into their language.

Evan Jones had begun translating parts of the Bible into Cherokee as early as 1822. When the Baptist board finally provided a printing press for his mission in 1841, Jones began in earnest to translate the whole Bible. His son John, who was more familiar with Cherokee colloquialisms, assisted him. Later John was sent east to college and divinity school where he learned Hebrew and Greek so that he could translate directly from original sources into Cherokee. Book by book, the two men produced a Bible that the Cherokees considered the best translation available to them. It was their practice to publish each book separately in their bimonthly magazine, the *Cherokee Messenger* (published wholly in Cherokee), and then to seek reactions from their readers. Passages that were unclear or did not seem to convey the true sense of the text to the average Cherokee were then revised and reprinted. The Cherokees, not the missionaries, were the judges of the translation. Other missionaries found this outrageous and believed that their translations were more accurate, but as one Cherokee who was bilingual put it (and Jones reported to his board), "Our translation is admitted to be the most correct"; "it is better Cherokee, more readily understood, and more gladly received by the full Cherokees [than any other]."[4]

Although the Joneses were committed to bilingual education, the Cherokee council ruled that its public school system (adopted in 1841), supported by Cherokee funds and taught by Cherokee teachers (all mixed-bloods), must be taught in English. Not until after John Ross's death in 1866 were the Joneses able to persuade the council to try their plan. In 1866, the council adopted a series of bilingual textbooks in arithmetic, geography, and history that were to be written by John Jones and published on the Baptist printing press. These books contained the text in English on one page and the same text in Cherokee on the opposite page so the full-blood and mixed-blood children could learn all of their subjects in both languages at the same time. Unfortunately, the Cherokee Nation lacked the funds to implement this plan fully. It was strongly opposed by the wealthier English-speaking parents who wanted nothing to do with the old language.

The most difficult problem faced by the missionaries among the Cherokees in the antebellum years was the existence of black slavery.[5] In the years 1794 to 1831, they largely ignored the question, but the emergence of Garrisonian abolitionism in 1831 and its claim that slaveholding was a sin that must not be countenanced by Christians gradually produced a crisis in mission work. Evan Jones always disliked slavery and in 1832–33 had persuaded some slaveholding Cherokees to free their slaves. But he was no Garrisonian. Most of his converts were too poor to own slaves, and the mountain area in which he worked was not suitable for plantations. When his board asked him in 1844 to report how many of his eleven hundred church members owned slaves, he replied that only four owned any, and these owned no more than two or three. He admitted that some of the Baptist missionaries had occasionally hired slave labor. He also told his board that neither he nor any other Baptist had ever preached against slavery because the Cherokee constitution and legal system accepted the institution. On this point Jones was not eager to meddle in politics.

Once the Baptist denomination in the United States split into southern and northern branches in 1845, the matter became more complicated. The Cherokee missionaries stayed with the northern Baptists (ultimately competing with southern Baptist missionaries for converts). Some northern Baptists adopted Garrisonian principles and produced a rival board to that which supported Jones. Fearing loss of support, Jones's board urged Jones to persuade his four slaveholding members to free their slaves or leave the mission churches. At this time there were seven Cherokee Baptist churches and ten branch churches. Jones was slow to carry out this request, for he knew it would arouse a storm of protest from the Cherokee slaveholders and that the federal agent (himself a southerner who had brought his own slaves into the Nation) might force his expulsion for meddling in Cherokee politics. Not until 1852 did Jones report that he had accomplished the goal and that the Baptist mission among the Cherokees was free from all collusion with slavery. Thereafter, Evan and John Jones became more ardent opponents of the institution.

The growing opposition to slavery by the Joneses did not hurt their position with the full-bloods, for they had little stake in the system and little sympathy for the wealthy mixed-blood elite who profited from it. Jones's friend Chief Ross (himself a slaveholder of mixed ancestry) told him to restrain himself on this divisive issue. Ross knew the surrounding slaveholding states feared that the Cherokee Nation might be a haven for runaway slaves and a station on the Underground Railroad if abolitionist missionaries got a foothold there. After 1850, the tension over "Bleeding Kansas" on the northern border of the Cherokee Nation further exacerbated the situation. In addition, the other northern-based mission agency, the American Board (also located in Boston), was putting the same pressure on its missionaries that Jones had been under. However, Samuel Worcester, superintendent of the American Board's Cherokee mission, strongly disagreed with the Joneses and adamantly refused to persuade his slaveholding converts to free their slaves or leave their mission churches.

As tension mounted after 1850, the mixed-bloods who dominated the Cherokee council passed several laws restricting the work of missionaries among blacks and demanding the expulsion of any missionary tainted with abolitionism. When Ross vetoed these laws, the slaveholders founded a secret, proslavery society called first the Blue Lodge and later the Knights of the Golden Circle. Membership was limited to slaveholders who agreed to vote only for office seekers who were slaveholders (a fact that caused great concern to the non-slaveholding full-bloods when they discovered it). In addition, members were committed to take the law into their own hands against any abolitionists, that is, to raise a mob and drive such persons out of the Nation. Some members of these societies broke up Baptist religious meetings and threatened bodily harm to the Joneses. This, in turn, solidified the full-bloods who feared that the proslavery faction would force the Nation into an alliance with the southern states (now threatening secession) and bring their country into a war that was not theirs.

In 1855 or 1856, the full-bloods formed their own secret society called the Keetoowah Society, partly as a counter to the Knights of the Golden Circle and partly to gain control of the Cherokee council. In effect, the Keetoowah Society was a political party created to wrest control of the government from the mixed-blood minority. But unlike White Path's Rebellion in 1824–27, this movement was much more carefully organized and politically sophisticated. It may well have drawn some of its ideas from the new Republican Party in the United

States. It certainly drew its chief support from the well-organized Cherokee Baptist churches and their Cherokee ministers. There seems little doubt that Evan Jones and John B. Jones were involved in the formation of the society and in supporting its goals. Significantly, however, the Keetoowah Society was not limited to Christians. Its constitution defined membership in terms of Cherokee-speaking persons committed to voting non-slaveholders into office and supporting a policy of neutrality in the growing animosity between the northern and southern states of the country. Although Keetoowah meetings opened and closed with Christian prayers, the society accepted as equals any traditionalists committed to their goals. Their meetings were held secretly, usually at night in the woods. They were conducted around a council fire, and the deliberations followed the traditional ceremonial and consensual procedures of ancient Cherokee councils. Ancient dances were performed; tobacco was smoked for its spiritual powers. The syncretic nature of this organization indicated the commitment of the Joneses to tribal unity and their unwillingness to draw a sharp distinction between Christian and pagan Cherokees.[6]

In the end, however, the federal government proved stronger than the Cherokee majority. John B. Jones had written to his board in Boston in 1859 that proslavery mobs were threatening their work but he was confident that antislavery feeling was growing. The board published his letter in its missionary magazine. When proslavery Cherokees showed the letter to the federal agent, a Georgian named Robert Cowart, in September 1860, ordered John B. Jones to leave the Nation within two weeks for "propagating abolition or anti-slavery sentiments among the Cherokees."[7] To avoid a possibly violent confrontation between the authorities and the Keetoowahs, Jones left. Nine months later (two months after the Civil War began), Evan Jones was forced to flee for his life to Kansas.

The story of the Cherokee Nation during the Civil War is too complex to describe in detail. However, John Ross appears to have favored support for the Union and would have welcomed military assistance in resisting the efforts of the Confederacy to force him into a treaty. Abraham Lincoln failed to send troops to protect the Indian nations in Oklahoma, and Ross felt compelled to make a treaty with the Confederacy lest it assist in a coup d'état against him by his proslavery opponents. When Evan Jones fled in June 1861, he carried word from Ross to the federal officials in Kansas to the effect that the Cherokees were loyal but needed military aid. Jones worked desperately to have troops sent to rescue the Cherokee Nation, feeling confident that Ross would abrogate his treaty with the Confederacy as soon as federal forces arrived. In June 1862, Jones accompanied a Union regiment into the Cherokee Nation, which defeated the Confederate forces there.

Unfortunately, a mutiny prevented the permanent occupation of the Nation. However, Ross agreed to return to Kansas with the retreating regiment. Two regiments of Cherokee volunteers (most of them Keetoowah members) were then formed to defend the Nation. Ross went to Washington, D.C., to negotiate with Lincoln. Though Lincoln seemed favorably disposed, a decision was postponed until the end of the war. From 1862 to 1865, the Cherokee Nation was engaged in its own devastating civil war, as the Cherokee Union soldiers fought bitterly against the Confederate Cherokees. John B. Jones returned to serve as chaplain to one of the Union Cherokee regiments, and for a short time Evan Jones served with the other. However, the latter spent most of his time in Washington with Ross trying to obtain a favorable treaty and raising funds to send food and clothing to the beleaguered pro-Union Cherokees.

In October 1865, the Cherokee council met and voted to adopt the Joneses (and their families) as full citizens of the Nation; this act also provided grants of land for themselves and their heirs. No other missionary obtained this mark of gratitude from the Cherokees. But the services of the Joneses did not end there. John, a Cherokee by adoption, joined a delegation sent by the council to Washington, where he took his father's place next to Chief Ross to negotiate, at last, a treaty that preserved the land and autonomy of the Cherokee people (despite strong government opposition on the grounds of Ross's initial betrayal in signing a treaty with the Confederacy).

The Cherokees loyal to Ross had voted to end slavery in January 1863, but this had little effect while the slaveholders retained their power under the Confederacy. During the treaty negotiations in 1866, John B. Jones quarreled with Chief Ross over a clause that granted Cherokee citizenship and equal rights to former Cherokee slaves. Ross shared the view of most slaveholding Indians that former slaves should be given their own tract of land in the West and not be included as members of any tribe. The federal negotiators sided with Jones, and Ross was forced to accept former slaves as full and equal black Cherokees. In the ensuing years, Jones worked hard to see that these freedmen received fair and equal treatment.[8] As missionaries, Evan Jones and John B. Jones felt obligated to help the Cherokees overcome the racial prejudices they had learned from the white man.

The Joneses returned to their missionary work among the Cherokees in 1866. They and the remaining native Baptist ministers reconstituted the scattered churches, rebuilt meetinghouses, and continued to evangelize among the unconverted. At the same time, they tried to help solve the new problems created by the building of railroads through the Nation, by illegal squatters who settled on Cherokee land or stole their timber and coal, and by the continual effort of Congress to denationalize them by creating a federal territory in Oklahoma prior to statehood—a program that included forcing the Cherokees to adopt private ownership of land and the sale to whites of any land not occupied by Cherokees. Evan Jones lost his health after 1868 and died in 1872, but John carried on his work.

John's hand was strengthened by the continued power of the Keetoowah Society (now no longer secret) and by President Ulysses S. Grant's new Indian policy. In 1869, Grant decided to appoint missionaries to be federal agents as a way of reforming corruption in the system. In 1870, he appointed John B. Jones as federal agent of the Cherokee Nation. John was the first Cherokee citizen to obtain this post and the first missionary to hold it. As federal agent, he used all of his skills and influence to protect Cherokee interests and to encourage the rebuilding of the war-torn nation. In 1872, he persuaded the federal government to give him sufficient cavalry troops to drive fifteen hundred white intruders out of the Cherokee Nation, burning the log cabins they had built as squatters, tearing down their fences and barns, and burning their fields of corn and wheat. He wanted to show the white frontiersmen that the Indians had rights that the United States government was bound to protect. Few whites in the West shared that view. Jones meted out the same treatment to cattlemen from Texas who drove their large herds through the Cherokee Nation before there were railroads to carry them to Kansas and ultimately to St. Louis and Chicago. The government had acknowledged the right of the Cherokees to tax such herds at a given amount per head. When the cattlemen refused to pay and threatened to shoot any Cherokee sheriff who tried to collect the tax, Jones used his authority to back up the Cherokees. He did the same with railroad companies that, by the Treaty of 1866, were allowed to build one railroad from north to south and one from east to west through the Cherokee Nation. These railroads took thousands of acres of Cherokee land for their tracts and stations, paying far less than its true value; they took Cherokee timber for their ties and bridges without paying for it; they killed thousands of Cherokee cattle as food for construction gangs (or when locomotives accidentally ran into them on the tracks) and refused to pay for them. Jones used his powers as federal agent to force the railroads to make good on all the claims for redress brought by Cherokees.

Although he gave up his salary as a missionary on becoming agent, he did not give up his missionary work. He continued to itinerate around the Nation, strengthening the eight mission churches; he also conducted regular meetings at the Baptist mission headquarters in Tahlequah (the Nation's capital). The Cherokee council had donated the use of 640 acres for the mission, and Jones hired experienced agronomists, nurserymen, and breeders to develop an experimental farm where they planted fruit trees and hybrid grains; they also bred horses, mules, hogs, and sheep so that Cherokee farmers could profit from the latest advances in scientific farming. He encouraged Cherokees to form agricultural societies and granges to hold annual county and national fairs to display their own successful crops, livestock breeding, and the household work of their wives and daughters. A white Baptist, married to a Cherokee, was effusive in his praise of John Jones's performance of his double responsibilities:

> Brother Jones exhibited unwearied industry since his appointment. While faithfully discharging his duties as U. S. Agent he has not left unperformed his missionary duties. Keeping up his appointments with his weekly Thursday evening prayer meeting at this place, and then mounting his horse, he has traveled to the most distant meetings in the various districts of the Nation, preaching in Cherokee. His labors seem almost superhuman. For the first time has the U. S. Agency truly exemplified in his social and business intercourse with this semi-civilized aboriginal people, the virtues of a Christian government. I have lived here fifteen years and can speak from personal observation.[9]

While Jones was preeminently concerned to protect the Cherokees from injustice, he was also ready to point out failings within their own social order. He protested discrimination against Cherokee freedmen when they were denied equal access to tribal land and equal participation in the Cherokee orphan fund. He criticized the tendency of the full-bloods to exclude all white men from entering the Nation, even those who could be beneficial through their skills and trade. He criticized the effort of the mixed-blood elite to alter the public school system. The elite wanted to place the full-bloods in "industrial training schools" where they would be taught useful mechanical skills and thus be limited to the roles of laborers or farmhands, leaving the public schools (with their broader, more comprehensive curriculum) to the more acculturated. Jones believed this plan would promote a caste system and reduce the full-bloods to second-class citizenship.

In his annual reports to the commissioner of Indian affairs, Jones spelled out a series of long-range programs that the government should promote to assist the progress of the Cherokees. He recommended that "the Government come to the aid of the Cherokees in their noble efforts to educate their children" by providing money for two high schools where "farming, gardening, and the mechanic arts should be taught." He stressed "the importance of having all the boundary lines of the Cherokees located and marked" so that whites could not claim ignorance when they trespassed or settled inside the Nation. He asked for mounted troops to patrol the borders against timber thieves, outlaws, and illegal whiskey dealers. The railroads brought in many lawless whites who were weakening the Cherokee efforts to live orderly lives. "The great majority of the [Cherokee] people," Jones wrote, "regret these [rail]roads as introductions of calamities rather than a blessing." He particularly implored Congress to resist efforts by the railroads and other special interests to detribalize the Indian nations and make Oklahoma a federal territory open to white settlement. "At each session of Congress bills are introduced and pressed for the establishment of a territorial government over the Indians and looking to the opening up of this country to settlement by the whites." These continued actions produced "among the Cherokees a deep feeling of insecurity." They felt such legislation would bring "still more crushing injuries." Thus, he said, "feeling akin to despair" was very generally prevalent. He believed that the common people would be the victims if "these evil prognostications" were realized. If "the government would give them assurance that white settlers would not be permitted to force themselves into their country—that the treaty guarantees [of tribal autonomy] would be maintained"— then the Cherokees would "work on the farms and in the shops, in

school and church" far more "joyfully and therefore more efficiently."
While Indian reformers in the East were arguing for detribalization
and private ownership of land by Indians, Jones was telling his superi-
ors, "The masses of the people . . . are utterly opposed to it. . . . I feel
it my solemn duty to protest against all the bills that will rob them
of their nationality [tribal identity], that will open the floodgates of
immigration and pour in upon them a population that will rob them
of their lands and overwhelm them with their votes, drive them to the
wall, finally sweep them out of existence. I protest against it in the
name of the pledged faith of the United States, in the name of honor,
justice, humanity and religion." [10]

Perhaps the most important aspect of the Joneses' work after 1866
was their effort to overcome the deep animosities between the pro-
Union and pro-Confederate factions within the Cherokee Nation. The
Confederate sympathizers, called the "Southern party," petitioned the
government after the war to divide the Nation into two self-governing
geographical areas. The Joneses supported the majority of the Cherokees in opposing this. They regretted that Chief William Potter Ross
(who succeeded his uncle, John, as chief in 1866) was so bitter toward
those in the Southern party that he would appoint none of them to
offices of any kind. Believing that this lingering division was detrimental to rebuilding the Nation, the Joneses persuaded one of their
ministers, Colonel Lewis Downing, to run against W. P. Ross in 1867.
Downing had been a leader of the Keetoowahs, a colonel of one of
the Cherokee Union regiments, and was a full-blood who spoke only
Cherokee. But as a Christian, he shared the Joneses' belief that charity
must be shown toward former enemies, that a live-and-let-live policy
was the only way to heal the factional scars. The Joneses encouraged
Downing to make overtures to those in the Southern party and to
promise them that he would treat them fairly and appoint them to
high offices. This aroused the bitter animosity of W. P. Ross and even
of some full-bloods loyal to the Ross party, but in the end, the Downing party triumphed. Downing's victory meant the fulfillment of the
Keetoowah Society's goal of full-blood domination of the council. It
also fulfilled the Joneses' goal of promoting tribal unity, peace, and
harmony after years of bitter factionalism.

From the point of view of the missionary movement, the Joneses'
chief accomplishment lay in their creation of a genuine Cherokee Baptist organization with its own native ministry, its own Cherokee-built

and Cherokee-sustained churches, Sunday schools, and temperance societies. This had been a major goal of theirs, but it was difficult to achieve among a people so poor and so unfamiliar with Protestantism and the separation of church and state. From early in his career, Evan Jones had established places along his preaching circuits where he held revival meetings, established prayer and Bible study groups, and selected pious, conscientious converts to lead a local branch of the mission church. Following the congregational autonomy of the Baptist persuasion, he allowed branch churches to license their own exhorters, evangelists, and preachers, and when he thought they were ready, he ordained them.

Since the days of Roger Williams, the Baptists had eschewed the idea of a learned, hireling ministry. They believed that the ability to preach was a gift of God and that the gospel should be preached without pay. They saw no need for learning, for the Holy Spirit carried the Word of God to sinners through the grace of God. Although this view was changing in the urban areas of the United States, it remained strong on the frontier. Because the Baptists practiced an egalitarian, democratic church order, they shared a common tradition with Cherokee egalitarianism. They tolerated each other's weaknesses and worked in cooperation as Christian brothers and sisters. Together they built their own meetinghouses, contributing to buy nails, hinges, and windowpanes. They supplied out of their own larders the food needed for revival meetings. They built a sense of community and fellowship that replaced that of the old communal villages and local councils and clans. In these respects, Christianity—and the sense of hope, self-respect, self-discipline, and spiritual power that Christianity provided—served as a crucial revitalization movement in each of their crises.

The Joneses did not convert all, or even a majority, of the full-bloods, but they did make Christianity a live option for them. Cherokees came to see that they could find strengths in Christianity that the traditional way no longer offered. And through native ministers and exhorters who preached the Bible in their own idiom and in terms of Cherokee cultural experience, the Cherokees were able to make Christianity their own and not the white man's religion. Above all, the Joneses helped the Cherokees see that Christianity had more than simply an individualistic approach to communion with the Great Spirit. They showed by their own commitment to the tribal welfare, as well as by the tribal loyalty they instilled in their members, that Christianity had a powerful binding, healing, and inspiring power for the Cherokee Nation. By enabling the Cherokees to find in Christianity the same sense of community loyalty, family loyalty, and national loyalty that had sustained them in the past, the Joneses helped them to bridge the gap between the best of the old and the best of the new. The Joneses did this not by altering the Cherokees' identity as a people but by enhancing it: they demonstrated that one could be a good Christian and still be a good Cherokee, not a carbon copy of a white man.

Part II
Accommodating the Old
Religion to the New

Chapter 6
Christianity and Racism: Cherokee Responses to the Debate over Indian Origins, 1760-1860

Thomas Jefferson, speaking for the prevailing scientific view of the varieties of the human complexion (or "races"), said in 1787, "The Indian is, in mind and body, the equal of the European." This view was widely held in Europe and America in the eighteenth century. It was also implicit in the Christian view that all humankind descends from one set of parents and hence all are brothers and sisters under the skin. Differences in complexion seemed to Jefferson to be the product of environment and custom. Consequently there was every reason for the new nation to adopt, in 1789, a policy toward the Indians that called for their ultimate incorporation into the United States as full and equal citizens (once they were uplifted from savagery by "Christianization" and "civilization").

Jefferson expressed some doubts that the African was fully equal to the European, and so did increasing numbers of scientists in the nineteenth century. For the most part, missionaries seem to have clung to the biblical view, though that became increasingly difficult for southern missionaries to accept once the abolitionist movement began. (Abolitionists considered Africans to be equal in mind and body and hence deserving of equal citizenship.) If God had made different kinds of human beings from the beginning, the concept of polygenesis threatened the biblical view of monogenesis. If the different kinds of human beings had somehow changed over time, that threatened the Christian belief in the fixity of species.

This essay discusses the gradual shift in scientific and Christian thought on the subject of the origin and equality of the Indian peoples from 1762 to 1860. It tries to indicate why most white Americans abandoned Jefferson's position and espoused the racial inferiority of Native Americans. Given this shift, it is not hard to see why the Indian adopted the position that he was superior

Coauthored by Walter H. Conser, Jr.

to Africans and then to maintain that the first red people were God's chosen people, not whites.

> Race as a meaningful criterion within the biological sciences, has long been recognized to be a fiction. When we speak of "the white race," "the Jewish race" or "the Aryan race," we speak in biological misnomers and, more generally, in metaphors. Nevertheless, our conversations are replete with usages of race which have their source in the dubious pseudo-science of the eighteenth and nineteenth centuries. . . . Race, in these usages, pretends to be an objective classification, when in fact, it is a dangerous trope.—Henry Louis Gates, Jr.

The study of race and ethnicity has currently taken on new significance both on the political scene and on the college campus. Ethnohistorians, sociologists, anthropologists, biologists, cultural historians, literary critics, and plain, old-fashioned intellectual historians (among whom we number ourselves) are struggling to redefine, demystify, deconstruct, and reconstruct the terms "race" and "ethnicity" in order to open up the values of America's multiracial culture to new understanding and appreciation. As Henry Louis Gates, Jr., has stated, there is a "direct correlation between economic and political alienation, on the one hand, and racial alienation, on the other"; many scholars "are collectively engaged" in the effort "to deconstruct, if you will, the ideas of racial difference inscribed in the trope of race" in order "to reveal the hidden relations of power and knowledge inherent in popular and academic usages of 'race.'"[1] This essay is a small contribution to this inquiry.

So long as they continued to fight for their national independence, the Cherokees honored their own myths of racial origin, but after 1794, when they made peace with the Euro-Americans, they were compelled to react to efforts imposing concepts of "race difference" upon them. Acceptance by tribal leaders of the federal policy of assimilation and of missionaries, who taught their children English, produced a variety of responses. Unfortunately, no Cherokee ever wrote an analysis of the issue in the years 1760 to 1860—hence the fragmentary, but we hope significant, evidence offered here.

Once Europeans realized that Columbus had not really found a short way to India and that the "red Indians" of the New World were not the Indians of the subcontinent of Asia and the East Indian Islands, debate began as to the origins of these "copper-colored" people of America. The scholarly (and not so scholarly) search for the true origins of the red Indians involved more than the question of whether they originated in Asia (and came to the New World across a northern land bridge) or came from Europe, Asia Minor, or the Middle East (via the Lost Continent of Atlantis) or from Phoenicia in Northern Africa (in storm-blown trading ships). For European Christians the first problem was how to fit them into the biblical history of racial origins, that is, from which of the three sons of Noah did they descend? Not being black, they could not be descendants of Ham, but they might have been Japhethites or Shemites. If descendants of Japheth, they belonged to the white race that peopled northern Europe; if descendants of Shem, they belonged to the Semitic race, perhaps from the Ten Lost Tribes of early Israel.

In the early nineteenth century, the so-called American School of Ethnography posited the notion of separate creations for each race of mankind. God created not only a white Adam and Eve but also a yellow, brown, black, and red Adam and Eve not mentioned in Genesis.[2] Most Christians considered this concept of polygenesis heretical, but others found it a "scientific" way to justify immutable biological differences among the human species, thereby invalidating efforts to alter the hierarchical superiority of the white (Caucasian or Anglo-Saxon) race over all others. This school of thought became popular as a wave of romantic nationalism redefined what it meant to be "an American" and justified racial discrimination not only against "red men" but against all other "inferior" races seeking amalgamation into the manifest destiny of the white Anglo-Saxon race.[3]

This essay examines two questions arising from the early efforts to define the racial origin of Native Americans: first, how did eighteenth- and early-nineteenth-century scholars come to disagree about whether they were descendants of Shem or Japheth, and second, how did the Indians react to the possibility that they might be Shemites and descendants of the Israelites? By confining ourselves to a discussion of these questions as they bear on the Cherokees, we hope to suggest the essential features of the problem. Our research indicates that no consensus was reached by white scholars about Cherokee origins, nor was there a consensus among the Cherokees as to the benefits of being identified as Shemites or Japhethites. However, among the missionaries to the Cherokees, the advantages of an Israelite connection seemed obvious. Similarly, among certain Cherokee converts (especially those of white-Cherokee ancestry, the so-called mixed-bloods) there was a tendency to favor this connection. To be descendants of the Jews brought the Cherokees within the fold of Christian history and prophecy, giving them an added claim to Christian concern and philanthropy as the once chosen and ultimately to be reclaimed favorites of God. However, full-bloods or traditionalists who resisted the efforts to make them over into the image of the whites rejected Christian efforts to co-opt them into the whites' sacred history. This reaction became stronger after 1828 when the frontier whites rejected the original governmental policy of assimilating the Indians into equal citizenship and supported instead Andrew Jackson's policy of segregating them in the West on reservations.

The question of the racial origin of the Cherokees (and other Native Americans) constitutes a significant aspect of the history of racism in the United States and has more than antiquarian interest. The Cherokees, as other southeastern tribes, adopted in the late eighteenth century the institution of black chattel slavery. There were many social, political, and economic reasons for this, but one of them was to maintain the distinction between red and black people in order to avoid the tendency of whites to lump all "colored people" among the ranks of inferior species.[4] In their effort to assert their own ethnic dignity and identity the Cherokee full-bloods frankly asserted that they were the first people created by the Great Spirit and were always his favorites; they would remain his chosen people so long as they adhered to his will and spiritual laws. To be "an American" would require, in their view, a pluralistic concept of ethnicity, for the United States would always be a multiracial nation. The Cherokees were not advocates of pan-Indianism because in their sacred mythology, it was the Cherokees qua Cherokees who were "the real people." Still, their fight for racial respect tended in that direction, for red people regardless of tribal differences were more favored by the Great Spirit than the sons of Shem, Ham, or Japheth.

Europeans first saw the Cherokees in the Old World when small delegations of them were brought to London in 1730 and 1762. In the year of this second delegation to meet the king, a biblical scholar published the first known effort to explicate their place in scriptural anthropology. Significantly, the anonymous author of this pamphlet concluded that they were descendants of Japheth, hence of the white race, and probably closely related to the Britons (perhaps out of a desire to cement English-Indian alliances against French and Spanish imperial rivals in the New World). Entitled *An Enquiry into the Origin of the Cherokees,* published at Oxford in 1762 and "sold by J. Fletcher in St. Paul's Church-yard, London," this tract was noteworthy in two other respects. It not only claimed that the Cherokees were included in the biblical prophecies of the apocalyptic war at the approaching end of human history, but it also noted that under divine will, the Indians of the New World would turn the tables upon the European invaders and would "distress and plunder them."

The circumstances surrounding the pamphlet and its author can only be reconstructed indirectly. In May 1762 a party of Cherokees escorted by Henry Timberlake departed Virginia for England. Born in 1730 in Hanover County, Virginia, Timberlake had repeatedly served in the Virginia militia. He lived among the Cherokees for several months and befriended several Cherokee headsmen, including Ostenaco, at whose request the trip to England was undertaken. In early July the Cherokees had an audience with King George III. The meeting was reported in the local London papers, and it was in response to questions concerning those reports that the *Enquiry* was written.[5]

Even though the author of the *Enquiry* remains anonymous, some information about him can be inferred. First, he was probably an Anglican clergyman. The pamphlet is full of classical quotations and biblical allusions. Questions concerning the proper interpretation of biblical passages and the proper application of biblical prophecies to contemporary affairs frame the essay. They also reflect a level of learning appropriate to an educated clergyman. Beyond that, the essay has the imprimatur of John Browne, vice-canon at Oxford. Finally, the publisher of the essay, James Fletcher, was an established London printer whose shop was located within the very shadow of St. Paul's Cathedral.

Three themes emerge in the pages of the *Enquiry.* First, because the Cherokees are described in the newspaper report as being "painted men," that is, decorating their faces and bodies with tattoos or paint, they are said to be related to the descendants of the biblical figure Meshek. The author avers that a similarity of manners indicates a similarity of origin and in this context compiles an inventory of traits that allegedly link the Cherokee and the progeny of Meshek. These characteristics, in addition to painted bodies, include shorn heads, dwelling in tents, holding property in common, and leadership by a head warrior (not a king). Beyond these common customs, the *Enquiry* argues, the Cherokees exemplify the very etymological meanings of the name of the family of Meshek, for the Cherokees are extended over a large area of land as befits the descendants of Meshek. In this bow to eighteenth-century anthropology, then, the *Enquiry's* author argued for the consanguinity of the Cherokees with the lineage of Meshek on the basis that similar customs indicate common, if distant, origins. For this author environment did not extinguish what he calls "family marks," for these marks—skin color, temperament, and so on—are the fundamental insignias of each of the races of the world.

Second, Meshek was the son of Japheth and the grandson of Noah. Thus, the *Enquiry* argues, the Cherokees are white. "All the Sons of Japheth are Europeans, i.e., white," states the author. Moreover, in line with their Caucasian racial origin, the *Enquiry* notes that the Cherokees, as descendants of Meshek, are culturally related to the Scythian tribes of Eurasia. But how could eighteenth-century Cherokees be related to ancient Scythians, separated as they are by such great distances? To this question the *Enquiry* merely cites two prevalent conjectures—the Indians came to North America over a land bridge from Asia or across through Iceland and Greenland and then migrated slowly to the south. The author of the *Enquiry* will accept either one of these explanations and is willing to leave it to others to make the final determination of the actual route. It was not unusual for commentators to trace the American Indian back to biblical roots, but they usually linked the Indian to the copper-colored descendants of Shem rather than to the fairer-skinned lineage of Japheth.[6]

Third, the author of the *Enquiry* suggests that, as the descendants of Meshek, the Cherokees and other Indian nations of North America may one day fulfill the prophecy described in the Book of Ezekiel and ravage their present European masters. This theme is based on the prophecy in chapters 38 and 39 of the Book of Ezekiel, in which Gog, the chief prince of Magog, coming from the north, attacks the people of Israel. Traditionally, interpretations of these passages have

highlighted the eventual defeat of the forces of Gog, as the Israelites, strengthened by their God, meet their opponents and decisively
subdue them. The author of the *Enquiry*, however, has chosen to emphasize the onset of the struggle and has placed the Cherokees in the
role of Gog.

By the eighteenth century, two broad patterns of explanation for
tracing the origin of Native Americans formed the intellectual context of the *Enquiry*. The first portrayed the American Indians as Jewish descendants. Thomas Thorowgood's volume, *Jewes in America, or,
Probabilities that the Americans are of that Race* (1650), was one of the
first English books to argue that the American Indian was one of
the Lost Tribes of Israel. John Eliot, the New England minister and
Indian missionary, wrote an approving preface to the second edition
of Thorowgood's book, and Roger Williams and others subscribed to
this view, thereby helping to make it a standard perspective in much
of the early American discussion.[7]

None of these volumes referred specifically to the Cherokees. However, James Adair's *History of the American Indian* (1775) provides a
useful example of this tradition as applied to that tribe. Furthermore,
his book offers a nearly contemporaneous contrast with the *Enquiry
into the Origin of the Cherokees*. James Adair was born in Ireland around
1709. Immigrating to America in 1735, he served as a trader among
the Cherokees and Chickasaws from 1735 to 1768. His book provided
an extensive description of life among the southeastern Indians; however, the organizing thesis of his volume was that Native Americans
were the descendants of Shem and the Jewish tribes. Adair argued that
external differences of color and the like that distinguished reds and
whites were explained by differences of custom. Native Americans,
like Europeans, were all descendants originally from Adam; there
was no separate creation of the races. Building on this point, Adair
discounted reports of Chinese or Scythian ancestry and stated that
the Indians were lineally descended from the Israelites, probably in
the dispersion after their defeat by the Babylonians. Adair recounted
various religious rites and marriage and funeral customs, as well as
traditions and habits of language, to demonstrate the Jewish origin of
the American tribes. The Jewish belief in Jehovah, for example, was
paralleled by the Indian worship of "Yohewah." Indians had prophets
and high priests, observed laws of ritual purification and cleanliness,
engaged in retaliatory punishment, and ornamented their bodies just

as had the ancient Hebrews. In all, Adair produced twenty-three different arguments, all purporting to demonstrate Jewish ancestry for Native Americans.[8]

In Adair's *History*, as in the anonymous *Enquiry*, common patterns of custom indicated common origins, but Adair reached radically different conclusions. The author of the *Enquiry* was unusual, not in his claim for the biblical origin of the Cherokees, but in tracing them to Meshek instead of to Shem and the Israelites.

The other theory, that of the Asiatic origins of American Indians, had an equally distinguished pedigree. In 1614 Edward Brerewood published his *Enquiries Touching the Diversity of Languages* in which he argued, through an appeal to affinities of custom and similarities of language, that the American Indian originated in Asia. Brerewood noticed that among the American Indians one found little of the arts and civility of Europe and equally little of the industry of China and Japan. Instead, the situation of the Indian resembled nothing so much as that of the "old and rude Tartars" of Mongolia, and only the future could tell whether they would develop into a civilized people.[9]

Brerewood's work found later echoes and restatements. John Ogilby's *America* (1671) reasserted that American aborigines had nothing at all to do with the Jewish Diaspora but instead reflected Scythian origins, born in "Tartary, which certainly was the first Nursery, from whence the Americans were transplanted."[10] Like Brerewood, Ogilby also compiled an inventory of customs, traits, and even physical similarities to prove the Asiatic origin of the American Indian. If Ogilby followed the familiar tack of comparing customs, Benjamin Smith Barton followed Brerewood's other lead and investigated language as a path to proving the Asiatic origin of the American Indian. Brerewood and Barton were not alone, however, in mapping out the linguistic landscape, for Thomas Morton's *New Canaan* (1637) and John Josselyn's *Account of Two Voyages to New England* (1674) had also pursued this way of demonstrating the Native American's Asiatic origins.

In his *New Views of the Origins of the Tribes and Nations of America* (1797), together with other published and manuscript materials, Benjamin Smith Barton conceded that compilation of similar customs was suggestive; however, he insisted that too much stress had been laid upon these alleged resemblances. To Barton's mind, customs were too easily modified by changing conditions or by adopting the traditions, manners, and traits of neighbors and invaders; they easily disintegrated into new forms and were not reliable indicators of points of racial origin. Language, Barton contended, though it underwent some changes, usually retained its own natural characteristics and thus provided a more scientific standard by which to assess possible origins.[11]

As a good Jeffersonian, Barton's invocation of scientific rather than biblical authority was characteristic and important. So too was his emphasis on a monogenetic account of human origins. Monogenesis, the descent of all human species from Adam and Eve, was the dominant ethnological assumption of Enlightenment philosophers and Christian theologians in the eighteenth century. Early writings on the origins of Native Americans were likewise almost entirely committed to monogenesis, especially once Pope Paul III declared in 1537 that they were humans and not animals.

An early challenge to monogenesis appeared in the writings of the Frenchman Isaac de la Peyrère. La Peyrère's *Prae-Adamitae* (1655) argued that God had fashioned two creations: the first one created the gentile race, which then spread throughout the world (including America), and the second created Adam, the forefather of the Jews. La Peyrère postulated that the deluge had not been worldwide but rather had only destroyed the Hebrews, leaving the descendants of the pre-Adamic creation in the New World, untouched and unknown to the Old World until 1492. In 1774 Lord Kames had suggested a polygenetic explanation for racial differences, and in 1799 Charles White argued that black and white people were two different species. But polygenesis was too heretical for most Christians, and not until the science of ethnology assumed legitimate stature in the nineteenth century was there real competition against the belief that all human beings were descended from one ancestor.[12]

Ethnological debates over polygenesis intensified with the breakdown of the environmentalist argument that prevailed during the Revolutionary generation in the United States. Though Jefferson and other deists were not biblicists (Jefferson doubted the universality of the flood, for example), they were convinced that biologically "all men are created equal," for all descended from one human pair, Adam and Eve. Differences among the various races or types of human species resulted from environmental differences or cultural customs (the Indians became tawny, one theory held, because they customarily rubbed themselves with bear fat). But environmentalism was challenged by Charles Caldwell as early as 1811, and reflecting the ethnological efforts to measure and explain the differences by European scientists such as Jean Lamarck, Johann Blumenbach, Petrus Camper, and Georges Buffon, American scientists began to doubt the concept of monogenesis.[13]

Dr. Samuel G. Morton, influenced in part by the new science of phrenology in the 1830s and even more by the measuring of human skulls by Camper and others, launched a major debate over the multiple creation of the different types of mankind that raged through the 1840s and 1850s. Although most Christian scientists (and churchgoers) rejected polygenesis, the books and articles of Morton and his pupil Dr. Josiah C. Nott, as well as the work of the well-known paleontologist Louis Agassiz at Harvard, forced the believers in monogenesis to choose between "scientific fact" and biblical "revelation." The debate centered upon the separate creations of blacks and whites, but in this debate Native Americans played an important role. If polygenesis helped some white Americans to overcome their guilt about slavery, it helped others overcome their guilt about the extermination of the Indians. Morton abandoned monogenesis in 1844, Louis Agassiz and Josiah Nott at about the same time. Morton reached this point by measuring skulls of the different races and concluding that they were clearly too different for too many centuries to be the result of environmental causes. Agassiz based his reasoning on anatomical structure. Nott relied on statistics alleging the inability of the African to cope in a free society. Similarly, the Native American was distinguished by his inability (and unwillingness) to become "civilized," coupled with prediction of his gradual extinction in competition with Europeans.[14]

But the majority who rejected polygenesis found sufficient evidence to establish racial hierarchies in the Bible. The basis of the biblical argument for the inferiority of the dark-skinned races was commonly traced to the sons of Noah. In defining the racial differences among red, white, and black Americans, many monogenists insisted that God had providentially differentiated Caucasians, Indians, and Africans by altering the color of Ham and Japheth. Shem, the progenitor of the red race, was the red or tawny color of his father, Noah. God altered Ham in the womb and he emerged black; Japheth emerged white. Thus from their births God had ordained the distinctions between the three races, though of course Adam and Eve were their common ancestors. After the flood, Shem's descendants remained in the Middle

East, though some went farther east as far as Siberia and across the land bridge to the New World; the descendants of Japheth went north and west to people Europe; the descendants of Ham went to Africa. Moreover, these interpreters contended that while Noah cursed Ham and his descendants, Shem and Japheth were blessed by him. Shem had the first commission to preach the truth of God's words, and the Jews flourished for this reason until they rejected Christ, but the Ten Lost Tribes wandered and lost the faith so that those who reached America had scarcely any traces of it left. Japheth's descendants picked up the mission of the Jews after Christ's death, and the Caucasians thus became the bearers of God's truth. In the 1850s two southern-ers, Samuel A. Cartwright and Samuel Baldwin, stressed the Jewish origins of Native Americans and their failure to retain their Jewish faith after immigrating to America. These wandering Jews, Cartwright and Baldwin argued, became less and less civilized as the centuries passed, until when discovered by the Japhethites in the New World, they were hardly human. Still, because they were the descendants of Shem, they did not make good slaves. God meant only the descen-dants of Ham to be slaves to the descendants of Japheth. Presumably, the Cherokees and other southeastern tribes who came to own black slaves in the nineteenth century shared in the right of Japheth because Shem was also blessed by Noah.[15]

The more fanatical racists of the antebellum era were outraged at the "amalgamationist" or integration theories of the Founding Fathers, the Indian missionaries, and the abolitionists. By midcentury, some southern Christians were utilizing "craniology" to substantiate the in-feriority of Indians to whites and coupling it with God's curse on Ham to defend the Indians' right to hold black slaves. For example, *The Due West Telescope* (quoted in the *Arkansas Gazette,* a paper that gave much attention to the Cherokees) published an article in 1858 that ex-plained the application of craniology to the differences between the red and black people in the United States and specifically repudiated the earlier views that Indians were descendants of Japheth:

> The Caucasian has eight cubic inches of brain more than the negro, and the Indian has two more than the negro. But why is it that the Indian, with only two cubic inches of brain more than the negro, cannot be reduced to slavery like the negro? . . . We answer by saying that the rational[e] is found in the fact that the Indians are the descendants of

Shem, and the right to hold them in personal bondage never was given
to the Japhethites . . . whereas God gave the right to hold the posterity
of Ham in personal bondage and hence not only the white race but the
Indians or red race hold the Hamites as slaves.[16]

Brain size accounted for, and justified, dominance of one race over
another—white over red and red over black—and God's curse made
blacks the slaves of both red and white. The article was quoted by the
Arkansas Gazette because the Cherokees were the western neighbors
of the Arkansans, and as a slaveholding state, the Arkansans wished
the Cherokees (a slaveholding tribe) to support the southern states in
their growing quarrel with the North over the westward expansion of
slavery. The Kansas-Nebraska Act had placed the Cherokees squarely
in between an abolitionist area and a strong proslavery area. Soon
they would have to decide whether to take sides in the white people's
fight over the peculiar institution that, in the eyes of the Arkansans
and Texans who bordered the Cherokee Nation, was ordained of God
and sanctioned by science.

Tempting though it was to the wealthier (and usually mixed-blood)
Cherokees who owned slaves to cast their lot with the South, they
were well aware that southern Christians found biblical justification
for the eradication of the Indians as well as for the enslavement of
the Africans. A writer for the *Mississippi Baptist* wrote an exegesis of
Genesis 9:27 in March 1860 to demonstrate that the Indians, as the descendants of Shem, were doomed to an even more certain extinction
than the sons of Ham. The text reads, "God shall enlarge Japheth, and
he shall dwell in the tents of Shem, and Canaan shall be his servant."

The entire sentence was prophetic and has been fulfilled in a remarkable
manner. The European nation has spread itself over the face of the earth
and doubtless Noah, with prophetic eye, gazed upon the waving forest
and mighty streams of the second "promised land," the then unknown
world of the West, where dwelt the children of Shem, long centuries before the idea of its discovery found birth in the fertile brain of Columbus.
There he beheld a remnant of that tribe which, in the old world, had for
so many centuries, held all the arts and blessings of a civilized life within
their domain. . . . He [Noah] beheld them [the Indians] in the shadows
of the towering mountains and by the margins of the silvery lakes of
the western continent, and the scenes passed in panoramic succession
before him; he saw the children of Japheth, enlarged by the hand of him
who then declared it through his prophet, landing on these unknown
shores and dwelling in the tents of them [the Indians]. And as the last

prophecy fell from the inspired lips, he saw the white-winged vessels that brought the degraded sons of Canaan from the burning wilds of Africa, to be civilized by the enlarged brain of Japheth (for God enlarged him mentally as well as physically).[17]

Prior to the 1850s, when regional tensions over slavery were overwhelming all other issues in the United States, most of the Cherokee slaveholders had been happy to accept Christianity and also to be designated as descendants of Shem. They had welcomed the efforts of the various missionaries to establish conclusive evidence for their heritage from the Lost Tribes of Israel. The most indefatigable of all the Cherokee missionaries in this respect was the Reverend Daniel S. Butrick of the American Board of Commissioners of Foreign Missions. Butrick was appointed a missionary to the Cherokees in 1817. Born in Winslow, Massachusetts, in 1787, Butrick served at several different mission stations in the Cherokee Nation from 1817 to 1838 and then marched with the Cherokees along the Trail of Tears to their new homes in what became northeastern Oklahoma. He died among them in 1847.

Butrick was one of a small handful of missionaries who tried to master the Cherokee language so that he could preach to them in their own tongue. He had great respect for the Cherokees, and they in turn respected him for his efforts to help them. He clearly did not share the new views of the "American School of Ethnography" but believed the Cherokees to be fully capable of doing everything that a white person could once they were educated and civilized. His fascination with the Semitic origins of the Cherokee people led him to undertake intensive research into their customs, sacred myths, and religious rituals. Much of Butrick's evidence was lost after his death, but enough survived for a friend of his to publish, in 1884, a twenty-page book entitled *Antiquities of the Cherokees*, which consisted of his notes on the Jewish features of Cherokee traditions. The anonymous editor of this tract noted that Butrick "spent most of his time" among the Cherokees, "writing, with the purpose, as he said, to show that the Indian [was] somebody," and not just a semihuman savage incapable of improvement as so many whites on the frontier believed.[18]

Most of Butrick's evidence for the Jewish origin of the Cherokees came from his firsthand study of their religion. He began this research in September 1835, when the Cherokees were in the midst of their struggle to remain on their ancestral land in Georgia, North Carolina, Tennessee, and Alabama. He was trying to gain support for their rights among white Christians, and with the help of the chief of the Nation (who wrote in support of his project to various elderly Cherokees who then served as his "informants"), he completed a manuscript by January 1837. At that time he offered it to John Howard Payne to publish. Payne, a well-known journalist, had visited the Cherokees, hoped to write a volume on their history, and published several important articles in defense of Cherokee rights against Jacksonian supporters of Indian removal.

Butrick knew that he had to overcome widespread western prejudice against the Cherokees. Shortly after his arrival among them, while he was preaching at Brainerd mission in the Tennessee region of the Nation, someone (perhaps Butrick himself) entered the following remarks into the journal kept at that station: "The sentiment very generally prevails among the white people near the southern tribes (and perhaps with some farther to the north) that the Indian is by nature radically different from all other men and that this difference presents an insurmountable barrier to his civilization." The missionaries, however, asserted, "[The] Indians are men and their children, education alone excepted, like the children of other men." There was nothing to prevent their rising to equal status with the whites.[19]

Butrick based his research upon the assumption that in the past there had been an "orthodox religion" among the Cherokees that closely followed that of the Jews. Over time, however, this orthodoxy had been "departed from," forgotten, or distorted. His task was to obtain from the oldest and best-informed men of the tribes (some of them more than one hundred years old) the most ancient forms of their religious beliefs and practices in order to prove their resemblance to Jewish practices as revealed in the Pentateuch. He was delighted to learn that there was a tradition of an ancient Cherokee prophet and lawgiver named Wasi whose position resembled that of Moses. The Cherokees called him "Wasi," Butrick claimed, because they had no sound any longer for *m*. Like James Adair earlier, Butrick found that some of their most ancient prayers were addressed to "Ye ho wah," which he was certain meant "Jehovah." His Cherokee informants also told him of an ancient religious leader who he believed corresponded to Abraham.[20]

Butrick was not able to discover any evidence of the survival of circumcision among the Cherokees, though certain Cherokees asserted of the neighboring Creeks that "some of them [were] circumcised."

He did find that in former times "the Cherokees wore long beards" (though their facial hair now was rather sparse), and he noted that "as the religious dances of the Jews were circular, so especially [were] those of the Indians." He also mentioned that "the ancient government of the Cherokees was a theocracy."[21]

However, his most convincing evidence came from some of the ancient religious stories or sacred myths of the Cherokees that, Butrick maintained, had been "handed down from parents to children entirely independent of any information derived from white men on this continent." These stories provided by his most elderly informants told of the creation and early history of the Cherokees. Butrick informed Payne that the Cherokee elders said "Man was made of red earth. The first man was red. The creator, having made man of red earth, blew into his mouth and that breath became a soul." Butrick continued, "The Cherokees say that the first man and woman were red people or Indians—that all before the flood were Indians, that the Indians were such of the descendants of that family as were not affected by the confusion of languages [after the fall of the Tower of Babel], and are of course the *real* people as their name [Ani-Yun-wiya] indicates." The "real" people were the original people, and Butrick's informants thus told him stories more or less similar to the story of Noah, the deluge and the ark, and the building of the Tower of Babel.[22]

Butrick also recounted the following version of the parting of the Red Sea by one of his Cherokee informants named Nutsawi: "Ye ho wah told the leader of the Indians that he must go to a country which he had given to them, but they would have to pass some great water before they got there. . . . They were flying from their enemies. But as soon as they came to a great water, Ye ho wah told their leader to strike the water with a rod and it should divide and give them a passage through and then flow together and stop their enemies."[23]

In one manuscript Butrick placed in parallel columns "A few promiscuous comparisons between Indian and Jewish Antiquities" that he thought John Howard Payne would find convincing:

Indians	*Jews*
Three Beings, eternal and in every respect, created all things in seven days.	In seven Days God created the heavens and the earth. Let us (Three Persons) make man in our own image.
Man was made of red earth and the	This man was called Adam, which

woman of one of man's ribs.

in the Hebrew tongue signifies one that is red, because he has formed of red earth.

At first no snakes or weeds were poison, but poison was communicated to them sometime after the creation.

God deprived the serpent of speech and inserted poison under its tongue.

Besides preaching and offering sacrifices, the priests, before the flood, also foretold events. They warned the people of the approaching flood, in case of this continued disobedience, but told them the world would not be destroyed by water but once; it would next be consumed by fire.

Upon Adam's prediction that the world was to be destroyed at one time by the force of fire and at another by the violence and quantity of water.

While the Son of God was on the mountain, after he had given the law, [he] commanded them to sing the hymns or prayers which they use morning and evenings at the same time they do sing them, viz. at day break in the morning and before going to sleep at night.

They were bound by their traditions to repeat their Phylactery sentences every morning between the dawn and sun rising and every evening between the time that the priests went in to eat their offerings and the end of the first watch.[24]

It did not seem to occur to Butrick that the Cherokees had first met European Christians as early as 1540, that Spanish priests had traveled among them in the seventeenth century, and that English and French missionaries had preached among them for more than a century prior to his arrival in the Nation.[25] Nor did he recognize that in many of these sacred myths the Cherokees were putting together biblical accounts with their own ancient myths and creating a syncretic approach to religious history that enabled them to keep some of the old and add something of the new; more important, he did not notice that in many of these syncretic versions of biblical and Cherokee mythology, the Cherokees were clearly seeking to express their own importance and their favoritism by the Great Spirit. For Butrick, the Cherokees, as descendants of the Jews, clearly had been among God's chosen people; but for Cherokees who knew nothing of Scripture before whites came, the effort to utilize the Jewish sense of chosenness had a far different function as they struggled "to be somebody" against the efforts of Indian-hating whites to reduce them to beasts in human form, or children of the Devil.

Some of the more sophisticated Cherokees who read Butrick's notes or heard him speak of his discoveries concluded that the stories were really variants of biblical accounts. The second principal chief of the Cherokees, George Lowrey, expressed some skepticism in 1835 about the authenticity of the remnants of Jewish orthodoxy among his people. Butrick duly took note of this: "On reading to Major Lowrey certain traditions, [as told by his informants,] he suspected that our aged friend [the informant] had received from certain Quakers, long ago in the nation, indirectly and without knowing whence it came, some of the information they had communicated."²⁶ What was more, when Lowrey talked more extensively to white persons about Butrick's efforts to prove that the Cherokees were Jews, he discovered that anti-Semitism was almost as pronounced among many white Americans as Indian hating. "Major Lowrey," Butrick wrote, "began evidently to be a little suspicious that any evidence of their being Jews would militate against their continuance in this country"—their ancient homeland.²⁷

Chief John Ross, on the other hand, was convinced that Butrick's Cherokee informants were relating genuine Cherokee myths and not variants of Scripture heard from early missionaries. Ross offered five reasons for believing that the accounts of Butrick's informants were to be trusted:

1. The Antiquarians [informants] who relate them are men of integrity and universally declare that they [the sacred stories] were handed down from their fathers &
2. The persons familiar with the above and other traditions and antiquities are generally such as have been from their childhood most entirely secluded from the whites, having no direct communication with them;
3. The most aged of the Cherokees—those who are a hundred or more years old are almost the only persons acquainted with the above traditions. . . .
4. The ancient Cherokees have generally held the white people and their religion in such contempt that there is no reason to suppose they would learn of [from] them. . . . [T]hey never conversed freely with white men respecting their religious customs &
5. Many of their customs do exactly resemble the customs of the jews as their traditions do.²⁸

Ross had accepted membership in a Methodist society in 1829, and he made frequent allusions in his public speeches to biblical stories that he thought gave hope of divine justice in their struggles. He must have expected the full-bloods (who constituted three-quarters of the Nation in 1835) to understand the symbolism of these stories. For example, in 1830, when Andrew Jackson first brought forward the policy of Indian removal and Congress accepted it, Ross said in a speech that he had printed for distribution among his people, "Let us not forget the circumstances related in Holy writ of the safe passage of the children of Israel through the chrystal walls of the Red Sea."[29] Ross believed that the God of Christianity would accept Cherokees as his people as easily as the whites, and this belief led him to support Butrick's position and to encourage his people to believe it.

Missionaries of the American Board were not the only ones who found evidence of Jewish ancestry for the Cherokees. The Reverend Thomas Roberts, a Baptist missionary, and Evan Jones, the Baptist schoolteacher among the Cherokees at Valley Towns in western North Carolina, made a concerted effort in 1823 to learn to speak and write Cherokee. They reported to their mission board in Philadelphia, "The construction of the language bears a striking resemblance to the Hebrew. Every modification of the verb is made by prefixes and suffixes as in Hebrew."[30]

However, other missionaries were unconvinced. The Reverend Cephas Washburn, also a missionary of the American Board, preached in the 1820s among those Cherokees who were living in Arkansas and who were presumed to be much closer to their original religious practices than those in the East who lived nearer to the whites. Washburn said in his *Reminiscences* that he found no evidence among the Arkansas Cherokees that they were descended from the Jews and in particular no evidence that they ever practiced circumcision.[31]

Washburn knew well Ta-he-e-tuh, one of the oldest Cherokee shamans, whom he called their "high priest." In 1820 he was more than one hundred years old. Ta-he-e-tuh told Washburn a story about a Cherokee hero who wrestled with a mighty adversary from the spirit world; the two of them struggled all night, and the Cherokee finally conquered the spirit at dawn by touching the sinew of his thigh. When Washburn pointed out that this was the story of Jacob wrestling with an angel that was included in the Bible, Ta-he-e-tuh "said the white people must have borrowed that story from the Cherokees to put in their good book."[32] He had no interest in claiming ancestry from the Jews. Nor did the great bulk of Cherokees (particularly among those called "full-blood," "traditionalist," or "adherents of the old religion") have much interest in identifying themselves with the Israelites. As one federal agent remarked, "Many Cherokees think that they are not derived from the same stock as the white, that they are favorites of the great spirit, and that he never intended they should live the laborious lives of the whites."[33] The anthropologist James Mooney, who did extensive research into the sacred myths of the Cherokees in the late 1880s, found many aspects of their ancient religion still prevalent, though he found no resemblance to anything in the Pentateuch. He did find, however, several creation myths that portrayed the Cherokees as the favorites of the Great Spirit.[34]

It must be said for Daniel Butrick that he dutifully recorded some of the ancient myths of the Cherokees in the years 1835 to 1837 even when they had no resemblance to anything in the Bible. However, he did not consider them the most ancient myths but rather the most recent departures from the orthodox religion of the Cherokees. He did not believe these variants would long survive the advent of Gospel Truth, and yet he should have seen the reasons for their continued hold upon the Cherokees. Many Cherokees lost interest in becoming Christians or in the possibility of attaining citizenship in white America when it appeared that they would always be only second-class citizens. This became evident as early as 1824 when the secretary of war, John C. Calhoun, addressed a letter to Governor George Troup of Georgia asking whether his state would grant citizenship to the Cherokees. Troup replied in a famous letter, "The answer is that if such a scheme were practicable at all, the utmost rights and privileges which public opinion would concede to the Indians, would fix them in the middle station between the negro and white man; and that, as long as they survived this degradation, without the possibility of attaining the elevation of the latter, they would gradually sink to the condition of the former—a point of degeneracy below which they could not fall."[35]

Knowing this, the Cherokee traditionalists saw only one option. They must assert their own separate racial identity and origin as a means to retain their growing sense of nationalism and separatism. By treaty, the Cherokees, as other tribes, were guaranteed the right to self-government under their own laws and leaders within their own boundaries. The desire to hold on to their homeland became tied to their desire to retain their own language, their own religion, their own ethnicity, and their own sovereignty. In 1827 the Cherokee people adopted their own written constitution and, in effect, asserted their independence as a nation; the only allegiance they felt they owed to the United States was to maintain peace and friendship, military and trade alliances. In the 1830s, the pressures of removal and the surrender of their lands led to a resurgence of their ancient religion; faith in their own myths of creation provided the substance for a patriotic fervor on behalf of national sovereignty.

Early creation myths that helped to sustain Cherokee ethnic identity were recorded by Butrick and Mooney.[36] The precontact myths were animistic or zootheistic, placing humanity in close and continual rapport with plant, bird, insect, and animal life; the spirits associated with the sun, moon, planets, fire, water, smoke, thunder, tobacco, and maize all played important roles in relating humans to nature and the cosmos. The key element in Cherokee religion was the necessity of spiritual harmony among all these interrelated elements.[37] Postcontact myths sometimes spoke of the separate creation of red, white, and black people by the Great Spirit. They served several purposes in the rising tide of Cherokee nationalism in the nineteenth century.[38] First, these myths declared that the red man was always God's favorite. Second, they proclaimed that the way of life given to each of the three races was different (hunting to the Indian, agriculture to the African, science and manufacturing to the European).[39] God did not expect or want changes made in their respective ways of life; hence efforts to civilize and Christianize the Indian were contrary to the will of the Great Spirit. Third, the Great Spirit had originally placed each race on its own continent (whites in Europe, blacks in Africa, reds in America). It was counter to the intent of the Great Spirit that the Europeans had taken the Africans into slavery from their homeland and had invaded and taken possession of so much of the Indians' God-given continent.[40] Those dislocations had created serious disharmony in the cosmos.

Further, it was alleged in one of the most common of the Cherokee creation myths that at the time of creation the Great Spirit had originally given the "Great Book," in which the whites found so much knowledge, truth, and power, to the red people; the whites had stolen that book from them, thus forcibly depriving the Indians of the knowledge that the Great Spirit had meant them to have—another source of disharmony and hence of sin in the world.[41] Insofar as traditionalists accepted the concept of a spiritual existence after death, they believed the Indians would go to a heaven without whites.[42]

Perhaps the most important and oldest of the Cherokee creation myths held that originally there was only a family of red people in the world, consisting of a mother, named Selu, a father, named Kanati, and a son. To this family was added a wandering "wild boy" adopted by Selu and Kanati. Wild boy was disobedient and persuaded the son of Selu and Kanati to kill Selu. Selu was the "Earth Mother" or goddess of corn, and after being mortally wounded, she told her sons that thereafter they must work hard if they were to grow their own food. Similarly, Kanati, god of hunting, shocked at the murder of his wife, left the two boys and told them thereafter they would have to take much trouble to find game to feed themselves.[43] Catherine Albanese suggests that this myth may reflect certain archetypal aspects of self-sacrificial Christ figures and of the curse of God upon Adam that henceforth he must live by the sweat of his brow.[44] However, the Cherokees had a static view of history marked only by the continual cycle of the seasons; they had no concept of teleology or "progress" from a beginning to an end of history.[45]

While it is understandable that many Cherokees, rejected by white America, would adhere even more strongly to their own belief in the separate creations of red, white, and black people, this placed them on the side of the polygenetic theory of the most militant white racists. It reinforced the white belief that red, white, and black were not "brothers under the skin," not all equally descended from Adam and Eve; it negated the missionaries' claim that "of one blood hath God made all nations." It left the Indians open to the belief of Indian haters that Indians had no rights that whites were bound to respect in "the second Promised Land." Many full-blood traditionalists, however, preferred to withdraw unto themselves rather than yield to the second-class citizenship that whites offered.[46]

A somewhat more difficult problem faced those Cherokees (perhaps 10 to 12 percent of the Nation) who adopted Christianity but who nonetheless wished to avoid total assimilation into the culture of the white race. These Cherokees, most of them Baptist full-bloods, struggled to dissociate Christianity from the white race. To them Christianity was a religion that any nation or people might hold and that allowed them at the same time to assert their own historical and ethnic identity. All Christian people, the Cherokee full-blood converts asserted, did not originate from Europe, Asia, Africa, or the Middle East. Christianity was not "the white man's religion," nor was it limited to those who descended from Adam and Eve. It was possible to accept the New Testament gospel without accepting the historical validity of everything in the Old.

This outlook was particularly strong among non-slaveholding Cherokee Christians. One of the common ways to justify slaveholding was to note that in the Old Testament the Jews had practiced a form of slavery, and God had held them to be his chosen people. The southern Baptists and Methodists among the Cherokees preached this God-ordained view of slavery, but the northern Baptists opposed slavery on the New Testament grounds of loving thy neighbor as thyself. One southern Baptist missionary reported that this heretical notion was being preached by Cherokee preachers ordained by the northern Baptist missionary Evan Jones. "I heard one of his preachers say," said the astonished southern Baptist missionary James A. Slover in 1861, "[that] if Abraham, David and all the ancient worthies of the Old Testament, being slaveholders, were here on earth, he could not fellowship with them."[47] Northern Baptist Cherokee churches (of which there were eight in 1861, containing more than sixteen hundred Cherokee members) would not allow slaveholders into their churches and rejected Jewish practices that condoned slavery. To the southern Baptists (and to most other southern Christians), this was unscriptural, but to the northern Baptist Cherokees it was a logical result of their attempt to sustain at the same time their belief in Christianity and their identity as a separate and distinct people with their own independent origin that in no way connected them with the descendants of Shem.

In the end, white efforts to co-opt the Cherokees into Christian history (as white Americans interpreted it) proved irrelevant. The Cherokees could not permit themselves to be considered descendants of Shem, Ham, or Japheth. They did not want to be lost Jews or accursed "colored people." And they could not become white.[48] The British writer of the *Enquiry* in 1762 could not persuade the Cherokees to associate themselves with the descendants of Japheth because that might lead to further distrust of "the irredeemable savage" who, as warriors of Gog and Magog, would someday turn against the whites and slaughter them. (More than one Cherokee ghost dance prophet spoke in such apocalyptic terms in the nineteenth century, but they could never arouse the Cherokees to follow their prophecies as the Shawnee and Sioux prophets persuaded their people to do.) Wisely, and through bitter experience, Cherokee Christians came to see that the validity of their faith did not, and must not, allow its message of spiritual freedom to ensnare them in the historical bonds of Euro-American racist myth and theory.

Nonetheless, the Cherokees, a conquered and minority people, were caught up in the history and the racial dilemmas of white America. Many Cherokees did own slaves; the Cherokees failed to preserve their homeland; many of them became Christians and adopted the white Americans' way of life, of speech, and of behavior. As the Civil War approached, the Cherokees were forced to choose between the North and the South; neutrality was not an option. The non-slaveholders (most of them full-bloods) sided with the North; the slaveholders (most of mixed ancestry) fought with the South. History engulfed the Cherokees in a tragedy that decimated them from 1861 to 1865, and in that fratricidal war it mattered little whether they were descendants of Shem, Ham, or Japheth or whether the first man was red.[49]

Chapter 7

Fractured Myths: The Cherokees' Use of Christianity

Sacred myths—those religious stories of a people that speak to questions such as How was the world created? Where did we come from? How should we live? and What happens after we die?—are a crucial feature of all religious traditions. In the early nineteenth century several missionaries collected versions of Cherokee myths sometimes in the hope of proving that the Cherokees were descendants of the Lost Tribes of Israel. Some Indians now claim that these stories were slyly manufactured to mislead or poke fun at the missionaries. Early anthropologists dismissed them as confused oral renderings of translations by interpreters of early missionary sermons. Ethnohistorians today are giving them more serious consideration on two grounds: first, because they indicate how new religious ideas were incorporated into old ones, and second, because they tell us what in Christianity seemed important or relevant to the Indians (most of whom took them very seriously). They also have much to tell us about how the Indians assumed the white man's prejudices against Africans while at the same time asserting their own spiritual superiority to whites.

This essay does not trace the origins of ancient myths. Rather, it examines "fractured myths," those amalgamations of Cherokee and Christian traditions, and their function as bridges from tribal religions to Christianity and as agents of incorporating Christianity into tribal religion. Through these efforts the Cherokees and other southeastern tribes were trying to preserve their Native American identity by asserting that God was red, the first man was red, the Indians were God's favorites, and it was the white man who, as a cruel and unjust oppressor, would ultimately be condemned by a just God and the world turned upside down.

The Great Spirit . . . mixing up the dust again, he blew upon it—and there stood before him A RED MAN! The Great Spirit smiled.—Seminole myth, c. 1819

The Cherokees saw that the first man and woman were red people or Indians—that all before the flood were Indians, that the Indians were such descendants of that family as were not affected by the confusion of languages [after the fall of the Tower of Babel].—Cherokee myth, c. 1833

Throughout the missionaries' and travelers' accounts of early-nineteenth-century contact with the Cherokees there are continual references to allegedly ancient myths that contain obvious references to events in the Old Testament. These references derive particularly from sacred stories in Genesis. Often described as "ancient" Cherokee myths by those who related them, these Indian myths seemed so clearly derivative that they were treated by their recorders as amusingly distorted sermons. Whether the interpreters had garbled the stories or whether they were altered by the Cherokees was unclear. Only those Christians eager for evidence that the Indians were descendants of the Lost Tribes of Israel took them seriously. Early anthropologists dismissed them out of hand. James Mooney considered them "worthless" because they were "so badly warped by Biblical interpretation." These myths may have contained parts of original Cherokee mythology, but they were utterly corrupted by biblical interpolations. An anthropologist searching for precontact myths and legends in pristine form could not take them seriously. As Mooney put it, "The Bible story kills the Indian tradition, and there is no amalgamation of the two."[1] It is the contention of this essay that there was significant amalgamation occurring. Taken in cultural context, these composite myths provide important insights into the Cherokees' effort to sustain and revitalize their identity.

As increasing warfare, epidemics, and cultural invasion from 1730 to 1830 undercut their original religious perspective on tribal history and religion, the belief system of the Cherokees suffered drastic damage. Their name for themselves, "Ani-Yun-wiya," meant literally "principal or real people."[2] The world they lived upon was traditionally described as a circular island of dried mud suspended from the stone arch of the heavens; the real people were at the center of that world, and when they died, the island (which floated on the water) would crumble and sink back to the bottom of the sea surrounding it. When strangers from outside their island appeared bringing new technical wonders and invincible military force, when none of their priests could draw upon sufficient spiritual power to defeat or hold back the invaders, it became obvious that the Indians were faced with sources of power beyond their ken. For their own survival they had to learn all they could about how these foreigners drew upon the ultimate sources of spiritual power and then, somehow, to use that power for their own survival. The priests of the invaders—missionaries—came to tell them about these powers, access to which somehow was contained within the "Great Book"—the Bible—which they held up as the source of all authority, human and superhuman. To what extent this new knowledge might be accessible to them and usable for their own preservation required serious consideration.

The ultimate defeat of the Cherokees in 1794, their acknowledged submission to the political authority of the foreign, white invaders, and their necessary transition from a fur trade economy to self-subsistent agriculture on small farmsteads forced drastic reorientations in every sphere of their lives. Between 1794 and 1830 the five southeastern tribes underwent a rapid period of acculturation. Ministers of five different evangelical Protestant denominations established missions and schools among them. This made Christianity at last, in William James's phrase, "a live option" for them. Choices had to be made for or against the old ways and the old religion. It was natural that an oral tradition that had always been open to new ideas would begin to assimilate new concepts; the Cherokees had been trading closely with the whites since 1690. However foreign the belief system of the whites may have been, there was no doubt about the extent of their knowledge and power. This power was assumed to be spiritual as well as military, political, and technological. The southeastern tribes, overwhelmed by white settlements impinging around them, the loss of their hunting lands, and a long series of land cessions, had to adapt to survive. They became farmers, moved with their wives and children out of their compact, stockaded villages, built log cabins, and like any other frontier family cut the trees and began plowing and planting on their own farmsteads. Some of them bought black slaves to assist them. They began to send their children to the missionaries' schools (where they also imbibed Protestant doctrines). They opened trade and intercourse with their white neighbors. They began to make written laws. So rapid was the transformation of their social order that by the 1830s they became known as "the five civilized tribes." Though comparatively few were converted to Christianity prior to their removal in the mid-1830s, several hundred eventually took the step, and the religious ideas and practices of Christianity became well known. At first the majority of Native Americans clung desperately to their old religious beliefs and practices, but much of this was increasingly unrelated to their new way of life. Others turned curiously but cautiously toward some comprehension of the new belief system. They were particularly interested in what seemed congruent to their own situation and history.

Most scholars since Mooney believe that the tribes of the eastern part of North America did not have a rigid or exclusive belief system. James Axtell writes that "native groups borrowed beliefs, myths, culture heroes, religious artifacts, ceremonies and even whole cultures from other groups of Indians," and "this continuing process of borrowing and transfer" led them "even to incorporate Christian items into Indian ways."[3] They were pragmatic; "purposeful change and adjustment was the norm." Axtell further notes that "although oral knowledge is tenaciously conservative, it is not changeless because it has a system of elimination. . . . [D]eities and other preternatural agencies which have served their purpose can be quietly dropped from the contemporary pantheon; and as the society changes, myths too are forgotten, attributed to other personages, or transformed in their meanings."[4] Because "traditional knowledge is very fragile" in oral societies and "depends on the memories of mortal people," epidemics, wars, and other disasters tend to "sever the links of knowledge that bind the culture together."[5] Tribes with "an urgent need to adjust" to rapidly changing conditions nevertheless try to do so "without surrendering their ethnic and cultural identity."[6] One of the ways they accomplish this is "to revitalize native culture . . . through the selective use of Christianity." They can "in time-honored Indian fashion add the power of the Christian God to that of [their] own deities and proceed to syncretize the beliefs and practices of the new religion with the deep structures of [their] traditional faith."[7] Or as another contemporary scholar, Gregory Dowd, puts it, the Indian consciously "sought to decipher the secrets of Anglo-American strength and made efforts to incorporate those secrets into their own way of living" and believing.[8] The Great Spirit might at any time have new knowledge, rituals, ceremonies, and predictions to enlighten and assist them.

This essay indicates how the Cherokees and other southeastern tribes developed an amalgamation of their traditional belief system and Christianity by means of fractured myths—that is, myths that purported to be ancient but that also incorporated historical events and heroic figures from the Old Testament. The myths claimed that major events in the Old Testament related to their own people as well as to whites. Although the process of amalgamation took several generations and is probably still in process, the most crucial period for the southeastern tribes was that between 1800 and 1830.

No translations of the Old Testament were made in the language of any of the southeastern tribes prior to their removal from the region in 1838; only oral versions circulated.[9] The large majority of extant fractured myths were written down by whites in that period, though some were obviously formulated earlier because they were considered so "ancient." Daniel S. Butrick, who recorded many of them, often prefaced his account by saying that his informants were very old men and that they had heard these from their grandparents: "Big Pheasant relates the history of creation received from his grandmother and handed down from the old men before they had any knowledge of whites." Big Pheasant's myth, however, said that the first woman was made from the rib of the first man.[10]

In the light of modern cultural analysis, these myths, however perceived by those who told them or wrote them down, mark the critical stage of the process of borrowing and transfer by which the southeastern tribes made Christianity useful to their revitalization. By insisting that the first man and woman were "red people," that they were "God's favorites," that they were the preservers of God's true ways (through a red Noah) when the rest of humankind had gone astray, and by appropriating to their own condition the oppression of Job and the imagery of the Red Sea (miraculously opened to the chosen and then closed to crush their enemies), the Cherokees and other southeastern Indians were consciously grafting their own identity into the universal history of humankind and preserving their own identity at the center of the universe till the end of time.

Some Native Americans welcomed the effort of missionaries to relate them to the Ten Lost Tribes of Israel. They thought this lineage would gain them more respect in the eyes of Anglo-Americans and link their destiny with that of Christianity. Others, of wider experience in white America, were aware of the endemic anti-Semitism embedded in it and argued that the Indians had enough against them without adding that burden. When Chief Cornplanter of the Senecas told a missionary, "It was the white people who killed our savior," the missionary replied, "It was the Jews."[11] Obviously the Indians divided history between whites and reds, the Christians between Christians and Jews.

By examining here some of the prominent themes in these fractured myths in terms of their effort to accommodate aboriginal beliefs to Christianity, this essay suggests a crucial step in the process of appropriating Old Testament ideas and heroes into a particularly Cherokee form of Christianity. But it also indicates that those who called themselves traditionalists may have appropriated the same myths, culture heroes, and historical events to bolster an anti-Christian tradition. Much depended on how the term "God" and related theological implications in the appropriations were translated into Cherokee, and that we do not know. It is not possible to ascertain with certainty when these myths originated or with which tribe. Although the process was a regional rather than tribal one, Cherokee versions of the myths have been chosen whenever possible.

If religion serves to legitimate a people's way of life, by asserting the supernatural reality or basis of its origins, values, beliefs, and hopes, then nothing seems more remote from the religion of the southeastern tribes than that of white, evangelical Protestantism. These tribes believed in the communal ownership of land, in sharing, in consensus decision making, and in human adaptation to the natural order of the fields, forests, and seasons. Evangelical Protestants believed that God commanded them to dominate nature, exploit its resources, and compete individually for wealth, power, and respect. The Indians prized generosity and burned the worldly possessions of their dead. The Protestants accumulated wealth and passed it on. The Indians had a matriarchal system based on exogamous clans. The Protestants had a patriarchal system based on individual self-reliance and competitiveness. The Indians thought little of death or the afterlife. The Protestants lived in constant anxiety over their admission to a better world after death. One religion stood for accepting the world as it was created and living within its natural boundaries; the other believed in making the world over. One was earthbound; the other otherworldly. One was pantheistic and polytheistic; the other Manichean and monotheistic.

There were some parallels, of course, of which missionaries made use. The Cherokee ritual of purification, or going to water, an annual rite involving immersion in a river and associated with obliterating hard feelings over quarrels with neighbors, was seized upon by Baptists to justify baptism by immersion as a ritual of salvation from sin. The Cherokees did have some fears of death if proper rituals were not performed (the spirit of the dead could haunt the family) and some concept of an afterlife however vaguely defined, and all Christians could play upon these themes. Witchcraft was recognized within both religions. And the frontier camp meetings were adopted by all denominations because the Indians found them akin to their protracted ceremonies that went on day and night for several days, including shouting, singing, prayers, and efforts to attain spiritual rapport with the forces of the supernatural world; camp meetings were also important social gatherings for people no longer living in compact villages. But such parallels were few, and the deeper meanings of the two theologies created a tremendous chasm difficult to bridge. Not even the concept of a triune deity could match the multitudinous powerful spiritual beings in the Indian supernatural realm, although some creation myths of the Cherokees spoke of three Creators.

It is not difficult to see why the Old Testament was of particular interest to Native Americans, for it provided knowledge of ancient times outside their own and it was very specific about the origins of humanity and the critical events that shaped human history. It told of the origins of different peoples and nations and languages. It opened up wider horizons and contained dramatic stories of God's (the Great Spirit's) dealing with humans through striking miracles, cataclysms, and heroic figures. Above all, it provided a picture of oppressed peoples whose prayers were heard and their rescue accomplished by supernatural power. The coherence of these vivid stories illuminated history in a dramatic way but with sufficient symbolic ambiguity to permit different interpretations. The Bible did not say Adam was red, but neither did it deny it. And at a time when the role of women was losing its power among the Cherokees and males were becoming dominant over their families, perhaps the negative view of Eve was of interest.

Examination of the impact of Christianity must start with the Cherokees' changing belief system and with those aboriginal myths that explained creation (cosmogony) and genesis (human beings), for it is the variation from the originals that makes the fractured myths significant. From what little we have left of that original belief system it appears that while the Cherokees had framed an understanding of the universe—the sun, moon, stars, and earth—and its interrelationships, they said little about the creation of men and women. As for the concept of sin, that entered their worldview only in terms of imbalances or disorders that broke the harmonious relationships between humans and nature or between humans themselves. Charles Hudson aptly says, "If there is a single word which epitomizes the Southeastern Indian belief, it is 'order.'" He explains further, "The Southeastern Indian concern with purity and balance was based upon the assumption that man lived in a just, well-ordered universe."[12] Other scholars emphasize harmony as the chief theme. John Phillip Reid in his study of Cherokee culture states, "The key to the Cherokee legal mind was the Cherokees' desire for social harmony." Fred Gearing writes that "the single focus which created pattern in Cherokee moral thought was the value of harmony among men. . . . The Cherokee ethos disallowed disharmony." Life was not, as in Protestantism, a constant moral battle among erring individuals prone to disobedience against a righteous God; it was a group effort to sustain harmony among themselves and with the orderly forces of the cosmos.[13]

There is consequently no emphasis upon a single Creator and his commandments to the first man. "In the beginning," says an old myth, "water covered everything. It was said, 'Who will make land appear?'"[14] This myth does not identify the speaker nor explain where the water came from. The most famous creation myth of the Cherokees begins, "The earth is a great island floating in a sea of water and suspended at each of the four cardinal points by a cord hanging down from the sky vault which is of solid rock. When the world grows old and worn out, the people will die and the cords will break and let the earth sink down into the ocean, and all will be water again. When all was water, the animals were above [in the Upper World] beyond the arch, but it was very much crowded and they were wanting more room."[15] The earth came into being not through the act of a Creator but through the familiar figure of the Earth-diver, in this case the water beetle (or in some myths, the crawfish) who dived deep into the water until he found mud and brought it to the surface where it floated; he continued this slow process until there was enough land for all the animals to live upon.[16] However, "when the plants and animals were first made, we do not know," the myth continues. "Men came after the animals and plants." The myth does not say how man appeared. The earth was circular, inhabited solely by red people, and the Cherokees (who called themselves the "real" or "original" people) lived at its center.

Disorder came into the world from the evil spirits who lived beneath the earth in the watery world and entered this world through springs, caves, or other holes in the earth. Disorder also came when people did not behave correctly with one another or when humans abused the animal world. Above the stone vault, in the Upper World, lived benevolent spirits (Thunder, Corn, Sacred Fire) who seldom interfered in the daily lives of human beings. The sun and moon passed over the earth and then circled up and around the stone vault to appear again in the East. One myth stated that when "Mother Sun" passed over the earth soon after its making, "a drop of blood fell from her to the ground and from this blood and earth sprang the first people, the children of the Sun."[17] Myths, now lost, may have told of three superior beings that later myths call the "Creators" or the "Masters of Life" or "Givers of Breath" who were responsible for giving life to human beings, but these myths have not survived except as we find them in the later "fractured myths" of the early nineteenth century. In the myths that James Mooney, John Swanton, or Frans Olbrechts and other anthropologists considered aboriginal, there are no examples that mention a "Great Spirit." There were, however, witches, "Raven Mockers," monsters (like the Uktena), "little people," and minor malevolent spirits whose mischief had always to be guarded against. There was no satanic figure. As Hudson says, the world being basically well ordered "so long as man lived by the rules" and guarded by special rituals against "wild" events or mischief, one "could expect to avoid misfortune."[18]

An early myth describes the first disorders in terms of lack of proper regard for the animals:

In the old days the beasts, birds, fishes, insects and plants could all talk, and they and the people lived together in peace and friendship. But as time went on the people increased so rapidly that their settlements spread over the whole earth, and the poor animals found themselves beginning to be cramped for room. This was bad enough, but to make it worse, Man invented bows, knives, blowguns, spears and [fishing] hooks, and began to slaughter the larger animals, birds, and fishes for their flesh or their skins, while the smaller creatures, such as the frogs and worms, were crushed and trodden upon without thought, out of pure carelessness or contempt.[19]

The animals held a council and to protect themselves decided to bring diseases upon man in self-defense. But order or balance was restored when the plants held a countercouncil and agreed to provide medicine for man. Man in turn agreed to kill only what he absolutely needed and to say a prayer of thanks to the spirit of any animal he had to kill. (Later, harmony was disrupted again when the white man urged the Indians into the fur trade; nineteenth-century myths returned to this theme.)

Another primordial myth of the Cherokees describes the first man and woman as superior beings but does not explain their creation; they evidently came down from the Upper World, lived for a time on earth, and then returned. But Cherokee history began with them: "Long years ago, soon after the world was made, a hunter and his wife lived at Pilot Ridge [in the heart of the Cherokee area] with their only child, a little boy." The hunter was called Kanati (later, the god of thunder); the wife was Selu, the corn goddess. The little boy—really the first human—had no name. The myth explained, among other things, the true role of males as hunters and warriors and women as cultivators of the soil and nourishers. They had equal status and importance. Trouble came into the world when a "wild boy" (also unnamed) appeared from the river; he was a child of the Under World. He made friends with the little boy and persuaded him to spy on his parents to discover the magical means by which they obtained game and corn for their meals. When Selu reprimanded the boys for this, they killed her (wild boy saying she was a witch). Thereafter Indians had to go to much trouble to raise corn and grow other foods. After the two boys discovered how Kanati miraculously obtained deer and other game, he became angry and returned to the Upper World whither Selu had gone after her death. Before he left, he taught them how to hunt as Selu had taught them to grow corn, but hunting and farming were no longer easy to do. The human race descended from these two boys, but the myth does not say where they obtained spouses. After they had made peace with the animals and developed *adonisgi* (doctors/ priests) to care for the sick and ward off evil spirits, life was generally peaceful and orderly until the white man came. The ensuing stress of constant warfare, recurring epidemics, and intensifying factionalism totally disrupted the Cherokees' lives and way of life, and by the early nineteenth century, the southeastern Indians were forced to reconsider their perspective on the natural and supernatural worlds. Doubtless this process had begun long before 1800, but so long as these tribes were independent and fighting for survival, they had paid little attention to the alternative religion the white man sometimes preached to them.

By 1800 the southeastern tribes were forced to recognize that the world was much larger and had more kinds of people in it than they had ever realized. Their own role models of Kanati and Selu had to be drastically altered as the warrior became a farmer and the cultivator became a domestic. Even the nature of creation and the genesis of man had to be reconsidered. It is then that one begins to find updated myths that speak of a Creator or three Creators who made three kinds of human beings—red, white, and black. They also had to place in their sacred myths the concepts of sin that the missionaries spoke so much about, to ask how the white man proved so much more powerful than they, to evaluate the Bible—the "Great Book"—from which the white man said all truth came, and to think of life after death in which the missionaries said the good would be rewarded and the bad punished.

The new creation stories exhibit wide variations in detail, but they all were concerned with the creation of red, white, and black people. They posit a concrete act of creation of human beings but say little about the creation of the world. The early missionaries found it very difficult to convince them that the earth was round, that eclipses could be predicted, that the earth went around the sun. As one missionary put it in 1821,

> The Cherokees are peculiarly inquisitive, and although they discover much grandeur in the works of God, yet the book of nature is to them in many respects sealed. And a minister not well versed in Geography, Natural Philosophy, Astronomy, and mathematics generally labours under many great disadvantages among them. . . . Last summer when at Creek Path, in answer to various enquiries of the Cherokees, I was led to make remarks relative to the figure, motions, etc. of the earth, the bulk,

relative situations, distances, etc. of several planets, causes of eclipses, etc. A gentleman living in the nation, considered by the Indians a very learned man, told them I spoke entirely wrong—that no one could tell the size of any planet nor shew its distance from the sun; that the earth was a plane—the sun, moon, and stars moved round it as it appears to them. . . . [A] complete knowledge of these subjects is necessary in order to explain them to the understanding of the Indians.[20]

The complexity of this new cosmology was too great, and the southeastern Indians (who believed they knew the facts of the earth as well as any white man) were not willing to accept the solar system without much more education. Hence they ignored this issue in their new mythology and preferred to bait the missionaries with ad hominem taunting: "Can any white man catch thunder? Can any white man catch lightning? Can any white man catch the wind?"[21]

Similarly they did not comprehend the complex theology of Christianity. It defied logic and experience. "Why did you kill your god?" they asked. "Who made the Saviour? Why did not God make man holy? . . . [W]hy did he let Satan tempt Eve?"[22] It was many years before they could begin to grasp the rationale for all this.

However, Christians did believe that a Creator had made man, and there were various theories among whites as to why different people had different complexions, temperaments, and customs. American science was in flux in the early nineteenth century as the most eminent anthropologists (still amateurs like Thomas Jefferson) debated whether different "races" were simply the product of environment (climate) and custom or whether they were created in different forms from the outset. Monogenetic theory fought polygenetic; the fixity of species fought the malleability of species. This was an area in which mythology could offer explanations.

Creation and genesis myths in this period took many forms, indicating their popularity and the unsettled nature of Indian speculation about this question. They differed as to whether there was one, two, or three Creators at work; some spoke of the creation of only red and white people; those that spoke of three Creators were not consistent as to whether they were all Indians; the myths differed as to how humans got their respective colors and over whether they were created from rocks, dust, earth, or clay. They all seemed to agree on the most important and pressing fact that each had been given a different vocation, and most agree that the red man was the favorite of the Creator(s). Some endeavored to show that the Creator had placed them in different parts of the world (the Indian in North America, the white man in Europe or England, the black man in Africa). And most clearly placed the black man in a position of inferiority and servitude to white and red men.

The most elaborate of these myths also served to blame the white man for disordering the natural separation of races ordained by the Creator because the white man had left his assigned continent, stolen the black man from Africa, and then invaded and stole the red man's land. Myths usually convey moral messages. In this case, the white man was responsible for the original sin that created havoc in the red man's and the black man's world. But the myths are also amusing in certain respects, for clearly the Creator was himself a bungler and failed to make all men properly red. He did not in all myths create the red man first. He made the white man less moral than the red but nonetheless gave the white man superior talents. How much of the red man's loss of control over his world was due to his own failings was ambiguous in most of these myths, but at the very least he lacked foresight. Searching for some moral order in their new subordinate position to whites, the southeastern Indians seemed to grant more power and even greater intellectual perception to the white man while clearly asserting the red man's superiority to the black man. Some of the blame clearly fell upon the Creator.

The Reverend Samuel A. Worcester recorded in 1829 a genesis myth that omits the creation of the black man but includes the creation of a woman: "Man was at first formed of earth. Two men were originally made by the Creator, an Indian and a white man. Each of these, after a season, became exceedingly lonesome, on which account the Creator formed a woman, also of earth, and gave them to him." Worcester pointed out to his informant that he had indicated the formation of two women ("them") but only one recipient. The informant said the woman was given to the Indian. Worcester commented in his notes, "It is obvious to remark the confusion which arises from blending the original tradition, which was probably that of the creation of one man only with the idea of the original creation of two, which doubtless sprang up after they had knowledge of white men" (but evidently before they had knowledge of black men?).[23]

A Creek genesis myth written down by the Reverend A. W. Loomis in the 1850s offers one of the many variants on the creation of three

men: "[There is an] old Indian tradition of three men who were originally all black. They came to a stream of water and one of them washed
in it and came out entirely white, and he was the father of the white
race. The second washed in the now turbid water and came out par-
tially white, and he was the father of the red men. The third, seeing
the water already too black, did not wash at all, except to touch the
palms of his hands and the souls of his feet, [and] therefore he remained black."[24] This account seemed to take no sides on who was
superior or which was the Creator's favorite.

John Swanton recorded another variation in which the first three
men were white, and after washing first, the white man remained
white; the second entered the stirred-up sediment and "was not quite
so clean and his descendants [were] the Indians. By this time the
water was very dirty and so the last man came out black and his
people [were] the negroes."[25] Swanton also noted a version that begins, "Three Indians were once out hunting"; they too found a pool
of water; they went in seriatim and came out with the usual three
colors.[26] Why the Creator made all three men of the same color is not
explained in any of these myths.

Stories that deal specifically with the bungling efforts of the Cre-
ator(s) exhibit other features. Two white men in Florida prior to 1819
recorded a Seminole myth that said that

> man was originally formed from the clay; that the Great Spirit submit-
> ted his creation to the influence of fire, but that his ignorance of the
> degree of heat necessary to give consistency caused the first batch to
> be over baked, black and crusty; these were the aborigines of the negro
> race. Again the Creator essayed, but endeavoring to avoid the error of
> the former attempt, he plunged into another, that of applying too little
> fuel. They were in consequence but half baked, of a pale ash color. These
> were [the whites'] first parents. But in the third and last effort, the Great
> Master created perfect models, both in shape and color, producing to the
> world the founders of the Indian tribes.[27]

The white men seemed to have seen this as a humorous story rather
than a sacred myth.

The Reverend Daniel S. Butrick, who believed the Indians were descendants of the Lost Tribes of Israel, collected many "ancient" stories
in the early 1830s with the aid of informants recommended for their
knowledge of ancient myths by the Cherokee chief John Ross. Butrick

said, "It is also stated that anciently the Cherokees supposed a number of beings—more than two, some have conjectured three, came down and made the world. They then attempted to make a man and woman of two rocks. They fashioned them, but while attempting to make them live, another Being came and spoiled their work, so that they could not succeed. They then made a man and a woman of clay, and being of clay, they were mortal. But had they been made of rock, they would have lived forever."[28] In addition to speaking of three Creators, the myth reflects an older view that humans were once immortal, which, as will later be seen, resonated with the story of Adam and Eve. It is not clear that the "Being" who spoiled the original pair was a satanic or evil spirit, but that seems to be implicit. Some of Butrick's informants had been converted to Christianity and may subconsciously have read the Devil back into an older myth.

The Seminoles, who had earlier and closer contact with Europeans than the Cherokees and were not finally defeated until 1843, told a more elaborate creation myth that was designed to assert the separate ways of red, white, and black men and to insist that the Creator never intended that the Indians should become Christians or agriculturists. This myth is important not only because most other southeastern tribes adopted it but also because it is an updated myth that, far from being a bridge toward Christianity, was a bulwark against it. It is attributed to the Seminole chief Nea-mathla, and he told it to an agent of the federal government in 1819:

> Father, it is not my wish to have my children made white men of. When the Great Spirit made man, he made him as he is and under three marks. He assigned to each a color at the creation [and] the duties of each, and it was never intended that they should mingle.
>
> Father, this was the way in which the Great Spirit made man. He stood upon a high place. Then, taking into his hand some dust, he mixed it and then blew upon it, sending it from his hand in front of him—then there stood up before him a white man!
>
> The Great Spirit was sorry. He saw what he had made was not what he aimed at. The man was white. He looked feeble and sickly. When the Great Spirit, looking at him said, "White man, I have given you life. You are not what I want. I could send you where you came from, but no, I will not take away your life. Stand aside!"
>
> The Great Spirit mixed up the dust again and, drying it, blew upon

it again—and there stood before him a black man! The Great Spirit was grieved. He saw now this man was black and ugly, so he bade him stand aside; when, mixing up the dust again, he blew upon it—and there stood before him A RED MAN! The Great Spirit smiled.

At this moment he looked up and saw an opening in the heavens and through it descended slowly three boxes. They came down at last and rested on the ground, when the Great Spirit spoke saying, "I have given life to you all. The red man alone is my favorite, but you shall all live. You must, however, fulfil each of you, the duties that are suited to you. These three boxes contain the tools you are to use in getting what is necessary to support you."

So saying, he called to him the white man. "White man," said the Great Spirit, "You are not my favorite, but I made you first. Open these three boxes and look and choose which you will take. They contain the implements you are all three to use through life."

The white man opened the boxes, looked in, and said, "I'll take this." It was full of pens and ink and paper and all the things you white people use. He looked at the black man saying, "I made you next, but I cannot allow you to have the second choice." The red man looked in the two remaining boxes and said, "I'll take this." That was full of beaver traps, bows and arrows, and all the kinds of things the Indians use. Then the Great Spirit said to the negro, "You take this [box]," and that was full of hoes and axes—plainly showing that the black man was made to labor for both the white and red man.

Father, thus did the Great Spirit make man, and in this way did he provide the instruments for him to labor with. It is not his will that our red children shall use the articles that came down in the box which the white men chose any more than it is proper for the white men to take the implements that were prepared by the Great Spirit for the use of his red children.[29]

Although this myth seems to separate the races by vocation, it also indicates that the Seminoles—as had all the southeastern tribes—had adopted the Euro-American practice of black chattel slavery. Its thrust is against further acculturation; it overlooks the fact that the Seminoles, like all the southeastern tribes, were always cultivators of the soil as well as hunters and trappers (though of course women did the cultivating prior to black slavery).

A variant of this myth among the Creeks, which begins with the three original human beings (all black) having bathed and assumed their racial coloration, was recorded by the Reverend A. W. Loomis:

[The three] started on their journey together and travelled till they came to a place in which the Great Spirit had deposited a great variety of articles arranged in three separate parcels. In one were books, maps, pens and papers, etc. and the white man choose these. In the second were bows and arrows, beads and feathers, and the like, and the red man caught up these; and there was nothing left for the poor black man but the spades and hoes and digging tools. Therefore [the Reverend commented after writing this down] . . . when we urged upon the Indians the advantages of education and the importance of sending their children to school, they answer, "Oh, learning is for you white people; the books were given to you, but to us, the bow and arrow; therefore the Great Spirit does not desire us to change our mode of living." [30]

As in Nea-mathla's myth, the purpose here was to hold back the thrust of white missionary efforts.

The myth of the three boxes appears to have derived from a West African legend that of course deals only with Africans and Europeans. [31] It indicates that Native Americans may have borrowed stories from their African slaves in formulating answers to the same kind of imperialism in America that had led to the disruption of African society. What these myths did not add, but which is clearly presented in other myths of that period, is the intention of the Creator to keep the races separated. He may have created them at the same time and place, but he did not intend to have them live together.

An old Cherokee chief named Arcowee discussed the original separation of the races by the Creator in a talk with the first Moravian missionaries in 1799.

The great father of everyone that breathes had from the beginning created all men, the red, the white and the black—the red he had placed toward the sunset [the Western Hemisphere], the whites at sunrise [Europe]. Now, after the expiration [of many years] one great day the white people had crossed over in great canoes and had received permission to build a city [on the red man's land]. They had not been satisfied with this, but had continually encroached more and more; this had occasioned disputes between the red and white people. Both had gone to war and herein they had both been wrong, for the Father who lived above disapproved of this and desires that all should be brothers. [32]

Chief Elk of the Cherokees, after telling the Moravians the story of Kanati and Selu in 1815, added to it the parting decision of Kanati before he left earth for the Upper World: "The father, before going upwards, drew a line between the two brothers and their dwellings. This line is the sea. . . . Finally, King George made bigger boats on the other side of the line and his people followed the same [westward course] of the sun until they finally came to the land on this side. . . . The brothers on this side were originally white, like those over the sea, but did not exercise the same care to protect themselves against the sun [and became red]."[33] This myth embodies the environmentalist theory of racial differences in complexion, but it also asserts the disobedience of the white-skinned brother who left the land assigned to him by the founder of the three human races and invaded the land belonging to his red-skinned brother.

This disobedience that brought such havoc to the red man was not always attributed to the white man across the sea. Sometimes the Indians blamed themselves. Perhaps they had made the wrong choice among the three boxes? Perhaps they had offended the Creator at some point? One myth said that the Great Spirit had first offered the skills of reading and writing to the red man, "but they didn't like it" so "then he turned to the whites and offered them the book. They took it."[34]

The story of the Garden of Eden seems to have been of great interest to the Cherokees. The missionary doctor Elizur Butler reported in 1826 that when he told this story of Adam and Eve to the Cherokees, they were shocked by it. "If you had an orchard," they asked, "and you told your children they might go into it and eat of the fruit of every tree but one, you would be very careful no wicked man should go and tell your children they might disobey you."[35] Yet the Christian God allowed Satan into the Garden; he was not a good father. But many were less literal minded. Cherokees recognized the symbolism in this story. However, making use of it, they did not blame the original woman. "God had forbidden man, on pain of death, to eat the fruit of a certain tree," said a myth recorded by Samuel A. Worcester in 1829. "Of this prohibition the wicked one took advantage. Influenced by him, the first man plucked the fruit of the forbidden tree; he looked on it; it was fair; he smelt it; it was fragrant. He tasted it and was ruined."[36] If the first man was red, as the Cherokees claimed, then he, not the first woman, was tempted by the Devil and fell.

Another myth involving the Edenic myth was reported among the Shawnees in 1850 when the Shawnees were close neighbors of the Cherokees. Here there are three men in the garden, and their punishment is a change in the skin color of the two who were most disobedient.

> In the beginning the Great Spirit created three men and placed them in a state of trial, forbidding them to eat of the fruit of a certain tree. But in the absence of their Creator, they made an examination and concluded that the fruit was good. Accordingly they took, each of them, an apple. But one of them put his into his pocket untasted. Another did the same after eating [only] a piece of his. The third devoured his entire[ly]. When the great spirit came back, he perceived that the apples were gone and became displeased. "Did I not tell you," says he, "not to eat of that fruit?" Whereupon the [first] one took his apple from his pocket [uneaten]. Unto him the Great Spirit said, "I give you the bible and knowledge of letters to guide you in the troubles you will fall into." Then the other took out his [apple] partly eaten. For his disobedience the Great Spirit changed the color of his skin [to red] and gave him His law in his heart only. The third, because of his having devoured the whole of his [apple], was blacked all over and left without moral obligation [or moral understanding].[37]

Thus the red man as well as the black man was punished by being made a "colored" people for disobedience to the Creator.

The Indians found a major cause for their troubles in the superior knowledge that the white man had obtained from the "Great Book" and the ability to read and write. If the red man was denied this skill by the Great Spirit, he was not to blame; if the white man stole it from the red man after the Great Spirit had given it to him, the white man was to blame; but if the red man lacked the patience or ability to learn to read and write, then he was at fault. Myths arose after 1800 that contained all three answers to the supremacy of the white man. Arcowee told the Moravians, "When the Great Father had created men, he had a great book which he had first offered to the red man with the command to read it. But they could not do this. Hereupon he offered it to the white man with the same command. When the latter saw it, he could immediately speak to this book."[38] Arcowee, however, was not opposed, as Nea-mathla was, to the missionaries' opening schools to teach the Indians to read. "The fact that the white man knew so many things which were not known to the red man" arose from his possession of that skill. "The time appeared, however, to be near when the red men should likewise learn to read it," and thus they would soon come to know as much as the white man did. Why the "Great Father" had not given the red man this ability was not explained.

Another myth involving the importance of the Great Book was re-corded from the Cherokees by John Haywood around 1810. This as-serts that the Great Spirit, discovering that the red man could not read the book, gave him a wampum belt that served the same purpose but taught him a different set of values and a different way of life:

They say the Great Spirit, created the heavens and the earth and all that is therein; that he then made a white and red man and set them upon the earth. To the red man the Great Spirit gave a book, who took and looked into it but could not understand it. The Great Spirit then gave it to the white man who read and understood it. To the red man the Great Spirit gave a tomahawk and a bow and arrows and taught him to subdue his enemies, love his friends, hate riches and bear hunger and abstinence, hunt the buffalo and bear for skins to make him warm and the deer and turkey for food. He taught him to love truth, to hate a lie, never to steal from his neighbor nor kill any but his enemies. He taught him not to be afraid though the winds blew, the lightning flashed and the thunders rolled. The Great Spirit then gave him a wampum belt which he fas-tened around his waist that he might recollect all that he had taught him. From the book, the white man learned a great many things—architec-ture, agriculture, fortification and machinery of various sorts. From the wampum belt the Indian learned patience, abstemiousness, to suffer pri-vation, hunger, thirst and fatigue, to endure heat and cold, poverty and misery, to bear pain without murmuring, to reverence the Great Spirit, love his friends, hate his enemies, and to seek revenge.[39]

As of 1810 the missionaries had made little impact upon the Chero-kees, who were just beginning to abandon hunting for farming. Con-sequently, this myth showed little concern for their not having the Great Book. What was important was impressed "in their hearts" and remembered in their wampum belt. Or, as H. B. Cushman heard a Choctaw say, their memory or oral traditions constituted "the book the Great Spirit ha[d] given the Indians; it [did] not lie."[40] After 1821, when Sequoyah had discovered a simple means to write and read Cherokee, the Cherokees' lack of the Great Book became less of a problem for those uninterested in acculturation, but while Sequoyah's syllabary made the Cherokees a literate people, it did not teach them all that the white man knew.

Other myths dealing with the white man's Great Book indicate that the Cherokees wanted very much to know its contents. At first, Chief John Ross had told John Payne, "The ancient Cherokees have generally held the white people and their religion in such contempt that there is no reason to suppose they would learn of [from] them"— or follow their doctrines.[41] But later the Cherokees believed that the Great Book had much that would be useful to them. The most staunch opponents of Christianity were the *adonisgi*. The Baptist missionary Evan Jones reported in 1829, "Some of the conjurors were very mad at our doctrine being spread so much about, as it condemns their way."[42] He boasted of confronting and humiliating these conjurers with his superior wisdom. In one letter to his mission board he noted,

> Several Indians called today, among whom was a celebrated adoniskee, Priest or conjuror, who some years ago had a great influence among the people. His popularity is now declining. Had a long, friendly conversation with him in which he displayed all his theology and, as an apology for its scantiness, said the people, in former times, possessed a great deal of knowledge of which the moderns were destitute. He said that the book possessed by the whites was first offered to the Indians by the Creator, but being unable to read, they did not understand it, consequently it was taken away and given to the whites, far to the East, beyond the Great Waters. The whites at first understood but little, but they studied and learned. And having the Book in their possession, were not liable to forget as the Indians were.[43]

Other Cherokees took the view that the white man's Great Book was of no concern to them. "When Sequoyah, the inventor of the Cherokee alphabet, was trying to introduce it among his people, about 1822," said James Mooney, "some of them opposed it upon the ground that Indians had no business with reading. They said that when the Indian and the white man were created, the Indian, being the elder, was given a book, while the white man received a bow and arrow. Each was instructed to take good care of his gift and make the best of it, but the Indian was so neglectful of his book that the white man soon stole it from him, leaving the bow in its place, so that books and reading now belong to the white man, while the Indian ought to be satisfied to hunt for a living."[44] The Indian's neglect of the book was obviously a great blunder.

"Soon after Creation," said another version of this myth, "while the Indian and the white man were together, God visited them and presented to the Indian a written paper. He was at first unable to read it, but after studying it for a while, was beginning to make out a few words when the white man very unceremoniously snatched the paper from his hand, read it without hesitation, and put it in his pocket. Hence the white man came to have learning while the Indians were unable to put language on papers." [45] Here the white man was to blame for the Indians' ignorance of reading. Yet another version blamed the Indian for having sold the book: "It is the tradition of the southern Indians of the United States that their ancestors once had a book and that whilst they had it, they prospered exceedingly, but that the white people bought it of them and learned many things whilst the Indians lost their credit, offended the Great Spirit and suffered greatly from the neighboring nations. That the Great Spirit took pity on them and directed them to this country [where they were able to live without competition from the whites]." [46]

In few of the creation or genesis myths is anything said about women. In the Christian worldview it was the woman who first brought sin into the world, and with her disobedience, man lost immortality and had to work by the sweat of his brow to survive. As the status of women declined among the Cherokees, it became easier to blame the woman for their problems. Because Eve was tempted by a snake, the role of snakes, which were already prominent in Cherokee mythology in the figure of Uktena, the monster snake, became more common in fractured myths. Was the snake a symbol of evil or "the wicked one" in disguise? How did women and snakes relate to the new views of death and the afterlife that Christianity was injecting into the Cherokees' worldview?

One answer to these questions was to say that the Superior Beings had ordained death because man was causing disorder on earth. "At first men were innocent and immortal. But after they began to multiply greatly, they became the envy of beings who dwelt above, who said, 'At this rate they will soon overflow the earth.' A motion therefore was made in heaven that man should be subject to death. The motion prevailed and the wicked one, the Chief of the authors of evil, undertook to bring about the object." [47] Thus Satan entered the Cherokee mythology. This myth goes on to describe the Edenic garden and says that "the first man" was tempted by the wicked one and ate the fruit and brought death to humankind. This appears to combine the Edenic myth with the older myth about the animal council that decreed disease because of man's carelessness and disregard for the animals. Samuel A. Worcester, who recorded it in 1828, did not point out how inconsistent it was to speak of overpopulation in the Garden of Eden where human reproduction was unknown. In any case, there was no red Eve to blame here.

Another myth of human origins also hinges on overpopulation but chiefly blames men's curiosity and disobedience to the sun god (here male, not, as is usual in Cherokee myths, female), and though a snake appears, he is not "the Chief of the authors of evil."

> The Intention of the [three] Creators was to have people live always. But the Sun, when he passed over, told them there was not land enough, and that people had better die. At length, the Daughter of the Sun, being with them [the Cherokees], was bitten by a snake and died. The Sun, on his return, enquired of her, and was told she was dead. He then consented that people might live always and told them to take two boxes and go where her spirit was and bring it back to her body, charging them that when they had got her spirit, they must not open the box till they arrived at the place where her body was. They did so, but just before they arrived they concluded to just open the box so as to look in and see her and then shut it again. But while doing this, the spirit escaped, and then the fate of all men was decided: that they must die.[48]

The connection of the snake with death appeared in another story that Butrick heard: "At first Serpents were not poison[ous]. No roots were poison. Man would have lived forever, but the sun, passing over, perceived that the earth was not large enough to support all in immortality that would be born. Poison was inserted in the tooth of the Snake, in the root of the parsnip, and elsewhere, and one of the first family [of man] was soon bitten by a snake and died. All possible means were used to bring him to life, but in vain. Being overcome in the first instance, the whole race was doomed not only to death of the body but to eternal misery."[49] Here the emphasis is on "eternal misery" of the soul after death, but no possibility of salvation is mentioned.

The Reverend Cephas Washburn when he was among the western Cherokees in the 1820s heard a creation story that reflected badly on women, saying they were flawed even in their creation:

> Oo-na-luh-nuh-heh [the Creator] made man out of red earth and afterwards, that man might think more than he would speak, he cut off a piece of his tongue out of which he formed a woman; so that the woman was all tongue, and this was the reason why women talk so much and think so little. . . . [The first woman] wandered away out of sight. . . .

[S]he found the snake. She did not wait for the snake to introduce conversation but, true to her tonguey [talkative] nature, she began to talk at once. . . . The snake soon discovered her weakness and calculated that he could make her an easy prey to his malevolent design.

This snake was indeed "the wicked one," and he talked the first woman into eating the forbidden fruit. She was thus guilty "of the first transgression of [the Indian] race" (being a red woman). "This talking and gadding propensity of women," said the chief who told this story, "was the reason the red people never admitted women into their councils and never trusted secrets to them." By this time there was much less respect for women than in former times; women had been reduced to a much less important role in tribal affairs by 1800, and Christianity helped to strengthen this development.[50]

Another myth concerning the low status of women, and the Creator's displeasure with them, concerned the disrespect shown by both men and women to the Creator in the early period of the world, but it had nothing to do with the Garden of Eden myth:

Away back in the first times, God lived on earth with men and he so arranged it that their hoes, plows, and all other tools worked without being guided. All a man had to do was to tell the hoe or plow where he wanted work done, and it was done by the tool itself. . . . One day [when] God was passing [by] . . . some wicked women passed a field where the hoes and plows were at work and said, "See what a foolish way to work." "Since you are not contented with my plan, henceforth do the work for yourselves," said He [to these women], and ever since the women have worked the fields.[51]

This was a Creek myth written down by John Swanton. Among the poorer Cherokees, women did continue to work in the fields throughout most of the nineteenth century, but by 1830 the more acculturated Cherokees came to hold the view of missionaries and whites generally that it was disgraceful for women to do field work. Whether there is any connection between this and the Garden of Eden, where food grew without work and God sometimes walked in the cool of the evening, and then the expulsion and the requirement that thereafter human beings work by the sweat of their brow, is hard to say.

As for the strikingly different views of Christians about life after death, rewards and punishments in it, and eternal hellfire for the unconverted, the Cherokees found several ways of incorporating these into their ancient worldview. Missionaries were shocked when they arrived in the Cherokee Nation to find that the Native Americans seemed to show so little concern about death or for life after death; this made it much harder for them to press the necessity of immediate conversion. When a Cherokee died, his relatives performed the proper rituals with the aid of an *adonisgi,* and then his spirit departed quietly for the West, "the darkening land," where it joined other Cherokees in a life very much like that they had led before death—hunting, attending dances, enjoying ball plays. (It was the white man, however, who dubbed this the "happy hunting ground.") The Reverend Samuel Worcester reported a conversation with an *adonisgi* about this in 1828: "The old man knew no tradition respecting a future state and thought nothing of any life beyond the present."[52] Another missionary reported in 1818 that the Cherokees told him "they had no expectation of anything after death, that they seldom or never bestowed any thought on these things, that they were not conscious of ever having done, said, or thought anything that was wrong or sinful. . . . Nor did all [that the missionaries said about repentance and salvation] appear to awaken enquiries on these momentous aspects" of their future.[53]

Yet every day the Cherokees saw friends and relatives who, having lost the spiritual compass of the traditional way of life, fell into drunkenness, violence, theft, and sometimes murder. For some of these the moral code of the Christian converts and a new fear of death may have forced them to examine the alternative more closely. But for others, the question of an afterlife continued to seem irrelevant. A visitor to one of the western tribes in 1817 remarked, "There are but a few Indians that will give an opinion respecting a future state. They say that such questions are only asked by fools and white people."[54] The Reverend Evan Jones, preaching among conservative Cherokees in the Great Smoky Mountains in the 1820s, said, "In their dark, uninstructed state, they seem to have no other fear of death than that which arises from the apprehension of the bodily pain with which it may be accompanied."[55] One old Cherokee told a New England missionary in 1822 that "before he heard of the Gospel, he supposed there would be a future life, that there would be but one place of residence and one class of men in the world to come."[56] He seemed to expect no distinction in the next world because of behavior in this one. The old full-blood chief Pathkiller told a missionary in 1828 that "when he was young they [the tribal elders] told him we [Cherokees] went to another country when we died, that there were many people in the great towns and villages, but they never talked much about this. He does not know whether they got the idea of a future state from their own minds or in some way from the book of God."[57] Many traditional Cherokees frankly said that Indians and whites would be separated after life. A Cherokee who had a vision in 1824 said that he had nearly died because of an illness: "At that time he had visited heaven where everything was beautiful, where the welshcorn grows without work and where the deer are plentiful and grow to the size of oxen. The Indians there were in very good health and had faces as round as the full moon and spent their time with constant diversion, like dances, etc. He had seen there Indians who had died a long time ago, but had met no white people there."[58]

John Haywood, however, described some of the hesitant steps being made toward a Christian position regarding life after death. In 1823 he reported,

> They believe that after death the spirits of all mankind go on one road some distance to a point where the road forks. When the spirit of the deceased comes to the point where the road forks, he is met by the messenger of the Great Spirit who conducts those who have led good lives along the right-hand path into a pleasant country which hath an eternal spring where game and everything else they want is plenteous; whilst those who have lived wicked lives, are forced by the messengers of the Great Spirit to take the left-hand road which leads to a cold, barren, country and where they are exposed to perpetual danger and frights of bad spirits and the farther they travel the more their difficulties and torments increase.[59]

One of the chief appeals of Christianity was its very concrete vision of the afterlife in heaven as a place of complete harmony where relatives and friends were reunited. Missionaries reported that more women than men seemed sympathetic to the view that Christianity would guarantee their ultimate reunion with lost loved ones. The Reverend Evan Jones reported that a woman came to him "interested in learning more of the future state" because she had recently lost a small child and had heard that she could be with it again in heaven if she were a Christian.[60]

Another feature of Christianity that made an impression was the belief that each individual was responsible for his or her own fate.

The evangelical Protestantism of that era was rapidly moving toward the Arminian concept of free will in salvation just as it had always believed in self-reliance and personal responsibility for one's action. For the Indians, the rapid breakdown of the tight restraints of community life created a greater gap between a "good" Cherokee and a "bad" Cherokee. Some apparently asked their *adonisgi* whether good and bad people ended up in the same place after death. Evan Jones talked to an *adonisgi* who had worked out a partial answer to this. He told Jones, "Man was created good and the Creator set the good way before him. Evil was afterward created and men had now their choice. Those who were bad, chose evil and were plunged into error and darkness and driven headlong with sin and misery. Jones remarked that "His [the *adonisgi's*] system [of theology] affords no remedy for evil [repentance, faith, grace]. He makes the future state to consist of four divisions: 1st, the good; 2nd, those who die in war; 3rd, the wicked; and 4th, wicked and lewd women."[61] The notion that there were different degrees of status in the afterlife dependent on behavior in this life was a new one in Cherokee theology. To concede this may have helped the *adonisgi* retain support. At the same time, of course, it was a serious concession to the more complex theology of Christianity.

That there was a new ethic evolving in Cherokee religion as a result of both the Cherokees' confrontation with their own social dislocations and the appeal of the alternative religion can be seen in many small ways. A Cherokee said in the mid-1830s, "Ye-ho-waah [one of the major spiritual beings] tells people how to worship and to feed and help the weak and the stranger." The *adonisgi* told them 'to abstain from all lewdness and from polygamy." The Great Spirit wanted their children "to be industrious and to mind [obey] their parents," and he told the wicked they might live "eternally in a lake of fire" if they did not reform themselves.[62] Polygamy had not been prohibited in the Cherokee Nation until 1824. Lewdness was a Christian concept of improper sexual behavior. Feeding the poor and strangers was part of the traditional hospitality ethic. Industriousness was part of the Protestant ethic. Obedience to parents was common to both religions. The lake of fire was Christian. Somehow all of these were being put together into a new moral system and a new spiritual imperative that would give meaning, order, and direction to their lives.

Biblical stories, such as those about Jonah, Noah, Job, the Tower of

Babel, and the parting of the Red Sea, excited interest and were retold in versions that fit the Cherokee worldview. Noah, for example, was a red man, so the only survivors of the flood were Indians. "The Cherokees say that the first man and woman were red people or Indians—" reported Daniel Butrick, "that all before the flood were Indians, that the Indians were such of the descendants of that family as were not affected by the confusion of languages [after the fall of the Tower of Babel], and are of course the *real* people, as their name [Ani-Yun-wiya] indicates."[63] The Jonah story was about two boys in a canoe, one of whom fell out and was swallowed by a big fish but cleverly managed to force the fish to regurgitate him.[64]

Even the story of Jacob's wrestling seems to have been adapted, although the Cherokee who told it to Cephas Washburn had no idea that it was in the white man's Great Book.

> A long time ago, there was one of our people, who was very good and Kul-lun-lut-teh-a-heh [the lawgiver] loved him very much. This good man was accustomed to pray very often, and the Being above often answered his prayers. One time he prayed for a thing that he wanted very much and he prayed for it very earnestly. While he was praying for it, Kul-lun-lut-teh-a-heh brought a very strong man to him and told him if he would overcome that man by wrestling, he would grant his petition. So they wrestled a long time, and in the conflict, the man from above put our ancestor's thigh out of joint and caused the sinew to perish; but our ancestor prevailed over his opponent at last, and gained the thing he prayed for. That is the reason why we do not eat that part of animals.

This appears to be a clear example of what Axtell refers to as an old myth being syncretized in order to fit new ones into the deep structure of traditional faith, thus preserving a tribe from "ethnic annihilation." When Washburn pointed out the similarity of this ancient Cherokee myth to the biblical account of Jacob wrestling with the angel, and had the interpreter translate that story to his informant, "he said the white people must have borrowed that story from the Cherokees to put into their good book."[65]

This same informant, a western Cherokee named Blanket, annoyed Washburn greatly because whenever the Bible was read to him, "he would, if possible, find some point of resemblance to [the Cherokees'] own traditions, and then he was sure to point out something which would tend to exalt his own people above the white people.

That, he would say, was borrowed from the Cherokees." Even Christ's suffering death to atone for the sin of Adam inherited by all human-kind only produced a parallel from Blanket. He told the story of a Cherokee named Crane-eater who, finding his brother too cowardly to suffer a whipping for stealing a horse, told the Cherokee police, "I am ashamed of him. . . . [H]e is a woman. I pity him. Untie him and let him go. I will take his place. I am a man, and though I have stolen no horse, I can bear the punishment which is due to him." And so the police whipped Crane-eater, the innocent man, to save the guilty man. "In this way," Washburn commented, "his mind was diverted from the atonement of Christ." But obviously something much differ-ent was taking place. Blanket was keeping the Cherokees at the center of human history.[66]

One of the most revealing and sophisticated efforts to incorporate Christian theology into the Cherokee religious worldview was that expressed by Ta-ka-e-tuh, the aged *adonisgi* of the western Cherokee whom Washburn interviewed early in the 1820s. Washburn said that Ta-ka-e-tuh was more than one hundred years old at the time and had come to the western area of the Cherokee Nation after 1819 with his nephew, Chief Takatoka. Ta-ka-e-tuh had clearly accepted large parts of the biblical story of creation and the concept of original sin and interpolated them into Cherokee sacred mythology. But he could not reconcile the New Testament message of brotherly love and for-giveness for sins within the strict Cherokee sense of divine justice. His concept of creation differed slightly (but significantly) from that of creation in Genesis: "First the earth was created; next, the sun, moon, and stars; then man; then birds, then land animals, then fishes and reptiles, and lastly vegetables and fruits to be good for man and beast." This order was more compatible with Cherokee mythology. Creation took place in six days, he said, but the Creator worked at night, leaving the daytime free for rest. Originally, there had been a seventh day of rest, but the Indians had gradually ceased to practice it long ago.[67]

Ta-ka-e-tuh retained the Cherokee view that continents were float-ing islands, that the first man was red, and that the Indians were God's chosen people. He had absorbed the story of Noah and the deluge, but, again, Noah was the only good man left in the world at that time, and he was a red man: "At first there was one man and one woman created. The first human pair were red." He accepted an environmental view of the different complexions among human beings with the exception of black people: "The varieties in the colour of the human race he accounted for by the influence of climate, except in the case of blacks. Black was a stigma fixed upon a man for crime; all his descendants ever since had been born black. Their old men, he said, were not agreed as to the crime thus marked by the signal of God's displeasure. Some said it was for murder, some cowardice, and some said it was lying. In this last opinion he seemed to concur." The curse on Ham may thus have been obliquely accepted by the Cherokees. The profound distinction of blacks from all others indicates the extent to which the Cherokees had accepted the racism of Euro-Americans.[68]

The great sticking point in Christianity for the Cherokees was the origin of sin and the punishment for it upon sinners. Ta-ka-e-tuh accepted the fact that when the first pair was created, the earth was a perfectly ordered garden—that was good Cherokee theology. But he adopted the Christian view that the first human pair had committed some transgression against God, broken some order he gave. Ta-ka-e-tuh did not know what it was. He said, however, "Some say it was eating the fruit of a tree which the Creator had forbidden." But according to Ta-ka-e-tuh, "It makes no difference what that disobedience was. God was very angry and He punished them in a great many ways." He created a much less pleasant earth, with thorns, briers, "poisonous vegetables . . . dreadful storms and tempests and earthquakes" and drastic changes in temperature. "The earth became unhealthy and all kinds of disease and plagues prevailed." The animals fought each other and "became unfriendly to man. The man and his wife often quarreled," "all kinds of pains and sufferings had to be endured, and now "all have to die," when at first they were immortal.[69]

The cause of their transgression was an evil, talking serpent that God had created. God had shut this serpent up "in a dark cavern in a rock," but he was able to talk to the first woman through a crack in the rock and persuaded her to violate God's law and then to persuade her husband to do the same. Part of their punishment was that God had infused into them the serpent's "own disposition" to disobedience to God's laws that were "written in their hearts." All of their posterity inherited this disposition. God was not to blame; "He never does evil or influences any to do evil; it was done by the serpent."[70]

Thereafter the human race became more and more wicked until there was only one good family left. Washburn asked how it happened that "amidst universal wickedness . . . this family was not corrupted also?" Ta-ka-e-tuh answered, "God . . . took away from this family the disposition of the serpent and gave them a disposition to do right." God then told this family "to build a great raft, which covered many acres, and to make a house on the raft," and "he told a pair of all kinds of animals . . . to go on the raft with the good family, and so they were saved alive when the flood came." After the flood the human race again grew numerous and returned to wickedness, "and so God gave them all up to be wicked but one man and his wife. This man He commanded to go away from all his relations and other people and to live by himself. This was the first of the Indian race." This effort to retain the spiritual superiority of the Indians and their specifically chosen role in history constituted an effort to use Christian mythology in such a way as to retain the ethnic identity of this chosen people. "When this man's posterity had become very numerous, the other nations found out where they lived, and they made war upon them, and often subdued them as punishment for their sins."[71] It appears that the Indian race had much in common with the Jews in the divine scheme of things, and Washburn noted, "Many of the Cherokees, when they become acquainted with the Jewish Scriptures and discover the resemblance of some of their own ancient customs to rites enjoined upon the Jews, are very ready to flatter themselves that they are truly descendants of Abraham."[72] (The effort of missionaries to find circumcised Indian tribes failed, though some southeastern tribes said they had seen such Indians. Washburn himself rejected any such Jewish ancestry for them.) God, Ta-ka-e-tuh said, got tired of saving these chosen people from their enemies only to find them returning to sin. "At last God caused them to come to this island, to separate them from the other nations and to keep them from becoming wholly corrupt." The separation indicated that by God's command the red people came to live on the island that was the North American continent.[73] But they had come eastward to this land.

"But here they became wicked and bad, and had wars, and at last God let the white men find out where they lived, and they came to this island and they have wanted to get our lands, and they have learned us a great deal of evil, and have made us fools with the firewater, and have cheated us out of our lands, and are driving us further and further to the west toward the great salt lake on the other side of which our fathers lived." History here meets ancient myth; the chosen red people came eastward across the Pacific to North America. But God had not yet deserted them: "We still hope for better times when our people will be delivered from their enemies and restored to their former superiority to all other people, and God will delight in us and dwell among us."[74]

Washburn found all of this interesting and said it seemed proof of their "monotheism" and their innate sense of morality. But when he tried to convince them of the new dispensation that came with the atonement of Christ for man's sins, the Cherokees failed to comprehend it. Ta-ka-e-tuh could not grasp either the concept of loving thy neighbor as thyself or forgiveness for sin. "When the moral precepts [of brotherly love] were explained in detail, he uniformly approved" of the idea, but "he often erred in making the application, especially as to who is our neighbor." Ta-ka-e-tuh saw no point in turning the other cheek against wicked attacks nor in failing to punish those who harmed the innocent. "He justified revenge as an act of simple justice, and the penal code of his people was formed on the basis of 'An eye for an eye and a tooth for a tooth.' The Savior's law of forgiveness and love to enemies, he pronounced utterly impractical." He expected all sinners to suffer after death and portrayed in vivid terms the endless torments they would have to endure forever. "He believed, and a few other old men like him believed, that some of the human race that were just and good to others and earnestly prayed for mercy, would in some way be saved, but in what way he could not tell." To the Cherokees, Washburn said, "God is a moral Governor and Lawgiver. Obedience secures His favor and is rewarded with eternal happiness. Transgression provokes His wrath and shall be punished with eternal torments. All men have transgressed; and if the dispensation of the law be carried out, all men must be condemned and punished. They know nothing of any other dispensation." To them it seemed inconsistent. "The great difficulty in the way of his belief was, why should a righteous God provide a way of escape for those who deserved the evils to which they were doomed, and why should he provide *such* a way in which the innocent suffer instead of the guilty, and that innocent one, His own, only, well-beloved Son?"[75]

Beneath this rejection of personal salvation for all who repent and accept the Messiah on faith, there was a problem Washburn did not recognize: the Cherokee religion was a corporate or tribal commitment; to allow each individual the right and power to opt out of the group was to promote tribal annihilation, just as if each Cherokee was given the right to own his own plot of land, sell it to whom he chose, and compete by himself in the white man's world for survival completely. Where then would the Cherokee people be? The greatest threat that Protestantism posed to any tribe was the concept that God dealt with his creatures on a one-to-one basis: individuals did wrong, and individuals who failed to ask forgiveness for these sins would be dealt with individually after death and at Judgment Day. There was no way under this to achieve order and harmony on a day-to-day basis. Life would always be a system of disorder until every last person in the world was converted. The Cherokees did not live with such cosmic disarray.

The Protestants in America were firmly wedded to the belief in the separation of church and state, making religion a purely voluntary and private matter, a concept that ran counter to the whole basis of tribal religion. In Cherokee theology the punishments that the spirit world inflicted upon those who failed to act in harmony with spiritual laws might at first bring only harm to the individual and his family, but ultimately could harm his clan and the whole tribe. Tribal rituals, not personal repentance, were necessary to sustain order. Missionaries who converted individuals dragged them from their families and put them at odds with the tribe; they were forbidden to participate in tribal rituals and ceremonies; they met only with those in their various sectarian churches. This was divisive and disorderly, contrary to the true spirit of harmony in the Nation.

The ultimate task of accommodating Christianity to Cherokee traditional patterns had to retain a sense of ethnic identity, tribal loyalty, and Cherokee nationalism and sovereignty. Herein lay the appeal of the Old Testament. Like the Puritan Calvinists in New England, the Cherokees found in God's covenantal relationship to his chosen people the only way to reconcile Christian (Protestant) evangelicalism with tribal solidarity. The events, symbols, miracles, and characters that, in the Old Testament, stood for the continuance of this covenanted relationship consequently appealed to them, for they upheld a special concern for an oppressed people over the whole of human history. Like the Puritans, they Christianized the Jewish covenant.

It is no coincidence that Chief John Ross (who was only one-eighth Cherokee but whose main support came from the full-bloods) chose to identify himself with the Methodists in 1829. He knew that President Jackson was about to persuade Congress to pass a law that would compel the removal of all the southeastern tribes from their ancient homelands. Over the next ten years, as he strove to prevent this, Ross frequently called for national fast days and days of prayer among his people. In his memorials to Congress Ross regularly used Christian imagery and references. In part he was trying to convince the church-going American public that the Cherokees were now fully civilized and Christianized and did not deserve to be removed to the Far West to live among wild and pagan tribes. But he was also trying to convey to his own people the belief that the Great Spirit and the God of Christianity were the same and that he was dedicated to saving the Cherokees, his chosen people, from oppression. In one of his memorials to Congress Ross even utilized the possibility that the Indians might be the descendants of the Israelites: "Some of you have said we were of the wanderers of that peculiar people whence true religion sprang. If it be so, imagine how glorious the effort to secure those wanderers a home—and such a home as may realize the bright predications which still exist unclaimed for the lost race of Israel. Who knows but our prayers may be the instruments to accelerate the fulfillments of that prophecy [of the Second Coming] and should they prove so, how can we offer you a return more exciting?"[76]

At this same time John Haywood told of a fractured myth that compared the Cherokees to the Jews fleeing from the pharaoh. "The Great Spirit took pity on them and directed them to this country . . . on their way they came to a great river which they could not pass, when God dried up the waters and they passed dry-shod."[77] But this was a story about ancient times, not of their oppression by Andrew Jackson. Thus the new mythology could serve both traditionalist and Christian Cherokees.

John Ross went further and compared the Cherokees' tribulations in 1830, the year the Indian Removal Act passed, to those of the perfect servant of God, Job. "My friends," he told the Cherokees,

> the people of the world are rejoicing at our misfortunes, and we are left to grieve and be sorrowful. What shall we do that will relieve us of our misfortunes? The Great Spirit above only knows what is best for us to do, and it is he alone that is able to pity or protect us should we trust in him. In older times there was a good man by the name of Job, who was very rich and believed that God would forgive those that put trust in him. This good man was unfortunate enough to lose all his property

in one day, taken from him by his bad enemies. . . . His misfortunes did not bring him to make use of any violent language nor did he blame the Great Spirit. . . . The Great Spirit in consequence of his cheerfulness caused him to gather again double the amount of property he had lost. . . . But if the President of the white people should cease to protect us and our rights and rob us of our rights, then I say to you . . . bear like Job. Like Job may you [as a people] be rewarded.[78]

One of the great strengths of Christianity was that it provided the possibility of supernatural help in times of overwhelming misfortune. Ross used a biblical symbol of righteousness to rebuke the injustice of a demonic but avowedly "Christian" America. The Cherokees had need of that symbolism after 1830.

Prior to 1835 the struggle between faith in the old traditional religion and the new Christian religion was waged on something like equal terms. The *adonisgi*, although they felt under siege from the scores of missionaries throughout the Cherokee Nation, found ways to adapt the old worldview and its mythology to many consonant aspects of Christianity and thus to give it new strength. The missionaries, by their all-out attack upon every aspect of paganism, only hurt their cause. In the fractured myths that evolved among the Cherokees between 1800 and 1835, we can witness the spiritual battle taking place in a particularly dramatic and illuminating form. As the anthropologist Edmund Leach has noted, "Myth . . . is a language of signs in terms of which claims to rights and status are expressed."[79]

The tensions between Cherokee traditional values and evangelical Christian values were far from reconciled in John Ross's day, though Christianity continued to attract members among the Cherokees. Probably only after the Cherokees were denationalized in 1898 and had to resign themselves to being a people without a country was it possible to yield the covenant ideal. Although Vine Deloria continues to argue that "God is Red," that Christianity has failed among the Native Americans, and that the Indians have more in common with Zionists and black nationalists than with assimilation or integration into an alien culture, a modus vivendi seems to exist today. Raymond Fogelson noted more than three decades ago in a study of the most traditional Cherokees in the Eastern Band that most of them still practiced some form of conjuring through *adonisgi*, yet they considered themselves good Christians. Moreover, even the conjurers were church members: "As far as can be ascertained," Fogelson wrote in 1961, "all of today's conjurors consider themselves to be good Christians and feel that their work is completely consistent with Christian doctrine." In the nineteenth century any Cherokee Christian who resorted to conjurers for help (whether in sickness, rainmaking, or divining) was subject to censure and church dismissal. Fogelson quoted a conjurer who said, "When I conjure, I go by the word of God. . . . In ceremonies, I use the name of the Lord. When somebody's sick, you take him to the creek and wet his breast by the heart. It's like the spirit gives him strength, like baptism. He can feel it. . . . If it wasn't [for] the power of the Creator, you couldn't make anything move." [80] The Cherokees seemed to have found at last a way to use the power of the Anglo-American invader to save their own people. Fogelson concluded this study of the persistence of Cherokee "magico-medical beliefs" by saying, "Here the close rapport between Christianity and conjuring does not seem to be a recent event." But just when it came about would be difficult to pinpoint. Certainly its beginnings seem to have been two centuries ago and to have gathered force from 1800 to 1830.

Chapter 8
Accepting Christianity, 1839-1860

More was involved in the adoption of Christianity by the Cherokees than the integration of their old sacred myths and Christian sacred myths. A new social order was in the making between 1830 and 1860, and it required a new moral and religious order. Gradually a group of ordained Cherokee converts arose to challenge the "conjurers" or priest/doctors called adonisgi of the traditional religion. Ancient religious practices (such as the annual rite of "going to water") were integrated into Christian rituals (in this case, baptism). The practice of medicine assumed new forms that enabled the adonisgi to practice his or her profession and still be a good church member. Voluntary church membership replaced the birthright membership in the old religion.

The policy of Indian removal had been so traumatic and appeared to be such a betrayal of treaty obligations and mutual trusts between Native Americans and white Americans that many Cherokee converts rejected their Christian commitment thereafter. But the missionaries who followed them west were chastened by the experience and embarrassed by the unchristian behavior of what they had thought was a Christian nation. The Cherokees started their own public school system so that they would be dependent no longer on mission schools for the education of their children. Missionaries became marginal in Cherokee life and their behavior more subdued. The less aggressive mission efforts from 1840 to 1860 permitted a gradual return of trust and a new and deeper interest in Christianity. Of particular importance in this rapprochement was the complete translation of the Bible into the Sequoyan syllabary in the 1850s, thus permitting the Cherokees to read and evaluate it themselves. This essay attempts to explain how this helped the steady growth of Christianity, though traditionalism by no means disappeared.

Removal from their ancient homeland created a severe political shock to the Cherokees but an even more profound spiritual shock. Cherokee religion was closely tied to the land—its sacred places, its flora and fauna, its history, and the spiritual beings who presided within it and linked human beings to the basic harmony of nature. It proved difficult to re-create this spiritual world in an alien environment totally new to them. Although some had turned to Christianity before removal, it had not been sufficiently absorbed to sustain these shocks. Most of the missionaries deserted the Cherokee cause after 1832, and the callous behavior of the government (representing "a Christian nation") impaired belief. Traditional religion, on the other hand, also lost relevance in the West, and its power was greatly weakened. The shaman might still be relied upon for certain medicinal aids or to avert natural calamities, but the transcendent view of the universe and the Cherokees' central place in it was shattered. The poor inevitably rekindled familial and clan ties, strengthening the sharing and cooperative values of their culture in order to survive, but those who were better off and held leadership roles turned to political concerns, self-reliance, and private enterprise to recoup.

Nevertheless, by a complex process difficult to describe, a new sense of Cherokee identity evolved between 1839 and 1855 that provided the basis for a major political revolt of the full-bloods against those of mixed ancestry. Its key elements were a syncretic combination of popular Christianity (led by Cherokee-speaking ministers) and a new tolerance for traditional dances, sports, and folkways among Cherokee Christians. Essentially, the Cherokees converted Christianity to their own needs and values, melding together at one level the Christian concept of God with the Cherokee concept of the Great Spirit or Great Provider; at another, their social ethic of sharing with the Christian ethic of sister- and brotherhood; and at a third level, their consensual method of decision making with the European concept of government by consent of the governed. They even conflated biblical stories and Cherokee myths.

Commonly understood, the difference between a full-blood and a mixed-blood was not biological or ancestral; a full-blood meant someone whose cradle language was Cherokee (and for whom Cherokee remained the primary, if not only, language). A mixed-blood was a

Cherokee whose cradle language was English and for whom it remained the first or only language. Over time, the difference between these two groups came to include many aspects of lifestyle, values, and norms. The mixed-bloods favored rapid acculturation, behaved like whites, and brought their children up by white values. Full-bloods kept as many of their old ways and values as they could. For those in the dominant Ross party, the ties of Cherokee patriotism united full-bloods and mixed-bloods throughout the removal crisis, but after 1846, a more specific definition of what it meant to be "a Cherokee" produced increasing estrangement. A mixed-blood would, confronting a white man, proudly proclaim his being "a Cherokee," but talking with other mixed-bloods, he might use the term "Indian" or "backward Cherokee" to deprecate those full-bloods of limited acculturation. Conversely, full-bloods began to speak of mixed-bloods as persons who had so far forsaken their heritage as to be more like white people than Cherokees.

Part of this animosity arose from the fact that so many of those who betrayed the Nation in making the false Treaty of New Echota were of mixed ancestry and English-speaking. The murderous factionalism from 1839 to 1846 often made mixed-bloods seem to be the chief opponents of tribal unity. Too many English-speaking Cherokees placed factional self-interest ahead of what was best for the tribe; the old ideals of decision making by consensus and the necessity of maintaining tribal harmony seemed to have given way to recalcitrant minority dissent. Mixed-bloods such as John Brown and John Rogers among the Old Settlers and those at the head of the Ridge-Watie party showed little concern for the traditional "Kituwha spirit" of tribal solidarity.

The distinction between full-bloods and mixed-bloods was complicated, however, by the fact that the Ross party itself was led chiefly by persons of mixed ancestry and none were more patriotic or loyal to tribal unity than John Ross and his family. The Treaty of 1846 had reunited the tribe politically, but differences separated those who had become so acculturated that they lived by the individualistic, acquisitive values of the whites and those who still clung to traditional communal values. The public school system exacerbated the division, and so did the growing social and economic division between the wealthier and poorer classes. The gap grew wider with each decade. Ross remained a beloved chief with whom the full-bloods felt comfortable despite his obvious preference for acculturation. He was respected because he always kept the full-bloods informed of his actions, helped them with their problems, and in difficult matters would call a general council of all the people to settle issues that the elected council could not resolve. His foremost priority was tribal unity. Although he wanted his people to learn up-to-date approaches to daily life, Ross did not force white cultural values on the full-bloods nor denigrate them for being "ignorant" or "backward." He always included respected full-bloods among his advisers and appointed them to the delegations to Washington, D.C. He wanted the Nation to adopt a market economy in order to prosper, but he let the full-bloods go their own way in their private lives hoping that the benefits of acculturation would eventually become apparent to them. He lived in the style of the wealthy elite, but he understood the needs and feelings of the poor, and he actively cultivated their support. Above all, he showed them respect.

The full-bloods were not, of course, a monolithic group. A few of them were wealthy and influential. Because most of them could read and write Cherokee in the Sequoyan syllabary, they were literate. They varied greatly in their adherence to traditional values and customs. Some were converts to Christianity. Some seemed to have little commitment either to traditionalism or Christianity. Much of the uneasiness among the ordinary Cherokees after removal derived from their sense of rootlessness. They felt cut off from the old ways and without a clear sense of direction for the future. All their energy went into scraping a bare subsistence from the soil; droughts and sickness constantly defeated them. Such solidarity as they had came chiefly from family and clan loyalties, a love of certain old ceremonies and sports, a faith in the practices of the *adonisgi,* and a commitment to the hospitality ethic. Most still practiced the ancient *gadugi* system of cooperative labor—sharing the work in heavy projects such as erecting school buildings, churches, or barns or clearing land with their neighbors. Ethnic identity was also sustained by oral folklore, sacred myths, and ancient dances and ceremonies. In addition, they shared a disdain for the hard-driving, materialistic, acquisitive ethic that whites associated with "progress." They found the whites and mixed-bloods generally "proud" or "haughty." Numerically the mixed-bloods were a subculture following white values and mores, but in terms of power and influence, the full-bloods were made to feel like a subculture. Under a democratic political system, the potential existed for a popular reversal of this situation if the full-bloods found the leaders and goals to organize it.

The key to the emergence of a strong and united political movement among the full-bloods lay in the gradual interaction between selected Christian ideas and traditional values. In part the new religious synthesis evolved as translations of the Bible into Sequoyan circulated more widely among the full-bloods, making it familiar to them in their own words. But the most important factor in the revitalization of Cherokee religious life was the growing corps of young, dynamic, and able full-blood preachers and pastors empowered by the Baptists and Methodists to preach the new religion in the Cherokee language and idioms. These full-blood preachers were committed as much to reviving tribal unity and sovereignty as to saving souls. They preached a social as well as a personal salvation through Christianity. Through them the term "a Cherokee Christian" ceased to be an oxymoron and became a new and positive identity. But it was not the same Christianity that the mixed-bloods and the more formal missionaries (the Congregationalists, Presbyterians, and Moravians) stood for. Cherokee ministers and Cherokee Christians retained too many elements of traditionalism in their lives to conform to the rigid standards of most white missionaries.

As the authority and leadership of this new syncretic religion passed into the hands of full-blood preachers and church members, the hostility between Christianity and traditionalism diminished. What had seemed in the early days of the missionary movement to be hostile, repugnant, and bizarre in the two faith systems gradually found a rapprochement—part of it subconscious and part of it deliberate.

The Christianity preached in Cherokee by native preachers gained a new authority. These men became new spiritual leaders and yet left room for the old authority of the *adonisgi*. The role of the *adonisgi* became complementary, not antipathetic, to that of the Christian leaders. Most important, Christianity ceased to be the white man's religion as "God" was redefined in terms closer to the meaning of the Great Spirit. The new aura and authority of the Cherokee version of Christianity provided new meaning, order, and direction in other ways. It gave the Cherokee majority a new sense of self-respect, of hope, of confidence. A new source of power was now available to the Christian Cherokees both as individuals and as a people. In fact, it became possible to define the pious Cherokees as the true children of God and not the treacherous and corrupt white people who claimed to be God's chosen people but acted contrary to Christian virtues. In the Cherokee form of Christianity the Native Americans remained God's favorite people, as the old Cherokee myths had maintained, and the covenant the white Americans thought they had with God belonged to his Indian children. Cherokee myths of creation were modified, and new explanations described how sin and suffering came even to God's chosen. Ultimately, the new linear view of history (from the creation of humanity to the millennium of peace, love, and justice for the chosen) provided an amalgamation of Cherokee ghost dance visions and Christian visions of a perfected world.

No more than 12 to 15 percent of the Cherokees were formally members of Christian churches by 1860, but the new syncretic worldview bridged the gap between Christian and pagan in ways that made formal membership unnecessary. Full-bloods could be brothers and sisters with those outside the church as well as those within. This syncretic worldview sustained the belief that the Cherokees were equal as a people and nation to the United States—equal, but separate; in it, but not of it.

Christianity had started badly among the Cherokees in the years 1800 to 1830. Few of the white men they met seemed to be admirable models for the religious values they professed to believe. It seemed odd to the Cherokees that missionaries would come to their community to refashion the Indians into Christians when so many whites needed reform even more. The "apathy and profligacy" of the whites residing among them, wrote one missionary, provided poor examples of the Christian way of life.[1] Many white men, when they came into the Nation, seemed to "consider themselves free from all the encumbrances of morality and religion."[2] In fact, some whites even took the pains to "endeavor to persuade them that there was no truth in gospel doctrines."[3] Nor were the actions of the Christian men whom they met as officials in the government of the so-called Christian nation much better, especially during the removal crisis. Most of the missionaries directed their efforts toward converting the mixed-bloods who spoke and read English. Some missionaries made it plain that they considered adult traditionalists beyond redemption. Missionaries in this period also aggressively denounced the Cherokee shamans or *adonisgi* and ridiculed the traditional practices and beliefs; any who became converts were required to shun as "evil companions" all who attended traditional ceremonies, even members of their own families and clans. As the first missionaries presented it, Christianity was a hostile and divisive force among people who needed unity and whose highest ideal was harmony. The missionaries separated church and state; the Cherokee full-bloods did not.

Cherokees were also disappointed that few of the missionaries bothered to come to their assistance during the removal struggle.[4] Chief Ross, who had joined the Methodists in 1829, appealed to the Christian God to help them in their hour of need: "Let us not forget," he told his people in 1830, "the circumstances related in Holy writ of the safe passage of the children of Israel through the chrystal walls of the Red Sea."[5] Ross appears to have been convinced by some missionaries at this time that the Indians might be the descendants of the Lost Tribes of Israel. But the God of Christianity paid no heed to the national days of prayer that Ross called. The fact that so many of the traitors who signed the Treaty of New Echota were mixed-bloods and Christians further tainted the image of that faith. Missionaries reported a strong upsurge of traditionalism during the years just prior to removal.[6]

The missionaries also noted strong anti-mission sentiment among the Cherokees after they moved to the new homeland: "Many of the [church] members are known to have backslidden," wrote Samuel Worcester, the superintendent of the Congregational mission at Park Hill in 1841; "a considerable number who were members in the 'Old Nation' have never joined any of the churches here."[7] His colleague Daniel Butrick reported, "There never was a time probably since we came to the Cherokee Nation [in 1817] when the missionaries were viewed with more suspicion than at the present."[8] Because Samuel Worcester had advocated removal after 1832 and employed as his translator of the Bible Elias Boudinot, the leader of the Removal party, the Cherokee council voted that he should be expelled from the Nation in the West.[9]

The earliest impact of Christian ideas upon Cherokee religion seems to have resulted from the efforts of the *adonisgi* to modify various Cherokee myths to accommodate some of the sacred myths of Christian thought. Facing the Christian challenge to their own conceptions of creation, human nature, human history, and the afterlife, the *adonisgi* incorporated Christian ideas into their sacred stories to give them more depth and to answer questions raised by the new religion.

These interpolations also sought to account for some of the foibles of humankind, to explain human sin and the defeats of the Indians, their comparative ignorance of technological mysteries, and their particular relationship to the Great Spirit. For example, the Cherokees had to alter their own ethnocentric creation myths in order to account for the creation of white people and black people. They had to explain why, if in their religion the red man was the favorite of God, the white man had the "Great Book" in which God seemed to have revealed all of the secrets that made the whites so powerful. They had to decide whether there was only one Great Spirit or whether the God of the Christians was a totally different divinity. They had to define more precisely what happened to the spirit of humans after their death—was there really a heaven and hell as the Christians said? Would people be punished in the next world for what they did in this? Because there was no single religious leader nor any group of *adonisgi* who coordinated Cherokee theological concepts, each *adonisgi* made his or her own adaptations; oral tradition was supposed to preserve older myths intact and un-corrupted, but changes rapidly crept in nonetheless. Ancient myths became subject to supplemental inspiration.

Many different myths evolved among the Indians (all claiming an-cient origin) to explain the different colors of humans: one said they were made of different colors of clay by the Giver of Breath or Creator; another said they were all made of white clay baked by the Creator for different lengths of time in an oven and so changed color; some said the Creator made three light-skinned men, but then each washed himself soon after creation in different shades of muddy water, which altered their color. Sometimes it was simply said that God mistakenly created black and white men first but found them repugnant to look at and so created a red man "who was his favorite."[10] Trying to account for females, one *adonisgi* said, "God made man red—of red clay— and made woman of one of his ribs."[11] Providing an explanation of the deluge that figured so prominently in missionary sermons, one *adonisgi* said, "When men were found to be incorrigible, at length a certain dog told his master to make a vessel and take his family and provision and seed to sow because Ye ho waah was about to bring a flood to destroy all their wickedness. . . . It was supposed that all kinds of animals went into the vessel. . . . [Afterward] the land be-coming dry . . . the man soon commenced preparing the ground for a crop. The family saved thus were red."[12] This syncretic version of

Noah and the flood conflated a group of complex ideas. It affirmed that the red man was God's favorite and, after the deluge, the only person left in the world from whom all others descended. It admitted the sinful nature of humans and God's punishment for sin. It seemed to some missionaries to prove that the Indians were lost Israelites because "Ye ho waah" was probably a corruption of "Jehovah" and "Yahweh." It also modified the old Cherokee myth of human beginnings in which the female was the cultivator of the soil and the male a hunter by stating that "the man" prepared "the ground for a crop."[13]

There were many versions of the myth that explained why the white man had been able to build great ships, cross the sea, conquer the Indian with his firearms, and provide iron, copper, and manufactured cloth for trade. All the white man's knowledge came from the "Great Book" (the Bible), his most prized possession. This book had once belonged to the Indians, but for various reasons they lost it. "It is said . . . that the book which the white people have was once theirs; that while they had it they prospered exceedingly, but that the white people bought it of them and learned many things from it, while the Indians lost the credit, offended the Great Spirit, and suffered exceedingly."[14] Another *adonisgi* told the Reverend Evan Jones that "the people in former times possessed a great deal of knowledge. . . . He said that the book possessed by the whites was first offered to the Indians by the Creator, but they, not being able to read, did not understand it, consequently it was taken away and given to the whites, far to the East, beyond the Great Waters."[15] Another version said that the white man stole the book from the red man.

The story of the Jews escaping from Egyptian captivity was appropriated to explain how the Indians got to the New World. When they sold the Great Book to the white man, the Great Spirit was angry with them; he punished them by making them live in bondage under the whites far from their present home. Eventually "the Great Spirit took pity on them and directed them to this country; . . . on their way they came to a great river which they could not pass, where God dried up the waters and they passed over dryshod."[16] A different story, common among the southeastern tribes by 1820, held that the Great Spirit originally designated different areas of the world for the different races—the black man in Africa, the white man in Europe, and the red man in America. He gave each of them different modes of life— to the white man, that of technology; to the African, that of agriculture and herding; to the red man that of hunting and trapping. This well-ordered world was disrupted by the covetousness of the white man, who used his inventive ability to build large ships with which he invaded Africa and then carried Africans as slaves to America, where he stole from the Indian his God-given land. This explained why disharmony in the cosmos came from the sins of the white man.

One Cherokee *adonisgi*'s effort to explain the origin of sin and life after death was recorded by Evan Jones in 1828:

> On the origin of man, he said Man was created good and the Creator set the good way before him. Evil was afterwards created and men had now their choice. Those who were bad, chose evil, and were plunged in error and darkness and driven headlong with sin and misery. His system affords no remedy for evil. He makes the future state to consist of Four Divisions: 1st, the Good; 2nd, those who die in war; 3rd, the wicked; and 4th, wicked and lewd women. All these were treated [after life] according to their deeds.[17]

These and many similar syncretic myths tried to reconcile traditional mythology with Christian revelation, history, and doctrine. They marked the first (and ultimately futile) step in the Cherokees' effort to combat the missionaries' challenge to their own theology and cosmogony. They were trying to assimilate new ideas into the old (to pour new wine into old bottles). The *adonisgi* hoped to demonstrate that their religion was perfectly sufficient to answer all questions raised by the missionaries. Thus there was no need to abandon the old way for the new. Moreover, as many *adonisgi* said to the early missionaries, "The God of the whites and of the Indians is not the same. . . . Indians were not created to follow your ways."[18] They even maintained that the Indian dead went to their own heaven, not to the white man's.

But the *adonisgi* suffered great loss of authority after removal (just as the missionaries did, though for different reasons). The spirits who had inhabited the various caves, lakes, rivers, and mountains in the East were not present in the new location. The herbs needed for medical purposes did not grow there. Invocations to totemic animals used in various rituals lost their meaning to the rising generation.

In the end, the Baptists and to a lesser extent the Methodists provided the most useful sources of religious revitalization after 1840. Baptists and Methodists did not insist upon a learned ministry, and their preachers therefore spoke to the average person in the language of the common folk. They also encouraged an itinerating ministry, and they reduced the complex theology of Calvinism to a more simple and comprehensible evangelical theology of an Arminian variety. Evangelical Baptists and Methodists preached, for example, that sinners could fall from grace and be redeemed a second time upon repentance, whereas Calvinists believed that true grace was never lost. Baptists and Methodists put more emphasis upon freedom of the will, the ability to choose whether to follow God or Satan. They believed in general redemption, that Christ had died for all who believed and not simply for the handful of predestined elect as Calvinists taught. They had a more simple, direct, and immediate concept of conversion, while their approach to church government was more participatory and egalitarian than that of more hierarchical denominations (such as the Catholic and Episcopalian). Among the Cherokees, the Baptist and Methodist preachers were willing to allow more latitude in judging who should be a church member and to be less strict in their discipline of those who slipped a bit from rectitude. Baptists also allowed each congregation to choose its own pastor. Methodists and Baptists both made regular use of revival meetings or camp meetings where lively preaching, loud hymn singing, and emotional excitement stirred up crowds of hundreds and lasted for several days. All of these aspects seemed unedifying and detrimental to the Congregational, Presbyterian, and Moravian missionaries among the Cherokees. As a result, the Baptists and Methodist denominations grew steadily in number from 1840 to 1860, whereas the other mission agencies remained small. Congregationalism actually declined.[19]

The three aspects of missionary work that made the Baptists and Methodists successful among the Cherokees were their itinerating missionaries (as opposed to the "settled mission enclaves" of the Congregationalists and Moravians), their employment of native, Cherokee-speaking preachers who could speak to the full-bloods in their own language, and their wide dissemination of published translations of the Bible and other religious texts written in the Sequoyan syllabary. The Congregational and Moravian missionaries disapproved of camp meetings (or protracted meetings) and thereby lost one of the most important means of reaching the full-bloods. Nor did they approve of itinerant preaching. The former they considered too emotional and unlikely to produce lasting conversion; the latter they believed useless unless an organized church with a learned minister was nearby to provide regular watch and care over those converted. But camp meetings and itinerant preaching were admirably suited to the widely scattered settlements of the Cherokees (as they were along the white frontier). The camp meetings attracted hundreds of Cherokees eager to take a brief holiday from the drudgery of house- and farmwork in order to meet with friends and enjoy a rousing spiritual meeting that, in some ways, was not unlike their own ceremonial dances. Camp meetings often lasted three to five days; in the spirit of the *gadugi* system, the Cherokees brought and shared the fodder for all the horses and enough food for the gathered throng. Cherokee women cooked the food communally, each family putting into the pots whatever they could bring for the occasion. The men erected the scaffold for preaching, made the seats, and sometimes built temporary arbors or shelters from the heat or rain. Preaching took place through most of the day and often far into the night. The Cherokees loved to sing, and hymnbooks in Cherokee provided the words. Ministers performed marriages as well as baptisms for new converts and communion services for old members. Fervent preaching, praying, and singing produced a high pitch of self-transcendence culminating in a sense of intimate rapport with the spiritual world as well as providing social solidarity. "The Cherokees, and Indians generally," said the Congregational missionary Daniel Butrick in 1850, "have such a desire to be together and enjoy each other's company, that I often find it no small task to keep the members of our own church at home when several hundred or a thousand were assembled a mile and a half distant [for a Baptist or Methodist camp meeting]."[20] Another Congregationalist, Charles Torrey, wrote in 1856, "A Methodist or Baptist meeting within a circuit of eight miles is almost sure to deprive me of a congregation [at the mission church]."[21]

Worcester and Torrey considered camp meetings a degenerate form of religious worship and expressed regret that the practice had ever been introduced among the Cherokees. They wanted the more restrained and staid Sunday services found in "respectable" middle-class churches. But, as their colleague Timothy Ranney noted, these exciting occasions and the cooperative planning, preparation, and direction of them gave the Cherokee common folk an important source of inspiration and social organization. Ranney said,

> The average attendance at [my] church has also been diminished, apparently considerably, by the large meetings held by the baptists in the

neighborhood. It is a matter of regret, and to some extent, of astonishment, that this influence is so great. . . . Once a month the baptists have a two-day meeting in the neighborhood. To attend these meetings people often come 40 or 50 miles. They generally begin to arrive on Friday evening and remain in the neighborhood until Monday morning. This of course requires a vast amount of labor and excitement in the families where they stop.[22]

Here the Cherokee hospitality ethic was strengthened by the sharing of home and food with these distant travelers. The same was true when traditionalists held ceremonial dances. The sharing of common bonds in thought, mood, experience, and hopes was a major feature of revitalization. Periodic gatherings of families and friends with a participatory ceremony that strengthened communalism and satisfied spiritual longings had always been central to Cherokee ceremonial life. Christianity simply provided a new form of shared exaltation, emotional transport, and communion with the other world.

Some Christian rituals seemed to have decided parallels to traditional rituals. For example, the form of baptism practiced by the Baptists was similar in both form and meaning to the Cherokee "purification" ritual called "going to water." The Baptist missionary Evan Jones described it this way:

Went to the Town meeting for the early spring ablution. The Adoneeskee, or priest, allowed me to accompany them, but when we came near the water, he directed me to take another path. Coming to the place, a stool was set down with a deerskin on it and some beads on the skin. The Adoneskee or priest muttered something which nobody could hear for about twenty minutes, the people all standing with their faces to the water. Then, with great solemnity, he walked into the water and scattered the sacred beads into the stream in all directions; the women then commenced plunging the children into the water, those [children] who were large enough, plunged themselves. The men went a little distance and dipped themselves. And the women went to a separate place and did likewise. This done, all retired to the house of the Adoneeskee, and, after listening to a long speech from the old man, they commenced eating cold venison which was prepared for the occasion.[23]

The purification rite was part of a celebration of the new year; following that rite, the "priest of the sacred fire" kindled new fire at the town council house, and from its embers each family relighted the fire in its own house. It was a community event of new beginnings and closely related to the concept of reconciliation, or wiping away of old quarrels and hard feelings in order to bring the community into harmony again. In earlier days at the purification rite (always held in a flowing stream), the people would let their old and worn garments drift off with the current and then don new ones for the new year, thus purified inside and out. The formula recited by the *adonisgi* at this ceremony invoked the spirits of the other world to bring harmony to the community. It is not difficult to see how this could be transformed into the Christian meaning of baptism as a divine forgiveness for sins, an effort to establish personal harmony with God in the presence of the community, and the sense of a new birth toward a life purified of evil thoughts and deeds, with commitment to friendship and fellowship toward all. All Baptist camp meetings ended with a march of the new converts to the river, where the Baptist preacher (native or white) invoked the divine presence as he dipped the spiritually reborn, who were usually dressed in new clothes. During this ceremony, the assembled throng sang hymns expressing their own commitment, and afterward a communion service was held with the sacramental meal of bread and wine.

Some Cherokees believed that this Christian ritual, like Cherokee purification, required regular renewal. A Cherokee named Watt Foster who attended a camp meeting with a white observer, William Potter, pointed out to Potter that a Cherokee woman, Mrs. Falen (or Fallon), whom they both knew, was being baptized. Potter remarked that he thought Mrs. Falen was already converted and baptized. "Yes," Watt said; that was true. "Why did they baptize her again?" Potter asked. "To make her stronger," Foster replied.[24] A Congregational or Moravian missionary would not have permitted this, but the Baptists and Methodists saw no harm in a renewed commitment. It was common for many Cherokees to experience new conversions or spiritual rebirths at different revival meetings. To Calvinists this was a mockery of predestination and preservation of the saints, but to Arminians it was an example of backsliding, repentance, and a strengthening of faith through grace. Baptists and Methodists saw religion as a continual struggle of the spirit versus the flesh. With pagans this struggle was more difficult, and more tolerance was needed toward backsliders. Often their hearts were willing but their temptations too great.

For this same reason, Baptist and Methodist mission churches, especially those over whom a native Cherokee was pastor, were less given to censuring and excommunicating members who occasionally slipped from moral order. Congregational and Moravian missionaries complained that this produced a lax, undisciplined, or corrupt form of church order. Persons were admitted too quickly into what should be a communion of disciplined saints; persons were allowed to remain as members of these churches who were often absent from Sabbath meetings, who were known to drink or swear or attend pagan rituals, and who failed to assert parental discipline over their children. One Congregationalist was shocked to find that even a Cherokee pastor was seen shucking corn on the Sabbath.[25]

The white missionaries of the more rigid denominations were so strict that often 40 to 50 percent of their members were excommunicated over the years for moral turpitude of one kind or another, but the records of Baptist and Methodist missionaries show almost no excommunications. Because Congregationalists and Moravians refused to make any concessions to Cherokee cultural patterns, they complained regularly of the "low standards" of their chief competitors. "The greater facility with which admittance is gained to the churches of the other denominations than to those connected with this Board," wrote one leading Congregationalist in 1850, "our missionaries regard as a great obstacle . . . to the salvation of souls, leaving many, when in a measure convinced of being in danger [of damnation] to repose confidence in a mere outward profession [to save them from hell]."[26] The Congregationalists and Moravians required six months or more of "probation" before any professed convert was admitted to baptism and another six months or more before he or she was admitted to communion. Probation was required before church membership was granted in these strict churches, but Baptists and Methodists held the doctrine of "growing in grace"; they admitted readily those whom they believed to be serious in their intentions (calling them "Seekers" after truth) and then utilized the church community to strengthen them in self-discipline and moral order. The "hasty and careless manner in which Mr. Jones [the Baptist missionary] and more especially the Cherokee preachers" admitted members to their communion, said another Congregationalist, resulted in "lowering the bars" to the church, which were to be kept high in order to properly distinguish the saved from the damned.[27]

As the membership grew among the Baptists and Methodists, the other missionaries complained of their "sheep stealing," that is, encouraging members of Congregational or Moravian churches to leave and join their competitors. This was particularly galling when those who left the church were often those who had been censured or excommunicated as inveterate sinners: "Three who were excluded from Mr. Worcester's church were soon received by the Methodists and made class leaders," reported one Congregationalist to his board.[28] But the reasons for this shift in denominational allegiance were not so simple. The rigid churches constantly stressed the failings of their converts and preached regularly about their sins; the more popular churches stressed their potential and their having started on the right path. Cherokees making the difficult transition from old ways to new needed encouragement and charity, not insistence upon impossibly high standards of behavior. Congregationalists preached to Cherokees as though they were preaching to New Englanders who had lived within the strictures of Calvinist orthodoxy since the days of the Puritans. "There would be no difficulty in having a very large church," wrote one Congregational missionary to his board, "if we were as lax as the Baptists."[29] Another wrote,

> When any of our members fall into sin and are called to account for it, they threatened to join the Methodists. In one instance, a member, being overcome by temptation and expecting the church would institute a course of discipline, he went off to the Methodists and was received by them though he was known to be deserving of censure, and was immediately made a licensed exhorter in their church. In two other cases where we commenced a course of discipline, the individuals desired us to go forward without delay to exclude them from fellowship, and then [they said] they would unite with the Methodists; and we learn from unquestionable authority, that they have been assured by the Methodists that they shall be received by them.[30]

It was considered highly unethical for one mission agency to accept the excommunicated member of another, for this made it impossible to maintain a general standard of how a true Christian should behave. It was also considered a major flaw in the practice of itinerant evangelism followed by Methodists and Baptists that they did not stay within their own geographical sphere of labor but "intruded" into the areas (Congregationalists would call them "parishes") in which other denominations were already established, had a church, and were cultivating the spiritual ground. Itinerancy led to Christian anarchy in its competition for gaining members. But these charges failed to consider that some forms of Christian thought and practice were more effective with the Cherokees than others, and itinerancy gave them a choice.

It was true, of course, that some Cherokees did see conversion, baptism, and the first communion as a kind of initiation rite that gained them entrance into the privileges of joining the new religious group. "It is, I find," said one Congregationalist, "quite a common idea with members of our mission churches to think every person must be admitted to church fellowship who desires to be admitted." [31] "[Among the Baptists] persons are urged to go all under the water, and are told that is understood to mean that is salvation," said a critic of the Baptists. [32] Voluntary church membership was an essential feature of all Protestant churches, but the more abstract concept of living a virtuous, Christian life by following certain forms of behavior came less easily to the Cherokees. A Methodist missionary admitted that many members of his church "believed they should go to heaven because they did not attend all-night dances and go to ball plays." [33] A Baptist convert told a Congregationalist that "the only articles" of the Baptist creed were "immersion and closed communion." [34] It took some Cherokees longer than others to understand that what was at stake in the new religion was a commitment to follow certain clear patterns of moral and social behavior, failure to do so being grounds for expulsion from the group.

The tendency toward syncretism grew out of the continuing desire of the full-bloods to keep as much as possible of the old way of life and its principles while benefiting at the same time from the spiritual order, meaning, and empowerment they found in Christianity. The missionaries forgot how long it had taken the Catholic Church to make its compromises with European tribal paganism and how many varieties of Protestantism sprang from the Reformation's effort to purify "corrupt" practices in Catholicism. Confusion among the Cherokees sprang from confusion among the missionaries. Or, to put it another way, compromise and pragmatic looseness were virtues in the religious transformation of any ancient culture. Congregationalists and Moravians suffered from their insistence that religiosity was a matter of private self-discipline; they ignored the fact that individual self-reliance was the polar opposite from the communal spirituality of the Cherokees.

Similarly, the Congregationalists and Moravians insisted that the native preachers in all denominations must have exactly the same cultural assumptions and doctrinal beliefs as the white clergy who ordained them. Because so few Cherokees met their exalted standards for the ministry, neither the Congregationalists nor the Moravians ordained or licensed a single native convert in the years 1835 to 1860. The Methodists and Baptists, however, readily licensed and ordained dozens of Cherokees and gave many of them complete ministerial charge of mission churches. Nothing did more to make Christianity a live option for the Cherokees than to have it preached to them in their own language by their own people. This practice (though officially the goal of all missionaries agencies) of creating a self-sustaining native ministry that would eventually make missionary work unnecessary had three important attributes. First, it overcame the tremendous gap between white preachers and their congregations and permitted the gospel to be transformed into the natural idioms of the Cherokee people. Second, it gave greater freedom to the interpretation of Protestantism both as theology and as church practice, for native ministers had comparatively little supervision once ordained. And third, it created a new corps of spiritual leaders, men of authority and power, to whom the Cherokees could look for moral order, direction, and goals. Moreover, these men (no women were ordained) understood the feelings of the old religious leaders, the *adonisgi,* and the attachment many Cherokees still had to them. Instead of aggressively attacking and denigrating them, they took the more pragmatic policy of seeking a division of labor with them. They won them over to the new religion by acknowledging their right to assume certain important roles in the cultural life of the community where it did not outwardly conflict with the church's role or where it seemed to supplement or complement it.

The concept of voluntary church membership required an important transition for the Cherokees from a religious system to which all belonged from birth and that was integrally related to all community activities (politics, sports, medicine, rites of passage, holy days, marriage, death, and ceremonies that warded off evil and gave thanks for divine intervention). The old religion had required ceremonies presided over by *adonisgi* for almost every event, from the meeting of a council to the frustration of witchcraft. Some steps had already been taken by 1839 to separate church and state, although Cherokee councils often invited missionaries to pray at their convocations. In the 1820s the council had passed laws against polygamy, infanticide, witchcraft, and Sabbath breaking, but Cherokee chiefs proclaimed national days of prayer in which the appeal for divine assistance was ambiguously worded to both the Great Spirit and the God of Christianity. The constitution adopted in 1827 proclaimed the principle of religious liberty, and traditionalists who interfered with Christian meetings were subject to fines and whippings. But all these actions had not ended traditional religious practices; they had simply raised the necessity for compromises. During the removal crisis some mixed-blood chiefs had promoted the slogan "Join the church and save the country," assuming that U.S. voters would not sanction driving a Christian people from their homeland. This had backfired and led to a revival of traditionalism. Full-blood traditionalists after 1839 sought to reunite religious beliefs and practices with nationalist goals and ideals. The growth of a native ministry provided the means.

Between 1839 and 1860 the Methodists annually licensed fourteen to sixteen "class leaders," exhorters, preachers, and ministers who were Cherokee—some of them mixed-blood and English-speaking but an equal number full-blood and Cherokee-speaking. The Baptists in this period kept in the field six to eight ordained native pastors and licensed another six to eight exhorters or evangelists. Both denominations encouraged lay participation by ordaining deacons of their churches and encouraging unlicensed exhorters to engage in evangelistic work. Little is known of the precise interaction between Cherokee preachers and their Cherokee congregations, for the ministry remained an oral tradition. Because Baptists and Methodists believed in a spirit-filled ministry, preaching through the power of the Holy Spirit, rather than a learned ministry carefully explicating doctrines and texts, native preachers did not write out their sermons any more than did white or mixed-blood ministers in these denominations.

Methodist "class leaders" were placed over groups of new converts and charged with leading them in regular prayer and exhortation and teaching them the Methodist "discipline" between the visits by the ordained, circuit-riding (and usually white) missionaries assigned to the Indian nations by the Arkansas Methodist Conference. These class leaders prepared new converts for church organization and, when talented, were themselves licensed as preachers and eventually as pastors. Baptist converts who displayed promise as ministers were encouraged to itinerate and give sermons; eventually they were licensed by the mission churches, and the most able became pastors of these churches. All native preachers and exhorters received tremendous help from the increasing number of books of the Bible that were being translated into Sequoyan, cheaply printed, bound, and disseminated by the Congregational and Baptist mission presses in the Nation. The mere fact that the Great Book of the white man was now available to the Cherokees in their own language encouraged its reading and study. At last the source from which the whites derived such power in the world was directly available to every Cherokee. Evan Jones, the Baptist mission superintendent who was an active translator and printer of the Bible in Sequoyan, said, "The gospel is gaining more and more attention. . . . [T]he natives used to view all we said as mere legendary tales in which Indians could have no concern"; gradually they learned that it had much to say to them as well.[35] Jones said that those parts of the Bible that by white people were often "passed over as matters of little concern" were "full of interest" to them, especially "the inspired history of the origins of Nations."[36] Like the Afro-American slaves in the United States, the Cherokees saw in the history of the Jews how a people who suffered for their sins still remained in covenant with the Great Spirit by their fidelity to their beliefs and practices and were eventually delivered from oppression. A God of justice who favored the poor and oppressed had new meaning for the Cherokees since their removal. They also found the Old Testament story of the Tower of Babel helpful in explaining the complexities of the world beyond their old boundaries. In the Jewish traditions of tribes and families who were closely knit and tillers of the soil as well as keepers of livestock they could find stories that seemed relevant to their lives. The spiritual wonders and miracles (not to mention witches) described in the Bible also bridged the gap between their old religion and the new one. And ultimately a linear view of history with a glorious redemption for the faithful at its conclusion became a source of hope. "That which we have received [through reading the Bible in Cherokee]," said a group of native ministers to the Baptist Board of Foreign Missions in 1847, "has opened our understanding. . . . Multitudes of our people can read and are desirous to have more of the book of God."[37]

The rapid growth of the Methodist and Baptist denominations from 1839 to 1855 was unquestionably due to the preaching of these native preachers and the translations they brought to every part of the Nation. "The secret of our success," said the Reverend Willard Upham, a Baptist missionary, "is no doubt to be found in the great employ of Native Agency, without which I think nothing extensive can be expected."[38] His brother, Hervey Upham, Jones's printer, agreed: "Nearly all our success with the Cherokees is through the Native Assistants, and if it was not for them, we could hope to accomplish but little."[39] Congregationalists and Moravians, of course, complained that not only were the native preachers woefully ignorant of theology but their exegesis of religious texts was often erroneous or naive as well. "The Cherokees will never be truly evangelized by such preachers as are furnished by the Methodists and Baptists," said Timothy Ranney in 1858.[40] "Say what we may of the efforts of the Methodist and Baptist missions elsewhere," said another Congregationalist, "they cannot be considered in any other light than a curse to this people."[41] Baptist and Methodist missionaries were fully aware of the difficulties their native pastors faced in correctly understanding the more complex biblical texts and did their best to give them some training. Evan Jones in particular, and his son John Buttrick Jones (both of whom were among the few missionaries to learn to speak and write the Cherokee language), did all they could to train their preachers and lay leaders in theology. The Joneses conducted monthly meetings at the mission station for all their preachers at which they spent two or three days going over those parts of the Bible that their native preachers found especially confusing. By 1848 all of the New Testament and several books of the Old Testament had been printed in Cherokee (Genesis, Exodus, Daniel, Isaiah, and Psalms among them). Jones instructed his preachers to mark those texts in their books upon which they needed further light. At these "meetings for the native assistants," Jones would take up their questions one by one and then engage in a general discussion with them about the best means of exegesis. "All are stringently charged [by Jones]," said his friend Daniel Butrick, who attended one of these training sessions in 1850, "never to attempt the explanation of a text of Scripture the meaning of which is to them doubtful." They were to bring difficult texts to these seminars for study first. Butrick said he was "truly delighted to meet with such a number of intelligent, pious, Cherokees, mostly in the prime of life, devoting themselves to the cause of godliness and the salvation of their people."[42] "The Epistle to the Hebrews has but lately been printed in Cherokee," Butrick continued, "[and the native preachers] found some difficulty in understanding certain portions of it, as they have no history of the Mosaic dispensation in their language. It was delightful to perceive their attention to the scripture and their thirst for knowledge on spiritual subjects." To criticize and scorn such dedicated men (as his colleagues did) for not knowing all that trained white seminarians knew seemed to Butrick the height of spiritual pride. He reminded the Congregational mission board that by 1850 the Baptists had six or seven times as many converts as the Congregationalists did. Furthermore, most of the members of the Congregational mission churches were elderly, whereas the Baptist converts were young.[43]

Despite the lack of written sermons by native ministers, it is possible to draw some conclusions about the various ways in which Christianity gradually gained a firm hold upon the Cherokees in these years and the role it played in giving the full-bloods a new source of self-confidence and unity. Clearly it served the personal needs of many, giving spiritual and group assistance, for example, to those addicted to whiskey; it provided an equally important sense of solidarity by serving crucial social needs; it inaugurated a new source of unity, organization, and leadership, and, perhaps most important of all, it managed to create a bridge between those full-bloods who were Christians and those who remained essentially traditionalists.

During the terrible trauma of removal and sickness that swept the Nation from 1838 to 1846, so many died that Christianity helped to provide a new approach to the possibility of life after death. Infants and children were especially vulnerable to disease, and missionaries told many stories of grieving Cherokee mothers who were consoled by the assurance that Christians would be reunited with their dead children and other loved ones in heaven. It is significant that two-thirds of the converts after 1839 were full-blood women. The number of children who had to be provided for in the national orphanage indicated the inability of the old clan system and the new nuclear family structure to care for orphans. Since 1794, some Cherokees had begun to move away from their old clan system and communal village life and adopted the white man's system of living in separate tracts of land with a one-family dwelling and a few acres of land capable of doing little more than supporting that family. Statistically the average Cherokee family consisted of five or six persons; this indicates both limitation of birth and a decline in extended families. Certainly the matrilineal system in which a woman could casually divorce a husband, keep her children and house, and expect her brothers to provide for them was greatly weakened. With the nuclear family came a patrilineal system in which permanent monogamy was the norm and husbands became the leading authority figures. Christianity reinforced this norm, and Christian marriage ceremonies stressed its divine authority. If Cherokee social revitalization had to be built around the stability of the nuclear family, Christianity was a strong bolster to that new way. In stressing patrilineal authority Christianity also stressed paternal responsibilities; the husband's duties toward his wife and family required self-discipline, hard work, and restraint against the problems of both adultery and alcoholism. A male Christian probably become a more desirable husband if his piety was strong. Certainly a wife could appeal to the brothers and sisters of her church and her pastor to support her in requiring sober, industrious, and monogamous behavior from her husband. As the clan system weakened, Christianity strengthened the family.

It also strengthened men and women against the dangers of intemperance; one issue upon which all missionaries agreed was the importance of the Cherokee Temperance Society and its pledge of total abstinence. Congregationalist and Baptist worked side by side in promoting this moral reform; the *adonisgi* had no such movement or responsibility. Moral behavior of both husbands and wives was further bolstered by Christianity's clearer statements regarding rewards and punishment after death for behavior during life. The old religion had only the most vague and undefined description of a next life; traditionally the peace of dead souls rested more on the performance of deathbed and burial rituals than upon the previous behavior of the deceased. Witches were generally dead souls doomed to wander the earth and cause trouble because their relatives had failed to perform some important aspect of death rituals; the *adonisgi* by appropriate ceremonies might identify and frighten off such malevolent spirits, but exactly where they went afterward was not clearly defined. When ancestors or old chiefs returned in dreams or visions, they usually carried messages about upholding traditional customs. The great strength of Christianity for the poor and demoralized Cherokees was its stress upon the Protestant virtues of self-control, self-restraint, self-discipline—the Protestant ethic of industry, sobriety, thrift, piety, honesty, and payment of debts. All this fit well with the new free-enterprise structure of the market economy. The moral code of this revitalization movement matched the economic necessities of accul-turation, and there was no return to the older economic order.

On the other hand, Christianity also reinforced important aspects of traditionalism, particularly for those who needed assistance in order to survive. All Christians were "brothers" and "sisters" de-spite clan or marital affiliation; they were bound by Christian duty to support one another in adversity. Church members thus were sur-rogates for clan members or for extended families no longer living together. Christianity strengthened the hospitality ethic of sharing, which was an important means of equalizing what little the poor had (and adding another level of obligation to the wealthy if they were Christians). The Bible commanded Christians to love one another, to share with the poor, to succor the needy; at this important level the poorer class (the full-bloods generally) found Christianity and the tra-ditional communal ethic of cooperation and sharing compatible and complementary. On this same score, the requirement that Christian brothers and sisters help one another reinforced the traditional *gadugi* system of pooling labor to perform tasks too great for a single family. In the ancient communal town the men were required to clear the ground for cultivation, which women then undertook. Men hunted in groups and protected the community in groups. They also built the large town council houses and playing fields together. So in the period from 1839 to 1855, Cherokee Christians banded together to build their meetinghouses and their shelters for protracted meetings. Virtually all mission churches of the Baptists and Methodists were built by their members, not by hired carpenters. Evan Jones reported to his board that in the years from 1841 to 1849 his members had con-structed fourteen meetinghouses, and in one year they had organized five camp meetings lasting three to five days. The total value of the fourteen meetinghouses he estimated at more than $3,360, and the total value of the food and fodder donated for 1849's revival meetings he estimated at $1,529.[44] When his board asked why they could not then provide money to pay their own ministers, Jones pointed out that it was easier to donate food from their farms and labor by their own hands than to raise cash among a people who seldom had any money at all and lived consistently in debt. As in the case of the hospitality ethic, Christianity reinforced the *gadugi* tradition and made it easier for Christians and traditionalists to work together. In building school-houses, for example, or raising a barn, traditionalists and Christians would be part of the same volunteer labor force.

Finally, the Cherokee full-blood community benefited from the Christian ideal of repentance from sin. In the breakdown of older tribal restraints, there were too many cases of drunken brawls, wife beatings, stabbings, and even shootings that tore at the fabric of the community. The terrible feuds of the factional strife between 1832 and 1846 made tribal unity impossible. But by utilizing both the tribal ideal of purification from hard feelings and the Christian ideal of forgiveness of one's enemies, it was possible to build reconciliation and to bring the Nation back together whether it was called the "Kituwha spirit" by traditionalists or "charity" by Christians.

Christianity also performed an important revitalization function by supporting both a linear view of history and a basic concept of separation of church and state. For example, it was obvious that Christian spiritual power could not always solve the problems caused by natural catastrophes except by prayer. What difference was there, then, between the *adonisgi*'s supplication to the Great Spirit to bring rain during a drought or end a pestilence of grasshoppers and the supplications of a Cherokee minister in similar prayers to God for help? Could not a Christian and a traditionalist agree to try both measures? Might not some Christians participate in both?[45] Likewise the Cherokee Christians accepted the secular nature of medicine or doctoring; this allowed them to utilize their skilled doctors (medicine men) just as Christian whites used their trained physicians. Originally missionaries had insisted that converts never utilize the services of *adonisgi* because they made incantations of spirit beings outside the Christian Trinity. But as missionaries, particularly among the Baptists and Methodists, conversed more with their converts, they had to admit that much tribal medicine was based on the use of beneficial herbs and treatments. Evan Jones said to one *adonisgi*, "I told him that God has given us all herbs, roots, and other substances possessing medical properties to be used in any way we know to be beneficial."[46] A female *adonisgi* asked Jones whether God condemned the practice of medicine entirely. He answered, "I told her all medical substances were free to be used with thankfulness to God."[47] The Baptists and Methodists took a pragmatic approach to medicine after 1839 and ceased to condemn any and all applications of the sick to an *adonisgi* for help. The Congregational missionary Timothy Ranney was shocked to learn in

1850 that some Baptist churches were now admitting *adonisgi* to membership if they professed to be Christians: "One of the candidates [for baptism in a nearby Baptist church] was a woman who maintains the reputation of being one of the best jugglers [*adonisgi*] in this neighborhood."[48] For Ranney it was impossible to be both a Cherokee shaman and a Christian, but not so for other missionaries.

Christianity even evolved a modus vivendi with the most sacred of all Cherokee religious ceremonies, the Green Corn dance. This was traditionally performed in midsummer when the first ears of corn turned green. It was a thanksgiving dance to Selu, the goddess of corn. But Cherokee Christians soon learned that it was customary in white America for Christians to give thanks for good harvests in their churches. Without too much distortion, prayerful thanks to the Great Spirit and to God for bountiful harvests could be equated in the same way the prayers for rain could be. Christians did not care for the dancing part of the Green Corn ceremony, but Baptists and Methodists might wink at it. At any rate, attending this annual ceremony and even participating in it was seldom a reason for censure or excommunication in the Baptist or Methodist mission church, much to the horror of the Congregationalists and Moravians.

Equally shocking to the rigid missionaries, the revitalization movement made it possible to separate Cherokee sports from Cherokee religion. Traditionally the Cherokee ball play was a surrogate for war and required traditional sacred rituals by the players beforehand (such as the scratching ceremony to thin their blood and drain off impurities). The more formal missionaries also disliked the fact that although the men performed in only a breechcloth, women as well as men attended the sport. In many ways the ball play had been secularized prior to 1839; it certainly was no longer a substitute for war. It had become an occasion for heavy wagers on the outcome of the game and for considerable consumption of whiskey before, during, and after each game (other reasons why missionaries forbade attendance). Still, it was clear that Christians had their own sports—horse racing, for example—that they attended where wagers were made and liquor was consumed. The Christian taboo against attending ball plays broke down after 1839 among Baptists and Methodists, and another bridge was built between Christians and traditionalists.

Revitalization, although it marked a further step toward separation of church and state, not only provided new spiritual power for those who became Christians, but it also brought a new unity between pagan and Christian full-bloods. It also gave a new religious meaning to history. Traditionally Cherokees had a cyclical view of humans' relationship to the universe; the seasons always returned and the earth renewed itself. Humans lived in harmony with this cycle by doing as little as they could to disturb the natural order. Religious rituals and sacred myths were dedicated to preserving that order. But as the old ways changed, and as Cherokees adopted the entrepreneurial, free-market economy, they embarked not only on a more individualist and acquisitive ethic but on the new perspective that the white man called "progress." Progress came from exploiting the resources of nature in order to enrich individuals and to produce more comforts for more people. Cherokees admitted the advantages of woven cloth, metal pots, and saddles and wagons. They could not make a living from the fur trade, so they had to enter the staple-crop system, the cattle-herding system, the wool-growing, hog-growing, and timber-chopping systems. They had to build gristmills and sawmills to market their surplus resources. But where did this all end? What was the spiritual purpose of profits and creature comforts and more speedy travel and communications?

Christianity provided an answer that both full-blood traditionalists and full-blood Christians could understand. The end result was to be the miraculous transformation of the world into a place of peace, justice, order, and the absence of pain, sickness, and war. The wicked and oppressive people would be removed; the poor, the oppressed, would receive power and equality. For Christians this meant that those who were truly God's chosen would regain control of the world from the hypocritical Christians and traitorous, factional Cherokees. For traditionalists this resembled the ideals of earlier ghost dance movements that were inaugurated by the visions of prophets and designed to restore the golden age of Indian life before the white man invaded, conquered, and oppressed them.

The connection between Christian millenarianism and ghost dance movement has been well documented. Less often noted was the important shift from a postmillennial to a premillennial view among many Cherokees after 1839. Those of mixed ancestry who adopted white people's ways, rose to wealth, and directed the Nation's destiny could believe, like white Americans, that human progress would, in the course of time, create an era of peace and prosperity for all. But to the full-bloods, for whom chronic poverty seemed unceasing, a pre-millennial hope of divine intervention to right the wrongs of the world made more sense. Hence the premillennialism of the Millerite movement and the Mormons had a stronger appeal to them in the 1840s and 1850s than the postmillennial concept of progress preached by most missionaries. In 1833 the Baptist preacher William Miller in New York predicted the end of the world and the Second Coming of Christ in 1843 or 1844. About the same time, Joseph Smith, the founder of the Mormonism, also predicted an imminent Second Coming and built a temple for Christ's return near Independence, Missouri. Millerites and Mormons reached the Cherokee Nation between 1839 and 1855 and were as successful among the Cherokees as they were among many white Christians.

In 1842 a missionary named Covel, sent by the American Board to the Cherokee Nation, surprised his colleagues by advocating pre-millennial doctrines; they called him a "literalist" or a "spiritualist." Covel tried to inculcate this idea at his mission school and found his Cherokee students very receptive to it. "He commenced talking with the children. Told them that Christ would soon come to raise all the dead saints and destroy the wicked and reign a thousand years. And those that would not repent and believe his doctrine would be destroyed."[49] Many Cherokees believed Covel's teachings, "some were alarmed and . . . [others] were frightened." But it was clear that he struck an important chord in Cherokee thought—the hope of a just society by divine intervention. Some of the missionaries considered Covel to be a covert Mormon. But the Mormons came into the Nation without any effort to hide their views. Their popularity was attested by the services conducted by three of them at the national courthouse in Tahlequah in the spring of 1847. House builders by trade, they were, like all Mormons, lay missionaries for their religion. "I became a popular preacher" said George Miller, the leading preacher of the three. "I was solicited by them to preach twice a week." One of the teachings of the Book of Mormon said that the Indians were originally white skinned but were cursed for rebelling against the truth of Mormon teaching many centuries ago; however, at Christ's return they would become white again and, if they converted, share in the glorious destiny of the chosen followers of Mormon. This was then, and has been often since, an appealing idea to many Cherokees. But George Miller's growing popularity "created a clamor of jealousy among the missionaries," he reported. They asked Chief Ross to expel him from the Nation. Ross said he could not because the Cherokee constitution mandated freedom of religion. Nevertheless, Miller decided to avert controversy and left for Texas in December 1847.[50]

The *Cherokee Advocate,* speaking for postmillennial, progress-oriented mixed-bloods, took note of the rage for premillennialism among whites at this time. An article printed on November 16, 1844, ridiculed the followers of William Miller and compared them to the ignorant Cherokees who had followed a ghost dance prophet in 1811–12. "The Catastrophe Preacher [Miller] and his enlightened followers are treading almost in the very footsteps of some old Cherokee Conjuror and his benighted followers," wrote the editor, a mixed-blood of some education and considerable religious skepticism. To the mixed-bloods, only a backward, ignorant full-blood would be taken in either by William or George Miller. But the mixed-bloods were coping well with the new social order and the full-bloods were not.

If the revitalization movement brought new hope, confidence, and unity among the poor full-bloods, it also increased the class division between them and well-to-do mixed-bloods. To those mixed-bloods who were not skeptics about religion, the message of Christianity was that of self-reliant individualism: "God helps those who help themselves." They had no more use for the older communal ethic and its ideals of cooperation, sharing, and solidarity than the Boston missionaries of Congregationalism. Congregational missionaries tended to stereotype the full-bloods as lazy beggars, ne'er-do-wells, and scapegraces who would rather live off others than work hard themselves. Some Congregational missionaries took such a negative view of Indians who came to their mission enclaves asking for food or a night's lodging that they sternly rebuked them and turned them away empty-handed. In one case this led the full-bloods to threaten the missionary for being coldhearted and for refusing to heed his own preaching about Christ's command to help the poor, clothe the needy, feed the hungry. Some of them threatened the minister's life, and he became so frightened that he left his mission church and never returned.[51]

Many missionaries not only refused to itinerate among the poor Cherokees in the outlying areas, but they deliberately confined their efforts to the English-speaking mixed-bloods. They concluded that it

was hopeless to try to reclaim the adult traditionalists from their benighted condition. As one Congregationalist said of his colleagues,
"They think they [the full-bloods] must be equal, if not surpass, the
first class of Cherokees, and thus fix their marks entirely beyond the
reach of all the common Indians." Further, "[They] visit only the better
families who can furnish good entertainment and neglect the poorer,
more degraded families and treat such with apparent coldness when
they call at the [mission] stations [seeking hospitality]." He urged his
brethren to leave their mission stations and travel out into the countryside to visit "the most ignorant, depraved, poor and filthy Indians."
"If we will not condescend to the poorest class of Cherokees . . . they
will either go to the Baptist or Methodist meetings where they can
find someone who does not feel above them, or they will excite such
opposition as we cannot withstand."[52]

But it mattered not; the Congregationalists and Moravians, even
had they left their missions and tried to reach the poor full-bloods,
were preaching the wrong message. Their message was attuned to the
mixed-blood bourgeoisie, those who were successfully adjusted to the
new middle-class ethic of mid-nineteenth-century America. The more
potent and meaningful Christian message for the two-thirds of the
Nation who were full-bloods was more than adequately spread by the
native ministers of the Methodists and Baptists. The Methodists were
divided in their appeal because, as members of the southern Methodist Church who accepted the importance of black slavery, almost
half of their converts were among the well-to-do mixed-bloods who
owned slaves.[53] The northern Baptists, whose headquarters was in
New England and who were steadily becoming more antislavery in
outlook, consequently garnered the major share of converts among
the full-bloods—almost twice as many full-bloods were Baptists as
were Methodists. Few if any full-bloods owned slaves, and slavery
had already become a significant mark of class distinction between
them and the mixed-bloods.

In the long run, it was the slavery issue that brought the new ethnic
identity of the full-blood majority to organizational unity—a unity in
which traditionalists and Christians shared a common definition of
who was a true Cherokee and what those qualities were that should
unify the Nation and inform its policies. When that time came, after
1855, the organizational strength and experience of the northern Bap-

tist Christians and the leadership abilities and charisma of the native Baptist preachers provided the guidance for the full-blood effort to drive the mixed-bloods from their influential role in Cherokee affairs. Only then was it clear how powerful the revitalization of Cherokee religious life had become.

Chapter 9
Cherokee Syncretism: The Origins of the Keetoowah Society, 1854-1861

Much has been written about the famous Cherokee Keetoowah Society, but many of the accounts are conflicting. Much of its history is shrouded in mystery because the society was, perforce, secret for most of its early years. Consequently its leadership, its membership, and its activities often must be discovered from sources written by its enemies rather than its supporters. In addition, the Keetoowahs underwent a radical reorganization in the 1890s, so the new organization was not the same as the original one.

This essay focuses on the role of the Keetoowah Society in the Cherokee Nation in the decades preceding the Civil War. One key to the power of the movement was that it brought together both full-blood traditionalists and full-blood Christians in the higher interest of unity and patriotism, or what they called the "Kituwah spirit." The originators of the Keetoowah Society appear to have been Baptist converts led by Evan and John B. Jones, and though Christian prayer was always part of its meetings, so too were ancient customs involving smoking tobacco and dancing. Two of the early leaders, Lewis Downing and Oochalata, became chiefs of the Nation after the political revolt.

Based upon original documents and all of the contemporary evidence available from other sources, this chapter demonstrates that religion and politics cannot be separated but they can be transcended in the greater interest of national survival. The Keetoowah movement is virtually unique in the history of Native American full-bloods and one of the outstanding illustrations of a syncretic religious-political society limited in membership to full-bloods.

The Cherokee Keetoowah Society[1] has been discussed by every major writer on Cherokee history since James Mooney, but no two agree on even its most basic aspects. The date of its founding has been variously given as 1857, 1858, 1859, and 1860. Its membership has been numbered at three thousand, seven thousand, eighty-five hundred, and seven-tenths of the Nation's males.[2] The society has been said to have consisted "exclusively" of full-bloods who spoke and read Cherokee or "chiefly" of the "poorer classes" or of the "uneducated." There have been historians who described it as an antislavery or abolitionist society and historians who said it never tried to oppose slavery. One school describes it as a traditionalist organization, another as an organization of Christian Cherokees. Some say it was founded and led by two white northern Baptist missionaries (Evan Jones and his son, John B. Jones), and some say that Chief John Ross dominated it; others say that a Cherokee Baptist minister (the Reverend Budd Gritts) founded and led it, and still others say that the traditionalist Pig Redbird Smith organized and directed it.[3] It has been called a revival of, a continuation of, and a reorganization of the ancient Kituwha Society that antedates the arrival of Europeans in North America. Some writers maintain that it preceded and some that it followed the formation of a secret proslavery society. Some say it was designed to maintain the neutrality of the Nation during the Civil War and some that it was formed to counter the prosouthern element in the Nation and align the Nation with the Union; others argue that it was an effort by the full-bloods to take control of the Nation from the mixed-bloods.

All historians agree that it was a secret society and that it was known as the Pin Society (or "the Pins") during the Civil War because its members wore crossed straight pins (or a single straight pin) on the left lapel of their coats or hunting jackets. Some say the two pins were placed in the shape of the Christian cross, and others say they made an "X" shape.[4] Most agree that it was limited to males, that it opposed the Ridge-Watie faction of the Nation, that its adherents were loyal to Chief John Ross (himself a mixed-blood, Christian slaveholder), and that after December 1861 its members fought for the Union against the Confederacy (although not formally, as members of the Union Army, until June 1862).

The greatest inconsistencies among the historians concern the

avowed objectives of the society and its ambiguous "constitution."
James Mooney said its "ostensible purpose" was "cultivating national
feeling among the fullbloods in opposition to the innovating tendencies of the mixed-blood elements"; that is, it was a reactionary, conservative, or traditionalist movement against acculturation or assimilation.[5] Annie H. Abel, quoting Albert Pike, the Indian agent sent to the
Cherokees by the Confederate States of America in 1861 to ally them
with the seceding states, said the Keetoowahs were "a Secret Society
established by Evan Jones, a missionary, and at the service of Mr. John
Ross, for the purposes of abolitionizing the Cherokee and putting out
of the way all who sympathized with the Southern States." Pike then
added that it was "really established for the purpose of depriving the
half-breeds of all political power."[6] The Cherokee historian Emmet
Starr said it was "a secret society for the purpose of protecting national
and community interests and for the fuller development of the nobler
qualities of individualism" and that "Budd Gritts, who was a Baptist minister, was prevailed upon to draft a Constitution and Laws of
government . . . which was compatible with the changing conditions
religiously and politically. . . . Almost without exception the Keetoowahs were either Baptists, Methodists, Presbyterians, a few Quakers
and a part of them worshipped according to the rituals of the ancient
Keetoowah" in the years "1859 to 1889."[7] E. E. Dale and Gaston Litton
said it was "originally formed to conserve the purity of Indian customs and traditions" and "was, largely speaking, anti-slavery."[8] Rudi
Halliburton states that it was founded by white abolitionist ministers
but says that "the abolitionist sentiments of the Joneses did not neces-
sarily transfer to the rank-and-file membership. . . . It would probably
be more correct to describe the organization as not being pro-slavery
than as being antislavery."[9] Grace Woodward wrote, "In 1859, Evan
Jones, the Baptist missionary, reorganized the ancient and secret Keetoowah Society, giving as his motive the desire to assist the Cherokees
in preserving the best of their ancient tribal traditions. Joneses' critics,
however, said that his real motive . . . was to originate or activate
an abolitionists society which could be counted on to support the
Union."[10] Gary E. Moulton, the recent biographer of John Ross and
editor of the Ross Papers, writes, "Beyond the desire to maintain old
Cherokee codes (probably the primary function), the society also may
have been led by the Joneses to favor antislavery positions. . . . It is
doubtful that Ross used the Pins for any political purpose."[11] Morris L.
Wardell said "its aims and objects were to preserve the religious and

moral code of an ancient Keetoowah Society," although "the members were Christians who were nevertheless impressed with the prospect that ancient tribal and religious rites were about to be lost." He added that "evidently to counteract the abolition influences of the Pin organization . . . the pro-slavery Cherokees organized Circles of the Knights of the Gold Circle."[12] T. L. Ballenger wrote, "The Keetoowahs are a group of fullblood Cherokees [and their purpose is] the 'perpetuation of the fullblood race.'" They stood for "unity and brotherly love" and their organization was "brought about largely through the efforts of the Rev. Evan Jones and his son." Ballenger states that in 1858 the Keetoowah Society instituted "a legal political entity that might be able to salvage the Cherokee lands and other possessions and perpetuate the nation in the case of a Northern victory. . . . The Reverend Budd Gritts, a prominent fullblood Baptist preacher," drew up its constitution.[13] Carolyn Foreman said the society was "limited almost entirely to the fullbloods" and at first its principal feature was the abolition of slaves. . . . The Keetoowah Society ha[d] always been reactionary in religion."[14] Marion Starkey said that its full-blood members "inclined to the philosophy that all men, whatever their color, should go free."[15]

These statements are not only inconsistent with each other, they are not consistent in themselves. Why would Christian missionaries form a secret society to preserve old tribal rituals? How could such a society protect community interests and also promote individualism? How could it seek "unity and brotherly love" and also the "perpetuation of the fullblood race"? Much of the confusion stems from the secrecy of the organization at the time, the lack of records of the society, the tendency to confuse the early phase of the Keetoowah movement with later phases, and what was probably a fluid, changing, pragmatic, and even expedient tendency among the leaders of the movement. There is also a tendency to attribute to the Keetoowah Society as a whole the views of the Joneses or John Ross and a failure to recognize that the Keetoowahs may themselves have been divided on some of these issues. Inasmuch as full-bloods are usually said to have constituted 65 to 75 percent of the Nation (though definitions of a "full-blood" differ), it would be strange if they agreed about all these complicated problems affecting the Nation at one of its most crucial periods.

The purpose of this essay is to provide a somewhat more precise definition of the founding, membership, structure, and purposes of the pre–Civil War Keetoowah Society by reference to its earliest known records, to contemporary papers of the Joneses and John Ross (and other participants), and to the general historical circumstances that surround its foundation and early years. From the analysis, I conclude that the Keetoowah Society was more political than religious and more innovative than conservative (even though it was limited to full-bloods). I also believe that it was nonsectarian and made no distinction between Christians and adherents of the traditional religion; that its central ideal was a patriotic commitment to Cherokee autonomy; that it believed national sovereignty and self-government required adherence to federal treaties; that it favored a policy of neutrality in the conflict between the northern and southern states (so long as that was feasible); that it was not an abolitionist or antislavery organization, although its members strongly believed that the mixed-blood, educated slaveholders were usurping power and trying to lead the Nation into a fatal alliance with the South; that it was created to counter the effect (or "conspiracy") of the proslavery organizations (Blue Lodges and Knights of the Golden Circle) by organizing the full-blood majority ("the masses" of common folk) for concerted political action within the existing electoral system; and that it embodied important aspects of a mutual-aid society (similar to the *gadugi* work group) among its members who were mostly poor and "uneducated." Later, when the Cherokees' social order broke down, in 1862, the Keetoowahs were as ready to resort to violence as were their opponents.

There is no evidence that the Keetoowah Society was either pro-Christian or protraditionalist but rather that it tolerated both in a syncretic blending of their shared values. Its meetings included elements of the new religion (such as Christian prayer in the Cherokee language) and of the old religion (such as smoking tobacco and stomp dances). Its emphasis upon brotherly love drew from both faith systems, but it saw this ideal in patriotic or ethnic terms. Its stress upon harmony, unity, and consensus decision making sought to transcend religious differences for the sake of national survival.[16] However, circumstantial evidence clearly ties the beginning of the Keetoowah Society to the northern Baptist missionaries who had taken a deep interest in Cherokee politics and were themselves threatened by the mixed-blood slaveholders and federal agents. The Keetoowah Society was undoubtedly encouraged and utilized by Chief John Ross in his own efforts to sustain national unity and survival through a balance of power. Perhaps the most important aspect of the Keetoowah Society is that its formation marked a new level of social and political sophistication among the Cherokee full-bloods. It demonstrated their ability to adapt the political and social functions of Euro-American voluntary societies and political parties to meet a crisis in Cherokee affairs and yet to do so within a traditional ideological structure as well as within the emotional and ethical symbolism of their own ethnic heritage. The society drew on its past to confront its future. To do so, the Keetoowahs utilized the fraternal experience, leadership system, and church organization gained from Christian missionary work in addition to drawing upon their memory of the traditional fraternalism and organization of their ancient Kituwah society.

Three important Keetoowah documents, translated from the Sequoyan syllabary in which they were originally written, throw light on the origin and purposes of the society. One was discovered by T. L. Ballenger in the published report of the Frank J. Boudinot case brought before the United States Court for Indian Claims in 1930.[17] The second, from an original now at the Smithsonian Institution, is included as an appendix to Howard Q. Tyner's master's thesis on the Keetoowah societies (University of Tulsa, 1949).[18] The third is a document used by Eula E. Fullerton for her master's thesis, "Some Social Institutions of the Cherokees, 1820–1906," at the University of Oklahoma in 1931.[19] Ballenger's document is a statement by Budd Gritts regarding the founding of the society in 1858. Tyner's document includes Gritts's statement but adds other records of the Keetoowah Society for the years 1859 to 1876. The Fullerton document, translated from Sequoyan in 1931 by Sam Smith (son of Redbird Smith and grandson of Pig Redbird Smith),[20] states in different words some of the same recollections of the formation of the society as those by Gritts. Most authorities consider Gritts, a full-blood who became minister of a Baptist mission church in the 1860s, to be one of the founders of the Keetoowah Society and one of its first "head captains." I have followed mainly the document in Tyner's thesis, which was probably translated by Levi Gritts, the son of Budd Gritts, in 1930.

In addition to these records, important information regarding the political and religious situation among the Cherokees that gave rise to the society in the late 1850s is contained in the letters of Evan and John B. Jones at the Baptist Historical Society at Colgate-Rochester Divinity School in Rochester. By placing all of this evidence in the broad context of Cherokee affairs in the years 1854 to 1860, a much clearer picture emerges of the origin, membership, organization, and purpose of the Keetoowah Society. Other contemporary documents from the papers of John Ross, the anti-Keetoowah Cherokees, and the various records of the United States and Confederate States officials add important details.

The year 1854 must be the starting point of the discussion, for that is when Congress passed the Kansas-Nebraska Act. By that act Congress broke the promise of the Missouri Compromise (as the northerners understood it) and opened the possibility of the extension of slavery not only into Kansas and Nebraska Territories but throughout the trans-Mississippi West as well. Because Kansas Territory lay along the northern border of the Cherokee Nation and because the Cherokees also owned a tract of 800,000 acres in southeastern Kansas (known as the Neutral Lands), the Cherokees became instantly embroiled in the rising tension between the northern and southern states over whether, through "squatter sovereignty," Kansas would become a free or a slave state. The slaveholders in Missouri and Arkansas on the eastern border of the Cherokee Nation, and in Texas on the southern border of Indian Territory, wanted Kansas to become a slave state. Because many Cherokees were slaveholders, their constitution and laws protected that institution. However, only 8 or 9 percent of the Cherokees owned any slaves, and they were the mixed-blood and intermarried whites who constituted the wealthiest and most acculturated. The other 92 percent of the Nation were poor subsistence farmers, most of them full-bloods.[21]

In the elected, bicameral Cherokee legislature, mixed-bloods had dominated the upper house and full-bloods the lower house since the 1820s. Part of the Keetoowah story is the revolt of the full-bloods against this situation. Chief John Ross, though of mixed ancestry and a slaveholder, had the confidence of the full-bloods, and he had been reelected chief in every election since 1828. Ross's chief concern was not the possible extension of slavery into Kansas but preserving the Cherokee Nation from being dragged into supporting either the North or the South in this controversy. The slaveholding Cherokees, particularly those of the Ridge-Watie faction, were not particularly fond of Ross and strongly tended toward sympathy for the South's position; in fact, by the mid-1850s this faction became known as the Southern Rights party. This socioeconomic division of the Nation had been increasing ever since removal and tended to divide the Nation not only between slaveholders and non-slaveholders, mixed-bloods and full-bloods, anti-Ross and pro-Ross, but into a class division between rich and poor. The anti-Ross faction contained most of the educated class and many intermarried whites, and it tended to look with a certain disdain upon the poorer or "unintelligent" masses as "backward" Cherokees.

In their effort to win control of Kansas Territory in the years 1854 to 1860, the slaveholders in the South, and some proslavery citizens of southern ancestry north of the Ohio River, formed secret societies to help send emigrants and arms to Kansas and to elect candidates to Congress favorable to states' rights and squatter sovereignty. They also supported filibustering expeditions to Cuba and Central America in the hope of annexing more territory capable of growing cotton. The organizations, called Blue Lodges and Knights of the Golden Circle (or "Knaves of the Godless Communion" by their opponents), were the counterparts of the Kansas Emigrant Aid Societies founded by northern antislavery activists. (Other secret societies flourished in the United States—for example, the Masons and the Know-Nothings; and flourishing third-party movements—the American party, the anti-Masonic party, the Liberty party, the Free Soil party—were well known to the Cherokees.) Soon after 1854, leaders of proslavery societies in Arkansas communicated with proslavery leaders among the Cherokees to see whether they were favorable to the southern cause, men such as Stand Watie, William P. Adair, and James M. Bell; some of those living in Arkansas were related to these men—E. C. Boudinot, John Rollin Ridge, George W. Paschal. The Arkansans urged them to form similar lodges in the Cherokee Nation and to use their influence against northern missionaries in the Nation who were allegedly sympathetic to abolitionism and "free soil." In addition, southern Methodist and southern Baptist mission agencies in the slave states were actively proselytizing in the Cherokee Nation to counter the efforts of these northern missionaries; these southern missionaries made it very clear that there was no antagonism between Christianity and support of the institution of African slavery.

In 1855 two Blue Lodges were formed in the Cherokee Nation and were gathering members to support slavery and its expansion. After all, if Kansas were to become a free state, it would provide a refuge not only for the slaves of white southerners but of Cherokees, so the Cherokee Nation must be made safe for slavery.

The Role of Evan and John B. Jones

Evan Jones, the superintendent of the northern Baptist mission activities among the Cherokees, had come to the Nation in 1821. He had supported John Ross in his opposition to Jackson's removal policy, worked chiefly among the full-bloods, walked with the Cherokees along the Trail of Tears, and in 1852 had expelled from his mission churches the four members (out of eleven hundred) who owned slaves. His son, John B. Jones, was born in the Cherokee Nation in 1824 and was ordained to work with his father in 1855.[22] Both of the Joneses had learned to speak, read, and write Cherokee and had not only won many full-bloods to Christianity but had licensed and ordained more than a dozen Cherokee-speaking full-bloods as preachers and pastors to preside over Baptist mission churches. When John Ross learned of the existence of the two Blue Lodges in the Nation, he immediately wrote to Evan Jones to alert him to the problem it would raise for his work and for the Nation. The letter, dated May 5, 1855, began by noting that these lodges might create division in the Nation over slavery and "create excitement and strife among the Cherokee people."

> It seems that there has been a secret society organized in the Delaware and Saline Districts auxiliary to a "Mother Lodge" in some of the States or Territories of the United States, and the enclosed copy is a form of the oath said to be administered to the members of the society. But I do not apprehend that the authors of this sinister plot can possibly dupe the Cherokee people into their own ruin and downfall, as the schemers, when found out, will only render themselves more odious to all who feel an interest in the prosperity and welfare of the Nation.[23]

The oath that these lodges were requiring of their members read:

> You do solemnly swear that you will answer such questions as may be asked you?
> Are you in favor of supporting slavery in Kansas, in the Cherokee Nation and in other countries?
> You do solemnly swear that you will, for the support of Slavery, support any person that you may be instructed to by the Mother Lodge for any office in the Cherokee Nation or anywhere else, and to assist any members that may get into a difficulty on account of being a Brother of the Secret Society and to keep secret the names of all the Brothers of the Society and other secrets of the Society?[24]

Ross did not have to tell Evan Jones what to do with this information. Many of his mission churches and members lived in Delaware and Saline Districts. Jones's house and mission headquarters were in Going Snake District just south of Delaware District. He and his son itinerated—as did the native Baptist ministers—around a wide circuit of preaching stations in the Nation, and they had a wide acquaintance with the full-bloods at whose homes they stayed when itinerating. The Joneses also had made many enemies over the years among the slaveholders and the southern-based missionaries. The northern Baptists were the greatest rivals of the southern Methodists in winning Christian converts.[25] Furthermore, the federal agents appointed to the Cherokees were all southern men, most of them slaveholders themselves. They had no use for abolitionists, and because the Cherokee and United States constitutions legitimized the practice of slavery, they considered it their duty to uphold the institution. A month after Ross's letter to Jones about the Blue Lodges, George M. Butler, then the resident agent, tried to have Evan Jones expelled from the Nation as "an abolitionist" but failed.[26] In October 1855 the Cherokee legislature held a debate, instituted by the mixed-blood slaveholders, that would have forced all missionaries to reveal their positions on slavery and subject those with antislavery views to expulsion.[27] The Joneses had a personal and professional interest in combating the Blue Lodges and the successor to them, the Knights of the Golden Circle.

In the first historical account of secret societies in the Cherokee Nation, published in 1866, D. J. MacGowan noted that "the Pin organization [the later name for the Keetoowah Society] originated among the members of the Baptist congregation at Peavine, Going-snake district in the Cherokee Nation."[28] MacGowan did not explain why, but the Pea Vine Baptist Church was headed at this time by Lewis Downing, who had been ordained by Evan Jones and later became one of the head captains of the Keetoowah Society. It is probable that Budd Gritts was a member of this church as well as Smith Christie, both of whom were also among the earliest head captains of the society. The Pea Vine Church was located less than fifteen miles south of Baptist Mission in Going Snake District, the site of the Joneses' homes. It was the oldest, largest, and most important Baptist church in the Nation. Originally it was known as the Amohee Church, located in eastern Tennessee. Its organizer and first pastor, Jesse Bushyhead, had assisted Jones in translating the Bible into Cherokee. Bushyhead reconstituted the church in a place called Flint, after the Trail of Tears.[29]

When Bushyhead died in 1844, Lewis Downing, a Cherokee-speaking full-blood who often was elected to serve in the National Council, became pastor.[30] For some unknown reason the church changed its name to the Pea Vine Church in 1858. The Joneses held revival meetings for hundreds of Baptist Cherokees at this church every year.

Among the letters John B. Jones sent to his mission board in Boston in the years 1855 to 1860 are several that provide important information with respect to the Pea Vine Church and to the increasing pressure he felt from proslavery forces. Without explicitly saying so, these letters make it clear that MacGowan was correct in identifying the members of this church as the founders of the Keetoowah Society. A week before the Keetoowah Society formally adopted its first constitution in April 1858, Jones told the board that he was disturbed by recent events at the church caused by the activities of the southern Baptist missionary James G. Slover. Jones had informed his board in 1856 that the southern Baptists were about to come to the Nation to try to win away the northern Baptist converts.[31] To his mind, they and the southern Methodists were the spiritual arm of the Blue Lodges. "The [southern] Methodists take slavery by the hand, encourage it, speak in its favor, and brand all who oppose it with opprobrious epithets. As they support slavery, of course slavery supports them."[32] As for Slover, he seems to have singled out the Pea Vine Church for his opening assault upon the heretical northern Baptists. Jones claimed that when he first heard that a new Baptist missionary was in the vicinity, he had expected to join hands with him in saving souls, but this was not to be the case.

> Instead of being a co-laborer and helper, he must from the antagonism of our principles, act as an opposer of our mission. He has been laboring here for some time and is about to organize a proslavery Baptist church. . . . I hear that some who were formerly with us, have joined his ranks. One man, by the name of Young Duck, who was a Deacon of the Pea Vine or Flint Church and had for several years been accustomed to preach occasionally, has gone over to Mr. Slover, the southern missionary, and is now in the employ of the Southern Board. . . . I understand that Mr. Slover is offering salaries for more [Cherokee] preachers. . . . He told me that he had been trying to get Mr. [John] Foster, who, you remember, was formerly my Father's interpreter.[33]

Slover, according to Jones, took "great pains to tell in certain places that he [was] not like the 'Jones Baptists.'" He said he owned "one 'nigger' and would own more if he were able." Jones added ominously, "In the Creek Nation the southern Baptists have the field." He made no mention in this letter of any effort by himself or his father to rally the Cherokees against those who supported slavery, but it is clear that he had a distinct interest in doing so. The political ramifications of this contest between the northern and southern Baptist missionaries became evident in the next letter Jones wrote to his board on July 12, 1858.

> Recently the Southern Baptist Board has established a mission here, the purpose of which, as now avowed by those most active in its establishment, is "To deliver the Cherokee Baptist churches from the thralldom of abolitionism." You know the meaning of such language in the mouth of a slavery propagandist. . . . Mr. Slover seems to be furnished with ample means for employing native help and to accomplish his purpose. We hear of his offering salaries to members of our churches to preach for him, and he has succeeded in inducing one man to go and preach the gospel of slavery.
>
> While we have the rich to oppose us, our own church members are principally full Indians. They are almost all poor, so poor that in many [white] communities many of them would be considered objects of charity. . . . Now remember that we are not only deprived of the contributions of the rich [Cherokees—the slaveholders], but their influence is used against us, even to prevent our own church members from contributing. . . . Again, we are surrounded by a very considerable population of Negroes, most of them slaves and many of them members of our churches. Of course, opportunities are occasionally offered of benefitting them in sundry ways, and when we can, we avail ourselves of such opportunities. Every such deed is watched and used to our detriment. An instance recently occurred. An old Black woman, on being freed by her mistress, gave her free papers into my father's hands for safe keeping. A claim was afterwards set up to the woman and repeated attempts have been made both by threats and persuasions to get them out of his hands. But all to no effect. He still holds the papers. Complaints have been made to the U.S. Indian Agent here from whom both my father and myself have received a note, each in consequence of the complaint.[34]

The complainant was William P. Adair. In this letter Jones enclosed a copy of Agent Butler's response to the complaint: "You have been reported to me as an abolitionist, teaching and preaching in opposition to the institution of slavery in this nation. You will please attest immediately to the truth or falsity of this charge." It was signed by Butler.

"This George Butler," Jones informed his board, "is a nephew of the late Senator [Pierce M.] Butler of S.C. and cousin of the late notorious P[reston] S. Brooks, and very much such a man as Brooks."[35] Jones obviously felt that the Baptist cause and the antislavery cause were now one and the same. Moreover, he felt that all the forces of authority, wealth, and influence were acting in concert to give dominance to the proslavery minority in the Cherokee Nation. Slover, the Methodists, Adair, Butler, and the founders of the Blue Lodges were all bent on pushing the Nation into the Southern Rights camp. (He did not mention that the southern slaveholders were themselves frightened by the strong showing of the new Republican Party in 1856 and its "free soil' platform.)

Because Baptists from the Pea Vine Church and other northern Baptist churches were running for election to the council in these years, religion and politics entered the hustings. "In every political election," Jones wrote in July 1858, "whenever a [Cherokee] Baptist happens to be a candidate for office, he is opposed as an abolitionist and sometimes successfully opposed on the ground only."[36] Jones probably referred to the defeat of Lewis Downing in his bid for reelection to the council in August 1857. Other Baptist Cherokees who ran for office in these years were Henry Davis, Smith Christie, David Foreman, Toostoo, Tannenole, and Budd Gritts. They did not all lose.[37] Jones also noted that the dominance of the proslavery faction in the National Council had led to efforts to clamp down on the northern missionaries: "Attempts have been made to compel us to conform our preaching and practice to the wishes of the slaveholders."[38] The records of the National Council show that in every session from 1855 to 1860, bills were introduced trying to expel or curtail the activities of "abolitionist" missionaries. Several of these passed but were vetoed by John Ross. In 1855 a bill required all missionaries to report their position on slavery to the chief and required the removal from the Nation of any missionary who advised a slave "to the detriment of his master." That this bill was aimed at the Joneses was evident from its preamble, which noted that certain missionaries had expelled church members "because they refused to emancipate their slaves." The Joneses were the only missionaries who had done this.[39]

The connection of all these events and of the troubles in the Pea Vine Church with the founding of the Keetoowah Society (and its rapid expansion through the Nation) was suggested by John Jones in a letter dated November 17, 1859—a letter that, when later published in the *Baptist Missionary Magazine,* led to his expulsion from the Nation:

> The Pea Vine Church has been very much affected by the new form which the opposition to our mission has taken. For many years the slavery question has been agitated here to injure our work and to prejudice the people against us personally as well as against our denomination. But notwithstanding this opposition, we have had free access to the masses of the people and the sentiments we have advocated have found very general favor except among the slaveholders themselves. It was seen that as Baptists increased, so opposition to slavery spread and strengthened. Southern Methodists and the irreligious opposed in vain. But about three years ago certain advocates of slavery conceived the plan of dividing the Baptists on this question. After about two years spent in planning and correspondence, the Southern Baptist Board sent a missionary here by the name of Slover. At first he openly advocated slavery, but finding it not as popular as was supposed, his policy was changed from that of open advocacy of slavery to that of merely encouraging and smoothing it over.
>
> Money has also been lavishly spent in buying up members of our churches. Three members of the Pea Vine Church and one excluded member yielded to the temptation and joined the pro-slavery Baptists as preachers, contrary to their convictions of right. One of these was a deacon, another the clerk of the church and something of a preacher, a third, a young man of considerable intelligence and talent [Thomas Wilkinson];[40] the excluded member was an unscrupulous lawyer. One of these is paid $350.00 per year, the others, $300.00 each.[41] With this force it was thought by some that the antislavery Baptists would soon be overcome, and the [Pea Vine] church and meeting house all go to the South. But the Lord has shown himself to be the guardian of truth and justice. Though these men have drawn away with them some ten or fifteen members and have baptized perhaps as many more, yet we think on the whole that the opposition to slavery has been strengthened by the very means employed to destroy that opposition. It was so plain that these men were bought that many turned away in disgust.[42]

In this same letter John Jones mentioned a surprising new phenomenon among the full-bloods—the rise of a spontaneous movement in 1858–59 against the proslavery party in the Nation. Jones did not refer to the Keetoowah Society, but he must have had it in mind. "Young men sprang up from obscurity and urged upon the people the sin of slavery more clearly and efficiently than ever before. Many also who were always opposed to it had their own sentiments more sharply defined in their own minds. We were expecting this division to effect our missionary Society very disadvantageously, but at the annual meeting we found the contributions of the Pea Vine church, where we expected the most effects, were larger than usual." [43] He also mentioned that he and the native ministers of his churches were traveling about "near the extreme western edge" of the Nation (near the Creek border) to counter the efforts of the southern Baptists. "Brother Downing [pastor of the Pea Vine Church] also, while accompanying the Principal Chief [Ross] to a council with the Osage Indians, passed through this country and held several meetings. . . . Toostoo, pastor of the [Baptist] church at Delaware Town, made arrangements for visiting the whole region once a month." When he could not go, he sent "the young men belonging to his church around to have meetings in every prominent neighborhood. . . . It ha[d] been determined to ordain a Cherokee brother, Henry Davise [Davis] as an evangelist and send him to this part of the country." [44] This may be the origin of the statements by Mac-Gowan and Mooney that the Keetoowah Society's efforts "extended to the Creeks." [45] In any case, it is clear from this letter that by 1859 the Joneses and their native preachers were engaged in an active counterattack against the slaveholders, the southern missionaries, and the Blue Lodges. Their movement also had ethnic and class implications.

Following John Brown's raid on Harper's Ferry in October 1859, hysteria over abolitionism permeated the whole Southwest; the presence of abolitionists as successful as the Joneses in what was considered part of "the South" (south of 36°30′) made them a focal point of attack from proslavery forces in Arkansas. John Jones said, "On account of our position on the slavery question, we also have to contend with strong opposition from many of the politicians both in the Cherokee Nation and the State of Arkansas. The border papers vilify us and stigmatize us as abolitionists and some of the slaveholders threaten us with the fist and the cowhide." [46] A prominent proslavery Cherokee said the Joneses would be driven out "if they had to resort to a mob to accomplish" it. [47]

When Agent Butler sent a sheriff to give Jones an order to leave the Nation in October 1859, Jones apparently called upon the full-bloods in the vicinity (presumably members of the Keetoowah Society) to intimidate him. The sheriff "was deterred from executing the order by fear of the common people," Jones wrote; they apparently surrounded the mission in a crowd preventing the sheriff from entering. "Anti-slavery principles both religious and political are taking a strong hold upon the Cherokee mind," Jones said.[48] Nevertheless, in November 1859, a bill was introduced into the council then in session "imitating the laws recently passed by some of the southern states expelling all the free Negroes from Cherokee soil. . . . It was, however, prevented from becoming law by the veto of John Ross, that most excellent and worthy man." Thus was the Cherokee government prevented from "following the cruel and inhuman example of some southern states."[49] The fact that the lower house, where full-bloods held a majority, supported this law indicates that they too shared a dislike for freed slaves.

The Keetoowah Society's Constitution of 1858

The Joneses were in sufficient difficulty from 1855 to 1860, even with their own mission board, to make no overt reference to the Keetoowah Society in any of their letters. Moreover, to do so would have broken the pledge of secrecy and weakened their best source of support. Knowing that their letters were subject to publication in the *Baptist Missionary Magazine*, they emphasized their struggle to expand their conversions and their dedication to antislavery. However, while these provide evidence of the spirit of the antislavery forces in these years, the crucial source of the origin and purposes of the Keetoowah Society rests in the document headed "Keetoowah Laws" (as appended to Howard Q. Tyner's thesis).[50] These laws consist of three different kinds of records. The first, which Tyner heads "Deliberation," is a short statement by Budd Gritts describing the decision taken on April 15, 1858, "to devise a plan" to organize the Cherokees in order to confront the many-sided crisis facing the Nation. The second part of the laws is a small group of statements that Tyner calls the "constitution" that Gritts drew up and presented to the originators of the society on April 20, 1858, and that was then adopted at the first national Keetoowah Convention on April 29, 1859. The third section contains a list of the "resolutions" or "regulations" passed at various intervals by various district and national conventions of the Keetoowah Society in the years 1860, 1861, and 1866.[51]

It is necessary to give part one, Budd Gritts's preliminary statement, in full, for it clarifies many aspects that historians have debated for so long with regard to the reasons for founding the Keetoowah Society. For example, its reference to the "reckless" or thoughtless behavior of certain Cherokees who were "taking sides with the South" and thereby abetting "those who owned Negro slaves" to assert control of the Nation may well refer both to the Blue Lodges and to its successor, the Knights of the Golden Circle, as well as to those Baptists at the Pea Vine Church who gave up their antislavery views to join Slover and the southern Baptists. Gritts's statement also links the founding of the society to the efforts of the federal agent and the proslavery faction in the council to drive the Joneses out of the Nation, for he says that the organizers of the society wished to protect "the teachers from the North" who were being "objected to and were being forced out of the Cherokee Nation." Gritts says many of the founders of the Keetoo-wahs believed that "if the Missionaries were gone, all the Cherokee people would go to the side of the South."

However, Gritts's statement must be read with caution. He is writing as a Baptist and close friend of the Joneses, but ultimately there may have been as many non-Christian full-bloods in the Keetoowah Society as there were Christians. More important, the internal evidence suggests that this statement was not written in 1858 but some time afterward, perhaps as late as 1866. Consequently Gritts may be reading back into the early discussions of the founders a prescience of the future that they did not have, or he may have been writing more for those who read it in 1866 than for those in 1858. His statement that "a small number of leading members of Keetoowah got together" on April 15, 1858, seems to imply that the Keetoowah Society already had members and leaders by that date who may have been meeting together and discussing the Nation's problems for some time. This meeting was not the first of its kind but simply the meeting that decided it was time to organize "confidential lodges" beyond the range of the Pea Vine congregation or the Flint and Going Snake and Delaware Districts and beyond the members of the Baptist denomination.

> On April 15, 1858, a small number of leading members of Keetoowahs got together and discussed the affairs of the Cherokees, the purpose and objectives for which they had always stood. They discussed what the final result probably would be caused by the existing state of affairs in the United States. The people of the United States were divided and it was clear they were about to fight. The Cherokees were situated too far in the South and the men were becoming reckless and seemed to be

taking sides with the South, but the leading cause was those who owned Negro slaves. It was plain the teachers from the North were objected to and were being forced out of the Cherokee Nation.[52] They believed if the Missionaries were gone all the Cherokee people would go to the side of the South, but they were mistaken. These matters were already understood by the Keetoowahs, and the Keetoowahs felt sure what the final result would be. They knew the relative members of the several states. It seems certain that the states of the South were entering into a conspiracy to abandon the union of states to set up a separate government. Keetoowahs had already studied their means of defense and knew the business followed by them.

We had already studied all about them; we decided best to affiliate with the North. I was then and there appointed to devise some plan that would be best for the Cherokee people and should place us in control of the Cherokee government. We fixed for the next meeting, April 20, 1858. On that day, I submitted my report or draft of a paper I had written. Also I made some remarks of explanation, all of which was in the dark of the night and in the woods. The report was approved and declared to be the law.

We felt confident it would be acceptable to the Cherokee people and we informed them and it was accepted all over the Cherokee Nation by confidential lodges.

The following year there was a general convention of the several districts and it was adopted there April 29, 1859.[53]

Obviously considerable thought and some organization preceded April 1858, more coherent bodies of members were formed into lodges in "distinct districts" in the year 1858–59.[54] At that time the two avowed aims of the organization were "to affiliate with the North" and to wrest control of the National Council from "those who owned Negro slaves." Gritts does not say that the society was designed to abolish slavery, although that is the way the Joneses seemed to be heading. The Keetoowah Society in 1858 was trying to head off the Nation's being led to take sides with the South. Implicitly they believed the Nation's security lay in honoring its treaty obligations with the United States.

The three short paragraphs that Gritts drafted for adoption by the organizers of the society on April 20, 1858 (and that were adopted as "the law[s]" of the society at a convention of Keetoowah lodges on April 29, 1859), do not follow the standard construction of a constitution. They constitute a set of general principles for a political movement—not unlike the Declaration of Independence or the social manifesto of a voluntary reform society. In effect, this was a Cherokee effort to define how a true Cherokee should think, feel, and act at this moment of national crisis.

> As lovers of the government of the Cherokees, loyal members of Keetoo-wah Society, in the name of the mass of the people, we began to study and investigate the way our nation was going on, so much different from the long past history of our Keetoowah forefathers who loved and lived as free people and have never surrendered to anybody. They loved one another, for they were just like one family, just as if they had been raised from one family. They all came as a unit to their fire to smoke, to aid one another, and to protect their government with what little powder and lead they had to use in protecting it.

This was an appeal to the old and ancient Kituwah spirit that, according to legend, had been at the basis of the Cherokees' social order long before the Europeans invaded their world. The belief that they were just like a family (as all are descended from Adam and Eve for Christians) stemmed from their own sacred myth that all Chero-kees originated from one pair, Selu, the Corn Mother, and Kanati, the hunter father.[55] To hark back to this idea of who was a true Cherokee was a means of transcending the differences between political parties and factions. It is a significant omission that no reference was made to the original seven clans of the Nation.[56] The "law" of Cherokee unity and love is a plea for national harmony, but because the Cherokees were now following a different concept of nationality—a more Euro-American one—with a written constitution, treaties, national bound-aries, and a centralized, democratically elected, bicameral legislature, the language of the manifesto had to be more abstract.

The second paragraph of Gritts's "law" contained some of the spe-cific grievances of the common people and patriot leaders. It identified enemies and described fatal tendencies of those who had lost the true Kituwah spirit:

> Now let us Cherokees study the condition of our government. We are separated into two parts and cannot agree and they [slaveholders? mixed-bloods? English-speakers?] have taken the lead of us. It is clear to see that the Federal Government [the United States] has two political parties, North and South. South are the people who took our lands away from us which lands the Creator had given to us, where our forefathers were

raised. Their greed was the worst kind; they had no love, and they are still following us to put their feet on us to get the last land we have. It is plain that they have come in on us secretly, different organizations are with them and they have agreed to help one another in everything. They control our political offices because our masses of people are not organized.

The sin of slavery is again conspicuously absent from the above list of grievances.[57] But the sense of past wrongs and a present conspiracy once again to take away their land is strong. For good reason "they [who] have taken lead of us" is left vague. Seeking to unite the whole Nation, the Keetoowahs shifted the blame to outsiders, the white southerners who had insinuated secret organizations among them to destroy the Nation. They were the same white people who took their ancient homeland in Georgia and who are once again on their frontier, greedy for more land. Those who cared to identify these conspirators with the old Ridge-Boudinot party, those who made the false removal treaty of 1835 with Andrew Jackson, were free to do so. But most good Cherokees were simply misinformed or had been confused in voting such people into the council.

The third and final paragraph in the "law" defined the organizational structure that would inform and unite the people.

> We therefore now declare and bind ourselves together the same as under our oaths, to abide by our laws and assist one another. There must be a confidential captain and lodges in numerous places and confidential meetings, the time and place to be designated by the captains. But we shall continue on making more laws. If any member divulges any secret to any other organization, it shall be considered that he gave [forfeited] thereby his life. But every time they meet, they must fully explain what their society stands for. They must have a membership role in order to reorganize [recognize] one another.[58]

On this note of secrecy and organization the so-called constitution of the Keetoowahs ends—as of April 1858. Significantly there is no definition of membership other than presumed agreement with the principles in these paragraphs. The leaders were clearly young full-bloods, but they were more sophisticated in the ways of politics than their parents and grandparents had been. They are relying on organization and appeal to transcendent ideas and to the leadership of those who have thought over the crisis and how to deal with it. Ray

Fogelson has suggested that the use of the term "captains" rather than chiefs, warriors, or headmen to designate the leaders may derive from the term *skagusta*, the name used to define a war chief or the head of the traditional cooperative work organizations called *gadugi*. Those who led the various contingents of Cherokees westward on the Trail of Tears were also called "captains," which indicates a civil, not a military, campaign and one in which the captain assumes responsibility for a wide range of duties to assist a civilian population.[59] Clearly the Keetoowah Society was not planning a military revolution but one of education, propaganda, and the use of the ballot box, just as, in the United States, the Republican Party was trying to use the electoral process to solve the slavery crisis.

In the Tyner document, eight paragraphs follow this brief "constitution" (numbered 4–11). They are each dated and constituted new "laws" or "regulations" adopted by a Keetoowah convention that took place secretly at Tahlequah between September 11 and 20, 1860. These eight paragraphs are followed by six (numbered 12–17) that appear to have been adopted by a previous convention on March 5, 1860. There is no explanation for why the September resolutions precede those of March. Next are two paragraphs (18–19) adopted at a "District Convention" dated June 20, 1860. These are followed by four paragraphs (20–23) dated September 20, 1860, that may be part of the group adopted at Tahlequah, and then four (24–27) dated December 18, 1860, and adopted at a convention whose location is not given. It seems best to consider these in chronological order rather than numerical so that the evolutionary nature of the various rules may be clear.[60]

The six paragraphs (12–17) grouped under the date March 5, 1860, probably resulted from a district convention. Whether there were by this time nine lodges, one for each electoral district, is not clear. Which district adopted these rules is not specified. Paragraph 12 reiterates the general list of dangers facing the Nation: "The Cherokees were about to disintegrate"; some people "intended to . . . destroy it"; "we resolve to stop from scattering. . . . We must love each other and abide by treaties made with the Federal government . . . we must abide by our constitution and laws. . . . Our society must be called Keetoowah." The rest of the resolutions describe the various duties of lodge captains (or "small captains"), district captains, and head captains and state that lodges must meet "four times a year." Here for the first time, on March 5, 1860, specific membership qualifications are given. Members are to be chosen in terms of "their habits, dependability, upright character and loyalty to [the] nation." More important, the captains (who seem to have been the membership recruiters) "must contact only a full blood Cherokee" (paragraph 17). Here the society adds an ethnic test to its ideological test, although it seems likely that the definition of a full-blood was not genetic but meant a person who spoke primarily or only the Cherokee language.[61]

Of the two resolutions adopted at the convention on June 20, 1860, the more interesting explains that lodges collected dues. Because the average full-blood was too poor to have much cash available, it was resolved, "In paying dues to our lodge the script [scrip] will be acceptable according to its value" (paragraph 18). Scrip was paper money, warrants, or "tickets" issued by the Cherokee treasury in the 1850s when the Nation was in debt by more than $200,000.[62] This scrip quickly fell below par value, but perhaps out of loyalty to the Nation as well as out of consideration to the poorer members, this Keetoowah lodge agreed to accept it as par, at least for the payment of dues.

The most important resolutions adopted in 1860 were those passed at Tahlequah between September 11 and 20 (paragraphs 4–11, 20–23). If normal procedures were followed, the convention was probably attended by the three head captains and three captains from each of the Nation's nine districts. (There is no record of how many attended, but from other information it appears that Lewis Downing, Smith Christie, and Budd Gritts were the three head captains at this time; all of them were northern Baptists.) The Tahlequah Convention adopted a four-point policy:

> First, their [the Keetoowah] constitution and laws are to be most sacred. Second, Federal and Indian treaties will be abided by. Third, in the division between North and South, we should not take sides with either. Fourth, we should not become citizens of the United States.

The policy of neutrality adopted at this time marks an important shift from the decision in 1858 to "affiliate with the North."

The convention then reaffirmed the basic ideals of Keetoowah: "All of the members of our Keetoowah Society shall be like one family . . . we must abide with each other in love. . . . We must not surrender under any circumstances. . . . Our government is being destroyed. We must resort to our bravery to stop it." However, there were several clauses in this paragraph (number 7) that seem to indicate a shift toward traditionalism: "We will from now follow our forefathers' traditions just as they met around their fire and smoked tobacco with joy and loyalty to one another. . . . Anything which may derive from English or white, such as secret organizations, that the Keetoowahs shall not accept or recognize." These statements may reflect a growing number of non-Christians among the membership. There are reports that some Keetoowah meetings included all-night dances and even ball plays.[63] Estimates claim that there were fifteen hundred to two thousand Keetoowah members in 1860; there were only fifteen hundred Baptist converts (though many more attended Baptist meetings); there were twelve thousand or more full-bloods (including women and children). If there was a shift toward traditionalism, it should be noted there was never any effort to criticize, much less repudiate, Christianity.

The only tradition that was specifically included (other than references to the sacred fire and smoking tobacco) was one made at Tahlequah in 1860 urging, "Like our forefathers in olden times . . . [w]hen anyone finished his speech, they all responded as one voice at once without hesitancy . . . we shall all speak [respond] at once, without anybody hesitating, with joy, and say 'woa'" (paragraph 4). An important new element in the definition of fraternalism and love was the addition on September 11, 1860, of a commitment to mutual-aid charitable care for all members:

> We declare this way. . . . When we have funds in our society, there shall be money provided out of our funds to buy medicine for our sick brother. [Also] . . . local captains shall receive benefits from our funds if any one of them should not own a horse and have to borrow. (Paragraph 5)

There is no indication whether the medicine practices were traditional or not. This mutual aid of the society was amplified in a resolution adopted at the Keetoowah convention of September 20, 1860:

> If any Keetoowah should get sick, or unable to take care of himself, all members of Keetoowah society who live nearby, shall look after him and visit him. And in case of the death of any Keetoowah they immediately must notify those that live afar, and those that receive the message, it shall be their duty to come. All brother Keetoowahs shall march in line to the grave following the dead. And each shall take a shovel full of dirt and put it into the grave. (paragraph 23)

Here, as Fogelson says, there are clear elements of the traditional *gadugi* organizations.[64]

The convention at Tahlequah ratified the earlier decision that only full-blood Cherokees were to be recruited for membership, but it went even further: "Only full blood, uneducated, and no mixed blood friends shall be allowed to become a member" (paragraph 6). This added a class test to those of ethnicity and ideology. An "uneducated" Cherokee was someone who could not read or write English, someone who had not attended a mission or public school long enough to be anglicized. Generally speaking, these were the poor of the Nation, small farmers whose parents had not been able to spare them from farmwork for schooling or whose traditionalism held that knowing how to write, read, and speak Cherokee was sufficient to be a good Cherokee.

Two months after the September convention at Tahlequah, Abraham Lincoln was elected. Now the predictions of an imminent division (and destruction) of the Nation in a white man's war seemed about to come true. The Cherokee Nation was also clearly split between the Ross party and the Southern Rights party. The possibility of neutrality seemed unlikely.

Between Lincoln's election in November 1860 and July 15, 1861, seven resolutions were added by various conventions of Keetoowahs. None of these mentioned any major political events—the secession of nine southern states, the formation of the Confederate States of American, Lincoln's inauguration, the firing on Fort Sumter, the early battles of the war. The new rules dealt with tightening up the structure of the society as it increased in size and importance: copies of the society's "laws" were to be provided to every lodge captain, but he was not to lend them out (paragraph 24); the treasurers of each district lodge were to provide reports to the three head captains; the secretary of any convention was to be paid for his services; quorums were set for conventions and procedures outlined for introducing new resolutions. In December 1860 a Keetoowah convention specified that individual members and not the captains were "to bring tobacco to smoke" (paragraph 25). After March 1861 any member who moved from one district to another was to be "given a sealed letter reporting his personal standing and reputation" by his lodge so that he might transfer to a new lodge (paragraph 29). This resembles the method Christian churches used (granting letters of dismission) when a member moved away and wanted to be able to join another church of the same denomination.

Perhaps the most significant new resolution was adopted on July 15, 1861: "If any urgent and important message from the chief of the Cherokee Nation should be received by Head Captains . . . it shall be the duty of the head captains to send out the message to all parts of the Cherokee Nation" (paragraph 30). Apparently as tensions mounted between the prosouthern and pronorthern factions among the Cherokees, Chief Ross wanted to be able to utilize the Keetoowah Society to spread his views and, in turn, to receive their views. Ross was under considerable pressure after January 1861 to sign an alliance with the Confederate States. The new Confederate government sent official agents to discuss the matter with him. It began to appear that if he refused to make an alliance, the mixed-blood, proslavery faction might try to take control of the Nation and make Stand Watie the principal chief. Such an effort might well receive military support from the Confederacy, whose troops were on the neighboring soil of Arkansas. The withdrawal in April of all federal garrisons from all the Indian nations in Indian Territory left those chiefs such as Ross, friendly to the United States, with no source of military support. Ross consequently needed to know whether he could count upon the Keetoowahs to defend him and the Cherokee constitution. Unfortunately no messages from Ross to the head captains have survived; however, they may have been delivered orally by messengers.

On May 17, 1861, Ross officially proclaimed the neutrality of the Cherokee Nation. Little is known of the specific political activities of the Keetoowah Society in the years immediately preceding the Civil War. Its primary task was organization and education. Some reports indicate that by the election of August 1860, the full-bloods had gained control of the National Council, but if so, the council took no action indicating the success of the Keetoowahs in this regard. Leadership remained in Ross's hands. The Keetoowahs simply provided him with the counterforce to balance the prosouthern faction. But meanwhile the secret organizations of the Watie party had made their own effective alliances, both within the Nation and with whites outside it.

Appendix A

I. Keetoowah Laws—April 29, 1859–Jan. 9, 1866.

Deliberation

On April 15, 1858, a small number of leading members of Keetoowahs got together and discussed the affairs of the Cherokees, the purpose and objectives for which they had always stood. They discussed what the final result probably would be caused by the existing state of affairs in the United States. The people of the United States were divided and it was clear they were about to fight. The Cherokees were situated too far in the South and the men were becoming reckless and seemed to be taking sides with the South, but the leading cause was those who owned Negro slaves. It was plain to be seen that Cherokee people without a full understanding were taking sides with the South. It was plain the teachers from the North were objected to and were being forced out of the Cherokee Nation. They believed if the Missionaries were gone all the Cherokee people would go to the side of the South, but they were mistaken. These matters were already understood by the Keetoowahs, and the Keetoowahs felt sure what the final result would be. They knew the relative members of the several states. It seems certain that the states of the South were entering into a conspiracy to abandon the union of states to set up a separate government. Keetoowahs had already studied their means of defense and knew the business followed by them.

We had already studied all about them; we decided best to affiliate with the North. I was then and there appointed to devise some plan that would be best for the Cherokee people and should place us in control of the Cherokee government. We fixed for the next meeting April 20, 1858. On that day I submitted my report or draft of a paper I had written. Also I made some remarks of explanation, all of which was in the dark of night and in the woods. The report was approved and declared to be the law.

We felt confident it would be acceptable to the Cherokee people and we informed them and it was accepted all over the Cherokee Nation by confidential lodges.

The following year there was a general convention of the several districts and it was adopted there April 29, 1859, and it appears on the opposite page.

> I Budd Gritts
> Head Captain Keetoowah
> Cherokee, (Name Keetoowah)

Keetoowah Society constitution and laws from Howard Q. Tyner, "The Keetoowah Society in Cherokee History," master's thesis, University of Tulsa, 1949.

CHAPTER I

1

Cherokee Convention

As lovers of the government of the Cherokees, loyal members of Keetoowah society, in the name of the mass of the people, we began to study and investigate the way our nation was going on, so much different from the long past history of our Keetoowah forefathers who loved and lived as free people and had never surrendered to anybody: They loved one another for they were just like one family, just as if they had been raised from one family. They all came as a unit to their fire to smoke, to aid one another and to protect their government with what little powder and lead they had to use in protecting it.

2

Now let us Cherokees study the condition of our government. We are separated into two parts and cannot agree and they have taken lead of us. It is clear to see that the Federal Government has two political parties, North and South. South are the people who took our lands away from us which lands the Creator had given to us, where our forefathers were raised. Their greed was the worst kind; they had no love and they are still following us to put their feet on us to get the last land we have. It is plain that they have come in on us secretly, different organizations are with them and they have agreed to help one another in everything. They control our political offices because our masses of the people are not organized.

3

We therefore now declare and bind ourselves together the same as under our oaths to abide by our laws and assist one another. There must be a confidential captain and lodges in numerous places and confidential meetings, the time and place to be designated by the captains. But we shall continue on making more laws. If any member divulges any secret to any other organization it shall be considered that he gave up thereby his life. But every time they meet they must fully explain what their society stands for. They must have a membership roll in order to reorganize one another.

Cherokee Convention.

April 29, 1859.

Approved by the National Convention, April 29, 1859—

Chairman

Vice President

Bud Gritts

Secretary

National Convention.

4

It shall be sacred where the brothers hold their meeting; lovers of their government, it shall not be a trifle matter, but they must have happiness, like our forefathers in the olden times that brought joy to anyone that would make a speech to them. When anyone finished his speech they all responded as one voice at once without any hesitancy to anyone. We will revive this practice, and when anyone speaks to us and discusses our laws and when he finishes and says "this is all you shall hear from me," we shall all speak at once without anybody hesitating, with joy, and say "woa."

This law approved September 11, 1860.

CHAPTER II

5

We declare this way in our Keetoowah Council. When we have funds in our society there shall be money provided out of our funds to buy medicine for our sick brother.

Be it further resolved that the local captain shall receive benefits from our funds, if any one of them should not own a horse and have to borrow.

6

Be it further resolved, that the Head Captains shall be the only ones authorized to appoint anyone to contact any candidates for new membership. Only full blood Cherokees uneducated, and no mixed blood friends, shall be allowed to become a member.

CHAPTER III

7

Under the Cherokee Constitution, after confidential conference a number of honored men began to discuss and deliberate and decide to organize secretly among friends whom they love, to help each other in everything. The intention is, first, their constitution and laws are to be most sacred. Second, Federal and Indian Treaties, will be abided by. Third, in the division between North and South, we should not take sides with either. Fourth, we should not become citizens of the United States. Now since these decisions have been made we will from now follow our forefathers' traditions just as they met around their fire and smoked tobacco with joy and loyalty to one another. They had never surrendered. We will also approve same. Our secret society shall be named "Keetoowah." All of the members of our Keetoowah Society shall be like one family. It should be the intention that we must abide with each other in love. Anything which may derive from English or white, such as secret organizations, that the Keetoowahs shall not accept or recognize. Now all above described must be adopted same as under oath to be abided by. We must not surrender under any circumstances until we shall "fall to the ground united." We must lead one another by the hand with all our strength. Our government is being destroyed. We must resort to our bravery to stop it.

8

We must have Head Captains chosen by members of Keetoowah.

9

There must be Captains in each district to supervise the district.

10

And every small lodge must have a captain.

11

Be it further resolved, the national organization of Keetoowah shall have a right to pass the laws in their confidential Council Meeting if it is for the benefit of the Keetoowah Society and if it does not conflict the constitution. Now if anyone takes our confidence lightly and divulges the work we must relinquish his life.

Tahlequah Cherokee Nation, September 20, 1860

CHAPTER IV

12

Few members of men of the society met secretly and discussed the condition of the country where they lived. The name Cherokee was in danger. The Cherokee Nation were about to disintegrate. It seemed intended to drown our Cherokee Nation and destroy it. For that reason we resolve to stop from scattering or forever lose the name of Cherokee. We must love each other and abide by treaties made with the Federal government. We must cherish them in our hearts. Second, we must also abide by the treaties made with other races of people. Third, we must abide by our constitution and laws and uphold the name of the Cherokee Nation. Right here we must endeavor to strengthen our society. Our society must be called Keetoowah. There must be three Head Captains, First, Second, and Third.

13

The Head Captains shall have the authority to appoint the secretary, also to select district captains who shall hold meetings twice a year in their districts, and they shall hold meetings of their lodges four times a year.

14

When the head captains meet they shall have the authority to enact laws of the Keetoowah society. District head captains shall have right to enact law when they deem it to be the best which does not conflict their constitution, but they shall not have a right to change this above law,—which was made at the head office. Any new applicants for membership of the society shall be investigated thoroughly by the society as to their habits, dependability, upright character and loyalty to our nation, before he can be admitted to be a member of a strong united Keetoowah society—to assist each other until they fail. But if any of them should join through fraud and divulges the secret works of Keetoowah and is convicted as such shall not reside or live among all of those Keetoowahs who live in the Cherokee Nations.

15

They must assist in upbuilding to carry on this great declaration. It must not be taken as a trivial matter. It was declared by honored men who live in Cherokee nation. Do you accept it? We the presidents approve it—

Keetoowah Cherokee Convention.

March 5, 1860.

CHAPTER V

16

Keetoowah Society shall extend an opportunity to take in new members, when they are worthy and approved. The Head Captain shall have authority to administer an obligation, or someone he may authorize, by saying "our society is of high standing, we are defender of our nation with our confidential society of Keetoowahs. You are joining a large group of Keetoowahs. You are promising to abide by the laws of this Society during all your life just as we have taken our obligation. We are friends. Is it your wish to take the obligation?" If the answer is yes, the Head Captain then must announce that they be accepted.

17

Be it resolved further by the Keetoowah Convention, we all had the authority to contact any applicant for membership. This practice will be stopped from now on—Captains shall have authority, or whoever they may authorize, to contact any applicants for membership and they must contact only a full blood Cherokee.

March 5, 1860.

CHAPTER VI

18

We hereby resolve by our Keetoowah Convention in paying dues to our lodge the script will be acceptable according to its value.

June 20, 1860.

CHAPTER VII

19

Be it resolved, upon any death of our members, the district captains shall have charge and made a record of it and they shall report same to Keetoowah headquarters every six months.

June 20, 1860.
Chairman—District Convention.

CHAPTER VIII

20

Be it resolved by the Keetoowah Convention that any important record pertaining to Keetoowah society must be written only in Cherokee.

September 20, 1860.
Chairman Convention
Secretary

CHAPTER IX

21

Be it resolved by Keetoowah Convention that the Head Captains who are elected by the Keetoowah Members shall not have a right to discuss or divulge the secrets of Keetoowah Society to any who are not members of our Society. The Head Captains must comply with this law. It shall be their duty to discuss and explain what Keetoowah stands for to the district captains who live in Cherokee Nation. If the district Captains are making any mistake upon their duties they shall take pains to explain to them in the most courteous way, and if any lodge should be weak they shall go visit the lodge and if it is impossible for them to go they should authorize someone to go who could explain thoroughly—

Chairman Convention
Secretary

CHAPTER X

22

Be it resolved by the Keetoowah Convention that the Head Captain of the society elected by the Keetoowah Cherokees and district captains and small captains who reside in different parts shall be captains continued during good behavior and good works, but if they should fail to do their duty could be expelled. If there shall be a vacancy caused by death or otherwise, the captains shall have the authority to fill the vacancy.

September 20, 1860.
Chairman Convention
Secretary.

CHAPTER XI

23

Be it resolved by the Keetoowah Convention, if any Keetoowah should get sick, or unable to take care of himself, all members of Keetoowah society who live nearby, shall look after him and visit him. And in case of the death of any Keetoowah they immediately must notify those that live afar and those that receive the message, it shall be their duty to come. All brother Keetoowahs shall march in line to the grave following the dead. And each shall take a shovel full of dirt and put it into the grave.

September 20, 1860.
Chairman Convention
Secretary.

CHAPTER XII

24

Be it resolved by the Keetoowah Convention, from now on the small captains shall have charge of the laws and shall take care of them as securely as they are able to. If some person who is a member of any other lodge should want to borrow the laws, they should refuse to lend it. When the small captains hold meetings of their lodges they shall read all the laws and they shall explain fully to all the members of Keetoowah. Be it further resolved that the Head Captains shall have the authority to furnish laws to small captains, if they do not have them in their district.

December 18, 1860.
Chairman of the Meeting
Secretary

CHAPTER XIII

25

Be it resolved by the Keetoowah Convention, when the small captains shall hold meetings it shall be the duty of the members to bring tobacco to smoke, so all of the Keetoowah members may smoke of them, but will not require just what size of tobacco they should bring.

December 18, 1860.
Chairman of the Meeting
Secretary

CHAPTER XIV

26

Be it resolved by the Keetoowah Convention from now on that there shall be a treasurer in each district and the district captain shall have authority to appoint a treasurer in his district. The district treasurer shall make reports or turn over the money to the district captain often.

December 18, 1860.
Chairman of the Meeting
Secretary

CHAPTER XV

27

Be it resolved by the Keetoowah convention, that the secretary of the convention shall be paid one dollar for all of the services rendered by him during the meeting and the money shall be paid out of the Keetoowah fund.

December 18, 1860.
Chairman of the Meeting
Secretary

CHAPTER XVI

28

Be it resolved by the Keetoowah Convention, when the district captains are in convention if over half of the members are present they shall notify the head captain that they are ready to transact business, and it shall be the duty of the head captains to deliver a message setting forth the necessary laws to be enacted by the district captains. When the district captains have enacted the laws they must report back to the head captains their acts, then the head captains shall study and examine the laws enacted by the law making body.

March 15, 1860.
Chairman of the Meeting
Secretary

CHAPTER XVII

29

Be it resolved by the Keetoowah Convention, if any Keetoowah member shall remove from one district to another district he shall report to his small captain and show that he is an active member of the district; He shall ask a recommendation from his captain to any other lodge in another district. If he has not shown active interest he shall be given a sealed letter reporting his personal standing and reputation to the district captains in the other district. When the report is received by the other district captains and if they are satisfied with the report they may accept him just like he was a new member of their lodge.

March 5, 1861.
Chairman of the Meeting
Secretary

CHAPTER XVIII

30

Be it resolved by the Keetoowah Convention, if any urgent and important message from the chief of the Cherokee Nation should be received by Head Captains to be looked into, it shall be duty of the head captains to send out the message to all parts of the Cherokee Nation. If anyone, or any one of us Keetoowah is called upon or chosen to take a message for them he shall willingly without hesitancy respond to the responsibility. We shall abide by the wishes of our head captains and remember our obligations as Keetoowahs and to do our part to the best of our ability.

July 15, 1861.
Chairman of the Meeting
Secretary

CHAPTER XIX

31

Be it resolved by the Keetoowah Convention, when the meeting begins they shall appoint a water carrier during the meeting and he shall be paid one dollar for his services.

January 8, 1866.
Chairman
Secretary
I Approve

CHAPTER XX

32

Be it resolved by the Keetoowah Convention, as soon as this law is enacted and shall become a law it will be their duty according to law to visit all the lodges in their respective districts and explain the Keetoowah laws.

Be it further resolved by the Keetoowah convention, that each district captain shall name a small lodge and make up a roll of names of the members of that lodge and report same to the head captains at first meeting held by Keetoowah Convention. The District Captain, or the Secretary, shall call the names on the roll.

Tahlequah Cherokee Nation

January 9, 1866.
Chairman
Secretary

Appendix B

The View of James Mooney

THE KEETOOWAH SOCIETY: This Cherokee secret society, which has recently achieved some newspaper prominence by its championship of Cherokee autonomy, derives its name—properly Kitu-hwa, but commonly spelled Ketoowah in English print—from the ancient town in the old Nation which formed the nucleus of the most conservative element of the tribe and sometimes gave a name to the Nation itself (see Kitu-hwagi, under Tribal Synonyms). A strong band of comradeship, if not a regular society organization, appears to have existed among the warriors and leading men of the various settlements of the Kituwha district from a remote period, so that the name is even now used in councils as indicative of genuine Cherokee feeling in its highest patriotic form. When, some years ago, delegates from the western Nation visited the East Cherokee to invite them to join their more prosperous brethren beyond the Mississippi, the speaker for the delegates expressed their fraternal feeling for their separated kinsmen by saying in his opening speech, "We are all Kituhwa people" (Ani-Kitu-hwagi). The Keetoowah society in the Cherokee Nation west was organized shortly before the civil war by John B. Jones, son of the missionary, Evan Jones, and an adopted citizen of the Nation, as a secret society for the ostensible purpose of cultivating a national feeling among the fullbloods, in opposition to the innovating tendencies of the mixed-blood element. The real purpose was to counteract the influence of the "Blue Lodge" and other secret secessionist organizations among the wealthier, slave-holding classes, made up chiefly of mixed-bloods and whites. It extended to the Creeks, and its members in both tribes rendered good services to the Union cause throughout the war. They were frequently known as "Pin Indians," for a reason explained below. Since the close of the great struggle, the society has distinguished itself by its determined opposition to every scheme looking to the curtailment or destruction of Cherokee national self-government.

James Mooney, *Myths of the Cherokees* (Nashville: Charles and Randy Elder, 1982), 225–26.

Appendix C

The View of Dr. D. J. MacGowan

Those Cherokees who were loyal to the Union continued in a secret organization for self-protection, assuming the designation of the Ketoowha society, which name was soon merged in that of "Pins." The Pins were so styled because of a peculiar manner they adopted of wearing a pin. The symbol was discovered by their enemies, who applied the term in derision; but it was accepted by this loyal league, and has almost superseded the designation which its members first assumed. The Pin organization originated among the members of the Baptist congregation at Peavine, Going-snake district, in the Cherokee Nation. In a short time the society counted nearly three thousand members, and had commenced proselytizing the Creeks, when the rebellion against which it was arming, preventing its further extension, the poor Creeks having been driven into Kansas by the rebels of the Golden Circle. During the war the Pins rendered services to the Union cause in many bloody encounters, as has been acknowledged by our generals. It was distinctly an anti-slavery organization. The slave-holding Cherokees, who constituted the wealthy and more intelligent class, naturally allied themselves with the South, while loyal Cherokees became more and more opposed to slavery. This was shown very clearly when the loyalists first met in convention, in February, 1863. They not only abolished slavery unconditionally and forever, before any slave state made a movement toward emancipation, but made any attempts at enslaving a grave misdemeanor.

The secret signs of the Pins were a peculiar way of touching the hat as a salutation, particularly when they were too far apart for recognition in other ways. They had a peculiar mode of taking hold of the lapel of the coat, first drawing it away from the body, and then giving it a motion as though wrapping it around the heart. During the war a portion of them were forced into the rebellion, but quickly rebelled against General Cooper, who was placed over them, and when they fought against that general, at Bird Creek, they wore a bit of corn-husk, slit into strips, tied in their hair. In the night when two Pins met, and one asked the other, "Who are you?" the reply or pass word was "Tahlequah—who are you?" The response was, "I am Ketoowha's son."

Dr. D. J. MacGowan, "Indian Secret Societies," *Historical Magazine* 10 (1866).

Chapter 10
Political Polarization and National Unity: The Keetoowah Society, 1860-1871

The fate of the Cherokee Nation was intertwined with that of the United States, and the issues of slavery and secession divided Cherokees as much as whites in the North and South. This chapter discusses the growing rift in the Cherokee Nation and the expression of that division in the further development of the Keetoowah Society and the organization of the Knights of the Golden Circle. Entanglement in the Civil War was costly for the Cherokee Nation, and yet despite widespread economic devastation and political animosity, by 1870 a new spirit of reconciliation and unity had emerged.

As the strength of the Keetoowah Society increased, so too did that of its opponents—men of education, wealth, and shrewd political skills. Little is known of the activities of the two Blue Lodges that Chief Ross believed to be operating in the Flint and Saline Districts of the Nation in 1855, but considerable information is known about the Knights of the Golden Circle, which was their successor. Most accounts date the formation of the Knights in the spring of 1859, but its records were secret and few have survived. Its adherents always alleged that it was created to defend the proslavery, prosouthern party from the aggressive behavior of the Keetoowahs. However, the Ridge-Watie-Boudinot party had been working closely together since 1832 when it was known simply as the Ridge-Boudinot party or the Removal party. Its more aggressive members had fomented considerable violence in the internal lawlessness of the Nation from 1839 to 1846; its leaders then had called for a separation of the Nation into two distinct Cherokee Nations each with its own distinct boundaries and government. However, prior to 1855 it had always operated openly, and its able leaders made no effort to hide its goals. From 1846 to 1855 it had abided by the Treaty of 1846, following which Stand Watie, as the new head of the party, had agreed to bury the hatchet and cooperate with the Ross party. During that decade those in the Watie party had contributed greatly to the economic development and political strength of the Cherokees. But after the Kansas-Nebraska Act, this faction had become more strident in its opposition to antislavery agitation, more antagonistic to Ross for protecting northern missionaries such as the Joneses, and more sympathetic with the white slaveholders in the surrounding states who were working frantically to convert Kansas into a slaveholding state. The Watie party frankly took the name "Southern Rights party" in the years preceding the Civil War, but recognizing that its adherents constituted a decided minority and that many of their actions were clearly subversive of the policies of the Ross government (and contrary to federal treaties), its adherents were undoubtedly the first to resort to secrecy. Clearly they put their friendship with the whites of Arkansas ahead of their loyalty to the Nation, and once again the old animosities toward John Ross broke loose.

Apart from the fact that antislavery Cherokees preferred that Kansas be a free state, and apart from the Nation's general concern over what would become of the Neutral Lands once Kansas became a state, the more conservative Cherokees realized that there were many Indian tribes living in Kansas and Nebraska Territories who had been placed on reserves there under treaties with the United States. To support the sanctity of their treaty rights against efforts under way to remove these tribes from Kansas required that the Cherokees themselves uphold their treaty obligations. Or, to put it the other way, the claims for Cherokee sovereignty under their treaty rights required scrupulous adherence to their own allegiance to the United States, and efforts to ally themselves with southern extremists who were already talking about secession would seriously damage their position.

The Knights of the Golden Circle, like the Blue Lodges, were dedicated to opposing abolitionism and promoting the cause of slavery and were fearful that a free state to the north of them would increase the possibility of runaway slaves perhaps aided and abetted by an Underground Railroad network extending to the antislavery Cherokees and missionaries. As in the case of the Blue Lodges, the formation of the Knights of the Golden Circle was instigated by white men from

Arkansas and constituted in effect a league of slavery advocates in that state and those in the Cherokee Nation.

But the Knights had other ramifications. It reflected in its origins the expansionist tendencies of the southern states as they sought more land for growing cotton (which was not apt to be a prime crop in Kansas). The man who first promoted the Knights was George Washington Leigh Bickley of Cincinnati, Ohio (in the prosouthern part of that state along the Ohio River).[1] Bickley started drumming up membership for the Knights (evidently his own invention) in the early 1850s as part of the Know-Nothing, anti-Catholic, anti-Irish movement. But as the Know-Nothing party faded, he switched his interest to colonizing and filibustering efforts in Latin America, taking his cue from the work of William Walker in Nicaragua and Narcisco Lopez in Cuba. Bickley styled himself the "President General of the American Legion, K. G. C." and sold membership in the KGC for ten dollars (mostly as a money-raising scheme for himself). Its membership and activities were secret because it was involved in illegal activities—sending groups of armed Americans into Mexico to settle and eventually to promote revolution and then request annexation by the United States. Bickley was ardently proslavery and tried to raise money chiefly in the South. He also shared the racist views of his day in his belief that the Anglo-Saxons were superior to any other race, especially those of mixed ancestry in Latin America. There is no known specific connection between Bickley and the formation of the KGC in the Cherokee Nation, but it seems likely that members of such an organization in Arkansas took it upon themselves to assist in the formation of such an organization.

No records reveal the names of those who started the first lodge or "encampment" of the Knights in the Cherokee Nation, but it was probably men closely related to the Ridge and Watie families, of whom there were several in Arkansas. Stand Watie was, by most accounts, the person who organized and led the Knights. Among those who may have influenced him were George W. Paschal (a white man from Fort Smith married to John Ridge's sister, Sarah), Elias Cornelius Boudinot of Fayetteville, Arkansas (the embittered son of Elias Boudinot), and Josiah Woodward Washbourne (also of Fayetteville and married to John Ridge's daughter, Susan). John Rollin Ridge, the son of John Ridge, though living in California as a newspaper editor in the late 1850s, was a member and ardent supporter of the Knights and used his newspaper to attack the Joneses, Ross, and the Keetoowahs.[2] Among the leading figures said to be members of the Knights in the Cherokee Nation were James M. Bell, William Penn Adair, Joseph A. Scales—all leaders of the Southern Rights party. When Stand Watie became principal chief of the Cherokee Nation in August 1862, after Ross went into exile, there ceased to be any need for the Knights, and it may no longer have kept any records.[3]

However, a copy remains of the "constitution" of the Knights of the Golden Circle as it was adopted in the Cherokee Nation. It is dated August 28, 1860, but there is general agreement that it was probably founded at least a year earlier. Its preamble reads, "We, a part of the people of the Cherokee Nation, in order to form a more perfect union and protect ourselves and property against the works of Abolitionist[s]—do establish this Constitution for the government of the Knights of the Golden Circle in this Nation."[4]

The various articles of the constitution laid out the membership qualifications and purposes of the organization: "No person shall be a member of the Knights of the Golden Circle in the Cherokee Nation who is not a pro-slavery man." "No person shall become a member of this order unless he be a citizen of the United States or of the Cherokee Nation." (This may have indicated joint membership by whites in Arkansas and Cherokees in the Nation.) "Each Encampment [lodge, branch] shall choose its own officers . . . by ballot." The constitution envisioned vigilante action and gave each encampment the right to act against abolitionists on its own vote: "The Captain, or in case of his refusal, then the Lieutenant has the power to compel each and every member of their Encampments to turn out and assist in capturing and punishing any and all abolitionist[s] in their minds who are interfering with slavery." The organization prescribed a treasurer and secretary for each encampment, but no officer was to receive any personal compensation. An oath of membership said, "You do solemnly swear that you will keep all the secrets of this order and that you will, to the best of your abilities, protect and defend the interest of the Knights of the Golden Circle in this Nation, so help you God." One scrap of material, dated April 29, 1861, gives a list of persons seeking admission to the organization at that time: J. L. Martin, J. S. Knight, J. M. Lynch, Jr., J. L. Butler, Thos. L. Rogers, L. R. Kell (all active supporters of the Watie party). Otherwise no membership lists are extant.

Long before 1859 the Southern Rights party of the Nation was aware of the organized effort by the full-bloods to take control of the Nation, but they were generally referred to as the "secret fellows" or "secret society." A letter from William P. Adair to Stand Watie in July 1860 indicates the rising tension in the Nation as these two secret societies began to confront each other. The letter concerned two men named George Smith and Charles Rooster who had committed some crime and were arrested by the Cherokee police—the lighthorse. But Adair charged that the leader of the lighthorse, Cah-Skey-Neh or Mankiller, had let them escape and that they were being protected, hidden in the homes of the "secret fellows" (the Keetoowahs) because they were members of that society. The crime they committed was evidently against one of Watie's party because Adair was very upset by their escape from justice:

> Geo. Smith and Chas. Rooster *did* give up, but Cah-Skey-Neh Mankiller, a Lieutenant of the Light Horse, permitted them to walk off without inter-ruption. Fifty men with guns appeared to watch after Geo. Smith and Chas. Rooster to *protect* them, though unauthorized by law. These fifty men were "Secret" men, and seemed to present rather a *defiant* front. . . . They are attempting to run over everything that is in any way connected with us. Men from all parts of the Nation (I mean these "Secret fellows") seem to take a hand in working for Smith and Rooster; Jo Shears and Jack Shears, and Geo. Scraper, etc. etc.—are doing all they can. The pris-oners are again in the woods—or rather in some of the houses of some of these "Secret fellows." . . . These *Secret* men have preferred charges against Stan Adair as Sheriff, and on yesterday, we preferred charges against Mankiller . . . for letting Smith and Rooster get away. . . . Times are exciting. Our friends must work. They must. We need not expect any quarter from our enemies.[5]

Soon after this the Keetoowahs became known as the "Pin Indians" or "the Pins." The formation of these two secret societies marked a hard-ening of the two existing factions in the Nation or, more accurately, a more cohesive formal organization of the activists in each faction. It clearly resembled the political polarization taking place in the United States in these years, revealing how intricately connected the Chero-kees' lives had become with those of white Americans. The full-bloods were no better able to keep separated than the mixed-bloods.

Because the "abolitionists" whom southern whites and Cherokee slaveholders most feared in the Nation were generally identified as the northern missionaries of the American Baptist Missionary Union and the American Board of Commissioners for Foreign Missions (both based in Boston), the focus of Cherokee attention was upon them. For five years, from 1855 to 1860, the National Council annually debated bills to restrict or expel these missionaries on the grounds that they were not just preaching the gospel but "meddling in politics." At every session some bill of this kind was introduced and passed by both houses of the Cherokee legislature only to be vetoed by John Ross. His vetoes proved impossible to override because of the loyalty of the full-bloods in the lower house to Ross's leadership.[6]

The missionaries of the American Board (mostly New England Congregationalists), led by the Reverend Samuel A. Worcester, stoutly denied that they were "abolitionists," admitting only that they were morally opposed to slavery as an institution but had no intention of trying to interfere with its existence. The Baptists, led by Evan and John B. Jones, held basically the same position. Evan Jones told his board that he never preached against slavery. But because Jones had—at his board's insistence—dismissed from church membership the four out of his eleven hundred converts who were slaveholders, he was clearly marked as a missionary who applied a political test for church membership. Moreover, in a quiet way, the Joneses did take a more active part in opposing slavery in the Nation. They clearly inculcated antislavery views into those Cherokees they trained and ordained for the ministry.

But there was a fourth party to this controversy beyond the Ross faction, the Watie faction, and the missionaries; that was the Bureau of Indian Affairs. It was the practice in federal appointments to make positions in the Indian Bureau matters of political patronage, and because the Democrats held power far more frequently than the Whigs after 1828, virtually all of the appointments—from that of secretary of the interior and commissioner of Indian Affairs down to the resident agents in each tribe—were Democrats. Moreover, since it was politically expedient to appoint as superintendents and agents persons approved by the political leaders of the states adjacent to the Indian tribes as the frontier moved forward, these offices were held by southerners and proslavery men. Virtually every agent to the Cherokees in these years was an ardent prosouthern man who owned slaves and brought his own slaves with him into the Nation. Agent George M. Butler, of a prominent South Carolina family, worked steadily to persuade the commissioner of Indian Affairs to expel Worcester and the

Joneses from the Cherokee Nation.[7] When Samuel Worcester died in 1859, his mission board was so deeply embroiled in the slavery controversy that it not only closed its Cherokee mission but also closed all its other missions with slaveholding tribes.

Agent Robert Cowart, from Georgia, who replaced Butler in 1860, concentrated his attention upon the Joneses. In this he was aided by the Knights of the Golden Circle, the Watie party, the whites in Arkansas (especially the newspaper editors), and the prosouthern commissioners and superintendents of the Indian Office; ultimately the secretary of the interior, Jacob Thompson, added his weight to Cowart's efforts. John Ross did all he could to help the Joneses, but John B. Jones inadvertently provided the cause for his own eviction in 1860. He allowed the *Baptist Missionary Magazine* to publish a letter in May 1860 in which he admitted that he and his father were strongly opposed to slavery and said that for this they were being persecuted by Cherokee slaveholders and whites in Arkansas: "On account of our position on the slavery question . . . the border papers vilify us and stigmatize us as abolitionists and some of the slaveholders threaten us with the fist and the cowhide."[8] In other letters to his board in Boston, Jones had indicated that slaveholders threatened "resort to a mob" against him and his father and that some secret parties were breaking up his revival meetings. The Reverend Willard Upham, a fellow Baptist missionary in the Nation, reported that the council was trying to take away his position as a teacher in one of the national schools; he also said that the Joneses had become fearful of riding about the countryside to their various churches because their lives were in danger.

However, the Keetoowahs had come to the assistance of the Joneses. They drove off those who tried to interfere with their religious services, and when Agent Butler sent a Cherokee sheriff to arrest John Jones for questioning about his activities in 1859, the sheriff "was deterred from executing the order by fear of the common people" who apparently gathered around to prevent the arrest.[9]

Cowart was assisted in his efforts to expel Jones by Elias Cornelius Boudinot, editor of the *Arkansan*, a fire-eating, proslavery paper in Fayetteville, Arkansas, as well as by Stand Watie and W. P. Adair. Boudinot saw Jones's letter in the *Baptist Missionary Magazine*, published it, and sent a copy to Cowart, indicating that it clearly showed that the Joneses were meddling in politics.[10] Watie and Adair then started a petition circulating among the Knights of the Golden Circle calling for the eviction of John B. Jones from the Nation as an "Abolitionist fanatic of the North."[11] When Cowart received the petition, it had five hundred signatures. To his mind this represented the will of the Nation (although the council itself had taken no action). On September 7, 1860, Cowart wrote to Jones:

> I learn from an article published in the *Arkansan* on the 14th of July last, that you are engaged in propagating abolition or anti-slavery sentiments among the Cherokees. . . . Added to the above, I have petitions by some 500 citizens asking your removal from the Cherokee Nation. You are therefore notified and required to leave the said Cherokee Nation by the 25th of this present month . . . otherwise Military Force will be employed to remove you.[12]

Evan Jones immediately went to see Chief Ross to ask his help, but Ross said it was too touchy a matter for him to become involved in. Because a military force would have escorted Jones to the Arkansas border, where he expected a mob of Arkansans to tar and feather him, Jones, with his wife and children, took a wagon in the night and, escorted by some of the Keetoowahs, made his way secretly to Missouri and then Illinois. His father remained behind.

When Cowart arrived in the Nation in June 1860, he had orders from the secretary of the interior, Jacob Thompson, to root out the Keetoowah Society. The commissioner of Indian Affairs, A. B. Greenwood, ordered Cowart to discover who "the counselors of this secret organization" were and who its members were and then to "proceed at once to break it up."[13] Cowart succeeded in getting rid of Jones (a presumed "counselor"), but he could not root out the Keetoowahs. After considerable effort, he told Greenwood, he was unable "to get anything that would do for proof . . . as regards those Secret Societies" and their "abolition plans."[14] Once Abraham Lincoln was elected, in November 1860, and the secession of the southern states began, the Cherokees came under increasing pressure from those in the states bordering Indian Territory to make their own position clear. The governors of Arkansas and Texas sent letters and emissaries to demand of John Ross that he express his support for southern rights, fearing that if he sided with the Union, his "warriors" might join with other Indians in a general uprising against the frontier. After the Confederate States of America was formed in February 1861, it appointed its

own Indian agents to negotiate treaties with all the Indian nations on
its western borders. Ross managed to fend off all of these overtures by
saying he wished to remain neutral (although he added that he had
signed treaties with the United States that he was obliged to honor).
He added, however, that as a slaveholding nation, the Cherokees had
much in common with the South and would take no action against it.
After Fort Sumter was fired upon in April and war was declared, Ross
issued a formal proclamation of neutrality.[15]

However, the Indian agent of the Confederacy, Albert Pike, was
successful in making treaties of alliance with all the other slaveholding
tribes (the Creeks, Choctaws, Chickasaws, and Seminoles). To add further pressure on Ross, Pike made secret arrangements with the Watie
party, which was eager for an alliance with the Confederacy. Watie
(again with assistance from white relatives and friends in Arkansas)
was provided with guns and ammunition for a volunteer force of
mounted Cherokees, ostensibly designed to protect the Nation and
border states from an invasion from Kansas. But the more important
function of Watie's volunteers was to threaten the Ross government
with a coup d'état if it did not soon change its mind about allying
with the South. This led to a dangerous and, for Ross, frightening,
confrontation between Watie's volunteers and the Keetoowahs late in
June 1861. Ross received word of it from Dr. James P. Evans, who was
visiting Webber's Falls where the confrontation took place. Evans was
a Watie man and evidently expected Ross to take action against the
Keetoowahs. "It seems," he wrote to Ross on July 2, "that on Saturday
last, the fragment of a Captain's company, met, as was their custom,
for the purpose of drilling and perhaps raising a flag of the Confederate States."[16] Clearly the company was part of Watie's volunteers.
Webber's Falls, at the fork of the Arkansas and Canadian Rivers, was a
stronghold for the Watie party, but the Keetoowahs had also organized
there, and through their efforts William Doublehead, a Ross man,
had been elected to the Cherokee Senate from the Canadian District.[17]
Evans's letter continued, "Before either object was accomplished, a
considerable number of full-blood Cherokees (estimated at one hundred and fifty) appeared upon the ground, armed and painted, under
the lead of Doublehead. I was informed a somewhat friendly conference took place, except that Doublehead accused Mr. Scales [the
leader of the troops] and perhaps others, of having threatened his life
and the company were deter[r]ed from raising the flag."

A day or two later, "Doublehead being from home, his wife left her home hurriedly and afterwards declared that a squad of armed men came to the house after night for the purpose of killing her husband." Evans said that Mrs. Doublehead probably mistook a squad of Albert Pike's Confederate troops, seeking food and whiskey, for a hostile mob, but that no real threat had been made against Doublehead. Evans learned, however, that "Dick Crossel and Doublehead, both had large body guards, that runners had gone out in every direction for the full-bloods, with the declaration that the half-breeds were all to be killed within ten hours." William Holt, a leader of the Watie faction in the area, "was very much excited" about this and "declared that if the tumult on the part of the fullbloods was not quelled in a short time, the halfbreeds would take the matter in their own hands and defend themselves, and if that should take place [in Webber's Falls] . . . the excitement consequent upon it would spread like wild-fire."

On the same day that Ross received this message, he dispatched a letter to John Drew, who was married to Ross's niece, Mary Coody; Drew was a slaveholder and friendly toward the Watie party, but his relationship to Ross made him loyal and dependable to Ross. Ross was extremely worried that fighting might break out at any time between the Knights of the Golden Circle and the Keetoowahs. He believed this would polarize the Nation and give Watie and Albert Pike the excuse to depose him and install Watie as chief. In his letter to Drew he wrote, "The object of this communication is to . . . ask your kindly interference to secure an amicable adjustment of the affair. We greatly regret to hear of difficulties among our people at any time and particularly so at the present time, when surrounded by the Commotions that exist among the People of the States. Please impress upon your neighbors the importance of harmony and good feeling and of avoiding every cause of dissension." [18]

Drew did manage to make peace in Webber's Falls, but two weeks later, Stand Watie was commissioned a colonel in the Confederate Army.[19] This should have been grounds for treason, but Ross dared not act against Watie. He had no forces to call upon other than the private society of Keetoowahs, whose existence he did not acknowledge at this time. Abraham Lincoln, after his inaugural on March 4, had sent a new agent to replace Cowart, but the man he appointed, John Crawford, was an ardent supporter of the Confederacy. And even had Crawford been inclined to support Ross against Watie, he had no United States troops to call upon, for in April, all troops in the Indian nations of Indian Territory had been withdrawn.

The Keetoowahs under Doublehead were officially correct in preventing the raising of a Confederate flag in the Nation, but they were not a legally recognized body. They were, however, ready to take the law into their own hands when threatened. Such a case occurred in that same month, June 1861, when one of their members withdrew from the Keetoowah organization and seemed likely to reveal its objectives and membership to the Watie party. The man was a Baptist preacher, probably one of those whom James Slover had converted to southern Baptist principles (perhaps Young Duck). The Reverend Henry F. Buckner, another southern Baptist missionary to the Cherokees, wrote a friend about the incident on June 26, 1861. He blamed "Jones and party" for the man's death.

> The Native minister, an inoffensive and pious man, was murdered— called out of his own house at night and shot; he ran—they followed and cut his throat. The cause is hard to ascertain. Three rumors here: 1st, Because he would not leave the Southern Baptist Church . . . 2nd, Because he had withdrawn from a secret organization known here by the term 'Pins,' he refusing to be united [with them] again; 3rd, Because of his money, of which everybody that knew him knew that he did not have a *red* [cent].[20]

Buckner thought the first cause was "the most plausible," believing that the Joneses, being "abolitionists," would resort to violence to stop the spread of the southern Baptist cause. But it seems more likely that the Keetoowahs, being unable to persuade the man to rejoin the society, feared that he might reveal its secrets and thus enable the new federal agent to do what Cowart had been unable to do, root it out with hard evidence. And if the agent did nothing, the Knights of the Golden Circle might start "calling out" Keetoowah leaders from their homes at night, as William Doublehead's wife suspected them of doing.

Buckner provides good evidence of the increasing tensions in the Nation in the advice he gave to a fellow minister, E. L. Compere, who was about to enter the Nation to join him. He told Compere not to travel through "the Southern part of the nation" near Lee's Creek and Flint District, for that was "the stronghold of these" Pin Indians.

However, farther west, "South of the Arkansas River" in the Canadian District and "from Fort Smith up the River to Webbers Falls," it was safe for a prosouthern Baptist to preach.[21]

Two major defeats for the Union Army that summer (one at Bull Run in Virginia on July 10 and one at Wilson's Creek or Oak Hills in western Missouri on August 10) led John Ross to believe that the United States might not win the war. Ross could not understand why no federal troops had been sent from Kansas to protect the Cherokee Nation. In June 1861, Evan Jones had left the Nation for Kansas, and it seems likely that he went as an emissary from Ross to find out just when the Cherokees might expect help. With Watie's troops policing the northern frontier of Kansas, it was not easy for Jones or any federal official to get word to Ross about the progress being made to send an expeditionary force into Indian Territory. Kansans were eager to do so because they feared either a Confederate invasion or, more likely, a combined Indian attack inspired by the Confederacy.

By the end of August, having heard nothing from Jones or the United States Indian Office, Ross concluded that he would have to abandon neutrality and, at least as a temporary expedient, make an alliance with the Confederacy. It was a gamble, but his chances of remaining in power much longer were rapidly diminishing, and he dreaded the possibility of a civil war between the Keetoowahs and Watie's regiment. He and his executive committee had decided on July 28 to call a council of the people to meet on August 20 "for harmonizing their views in support of the common good and to remove false allegations as to the opinions of the 'full blood' Cherokees on the subject of slavery and of their sentiments towards the white and 'Half breed' citizens."[22]

On August 10, Watie's regiment had taken part in the Confederate victory at the Battle of Wilson's Creek, and Watie seemed to many to be a heroic figure. Consequently, when the popular council met at Tahlequah on August 20–21, it agreed that for the sake of unity and harmony so essential to the Nation's survival, it would grant Ross the power to do whatever he thought best, even if that meant signing a treaty with the Confederacy. Ross had told them, "Union is strength; dissension is weakness, misery, ruin."[23] The Keetoowah Society may have understood that Ross was likely to make a treaty with the Confederacy only to bide for time until a federal army could enter the Nation. Or it may have simply decided to trust Ross to do what was best for the Nation. Certainly such a treaty would strengthen Ross's leadership and weaken the case for a coup d'état by the Watie faction. This was also the view of Watie's closest supporters. Two of them, W. P. Adair and James M. Bell, wrote to Watie after the council, "You have doubtless heard all about Ross's Convention, which in reality tied up our hands and shut our mouths. . . . The Pins already have more power in their hands than we can bear, and if, in addition to this, they acquire the treaty making power, you know our destiny will be unalterably sealed."[24]

In fact, the Watie party felt so desperate at this time that some of its members advised Watie to use his troops to take over the Nation at once so that he could have "the treaty making power." It was essential, Adair and Bell said, to "have this pin party broken up." "Now is the time for us to strike, or we will be completely frustrated."[25]

Their suspicions were correct. Ross intended to use the treaty to provide himself with an armed force to counter Watie's regiment. In a letter to General Benjamin F. McCulloch, the commandant of the Confederate forces in the West, on August 24, he said, "We have deemed it prudent to proceed to organize a regiment of mounted men and tender them for service. They will be raised forthwith by Col. John Drew."[26] Ross knew that the Keetoowahs would be the first to volunteer to serve under Drew, for that would legitimate them as an official arm of the Ross government. Ross also specified to McCulloch that Drew's regiment was to be used only "for service on [the Nation's] northern border" against a Union invasion. And when the treaty was drawn up and signed on October 7, Ross was given promises that the Cherokee regiment would not have to fight outside the Nation or against other Indians. Whether McCulloch knew that Drew's regiment consisted of Keetoowahs is not clear, but he did report, "Colonel Drew's Regiment will be mostly composed of full-bloods, whilst those of Col. Stand Watie will be half-breeds, who are educated men and good soldiers."[27]

The Knights of the Golden Circle were not disbanded after Watie became colonel of the Confederate volunteers any more than the Keetoowah Society was abandoned after the formation of Colonel Drew's regiment. The two societies remained secret societies united by their own organizational oaths and under their own leaders. This became evident when the time approached for the start of treaty negotiations with the Confederacy at Tahlequah. On September 24 the Knights of the Golden Circle slipped quietly into the town, put up at one of the local hotels, and began distributing leaflets to undermine Ross's leadership. It was also reported that they concealed rifles in the hotel and might have plans to disrupt the treaty proceedings. In their own mind, they may simply have been gathering to prevent the Keetoowahs from a show of force. Some Ross supporters thought Watie might bring in his regiment and try to take control. A letter written to John Ross by John W. Stapler, his brother-in-law, on September 25 informed him, "Our town is filling up with Strangers. . . . [James M.] Bell's company [of Watie's soldiers] arrived here late last night. E. C. Boudinot [is] with them and Stan[d] Watie with his companies expected tonight. The issuing of the inflammatory sheet denying unity of feeling . . . [is] endangering a bloody Civil Conflict."[28] One of the Keetoowah leaders, Anderson Downing, a relative of Lewis Downing, "was killed last night" (presumably by the Knights). The "inflammatory sheet" that Stapler mentioned said,

> Whereas we, the undersigned Citizens of the Cherokee Nation, being Satisfied from unmistakable evidence that our lives are emperiled on account of our political opinion and that we have narrowly escaped assassination several times recent from a secret organization which has its ramifications in many portions of our Country. . . . Therefore, be it Resolved, lst, we will take such steps as from time to time may become necessary for the defense and protection of our lives. . . . 2nd, That we wish peace and friendship with all the world. . . . 3rd, That we will do all in our power to preserve the identity and Separate individuality of the Cherokee Nation. . . . 4th, That the Constitution and Laws of our Country recognize the institution of African Slavery and we will oppose any change in that Constitution and those Laws in this respect by abolition influence. 5th, That we recognize no distinction between Cherokee Citizens on account of colour and will do all we can to do away with any prejudices that may exist between "Halfbreeds and Fullbloods."[29]

However, the treaty-making process went forward without incident from October 2 to October 7, when it was duly signed by Ross. The National Council then met and in full session (and probably with the full-bloods in control of both houses) ratified the treaty on October 9.[30]

A kind of unity was achieved, but in fact it was simply a balance of power between the Ross party and the Watie party.

The first test of the treaty with the Confederacy and the loyalty of Drew's regiment to Ross (or the Keetoowah ideals) rather than to the Confederate Army commanders came two months later, when the Creek Nation (which had signed a treaty with the Confederacy on July 10) divided and roughly one-third of the Creeks (most of them full-bloods) asserted their loyalty to the United States. This faction was led by Chief Opothleyoholo, who had expressed astonishment when Ross had signed a treaty with the Confederacy. Ross's efforts to appease Opothleyoholo failed, and the loyal Creeks gathered themselves together in opposition to the Confederate faction. Because many Creek slaves ran off to join the loyal faction and Opothleyoholo seemed about to seek refuge with his followers in Kansas, the chiefs of the Creek Nation, who had signed a treaty with the Confederacy, asked help from the Confederate Army to put down this rebellion. The Confederate commanders agreed and on November 14 ordered part of Colonel Drew's regiment to move to the Creek capital. There it was to join with Creek and white Confederate forces to attack Opothleyoholo's supporters. The first engagement at Round Mountain on November 20 was a defeat for the Confederate force, and Opothleyoholo continued his march toward Kansas. Drew's force of 480 men and officers did not catch up to the running engagement until December 5. A conference was arranged with Opothleyoholo's force prior to an attack, but he would not yield. On the eve of the battle, the Keetoowahs in Drew's regiment met secretly and concluded not to fight against Opothleyoholo. Drew reported that 420 of his officers and men deserted, many of them joining Opothleyoholo and some fighting at the Battle of Bird Creek on December 9 with Opothleyoholo's men against the Confederate force consisting of Creeks and Texas militia. Again the Confederates failed to defeat Opothleyoholo, and he continued his retreat. Some of Drew's deserters went with him all the way to Kansas. Others drifted back on their own into the Cherokee Nation. Several went to Ross's home in Park Hill and asked his help to avoid being court-martialed.

Drew was highly embarrassed, and Ross was caught in a dilemma. Ross did not want any of the Keetoowahs shot for desertion and aiding the enemy, but he was still allied to the Confederacy. His solution was to take part of the blame on himself and place part on the Confederate commander. He argued that he had been promised that Cherokee troops would not fight outside their own nation and would not fight other Indians. These pledges had been broken. The deserters were confused, he added, because he himself had told them they would not have to fight other Indians. Eventually, he brought all the deserters together, reprimanded them for their behavior, and then, with the agreement of Colonel Douglas H. Cooper of the Confederacy, readmitted them to Drew's regiment.[31] Watie and his friends were contemptuous of the deserters and Ross's pardoning of them.

The next test of the Keetoowahs in Drew's regiment came in June 1862 when the United States finally mustered an Indian Expeditionary Force to enter the Cherokee Nation. By then, Evan and John B. Jones (who accompanied the expedition) had convinced the officials of Kansas and the United States that Ross's treaty was simply an effort to stall for time and hold off Watie's threat to his leadership. The Union expedition was viewed as an effort to rescue Ross from his difficult position. Colonel William Weer, its commander, was confident that Ross and Drew's regiment would welcome the expedition as soon as it arrived. And he was right.

After a brief battle at Locust Grove on July 3, 1862, in which the Confederate forces of Colonel J. J. Clarkson were badly defeated, most of Drew's forces deserted a second time. But this time they enlisted in the Union Army and formed a second regiment of Cherokees to join the regiment made up of those who had sought refuge in Kansas and were part of the expeditionary force.[32] Lewis Downing became chaplain of one of the two Cherokee regiments (later known as the Cherokee Home Guard), and at different times during the rest of the war, John B. Jones, Budd Gritts, and Evan Jones served as chaplains of one or the other of these regiments. It was now evident to all that the Keetoowahs had not joined Drew's regiment to fight for the Confederacy but to implement Ross's policy of stalling for time until the Union came to his rescue.

When the expeditionary force reached Ross's home at Park Hill on July 12, he was surrounded by other members of the Keetoowah Society. They put up no fight, and while Ross at first declined to surrender, he finally agreed to "house arrest." On August 2, when the expeditionary force had driven the Confederates out of the Nation and into the Creek Nation to the west, John Ross and a large entourage of family and friends departed for Kansas while the two Cherokee Home Guard regiments remained to hold the Nation for the Union. When Ross reached Kansas and was taken to General James Blount, the commanding officer of the region, he stated that he had always been loyal to the Union and blamed the United States for failing to provide him with any military support when he was invaded by the Confederate forces. He had been compelled, against his will, he said, to sign a treaty with the Confederacy, in order to preserve his people from an internecine war. Blount allowed him to travel to Washington to discuss all this with President Lincoln.[33] Evan Jones was later made a Cherokee delegate to work with Ross in Washington (later they were joined at different times by Lewis Downing and Smith Christie), but no treaty with the United States was concluded until 1866.

This succession of events seemed to demonstrate conclusively to the Watie party that Ross had acted the part of a hypocrite throughout. No sooner had he left the Nation than Watie returned with his regiment. The Cherokee Home Guard, lacking ammunition, was forced to return to Kansas. Watie's supporters then held a council and elected him as principal chief of the Cherokees at Tahlequah on August 21, 1862. Ross thereafter was known as the "chief in exile." The treaty with the Confederacy was affirmed, and there followed a bloody war of vengeance against anyone identified as a Keetoowah or "Pin," which drove many thousands of Cherokees into Kansas in flight. Watie's council passed a law making every Cherokee male between the ages of sixteen and forty-five eligible for armed service in the Confederacy. Any who refused conscription were to be shot as traitors.

During the winter and spring of 1862–63, the Cherokee regiments were situated in Kansas and then Missouri. Their camp at Cane Ridge, Missouri, was within sight of Cowskin Prairie in the Cherokee Nation, but they lacked the support from Union troops to return to the Nation until the late spring of 1863. They did, however, cross over briefly into Cowskin Prairie in February 1863 in order to hold a council loyal to John Ross. This council reelected him as principal chief (though he was still in Washington); it passed a law abrogating the treaty with the Confederacy; and it proclaimed all those loyal to the Confederacy to be traitors and confiscated all of their homes and businesses. This confiscation act was to be a major issue after the war. On February 19, this council also passed a law emancipating all the slaves—a largely ineffective act, as most of the slaves were still under the control of their mixed-blood owners who were loyal to the Confederacy. Lewis Downing was made acting chief in Ross's absence.[34]

In the spring of 1863 a second expeditionary force was sent into the Nation by the United States. It succeeded in administering a major defeat on the Confederate forces at the Battle of Honey Springs on July 17.

But it did not follow this up. Instead, most of the army returned to Kansas, leaving only a brigade made of three Indian regiments at Fort Gibson to protect the Nation. This proved totally insufficient, and soon Watie's regiment was back in action, waging a scorched-earth policy despite futile efforts to capture him by the Cherokee regiments at Fort Gibson. Countless harrowing episodes took place as Watie's men and the Home Guard waged their attacks and counterattacks throughout the Nation from 1863 to 1865. When not engaged with each other, as they seldom were, they roamed through the countryside wreaking havoc on anyone associated with "the enemy"—in the process looting, burning, and harassing men, women, and children. Whose vengeance was greater or worse would be hard to estimate. It was a civil war among unrestrained guerrilla forces that took more than four thousand lives and devastated all that the Cherokees had built up since 1839. Many who had followed the expeditionary force back to the Nation in the spring of 1863 returned to Kansas for the duration of the war. Watie was never caught, and the Union forces at Fort Gibson, surrounded by several thousand Cherokee families seeking protection nearby, were further decimated by epidemics of cholera, malaria, and dysentery.

When the war finally ended in April 1865, the Nation was in ruins and the two opposing parties were so bitter toward each other that they each sought to make their own peace terms. Ross wanted a reunited Cherokee Nation under the leadership of those who had supported the Union; Watie wanted the Nation divided into two separate countries each with its own boundaries and government. The treaty commissioners, who had originally been sympathetic to Ross, turned against him when they began to read some of the statements they found in captured Confederate documents in which he had expressed what appeared to be wholehearted support for the Lost Cause. Ross further annoyed President Johnson's treaty commissioners by insisting on reparations for all Cherokee losses (because of the lack of United States protection) and by refusing to make concessions to railroad rights of way and land grants.

The Watie party was far more complaisant in its effort to obtain its own treaty, and it did all it could to blacken Ross's name and impugn his motives and loyalty. It was in the war of words and petitions and memorials between the Ross (or loyal) delegation and the Watie (or southern delegation) that the Keetoowah Society came under closer scrutiny. The Ross party began to speak of it as the "Loyal League" and argued that it was founded before the war and continued, secretly, through the years 1861 to 1862, finally blossoming into the Cherokee Union regiments. The Watie party portrayed the Keetoowah Society as an abolitionist movement that began long before the secession crisis and that existed simply to support the animosity of the full-bloods against the more acculturated and civilized mixed-bloods. Its origin even was traced back to the days of the division over removal. To Ross the Keetoowahs were the noblest of Cherokees, the Knights of the Golden Circle the worst. To Watie and his friends, the Keetoowahs were little more than murderers and thieves (they indicated no knowledge of the Blue Lodges or Knights).

Ross may have first begun to think of the Keetoowahs as the Loyal League in 1862 when he reached Washington, D.C., and was trying to impress Lincoln and the public about their obligations to support his beleaguered people. Ross's wife, Mary Stapler Ross, had been born into a well-to-do Quaker merchant family in Philadelphia, and from 1862 to 1866 they lived in her family home at 708 Washington Square. It was probably she who persuaded a group of her friends to sew an American flag and inscribe it to the Keetoowah Society. It was said later to be one of the "cherished relics" of the society—"a United States flag, across which in golden letters is inscribed, 'Presented to the Keetoowahs, Friends of the Union, by Ladies of Philadelphia, 1862.'" Some accounts describe it as also having some letters in Sequoyan sewn into it.[35]

On July 7, 1864, Ross's nephew, Daniel Hicks Ross, wrote to him from Fort Gibson speaking, he said, "on behalf of the Ketoowha Society, that large and loyal class of Cherokee citizens who, in point of fact, constitute[d] 7/10ths of the male population."[36] But he did not refer to it as "the Loyal League." In February 1865, Ross told William P. Dole, the commissioner of Indian Affairs, "We represent the Cherokee Nation, who are *now* and *ever have been decidedly loyal.*"[37] But not until the treaty negotiations were under way in January 1866 did the Ross delegation begin to speak of the Loyal League. Some historians have concluded that the Loyal League and the Keetoowah Society were in fact two distinct organizations. Morris Wardell, for example, spoke of the "abolition influence of the Pin Organization and the Loyal League."[38] But it is my considered opinion that there never was a distinct Loyal League, that it was simply a propaganda device concocted by Ross in 1866 to counter the scurrilous attacks of the southern delegation and burnish the image of the Keetoowahs, whose bloody reprisals against the Knights of the Golden Circle did not bear the light of day. I am also inclined to believe that the Knights of the Golden Circle has probably received more attention as a cohesive secret organization than it deserves.

The first clear reference to the Loyal League that I have seen occurred on January 31, 1866, in a pamphlet entitled *Communication of the Delegation of the Cherokee Nation to the President of the United States*. It was signed by all the members of the Ross delegation except Ross because it was a testimonial to Ross's character and leadership. The signers were Smith Christie, White Catcher, Daniel H. Ross, Thomas Pegg, Samuel H. Benge, and James McDaniel. It stated, "For several years before the outbreak of war, there was in our midst an element inimical to our institutions . . . susceptible of becoming exceedingly dangerous when fondled and nursed by such spirits as Albert Pike and backed by the powerful army of Gen. Ben McCulloch. This element was headed by Stand Watie . . . and stimulated by such sheets as the *Arkansan*, published . . . [by] his nephew, E. C. Boudinot." This party was now in Washington trying to persuade the United States that "the Chief of the loyal Cherokees [was] disloyal." "With this element in [their] midst [in 1861], organized into Lodges of Knights of the Golden Circle," Chief Ross had proclaimed neutrality, which "nine-tenths of the whole" Nation endorsed. "In order to uphold the peaceable, friendly policy always inculcated by their Chief with the United States . . . and alarmed at the teachings of the party to whom we have alluded, the masses of the Nation had organized into a *Loyal League* (the first on record) pledged to an unfaltering support of their principles, and to keep from office and power every man suspected of treasonable designs against the Nation and the Federal Government."[39] Clearly they were speaking of the Keetoowah Society but preferred the term more popular in the northern states for the kind of patriotic societies that during the war adopted the name "Loyal League" in order to distinguish themselves from northern Democrats and Copperheads. But the primary loyalty of the Keetoowah Society was to the Cherokee Nation and its ancient Kituwah spirit, not to the United States. So far as the United States was concerned, the Keetoowahs were loyal to the treaties made with it, but by and large they saw the Civil War as a white man's war, not theirs.

This pamphlet or memorial claimed that the treaty with the Confederacy in October 1861 was imposed "under duress" by Lincoln's failure to provide these loyal Cherokees with military support. It went on to say that when Colonel William F. Cloud escorted Ross (under arrest) to Kansas in August 1862, "over two thousand" Cherokee refugees there "(now soldier[s] of the Union) cluster[ed] around him and rejoice[d] at his safe arrival within the Union lines." At the time of the signing of the Confederate treaty, this pamphlet continued, Ross was in despair of saving his country and acted only to buy time. "These were the sentiments of our Chief, perfectly understood by his friends, over two thousand of whom were members of the 'Loyal League.' " Ross had praised these men for refusing to fight against Opothleyoholo at Bird Creek and for fleeing to Kansas to join the first Indian regiments organized there.

In response to this pamphlet, E. C. Boudinot and William P. Adair of the Southern party delegation wrote their version of events in February 1866 (the exact date is not given). Boudinot and Adair maintained that the Cherokees had been divided ever since removal and that over the years the division was known first as the Treaty party versus the anti-Treaty party, then as the Ridge and Ross parties, and "in 1856 as the 'Pin' and 'Anti-Pin' " parties. Now they were called "the 'Northern' and 'Southern Cherokees.' " But the bitterness between these two parties had nothing to do with the Civil War itself. Referring to another memorial of the Ross party, Boudinot and Adair quoted the following passage, which they considered self-serving:

> When the rebellion broke out, the Cherokees were divided into two parties, the loyal and disloyal. Both had been thoroughly organized for two or three years and prepared for the struggle. Under the lead of Stand Watie, lately a general in the rebel army, the disloyal element (small in numbers but backed by strong influences from the rebellious States) had been organized into "Blue Lodges" and "Knights of the Golden Circle." The loyal masses, by a general movement of the populace, had organized into a "Loyal League" known as the Keetoowha Society, but by the rebels it was called in derision, "The Pin Society." This Loyal League embraced the great mass of the men of the Cherokee Nation, especially the fullblooded Indians.[40]

This was a more accurate statement by the Ross party than the one made to President Johnson on January 31, 1866. Boudinot and Adair,

however, described this as "a malicious misrepresentation from beginning to end . . . a miserable attempt to represent an infamous,
secret inquisition, proscriptive in design and murderous in intention,
as a commendable and praiseworthy association. The 'Pin Society'
was organized *five years* before the war [in the spring of 1856] when the
words 'loyal' and 'disloyal,' now so common, were unknown within
the broad limits of the Republic and years before the idea of *secession*
was thought of or dreamed of in Indian country."

Boudinot and Adair were here as self-serving as the Ross party.
Secession was certainly known and talked of by mixed-blood and
intermarried white Cherokees even before 1856, and the Keetoowahs
said in their constitution that there was clearly a trend in the Nation
to lead the Cherokees to break their alliance with the United States
and ally themselves with the South. Furthermore, the Blue Lodges
were also well known in the Nation by 1855, and they were clearly
dedicated to slavery and southern rights. Boudinot and Adair transformed the Keetoowah Society into nothing more than a party plot
by Ross to subvert the Cherokee government: "The purpose of this
secret society was to secure and perpetuate the power of Mr. Ross
and his friends by arraying the great mass of full bloods against the
half-bloods and white men of the Nation; to inflame and excite the
innate prejudices of caste among the Indians, and thus enable demagogues, peculators of public funds, and murderers to enjoy in security
their ill-gotten gains." In fact, it was the mixed-bloods of the Watie
party who were creating a sense of caste in the Nation by their constant degradation of the "backward" and "unenlightened" full-bloods,
and it was they who were enriching themselves at the expense of
the Nation's poor subsistence farmers. From the point of view of "the
masses," the mixed-blood minority was dominating the council for its
own greedy purposes. Ross was in the ambiguous position of medi-
ating between two opposing forces, and the Keetoowahs proposed to
give him a counterweight to rebalance the scales, which were moving
in the direction of the mixed-bloods and away from the Nation's best
interests.

The Boudinot-Adair pamphlet went on to argue that the point of
"this 'League'" was not to vote in the full-bloods but to assassinate
the leaders of the Watie party. "It is well understood that at such
[secret] meetings, the question of assassinating prominent citizens of
the Nation, obnoxious to the order [the League], was frequently dis-

cussed and *voted upon; murders* were committed in pursuance of their decisions." That murders were committed on both sides is undeniable, but Boudinot and Adair chose not to recall how the Ridge-Boudinot party had used the concept of "blood revenge" to justify six years of murders by various gangs from 1839 to 1846. Their point was to prove that "no question of United States politics entered into their disagreements" and that "the war afforded a good excuse for arraying the two parties in arms against each other" in bloody guerrilla warfare. Boudinot and Adair were working here, and in subsequent pamphlets, to justify their request that they be allowed to live in a separate country under their own government: "For thirty years we have had neither a community of interests, tastes or aspirations. We are two different people." Ross, however, was trying to justify the unity of the Nation. Ross undoubtedly had the majority on his side; unity was essential to the Nation's survival.[41]

On May 12, 1866, John B. Jones and five other Ross delegates (but not Ross) signed and printed another tract that was sent to the commissioner of Indian Affairs. In it they refuted Boudinot's claim that there was such enmity between the Watie party and the Ross party that they could never live under the same government: "Already two-thirds of the disloyal are home again living in absolute security [in the Nation]." They listed some of the leading officers in Watie's regiment among these. Referring to the Southern party delegates, they said, "It is not peace, security and fraternity these lately disloyal leaders want—it is political power. They know full well that they and their whilom followers will be safe among the loyal men. . . . But they know too that the men who organized the Knights of the Golden Circle in 1859 . . . will not soon again be honored with public confidence in the nation."[42]

By 1866 both factions were willing to reinterpret history to fit the exigencies of their particular goals. Both tried to destroy the respectability of the other. Ross won this contest, and the Watie faction was not able to divide the Nation into two distinct governments. But when Ross died and his nephew, William Potter Ross, became chief in October 1866, it was clear that mutual distrust remained strong. W. P. Ross was bitter over the behavior of the Watie party and held it to blame for the guerrilla war and scorched-earth policy that decimated the Nation. He would not appoint any of its leaders to important offices or to the delegation to Washington on the Nation's business. He seemed determined to perpetuate the harsh feelings the war had generated.

Evan and John B. Jones, who returned to the Nation (now as honorary citizens) and to their missionary work in 1866, remained on close terms with Lewis Downing and the other Keetoowah leaders. They did not believe that W. P. Ross was serving the Nation well by keeping it divided in the face of mounting efforts by land speculators, railroad magnates, cattle ranchers, business entrepreneurs, and frontier squatters to utilize the Nation's resources to enrich themselves. Especially pressing were the persistent efforts of Congress to turn the Indian Territory into a federal territory, divide the communally owned land of all the tribes into private plots, and then denationalize the tribes and open the area to white settlements under what would shortly become a white-dominated state government. The Joneses believed that a more charitable approach would be to support reconciliation between the two factions.

In 1867 they persuaded Lewis Downing to break with W. P. Ross and to make overtures to Watie and his followers, promising them a fair share of offices and a role in policy making if they would support him against Ross. Some of the Watie men, notably William P. Adair and Joseph A. Scales, agreed to do so. Watie, who was still living in the Choctaw Nation, took no part in these secret negotiations. Although many Keetoowahs were torn by their loyalty to the Ross family, enough of them supported Downing to gain his election. Downing was the first full-blood (defined as a person who did not speak, read, or write English) to become principal chief since 1827. He was elected for a second term in 1871. Under the Downing party, the Cherokee Nation enjoyed a more peaceable Reconstruction era than that which prevailed in the war-torn Confederate States, and the Cherokees gained a renewed sense of harmony.[43] Slowly they returned also to a semblance of prosperity in their war-torn nation.

With the election of Lewis Downing the Keetoowah Society was able to relax its vigilance and its militance. It became a social rather than a political organization. Its original objectives had been achieved. The full-blood majority was in control of the Nation. The institution of slavery was abolished. The gap between the wealthy slaveholders with their large plantations and the non-slaveholding farmers with one horse and a plough had been substantially narrowed. The death of John Ross in 1866 and of Stand Watie in 1871 seemed to mark the end of the long feud that had divided the Nation since the removal controversy. Downing and his party owed nothing to either party but were in fact a coalition of the moderate elements in both. Some Keetoowahs resented Downing's defection from William P. Ross, the handpicked heir of the old chief. Some Watie supporters, such as James M. Bell, E. C. Boudinot, and William N. West, continued to nurse their old animosity toward the full-bloods, whom West referred to in these years as the "hog and hominy class." But the majority of the Cherokees were far more concerned to sustain the new harmony and the old Kituwah spirit that enabled them to speak with one voice against all the white factions that wanted to take over their country.[44]

If any Keetoowah conventions were held or any bylaws passed by them between July 1861 and January 1866, they are not included in the extant Keetoowah documents. The Tyner document does include two resolutions passed on January 8 and 9, 1866 (paragraphs 31 and 32).[45] The first simply states that "a water carrier" was to be appointed and paid for his services at each convention; the second states that district captains must "visit all the lodges," "explain the Keetoowah laws," "make up a roll of the names" for each lodge, and "report the same to the head captains at Convention." This seems to indicate that during the war the lodges acted on their own, or else, being mostly confined to the area around Fort Gibson, there were easy means of knowing who was in what lodge. After peace occurred in April 1865, those living at Fort Gibson or in Kansas returned to their old homes or went to build new ones. The Keetoowah resolution of January 1866, calling for visiting the lodges, was designed to reconstitute the organization. Still, it is not clear why there were no records or laws passed from 1866 to 1870 unless they have not survived. Probably the massive effort needed to rebuild the Nation absorbed most of the Keetoowahs' time. In addition, the organization of the Downing party was itself a majority activity for some, whereas those favoring W. P. Ross may have been alienated from the society. Those with political goals could run for office now and try to implement changes through a council dominated by full-bloods under a full-blood chief.

In 1870 the Keetoowahs passed a bylaw that ended the secrecy of the society, which had probably not been an issue since 1866.[46] Those who lived in the 1870s spoke highly of the great Keetoowah conventions at Tahlequah every August. One Cherokee recalled that "several thousand were usually present at the conventions in the period of the early and mid-seventies. . . . In the afternoons there was usually preaching and singing in the Cherokee language. The mornings were devoted to consultation and there were speeches by leaders. . . . [B]arbecued meats were provided in abundance with fish and fowls . . . and big kettles full of black coffee."[47] Women and children participated in the festivities, and patriotic feelings mixed with Christian and traditional activities. Reconciliation was the spirit of Christian charity and of Kituwah harmony.

The Keetoowah Society found it necessary to reorganize and re-turn to secrecy in 1876 as new divisions emerged about the course the Nation should take. In the 1890s the Keetoowahs split into two groups that later became known as Keetoowah Society Incorporated and the Nighthawk Keetoowahs.[48] But there were different causes, different leaders, different goals. The original Keetoowah Society of 1856 was directly related to the great national schism within the United States and its ramifications within the Cherokee Nation. By 1870 that crisis was past, and the Kituwah spirit found new paths to travel.

Appendix A

The View of the Reverend Stephen Foreman of the Watie Party

I asked myself why I was so obnoxious to the Pins or Ross Party, as I choose to call them. . . . The whole secret, however, I supposed, was that I was a Watie man. I never had denied that I was, in some particulars, and the Pins knew it; the fact was, the Pins made me so. They themselves had drawn a line of distinction between themselves and the half-breeds, and being a half-breed, I naturally fell on the Watie side. And not only so, but I had from the beginning opposed the Pin organization, and said much against it publicly, because I thought I could see ruin written on the very face of it. From what I could learn from various sources their object was 1st, to get the government of the Nation in their own hands; 2nd, to rid the Nation of slavery; 3rd, with the appearance of law, to carry all measures that would help their cause or render them popular.

The two Joneses, I thought, were the originators of the Pin organization. Chief Ross was knowing to the whole plan and sanctioned every measure,

Diary of Stephen Foreman, July 16, 1862, Western History Collections, University of Oklahoma, Norman, Oklahoma.

I firmly believed. So far, I thought I could see their plan working admirably. Last fall the two branches of the National Council were nearly all Pins. And at the Bird Creek fight they all, to a man, nearly, fought on the Federal side, with Opath-le-ah-holah, thus turning traitor to the Confederate Government which they were sworn to support, and trampling upon the law they passed appointing themselves officers and soldiers in the Confederate service. But it made no difference at all, for when it was necessary to do business in council, they came and took their seats as usual, thus acting in a twofold capacity— one day a soldier, and the next a councillor. Some of these very persons made and ratified the Treaty under which they were clothed and fed and paid all last winter, and where are they? Why after lying about [Fort] Gibson and near Chief Ross's, spending thousands of dollars for the Confederate Govt., they turn over to the Feds [in July, 1862], join the Northern Army, and take the oath to support the Lincoln Government. And then they come and rob and kill, and it is all right with Chief Ross because it is carrying out the policy of the Pin party.

Appendix B

A Confederate View of the Keetoowahs

[In 1866, when two opposing delegations from the Cherokee Nation were vying for recognition by the federal government, a series of pamphlets were printed by each explaining why they were entitled to support. The delegation headed by Chief John Ross issued a memorial addressed to President Johnson stating that the delegation headed by Stand Watie represented those "disloyal" Cherokees who had been members of "Blue-lodges and Knight[s] of the Golden Circle" who supported the Confederacy; the majority of the Nation, this memorial said, "had organized themselves into a 'Loyal League' known as the Ketoowha Society. . . . This Loyal League embraced the great mass of the men of the Cherokee men, especially the fullblooded Indians." This memorial was rebutted in a pamphlet entitled *Reply of the Southern Delegates* and allegedly written by E. C. Boudinot. It describes the Keetoowah Society as a strictly political group formed to overpower the progressive mixed-blood

Reply of the Southern Delegates (Washington, D.C.: McGill and Witherow Printers, 1866), 5–6. The memorial is signed on the last page by Elias C. Boudinot and Wm. P. Adair.

chiefs. After quoting the Ross memorial's statement about the "Loyal League," the author says:]

This is a malicious misrepresentation from beginning to end; it is a miserable attempt to represent an infamous secret inquisition, proscriptive in design and murderous in intention, as a commendable and praiseworthy association. The "Pin Society" was organized five years before the war, when the words "loyal" and "disloyal," now so common were unknown within the broad limits of the Republic and years before the idea of secession was thought or dreamed of in the Indian country. The purpose of this secret society was to secure and perpetuate the power of Mr. Ross and his friends, by arraying the great mass of the full-bloods against the half-bloods and white men of the Nation; to inflame and excite the innate prejudices of caste among the Indians, and thus enable demagogues, peculators of the public funds, and murderers, to enjoy in security their ill-gotten gains.

This is no empty declamation; it is the expression of facts as testified to by many who formerly belonged to the society, but abandoned it upon ascertaining it diabolical objects, and have ever since remained its most steadfast and bitter opponents. The better class of the members of this "League" and many of the most intelligent and influential full-bloods among our people, repudiated the brotherhood in disgust before the war, and have acted with what is termed the "Watie Party." The members of this society held their meetings upon the hilltops and in the deep recesses of the valley; not, as shamelessly alleged, "to inculcate fidelity to treaty obligations upon the young and old," but rather to deliberate upon the most effective plan to crush their hated opponents, and secure absolute power in the hands of the favored few not included in the general proscription.

It is well understood that, at such meetings, the question of assassinating prominent citizens of the Nation, obnoxious to the order, was frequently discussed and voted upon; murders were committed in pursuance of their decisions. The attempt, at this late date, to claim for this wicked association, peculiar "fidelity to treaty obligations," which was not entertained in common by every man, woman, and child in the Indian country, is as absurd as it is untrue. The "Katoowha Society" had its signs, grips, and pass-words; its members, at one time, wore a pin as a badge of membership and identity; and this becoming known, furnished an appropriate name for the mysterious organization by which it will ever be known—"The Pin Society."

The bitterness between the "Pins" and the "Anti-Pins" was intense; no question of United States politics entered into their disagreements; theirs was a deep-seated, inextinguishable hate, nurtured by long years of bloodshed and murder; the former were truculent, overbearing, and unscrupulous; too foolish to use their power with wisdom and discretion, they made themselves detested by every advocate of law and progress, and ruthlessly trampled under foot every consideration of justice and right; the latter, though a minority, could not, and would not, brook the unsufferable indignities and persecutions to which they were daily subjected; the consequence was, many collisions took place between them and much blood was shed.

The war afforded a good excuse for arraying the two parties in arms against each other. . . .

Appendix C

February 14, 1876

Reorganization

1

After the secret Keetoowah Cherokee Convention, leading men defenders of the country, began to discuss what we Keetoowahs were leading to. We have been united together for many, many years—on account of Keetoowah Society. At this time it might seem that our society was scattered on account of other or different lodges, societies, and companies being organized amongst our own people. The purpose of some is greed, some to oppress your own fellow man of his character; some to swindle, some to assist railroad companies, some to deprive each individual of his property, some to destroy the Cherokee National Government. For these reasons it would seem that the Keetoowah Society might have weakened. Consequently it might seem that the real defenders of our country and defenders of our government are failing to progress along as it should because of the things mentioned above. These other societies conflict with the Cherokee Constitution and laws, and for that reason we are liable to lose our independence. From the way it looks now we are liable to lose our government; for that reason (for friends listen and think of the conditions of our lives), for that reason we resolve by the Keetoowah meeting that we reorganize our old Keetoowah society as friends, loyal to each other, to abide by our old laws.

Keetoowah Society constitution and laws from Howard Q. Tyner, "The Keetoowah Society in Cherokee History," master's thesis, University of Tulsa, 1949.

Chapter 11
Fighting against Civilization: Ghost Dance Movements in Cherokee History

Most Americans are now aware that what is called "the last of the Indian battles" at Wounded Knee in 1890 was really a slaughter of men, women, and children consequent upon the rise of the ghost dance movement among the western tribes. When the Bureau of Ethnology sent James Mooney to investigate this massacre, he wrote a book noting that similar nativist movements had occurred many times before among other tribes. He identified one of these in the Cherokee Nation in 1811 when the missionaries were making their first serious inroads and the old way of life seemed threatened by rapid acculturation. In times of religious, social, and political crisis, Native American prophets tend to arise who, through dreams and visions, predict that the Great Spirit will soon intervene in human affairs on behalf of justice to his red children. Furthermore, he will send some catastrophe to destroy the white people and return to the Indians the lands taken from them.

Apocalypticism also appears in several parts of the Bible, and it is well known that the ghost dance movement among the Plains Indians included references to the second coming of Jesus. This essay examines some of those movements among the Cherokees and takes special note of a peculiar movement, by a disgruntled faction in 1867, to arouse the people to join a military effort to drive the white people out of the West. The movement, though not a typical ghost dance, deserves attention because it indicates that even after generations of acculturation, many Cherokees remained ready to risk everything for a return to the old days.

What are ghost dances, and why has so much been written about them in recent years? In one sense, a ghost dance is a desperate plea for supernatural intervention in their affairs by a people whose old cultural structure has been shattered. In another sense, it is simply part of a continuing effort among a downtrodden minority to restore their own dignity under a restructured faith system that will provide meaning, order, and direction to their lives. The first definition is commonly used to describe the classic ghost dance movements of the Shawnees under Tenskwatawa in 1805, the Paviotsos under Wodziwob in 1870, and the Sioux and others under Jack Wilson (Wovoka) in 1890. The latter definition applies to the continual efforts of most Native American groups to incorporate new elements into the sacred myths and symbols of their traditional worldview. The great attention paid by scholars to spectacular ghost dance movements is part of the commendable effort to reverse the negative definition of them as the superstitious catastrophism of a vanishing primitive people and stems in part from the raging millennial outlook of white America, which has created its own catastrophism.

Partly because of the massacre in 1890 at Wounded Knee, South Dakota, and partly because of white malaise over the destruction of indigenous peoples and the seizure of their lands, early ethnohistorians focused upon the sensational aspects of ghost dance movements and saw them as "the death throes of a vanishing race." Thus the long debate over the meaning of classic ghost dance movements once tended to deemphasize the less spectacular intratribal movements that constituted the ebb and flow of most cultural transformations. Since 1956, however, when Anthony F. C. Wallace established the concept of "revitalization," ethnohistorians have depicted these movements as part of a general cultural transformation among Indian groups that catalyzed accommodations of syncretistic ideas and practices that sustained their identities and revived their tribes. "Cultures *can* change within one generation," Wallace noted, quoting Margaret Mead, but more recently Alice Beck Kehoe has again suggested that "cultural distortion is not inevitably precipitous and dramatic."[1]

Ethnohistorians need to find ways, first, of differentiating between rapid, precipitous cultural transformation and long-term, gradual, or spasmodic revitalization; and second, of assessing cultural deprivation (in terms of causation and time span) relative to the incremental or episodic crises that produce cultural and religious restructuring. If they are to become true comparatists, ethnohistorians must train themselves, as David Aberle put it, to measure precisely the "relative deprivation" that disparate peoples undergo when their cultural microcosms are disrupted, and they must do so having first ensured the legitimacy of their expectations by examining, sensitively and with open minds, the surviving evidence. Was the loss of the bison in one generation, for example, more devastating to the Plains Indians than the loss of their homeland to the southeastern nations? Is a catastrophic ghost dance movement (with whatever revitalizing it may bring in the long run) more indicative of successful cultural accommodation than a series of reconciled disputes between traditionalists and acculturationists? What, ultimately, is the significant difference between a pan-Indian or intertribal revitalization movement and a revitalization movement within one tribe? The long-neglected ghost dance movement that took place among the Cherokees in 1867—a movement that, upon analysis, appears clearly to have been a false ghost dance—throws into bold relief the necessity of learning not to confound phenomena that resemble one another superficially. The study of it and similar false ghost dances may shed new light on what is true and false in all of them.[2]

Cultural Crisis and Revitalization, 1807–1895

The Cherokees, like the Navajos and some other large tribes in the West, did not participate in the ghost dance movements of 1870 and 1890 that swirled around them. W. W. Hill and others have suggested that the Navajos and Cherokees shared a fear of the dead that made them wary of the return of ancestral ghosts prophesied by these movements. However, James Mooney in his seminal study of these movements noted that many Cherokees participated in an important ghost dance movement in 1812–13. He attributed this movement to the influence of the Shawnee messengers of Tenskwatawa who visited the neighboring Creeks in 1812. Recent research indicates that a series of dreams and visions by Cherokee prophets began early in 1811, prior to the visit of Tecumseh and the Shawnee messengers to the Creeks. The prophets spoke of the imminent, cataclysmic destruction of the whites, the restoration of the dwindling game, and a return to the golden age of precontact life; they provoked the burning of European clothing and manufactured goods and urged the revival of traditional dances and ceremonies. Apparently, the Cherokees were not inherently opposed to such restoration movements. Yet, although they underwent many culturally disruptive crises in the nineteenth century (notably, removal from their homeland and murderous internal strife in the West), they do not seem to have gone through such a movement. They did, however, experience a series of internal crises in their search for a more satisfying religious perspective. A brief synopsis of this series of religious movements, which contributed to the cultural accommodation of the most "civilized" tribe in America in the years 1807 to 1895, will bear this out.[3]

1811–1813. A ghost dance movement led, according to some accounts, by the prophet Tsali arose after a vision talk with some ancestral ghosts who instructed the Cherokees to stop plowing up Mother Earth, to give up the customs of the whites, and to regain some of their sacred towns lost in treaties. This followed a critical dispute between the upper and lower towns and the assassination of Doublehead as retribution for a corrupt bargain he had struck in selling Cherokee hunting grounds to the United States. In 1808–10 the first written laws had seriously restricted clan revenge and matrilineal inheritance. In 1811, after negotiations with the Jefferson administration, more than eleven hundred Cherokees moved to Arkansas and claimed a right to exchange their lands in the East for new lands in the West. That year, a series of earthquakes strengthened the ghost dance and led to predictions of the end of the world and the disappearance of whites in a hailstorm and an eclipse. Ultimately, the necessity of coping with the Creek War dissipated the movement as the Cherokees chose to side with the United States.[4]

1824–1827. White Path's Rebellion was a peaceful revolt by the full-bloods (persons whose primary tongue was Cherokee), who objected to the rapid centralization of national authority, scores of new laws, and increasing missionary evangelism. A council of rebellious chiefs ordered the rejection of Christianity and the market economy. The rebels finally yielded to the mixed-blood chiefs and supported a written constitution in 1827 on the grounds that the imminent election of Andrew Jackson might force the Nation from its homeland and that it was necessary that the Cherokee Nation be united to save itself.[5]

1832–1838. Missionaries reported a strong resurgence of traditional dances and ceremonies and a rejection of missionary efforts during the removal crisis; removal of the Cherokees temporarily ended this movement.[6]

1840. The Reverend Samuel A. Worcester reported a widespread interest in astrology after he began publishing a zodiacal almanac in Cherokee. The Cherokees, he said, besieged him with requests for pictures of the signs and for more information on how the courses of the moon, sun, stars, and planets, all-important in traditional sacred mythology, influenced human health and controlled the weather. The Cherokees, trying to reestablish their farms in a strange climate with new diseases, sought new ways to order and control their lives.[7]

1842. During the traumatic years of readjustment following removal, a missionary teacher aroused a religious revival when he preached the Adventist doctrines of William Miller, who predicted the return of Christ in the year 1843–44. The failure of this Second Coming and the dismissal of the missionary ended this premillennial movement.[8]

1847. Two Mormons attained great popularity by preaching their own form of premillennialism. This followed several years of feuding and murders by an armed faction that opposed the leadership of the elected chief, John Ross. The Mormons left for their own reasons after encountering some opposition, but Mormonism continued to thrive as the Cherokees struggled to cope with starting over in the West.[9]

1855–1865. As the threat of civil war in the United States grew, two competing secret societies formed—the Knights of the Golden Circle, composed of mixed-blood slaveholders who upheld black slavery among the Cherokees, and the Keetoowah Society, limited in membership to full-bloods and dedicated to rebuilding tribal solidarity, to preserving traditionalism, and thus to reversing the dominance of mixed-bloods in Cherokee political affairs. During the Civil War, these two groups engaged in a bloody conflict that destroyed all that the Cherokees had rebuilt after their removal. In 1867 the full-bloods gained control of the National Council.[10]

1890–1895. Following the passage of the Dawes Act and the decision of the U.S. Congress to create a territory out of what is now Oklahoma, the Keetoowah Society revived and split in two. The new organization, called Nighthawk Keetoowah, rejected compromise over the division of tribal land among individual owners of private plots and adopted a strong traditionalist attitude of sustaining sacred ceremonies, dances, and rituals. This traditionalist movement continued long after Oklahoma became a state in 1908.[11]

These eight cultural crises among the Cherokees clearly mark their continual, though sporadic, efforts to reconcile old and new religious perspectives in order to sustain tribal unity and maintain control over their world. They suggest that revitalization need not be associated with a single prophet or doctrine or result from a single watershed. They also indicate a lack of continuity from one religious movement to another. While the Keetoowah movement demonstrated the hold of traditionalism, it was implemented by Baptist missionaries and led by Baptist converts. Christianity steadily increased its hold on the Cherokees, although medicine men were admitted to Cherokee Baptist churches and continued to practice tribal medicine. Christianity was itself a revitalization movement, but fewer than 15 percent of the Cherokees were Christian. Ethnohistorians need to explain more clearly why some tribes took a modular or pragmatic path to cultural survival, while others risked the spectacular, magical millennial path.

Impetus and Definitions of Ghost Dances

Far from answering this question, recent studies of ghost dance movements have further complicated it by searching for a single underlying motive. Kehoe's study of Jack Wilson's movement in 1890 argues that Kicking Bear, the Lakota Sioux chief, distorted the movement's true meaning by positing a "magic, bulletproof shirt" that justified a military assault against the oppressive white man. "Jack Wilson," Kehoe says, "was a prophet of peace," but Kicking Bear wanted war; thus "a Prince of Peace was again betrayed." Wilson said the ideal embodied in his vision was "a clean, honest life" that would ensure "earth renewal." Kicking Bear had "to distort the true Ghost Dance religion" in order to advocate forceful expulsion of the whites. "The true ghost dance," Kehoe maintains, held that "if every Indian would dance" the dance prescribed in Wilson's vision, then "the great expression of faith and love would sweep evil from the earth, renewing its goodness in every form, from youth and health to abundant food." The ghost dance adapted from Wilson revitalized a group of Dakota Sioux living near Prince Albert, Canada, who incorporated it into their traditional Medicine Feast. This "New Tidings Movement," which lasted until the 1960s, was "an example of the real Ghost Dance religion, a revitalization of traditional . . . beliefs and ceremonies," a "creative pruning of unobtainable or anachronistic elements, such as emphasis on bison." [12]

Russell Thornton in his analysis of the ghost dances of 1870 and 1890 argues that "the basic object" of these movements "was the return to life of deceased populations of Indians." Though no ancestors returned to life, Thornton found an increasing birthrate after 1890. For him, the test of the revitalizing element in true ghost dances lies in objectively verifying the increasing population of the tribes that most actively supported them. Although the more spectacular predictions of the ghost dances of 1870 and 1890 (the elements that fascinated early anthropologists) failed to materialize, Thornton as well as Kehoe finds the movement ultimately successful. Yet each finds a different truth underlying Wilson's movement. [13]

Henry F. Dobyns and Robert C. Euler in their analysis of the ghost dance of 1889 among the Pai Indians argue more simply that the failure of the predictions of the prophet Wodziwob led to a breakdown of religious solidarity in the tribe. Once "Pai religious unity" was broken, the way for a more functional "diversification of religious practices and belief" was opened. The ghost dance movement was thus a catalyst of cultural transformation; it separated church and state and allowed for religious pluralism. Some Pais became Mormons, some joined Protestant churches, some remained traditional, some became skeptics; this proved to be an effective adjustment to the religious pluralism of the dominant white society. Still, Dobyns and Euler conclude that the Pai ghost dance "never achieved . . . an effective revitalization function" in any general sense. Was their movement, then, a false ghost dance? Is successful revitalization the test of a true ghost dance? That is, if revitalization takes place as a result of post–ghost dance adjustments despite the failure of the prophets' spectacular predictions, is it merely an unintended consequence of purposive action, assuming that Wallace is correct in describing revitalization as "a deliberate, organized, conscious effort by members of a society to construct a more satisfying culture"?[14]

This debate over "true" ghost dances, particularly why ghost dances now are so commonly seen as revitalization movements, requires a definition of "false" ghost dances. Obviously, a ghost dance was not false simply because its prophecies never materialized. The Cherokee ghost dance of 1867, discussed below, was false not because it failed to revitalize but because it was concocted for political purposes by self-interested individuals who hoped to manipulate unsuspecting Cherokees for their own aims; the perpetrators had no faith in its claims themselves. It may have stirred some full-bloods to revive traditional religious rituals, but that was not its true purpose. This ghost dance movement lacked a clearly identified prophet, although it had messengers, some sincere; it lacked both a specific dance or ceremonial element prescribed to trigger the hoped-for event (though it encouraged traditional Cherokee dances) and a doctrine of moral renewal or personal redemption. In fact, sacred elements are almost entirely absent from the surviving evidence. Nonetheless, this false ghost dance caused considerable turmoil in the Nation and aroused serious concern among observers.

A true ghost dance included a prophet, a vision, a doctrine, and a ritual received from what the prophet believed to be a genuine supernatural source.[15] This message centered on promises of divinely guided cultural renewal and coherence, restoration of tribal land and other resources, and imminent destruction or expulsion of the European invader and oppressor. The process of ridding the region of whites might take the form of a supernaturally induced cataclysm (such as an earthquake, tornado, or hailstorm), a supernaturally led Indian uprising, or an armed attack on the whites by a union of the oppressed and certain allies (Spanish, French, British, or Mormon). The essential ideological features of true ghost dance movements were the rejection of European concepts of progress through the subjugation of nature, the rejection of the individualistic ethic of material acquisitiveness and the market economy that encouraged it, and the rejection of the European assumption that whites were the chosen people of God, with a manifest destiny to rule the world and bring about the millennium on earth as it was in heaven. A true ghost dance asserted that the red people were the chosen ones of God; that sharing, cooperation, and communal ownership of land constituted the true social ethic for human beings; that the Great Spirit required a harmonious balance among man, nature, and the supernatural; and that stability, not change, was the ideal order. In essence, a ghost dance was ethnocentric. It asserted that North America belonged to the indigenous peoples, whose way of life was divinely ordained for that continent; that the Europeans were invaders who had abandoned the region the Great Spirit gave them (and dragged the African from the land divinely granted him); and that true harmony would exist in the universe only when each race followed its divinely ordained ways in its own domain. The true purpose of a ghost dance was to restore aboriginal power, dignity, order, self-control, and political autonomy to the red men of the New World, their Old World. In most cases this meant rejection of the material goods and livestock obtained from the Europeans. Syncretistic elements are apparent in the late-nineteenth-century ghost dances, especially in terms of Christian symbolism (messiah, millennium, revivalism, the Second Coming of Christ, and so on).

It is probable that the ghost dances that predicted military assistance from white allies constituted efforts to attract persons skeptical of total reliance on supernatural magic, whereas ghost dances that relied wholly on supernatural intervention were supported by those skeptical of the military efforts that had so often failed them. The fact that the false ghost dance described below predicted assistance from European and Mormon allies in a war against white Americans places it in the category of the ghost dances that led to Pontiac's confederacy and Tecumseh's war.

The Ghost Dance Movement of 1867

Although the manipulators of this false Cherokee ghost dance included some full-blood or traditionalist leaders, the movement was essentially directed by highly acculturated mixed-bloods. Fearing that a new traditionalist party was about to remove them from power in 1867, these mixed-bloods and their full-blood allies fabricated and disseminated in revivalist meetings a messianic call to arms against all whites west of the Mississippi. They asserted that a military alliance with many neighboring tribes existed or was coming into being and that specifically "European powers" would provide arms and supplies. The evident absence of a specific prophet and specific dances and ceremonies may be crucial to its falseness, but the movement's ultimate goal of imminent, miraculous restoration of the land to the indigenous peoples and the expulsion of the white man clearly lies within the definition of a true ghost dance. The popular reception by the Cherokees of the message of restoration of autonomy over their nations and natural resources was also typical of a true ghost dance. That this movement spread quickly indicates the tremendous cultural tensions facing the Cherokees following the devastation visited upon them during the Civil War and the confusion among them resulting from new congressional efforts to promote territorialism and from the government's effort to stipulate the admission of all former slaves to full Cherokee citizenship in the peace treaty of 1866. What brands the movement as spurious is that its purpose was to sustain mixed-blood rule in the name of traditionalism.

Origins

The movement began in the summer of 1867, when the Cherokees were suffering from the aftereffects of the internecine strife engendered by the Civil War. During the war the Cherokee Nation had been divided between those who sided with the Confederacy and those who sided with the Union. Although this division appeared to grow out of the conflict between slaveholding and non-slaveholding Cherokees, it had far deeper roots. Cherokee historians have traced these roots back to the crisis over Indian displacement in the 1830s, when the Nation developed a group of leaders (most of them mixed-blood slaveholders) who concluded in 1832 that it was futile to fight removal from their ancestral homeland. Failing to persuade the Cherokee council to accept the inevitable, these leaders made their own treaty with the United States in 1835. The Treaty of New Echota was never ratified by the council, but it was ratified by the U.S. Senate. Its signers, the Removal party, were branded traitors, and after the U.S. Army forcibly removed the Cherokees in 1838, three of the most prominent leaders of that party, Major Ridge, Elias Boudinot, and

John Ridge, were murdered. Several years of near civil war followed as the Removal party sought to avenge their deaths. In 1846 a treaty ended the conflict, but the rivalry between the two parties was by no means forgotten.

The division took new form in the 1850s as an antislavery movement among the Cherokees. Most of the full-bloods were too poor to own slaves, and in any case many of them were members of the northern Baptist mission churches, which prohibited their members from owning slaves. In 1855 two secret organizations formed within the Nation. The more radical proslavery leaders joined the Knights of the Golden Circle, and the more extreme antislavery leaders joined the Keetoowah Society. The Knights of the Golden Circle sought to stamp out all antislavery activity and to expel the northern Baptist missionaries. The Keetoowah Society (with which the Baptists were closely associated) sought to keep the Cherokees neutral in the mounting sectional division among white Americans. To do so, the society bound its members to elect only non-slaveholders and non-English-speaking Cherokees to office; its membership was limited to full-bloods. The Keetoowahs (later called "the Pins") included both Christians and traditionalists. The Knights of the Golden Circle, a small body, was closely allied with the wealthier, English-speaking Cherokees (perhaps 30 percent of the population). The mixed-bloods controlled the National Committee, or upper house of the council; the full-bloods controlled the lower house.[16]

A third group, led by Chief John Ross and his family and their close friends, mediated between the two factions. The Ross family was of mixed ancestry; they were well-to-do slaveholders committed to acculturation. But because Ross, who had first been elected in 1828, had firmly opposed the Removal party and held the Nation together during the bloody years after 1839, he was regularly elected chief with the general support of the full-bloods. He favored a policy of neutrality in 1860 and thus was not trusted by the proslavery party; he allied the Nation with the Confederacy in 1861 but repudiated the alliance in 1862 and fled north under the protection of the first invading Union military force. For the next three years, the Confederate and Union Cherokees fought each other, decimating their once thriving nation. Stand Watie, who became a general in the Confederate Army, was the leader of the Southern party and a nephew of Major Ridge of the Removal party. After the war, the Southern party sought to divide the

Nation into two autonomous Cherokee nations, one for the Southern party and one for the Union party. Just prior to his death in 1866, John Ross signed a treaty with the United States that prevented this division, but it did not put an end to the bitter rivalry between the two groups.[17]

After Ross's death, the Cherokee council elected his nephew, William Potter Ross, chief to complete his term, which ended in 1867. The assistant chief was Colonel Lewis Downing, a full-blood and an ordained Baptist minister who had fought with the Union forces. "Will" Ross was also a Union veteran, but he had graduated from Princeton College and was committed to his uncle's policy of acculturation. He was so bitter toward the Southern party that he refused to appoint any of its members to office, prompting the Southern party to send its own delegations to Washington in 1866 and 1867, claiming to have been treated unfairly and continuing to push for a division of the Nation. Ross had been a slaveholder and, like his uncle, a southern Methodist. Downing had been a member of the Keetoowah Society and was a protégé of the northern Baptist missionaries Evan Jones and John B. Jones, his son. They had served as chaplains in the Cherokee regiments of the Union forces and returned to the Nation in 1866 to reestablish their mission churches among the full-bloods.

In the spring of 1867, when it appeared that Will Ross would again be a candidate for principal chief, Downing and the Joneses decided that it was in the best interest of the Nation to achieve a reconciliation with the Southern party. Downing therefore became a candidate for principal chief, in opposition to Ross. He also appears to have made some agreement with the leaders of the Southern party, offering them important offices in exchange for their support. If Downing was elected, it would be the first time since 1827 that a full-blood had become principal chief. The full-bloods seemed about to realize the goal of the Keetoowah Society by regaining control of the Nation from the mixed-bloods. Ross, lacking his uncle's respect for, and rapport with, the full-bloods, considered this a step backward; he was angry with the Joneses for deserting him and his uncle's party, and he was determined to do all he could to keep the Southern party from regaining power. Ross and his collaborators are considered, then, to have instigated the false ghost dance movement.[18]

The Observations of William L. G. Miller

Under the Cherokee constitution, elections took place on the first Monday in August. All male adults were eligible to vote. Though the results were generally known the day after the election, the votes were sealed until the council met in November, made an official count of the votes (after examining contested votes or cases of alleged fraud), and proclaimed the winner. It was during this hotly contested election that the ghost dance movement took form. There had been some violence among the opposing factions at the polls, and while the votes seemed to indicate that Downing was the winner, the considerable turmoil that prevailed between the election and November obscured the outcome. Ross would not concede defeat.

There appears to be only one document describing this ghost dance. No official records mention it. None of the extant papers of Ross, Downing, or the Joneses mention it, and no surviving papers of members of the Southern party allude to it, which may indicate that William L. G. Miller, who described the movement, and Lewis Downing, who supported Miller's claims, may have exaggerated its importance. But there is no doubt that the ghost dance occurred. The document that does survive, in the archives of the commissioner of Indian affairs, is very explicit. Miller, a native of Scotland, had resided in the Cherokee Nation for many years. He had been a merchant, doctor, and lawyer; he had learned to speak, read, and write Cherokee. Downing respected and trusted him and told him that, if elected, he would appoint Miller his executive secretary (a post not mentioned in the Cherokee constitution but essential to a chief who could not speak, read, or write English). The Joneses, among others, distrusted Miller, suspecting that he provided the federal government with information about internal Cherokee affairs. From his subsequent career in the Nation, it appears that Miller was loyal to Downing and did his best to support the full-bloods and the national interests of the Cherokee people.

Although Miller described the ghost dance movement as a concoction of Downing's political opponents, it hardly seems likely that it would have been undertaken had the Cherokee Nation not been rife with fear and anxiety about the future. Even a false ghost dance movement drew upon the more or less permanent cultural confusion, angst, and hopes of Native American peoples from the days of the first European devastations of their cultures. The perpetrators of the hoax were no doubt aware that the war raging to the west of them between the U.S. Army and the Plains tribes concerned all Native Americans, raising fears of their wholesale extermination by frustrated white homesteaders. Ghost dance movements were common among the Plains Indians from 1865 until the massacre at Wounded Knee in 1890.

The three conspirators took advantage of the general uneasiness and rumors rampant among the Cherokees. Miller identified them as James Vann, Lewis McNair, and Sis-quo-nee-tah (Little Pig). Vann was a member of a wealthy mixed-blood family, most of whom had been slaveholders, allies of the Confederacy, and members of the Southern party. However, he had joined the Union forces during the war. He had been elected assistant chief in 1867, but not as a Downing party candidate; he was a Ross party man. Lewis McNair also came from a slaveholding mixed-blood family associated with the Ross party. Sis-quo-nee-tah, a full-blood loyal to the Ross party, had just been elected to the council; he probably represented that group of full-bloods who saw Ross as the natural heir to his uncle's leadership role.

As Miller noted, Sis-quo-nee-tah had a more traditionalist outlook than Vann and McNair and may have been their link to the full-bloods. He may even have belonged to the Keetoowah Society. When elected to the council, he expressed resentment that the constitution required all officeholders to take an oath stating their belief in "the being of a God or a future state of reward and punishment." This had been written into the constitution in 1827, when John Ross was trying to convince white Americans that the Cherokees were a civilized, Christian people who did not deserve to be removed to live among the "wild, savage" Indians of the West. It is probable that when full-bloods took this oath, it was administered in Cherokee, and that the word for "God" was the same as that for "Great Spirit." But Sis-quo-nee-tah resented it, just as he resented that Ross's opponent was an ordained Baptist minister.

None of the three instigators of the false ghost dance movement was a prominent leader, although Miller was probably correct to surmise that Will Ross was aware of what they were doing and at least tacitly approved of it. Miller implied that all three men were easily flattered and had a high sense of their own importance. They may have enjoyed giving "wild and visionary" speeches around the Nation to excited crowds. Miller had been aware of the movement from the time of the election in August but at first ignored it. As it attracted more and more adherents, he became alarmed, fearing that it might lead to "an insurrection." Downing might be assassinated and the Cherokees linked to the rebellious Plains Indians; they stood to lose what little autonomy they had left. Certainly the movement was designed to wave the "bloody shirt" against any rapprochement with the Southern party. The situation seemed particularly perilous because the federal agent to the Cherokees had recently died and his successor had not yet arrived. Lewis McNair, the only bilingual member of the trio, claimed to have received dispatches from "European powers" supportive of a general uprising. Miller wanted to make certain that the commissioner of Indian Affairs pinned the blame for any disturbance upon the Ross party, which, he said, was "very much discontented at their signal defeat" and "talk[ed] strongly of contesting the election" when the council assembled.

The most curious aspect of the movement was not its claim that a pan-Indian alliance supported by European powers would soon sweep all whites back across the Mississippi River, but the assertion of the false prophets that the Europeans would be assisted by "the Mormons, the only American white friends of the Indians." If Ross plotted this hoax as shrewdly as Miller implied, it seems odd that his minions would claim that the Mormons would participate with the Cherokees in the "massacre of all the whites and half breeds, except the supporters of W. P. Ross, who they will make chief." The Mormons now were hated and feared in the United States even more than the Europeans. Miller was surely wrong to believe that Ross had "made a speech strongly at variance with his pretended patriotism and friendship for the United States." Miller may have been trying to influence the commissioner against Ross in anticipation of Downing's being counted out by the council. If Ross could bring some of the full-bloods in the lower house to his side, he might become chief yet.

Although Mormons had lived and proselytized among the Cherokees prior to the Civil War, there is no evidence that any Mormon missionaries were present in 1867. However, Mormonism did appeal to many Native Americans because the Book of Mormon foretold that, ultimately, the Indians would become a "white and delightsome" people and would be accorded the honor they deserved as descendants of the Lost Tribes of Israel. Mormons were active in the late 1860s among the Utes and Paiutes to the west. These tribes had developed their own true ghost dance movement by the end of that decade.

Some credulous Cherokees may have believed that the Mormons, persecuted like themselves by the United States, were logical allies. But why Ross would want his party associated with them is not clear. Possibly Vann, McNair, and Sis-quo-nee-tah were left to their own devices on their errand and thought that Cherokees sympathetic to Mormon millennialism might be attracted to the Ross party by this claim of Mormon military assistance. In any case, Miller was convinced that this was "just the kind of element the Mormons would operate on"; he urged the commissioner to arrest and prosecute the "emissarie" from that church who was involved, but he never identified him. It was as convenient for Downing as for Ross to be able to point to outside agitators as the cause of any trouble that might ensue.[19]

Miller's Letter to the Commissioner of Indian Affairs

At this point it is important to cite in full the body of the letter that Miller wrote to the commissioner on October 2, 1867.

I have promised to myself to volunteer no more information to the Government as it has more than once endangered my life. From the fact that the U.S. Officials have given up my name to unscrupulous persons, implicated, and I have incurred considerable risk from the fact that I was not aware of what I regarded as a breach of confidence until some time after the mischief was done; as for instance in the case of the speech [sic] made by the late John Ross, Chief of the Cherokees, December 1861, which was published in a pamphlet issued by the Hon. N. D. Cooley, late commissioner of Indian affairs, in which my veracity was allowed to be impeached; and I was denied the right to vindicate myself or prove the truth of what I had so faithfully and disinterestedly reported—a thing easily done at the time, as I understand that Mr. Cooper, formerly a General in the rebel service, was then in Washington and could have verified the truth of the speech from memory. He being present on the stand at the time the speech was delivered and following in a speech of the same purport.

This I did not know anything about until very lately, the Ross Delegation being characteristically very reticent on the subject, doing their work insidiously. But in certain quarters I have been made to feel the effects of their conduct. The Rev. J. C. [B.] Jones and Capt. [Smith] Christy, knowing [know] my report to be true, as does every one who was present. But the Ross's have long imbued their followers with the belief that I am a government spy, which circumstances in the last War, has [*sic*] confirmed. This is a dangerous distinction, and in my case very unprofitable.

But I consider what I have to relate *now* of such vital importance to the United States and the loyal Cherokees, that it outweighs every other personal consideration. But I shall so state what has come to my knowledge as to leave you to be the judge of its importance and to draw your own inferences.

It appears from reliable information, Col. Lewis Downing being my principal authority, that Capt. James Vann, 2nd chief elect, resident of Flint District; Sis-quo-nee-tah, or Little Pig, a Councillor of Canadian District, and Lewis McNair, of Coo-wee-scoo-wee District, and perhaps others, have for some time back been making various inflam[m]atory speaches in several places in the Cherokee Nation, tending, as I apprehend, to incite the Cherokees against the United States and the party who supported Col. Downing in the last election for principal Chief.

The speaches were represented as being wild and visionary, but none the less mischievous in their tendency among the credulous, and this fact weakens their effect among the thinking portion of the community, who are the majority. It may be as well to mention that the speakers are men who have a very large share of self esteem and conceitedly attach a *very* great importance to their powers, influence and ability and Wisdom, and are just such men as are easily led by flattery on fair promises, and on the whole well calculated to the tools in the hands of bad designing men who could gain their confidence, and take advantage of their antipathies and prejudices.

From what I can gather, the speakers claim to be in communication with some of the European Powers who, they say, sympathize with the Cherokees, and have combined to revenge them on their enemies, the United States and all who are opposed to them among the bad Indians friendly to the United States, particularly including the Downing Party and the Southern Cherokees. And that these *Great Powers* have combined to send a *great army,* in conjunction with the only American white friends of the Indians, The Romans (the *Mormons* are called by this name in the Cherokee language), and that with this army, which is to include a million of the Indians of the plains, well armed and well provided for, they will come into the Cherokee Nation this fall and massacre the whites and half breeds, except the supporters of W. P. Ross, who they will make chief, and then sweep the country from the nation to the Mississippi, and give it all up, with the spoil, to the Great Cherokees and their friends, for their own use, and defend them in the possession.

They pretend to read translations from the communications received from these Great Powers, confirming the truth of all these promises. L. McNair, being the interpreter and translator. They claim that the Agent of these Great Powers have [has] been among them for some time, that he has conversed with many of the same subject, and that he is now in the Creek Nation prosyliting [*sic*] the Creeks.

Little Pig is to gather up a Cherokee force to go out and meet the great army and get ammunition and arms. But before he goes, he is to cause the assassination of all opposing leaders, and those who betray the secret. Particularly those who will oppose his taking his seat in Council on account of his ineligibility from his absurd disbelief in a God, or a true state of rewards and punishments [after death].

There are many reasons why I believe this to be true, although it was only yesterday that I learned the particulars given. I have heard McNair, in his broken way, speak to the same effect, but so obscurely that I did not then understand him. I have also heard other Indians hint mysteriously at the same, but supposed it an election trick, put up by Mr. Ross or his friends, and treated it with contempt. I have also heard of families moving away from the route of the great army on the Verdigris [River], but attributed that to fear engendered by the existing war with the Indians of the plains.

I cannot say that W. P. Ross has knowledge of this, but I believe he has, for some time ago, since the election, a woman informed me that he had made a speach strongly at variance with his pretended patriotism and friendship for the United States. We know that he undervalues Col. Downing, chargeing [*sic*] that he will be ruled by Mr. [John B.] Jones and myself, forgetting that John Ross was advised for years by Rev. E[van] Jones. His friends, at least, make threats, talk strongly of contesting the election, and in any case preventing Col. Downing taking his seat as Executive of the Nation. That they are very much discontented at their signal defeat [in August] and the unmistakable rebuke to their unmeasured arrogance, is certain, and how far the speaches of Vann, Little Pig, and McNair has [have] to do with this is uncertain, but to my mind it forms just the kind of element the Mormons would operate on, to the greatest advantage, and I cannot avoid thinking that all our late Indian difficulties are due to them or to men equally unprincipled.

That this did not originate with the Cherokees is sure, while I think that there is a pretended, or real, emissarie of the Mormons at the bottom of it. That he should be taken, tried, and punished to the extreme of the law, seems to be a duty. Who is to do it? It can be done by judicious management through the misguided fools, Capt. Vann, Little Pig, and McNair. Col. Downing will aid all he can, but in any case will fasten the charge upon these men by persons hearing the speaches. Again, it is for you to decide whether or not there may not be just apprehension of an insurrection in the Cherokee Nation which it may be proper to prevent for the sake of peace on the frontier.

I write this with the consent of Col. Downing; had there been an agent [of the federal government here at this time] I would have written through him, or notified him, of the facts. I now leave the matter with you, begging that you will acknowledge the receipt of this, so that I may know it has reached you.[20]

There was no Cherokee insurrection in the fall of 1867. The religious fervor Miller saw among some of the full-bloods faded away. The council met peacefully in November and duly ratified Lewis Downing's election as principal chief. James Vann became assistant chief. The federal government took no action in response to Miller's letter. Whatever excitement had been generated by the false ghost dance ended with the failure of the prophecy. At the end of his four-year term in 1871, Downing was reelected.

The Movement's Outcome

A peaceful revolution placed the full-bloods in control of their own government for the first time in forty years. The tensions within the Cherokee Nation continued, as the reorganization of the Keetoowah Society in later years demonstrates, but the apparent enthusiasm of many Cherokees for any miraculous event that could restore their land and autonomy to them indicates the potential of this movement. Its leaders had exploited real anxieties. Miller noted the revivalist enthusiasm and excitement generated by the messengers of the hoped-for restoration of political autonomy. Undoubtedly, many full-bloods did revive their old dances and ceremonies. Had some prophet emerged with a vision giving divine sanction to the movement, and had he prescribed certain songs and rituals, a true ghost dance might have arisen from it.

Conclusion

Ethnohistorians need to refine the definition of the ghost dance or revitalization movement to differentiate the secular from the religious, the sporadic from the spectacular, and the potential for millenarianism from the revitalization latent in that potential. As

Cherokee history in the nineteenth century demonstrates, a large tribe, divided between those favoring rapid acculturation and those reluctant to abandon traditionalism, may follow two distinct, though interrelated, paths to revitalization. Both seek order, control, direction, and meaning for their lives. Both long for tribal unity and autonomy. But the faction favoring rapid acculturation opts for politically structured order, whereas the traditionalist faction seeks a syncretistic religious structure. Secular and religious revitalization may therefore proceed side by side, although the two factions may be suspicious of each other.

Duane Champagne has suggested that, while "the literature on revitalization movements and that on state building are almost mutually exclusive," nevertheless "there are some common historical and social structural factors that underly both." In the case of the Cherokees, state building was the choice of the strong mixed-blood faction (constituting 25 to 35 percent of the population), whereas religious and social alternatives were preferred by the full-blood faction. Because the Cherokees were a large tribe, ranging from sixteen to twenty thousand members, with a territory of ten million to twelve million acres, both social and geographical separation of these two groups was possible. They shared power in electing representatives and chiefs for their bicameral legislature, but the mixed-bloods dominated tribal political affairs from 1827 to 1867. The mixed-bloods adopted English in speech and writing, embraced Christianity, sent their children to mission schools, entered the cash-crop agricultural system of the surrounding states, utilized black slave labor, and modeled Cherokee political structure on the U.S. Constitution. If this group had a source of spiritual revitalization, it was evangelical Christianity.[21]

The full-blood majority, while accepting the necessity for an agricultural system and political centralization, remained more traditional in beliefs and values. They engaged sporadically in millenarian movements or other religious revivals (Millerism, astrology, Mormonism). These had little continuity and no outstanding prophets; they were viewed with amusement or contempt by the mixed-bloods. Sequoyah's invention of a simple way to write the Cherokee language in 1821 made the full-bloods literate in their mother tongue and lessened their interest in social acculturation, but the dominance of the mixed-blood minority forced the adoption of English as the official language, encouraged the influx of five missionary agencies, and strengthened the Cherokees' commitment to a market economy. By 1860, perhaps three thousand Cherokees were members of Christian mission churches (most of them were Baptist and Methodists). Mixed-bloods who were not church members nonetheless identified themselves as Christian in outlook and passed laws complementary to Christian morals (they outlawed polygamy, witchcraft, infanticide, and gambling). While about fifteen hundred fullbloods were members of mission churches (chiefly northern Baptist), the majority of them did not identify themselves as Christian in outlook. The mixed- and full-blood factions correlated closely to a growing class division between rich and poor, English-speaking and Cherokee-speaking, slave-holding and non-slaveholding.

Out of this tension grew the movement of the full-bloods to join a populist political movement after 1865 to sweep the mixed-bloods from power. The success of that movement in 1867 demonstrated the political sophistication of the full-bloods but not their religious acculturation—hence the effort by William Potter Ross and his allies in 1867 to utilize the potential for millenarianism to divide the full-bloods and prevent the overthrow of mixed-blood domination. Miller and Downing, as leaders of the populist movement, were sufficiently worried about Ross's tactic to seek federal help, although that was itself dangerous; nothing angered the Cherokees more than interference in their internal affairs by the government of the United States.

All of this suggests that ethnohistorians need to recognize the difficulty of making broad generalizations regarding ghost dance movements and revitalization and to stick closely to the contextual circumstances within each tribe over long periods. Abstract theorizing about true and false ghost dances can be misleading. We may find good examples of revitalization among the Senecas or identify the distinguishing features of the spectacular, intertribal ghost dances of 1870 and 1890, but we should not extrapolate broad constructs from these special cases. There is more to be learned by careful study of the unique characteristics of traditionalist religious revivals among the wide variety of Native American peoples.

Epilogue
The Fast Day Proclamation
of Chief Lewis Downing, 1870

When Chief Lewis Downing wrote this Fast Day Proclamation in
the fall of 1870, the Cherokees were facing serious challenges to their survival
as a nation. The railroads were starting through the Nation—one from north
to south, one from east to west. Congress had promised millions of acres of
land to the railroads in 1866 that would be delivered once the Indian tribes in
Indian Territory were denationalized. Eager for that day, the railroad lobbyists
were pressing Congress to turn Indian Territory into a federally controlled
territory preparatory to statehood (ultimately the state of Oklahoma). At the
same time, hundreds of white men and freedmen were coming into the Cherokee Nation, assuming that it would soon be turned over to homesteaders,
prospectors, and other entrepreneurs. The federal government was refusing to
honor its treaty obligations to remove these intruders. The Boudinot Tobacco
Case, decided in that year, destroyed the hope of the Cherokees that they could
become manufacturers of tobacco without being taxed by the government; competing white chewing-tobacco entrepreneurs in Arkansas had persuaded the
government to end that "unfair competition." Worst of all, a highly influential group of Indian reformers in the East had concluded that the only way
to help the Indians was to give each of them a plot of ground, abolish their
tribal government, and make them citizens of the United States—a reform
movement that triumphed in 1887 with the passage of the Dawes Severalty
Act—the death knell of independent tribal existence on their own land base.
Downing was probably also aware that within a year after this proclamation,
Congress would end the long practice of negotiating with Indian tribes by
treaty, giving Congress the power to tell the Indians what was necessary for
their own good.

Lewis Downing had fought for the Union as a colonel during the Civil War.
He was elected chief in 1867 and again in 1871. He was a full-blood (speaking

only Cherokee) and an early organizer of the Keetoowah Society. He was an ordained Baptist minister. His proclamation indicates how far the Cherokee people had come in 1870 toward being themselves "a Christian nation."

It is proper, and becoming, for all people, at all times, to humble themselves before Almighty God, and to confess their sins, and to implore his forgiveness, guidance, and protection through Jesus Christ. But the necessity of so doing, is especially apparent and urgent when people and Nations are in circumstances of distress and danger, and when threatened with public calamity.

As an encouragement to prayer and supplication, under such circumstances, we have only to turn to the promises of God, that when his creatures cry to him for succor in distress, or for protection in weakness, that His ear will be ever open to hear the prayer of sincere and earnest men. We can turn also to the repeated instances in which God has heard the prayers of distressed Nations, and listened to their confessions of sin, and protected them by His power, and warded off calamities.

Nineveh, when the edict of the Almighty had been issued for her destruction, proclaimed a fast, and all the people, from the King to the beggar, prostrated themselves in humiliation, and lifted up to God the cry for deliverance. The heart of Jehovah was moved to pity and the decree was annulled, and he repented him of the evil that he had determined against that city. Thus God, by both word and action, has declared Himself to be a prayer-hearing God.

Today, the Cherokees, and the whole Indian race are in distress and danger. Powerless we lie in the hands of the government and people of the United States, as did the Jews in the hands of Ahasuerus and the Persians. The United States can bring the weight of forty millions of people, and untold wealth, power, and skill to crush us in our weakness.

Not only have they the power thus to crush us, but with very many, the disposition is not wanting. Already the cry for the extermination of Indians, is heard from quarters, so high and influential as to give harm to the whole Indian Race. Especially are we alarmed, when we read in the short history of the United States name after name, of mighty nations of red men who once occupied this vast continent, but who are now swept from the face of the earth before the white man.

Amid the general decay of Indian Nations and the annihilation of the vast majority the five nations of the Indian Territory have not only survived but increased in numbers—accumulated property—advanced in civilization, adopted the Christian religion, and are now building churches and school houses; establishing printing presses, and agricultural societies, and making more rapid strides in civilization than ever before.

All this prosperity under God and His gospel, we owe to our separate national existence, and the protection and security afforded by our treaties with the United States. Although their treaties have been frequently violated, and their protection has been but partial, still they have served to prevent the tide of immigration from flooding our country, and to thwart the rapacious land grabbers, and liquor sellers; and to check injurious legislation by Congress. But avaricious men, and the enemies of the Indian, have opened their batteries on Indian treaties and threaten their annihilation. Efforts are being made to annul and destroy all of our treaties, and thus to tear away our only human defence, and leave us to be the sport of capricious legislation and unjust administration, and the victims of unscrupulous speculators.

Even now, before these treaties are annulled, the sacred obligations of the United States to protect us are to a great extent rendered nugatory by unjust decisions, and unwarranted official rulings.

Our adopted citizens have had their business houses closed by order of the United States Officials, to the great injury of our community, and are compelled to obtain in Washington, license to transact business.

The tax gatherer stands ready to enter our country and wrench from us our scanty earnings. Already the manufactories of our citizens have been seized and sold, under the operation of tax laws, from which the United States are sacredly pledged to exempt us.

Now, the organization over us by force of Territorial or State government is urged. Our title to our lands, and invested funds, has been questioned. The very foundations of our National and individual existence are threatened. The demand is made in influential quarters, that the Government of the United States shall disregard its sacred pledges and raise the flood gates, and let in upon us a stream of immigration to overwhelm us.

Our rights and liberties are trampled in the dust; our citizens are arrested by United States Marshals, contrary to law, dragged to prison in a foreign state, arraigned before a foreign court, and acquitted or condemned at the caprice of Judges and Jurors of a strange tongue, in a foreign land, who have no sympathy with us, and no regard for our rights or liberties.

Viewed in every light, and from every stand point, our situation is alarming. The vortex of ruin, which has swallowed hundreds of Indian Nations, now yawns for us.

In these circumstances of distress, where shall we go? Whither shall we flee for help?

Our Delegations, our lawyers, and friends have failed to stay the onward progress of usurpations. Our prayers, memorials, and petitions have fallen unheeded on the ears of Congress and Departmental officers.

To God, then, the Ruler of the universe. To Him who holds in His own hands the destinies of Nations, great and small, and who disposes of Emperors and Kings, together with their Empires and Kingdoms, according to His own good pleasure. To the Lord our God, let us go with our case. Let us pour out our prayers into the ear of the Merciful Jehovah, who, in the days of old "hath scattered the proud in the imagination of their hearts. He hath put down the mighty from their seats, and exalted them of low degree." To him let us confess our sins, and pray for National preservation, and for individual protection. In this let us unite with one heart, and one voice, and with deep earnestness of soul.

Now therefore in view of our critical condition, I, Lewis Downing, Principal Chief of the Cherokee Nation, do hereby set apart, and appoint Thursday the seventeenth (17) day of November A.D. 1870, a day of National Humiliation, fasting and prayer. And I do hereby call upon all the people of the Cherokee Nation, to observe the same, strictly, earnestly, and sincerely. Let christians of every name, throughout the whole nation, lay aside their ordinary business engagements, and assemble at their various places of worship, and unite in earnest prayer and supplication to Almighty God for National preservation. Ask God to incline the hearts of the rulers and people of the

United States to observe strictly their solemn pledges not to trample down our rights and our liberties. Pray God to secure to us our country, and our homes to save us from usurpation, which fill our land with the foreign officers, who drag us before foreign courts, and cast us into foreign prisons, without color of law; which levy unjust taxes, and confiscate our property to satisfy the same, which lays unjust and oppressive restrictions on a portion of our citizens to the injury of all. Let us beg of God to save us from usurpation which threatens to destroy the last vestige of self government that remains to us, and to open our country to white immigration, and thus take from us our homes, and destroy us as a people. Let us humbly ask God to save [us] from these calamities, and from all other and give us peace, to protect us by his own power. And thus preserved, we may become a nation devoted to God, loving him with all our hearts and earnestly laboring in his service. A nation redeemed by the blood of Jesus Christ his son.

Given from under my hand, and the seal of the Cherokee Nation, at the Executive Department, Tahlequah, C. N. on this 17th day of October A.D. 1870.

Lewis Downing
Principal Chief of the Cherokee Nation

From the *Cherokee Advocate*, October 22, 1870.

Notes

Chapter 1. Native American Reactions to Christian Missions

1. Robert K. Berkhofer, *Salvation and the Savage* (New York: Atheneum, 1976).

2. See A. F. C. Wallace, *The Death and Rebirth of the Seneca* (New York: Vintage Press, 1972).

3. See James Mooney, *The Ghost Dance Religion and Wounded Knee* (New York: Dover, 1973).

4. See Arrell M. Gibson, *The American Indian* (Norman: University of Oklahoma Press, 1980), 102, 472, and Henry W. Bowden, *American Indians and Christian Missions* (Chicago: University of Chicago Press, 1981), 54–55.

5. Bowden, *American Indians,* 76–90.

6. Gibson, *The American Indian,* 349.

7. Bowden, *American Indians,* 117–32, and Neal Salisbury, "Red Puritans: The 'Praying Indians' of Massachusetts Bay and John Eliot," *William and Mary Quarterly* 31 (January 1974): 28–53.

8. James Axtell, *The Invasion Within* (New York: Oxford University Press, 1985), 4.

9. Quoted in James Mooney, *Historical Sketch of the Cherokee* (Chicago: Aldine Publishers, 1975), 103.

10. Quoted in William G. McLoughlin, *Cherokees and Missionaries, 1789–1829* (New Haven: Yale University Press, 1984), 60.

11. Quoted in Henry T. Malone, *Cherokees of the Old South* (Athens: University of Georgia Press, 1956), 96.

12. Robert S. Walker, *Torchlights to the Cherokees* (New York: Macmillan, 1931), 178.

13. Brainerd Journal, May 29, 1818, 109, Papers of the American Board of Commissioners for Foreign Missions, Houghton Library, Harvard University (hereafter, ABCFM Papers).

14. McLoughlin, *Cherokees and Missionaries,* 190–91.

15. Quoted in William G. McLoughlin, *The Cherokee Ghost Dance: Essays on the Southeastern Indians, 1789–1861* (Macon, Ga.: Mercer University Press, 1984), 269.

16. McLoughlin, *Cherokees and Missionaries,* 39.

17. See McLoughlin, *Ghost Dance,* 253–60.

18. Ibid., 274.

19. Axtell, *The Invasion Within*, 78, 80.

20. See Charles Hudson, *The Southeastern Indians* (Knoxville: University of Tennessee Press, 1976), 120–83. Other terms of harmony were order, balance, and equilibrium.

21. Cited in McLoughlin, *Cherokees and Missionaries*, 203.

22. Ibid., 203.

23. Ibid., 198.

24. Ibid., 39.

25. See Daniel J. Boorstin, *The Lost World of Thomas Jefferson* (Boston: Beacon Press, 1948), 82–88. See also William G. McLoughlin and Walter H. Conser, Jr., "The First Man Was Red," *American Quarterly* 41 (Spring 1989): 243–64.

26. Michael Coleman, "Not Race but Grace," *Journal of American History* 67 (June 1980): 41–60.

27. George Fredrickson, *The Black Image in the White Mind* (New York: Harper and Row, 1971), 2, and William Stanton, *The Leopard's Spots* (Chicago: University of Chicago Press, 1960).

28. Quoted in McLoughlin, *Cherokees and Missionaries*, 13.

29. Brainerd Journal, March 20, 1820, ABCFM Papers.

30. Quoted in Walker, *Torchlights*, 244.

31. Ibid., 21.

32. McLoughlin, *Cherokees and Missionaries*, 36–45.

33. The Moravians were, in the end, allowed to remain after they reluctantly, and against their better judgment, did open a boarding school.

34. See Dorothy C. Bass, "Gideon Blackburn's Mission to the Cherokees," *Journal of Presbyterian History* 52 (Fall 1974): 219.

35. McLoughlin, *Cherokees and Missionaries*, 56–78. Blackburn said, "I have laboured with some of the chiefs to have an attempt made to have a few simple laws passed by their Nation and reduced to writing and have some one of themselves to act as Secretary of State and that no law should be in force unless committed to record." Ibid., 78. In this he was not successful.

36. Ibid., 80.

37. Ibid., 134–35.

38. Ibid., 117–22.

39. Ibid., 203.

40. Ibid., 209–10, and McLoughlin, *Ghost Dance*, 385–96.

41. McLoughlin, *Cherokees and Missionaries*, 202–3.

42. Quoted in Ibid., 205.

43. Ibid., 207.

44. Ibid., 208.

45. Quoted in William G. McLoughlin, *Champions of the Cherokees: Evan and John B. Jones* (Princeton: Princeton University Press, 1990), 72.

46. Ibid., 72.

47. McLoughlin, *Ghost Dance*, 112–52.

48. Quoted in Ibid., 143.

49. See the discussion of White Path's Rebellion in McLoughlin, *Cherokees and Missionaries*, chaps. 18 and 19.

50. Quoted in William G. McLoughlin, *Cherokee Renascence* (Princeton: Princeton University Press, 1986), 392.

51. Henry Clauser to the Moravian mission board in his journal, March 25, 1837, Moravian Archives, Bethlehem, Pa.

52. Daniel Butrick to Samuel Worcester, January 1, 1819, ABCFM Papers.

53. A typical example of this reaction was a statement of Chief Chulioa regarding the Moravian missionaries. He told the federal agent, "We have heard that the missionaries were too proud to converse [with the Cherokees in their own tongue]." Quoted in McLoughlin, *Cherokees and Missionaries*, 51.

54. Daniel Butrick to Samuel Worcester, January 1, 1819, ABCFM Papers.

55. Daniel Butrick in his journal, November 6, 1824, ABCFM Papers.

56. The first three Methodist circuit riders to marry Cherokees were Richard Neely (in 1825), James J. Trott (1828), and Nicholas D. Scales (1827). McLoughlin, *Cherokees and Missionaries*, 175.

57. Quoted in McLoughlin, *Cherokees and Missionaries*, 290.

58. For the reaction of the Methodist mission board to the behavior of the circuit riders and Trott's reaction to that, see McLoughlin, *Cherokees and Missionaries*, 291–92, 295–96.

59. Ibid., 297–99.

60. For biographical details of the career of Evan Jones, see McLoughlin, *Champions of the Cherokees*.

61. Daniel Butrick to Willard Upham, enclosed with the letter of Evan Jones to the Baptist board, February 18, 1847, American Baptist Missionary Union Papers, Baptist Historical Society, Rochester, N.Y. (hereafter, ABMU Papers).

62. Lewis Downing et al., enclosed in a letter of Evan Jones's to the Baptist board, April 6, 1847, ABMU Papers.

63. For a discussion of the Keetoowah Society, see McLoughlin, *Champions of the Cherokees*, 245–48 and passim, and Emmet Starr, *History of the Cherokee Indians and Their Legends and Folklore* (New York: Kraus Reprint, 1969), 143, 258, 479–84.

64. Margaret C. Szasz, *Indian Education in the American Colonies* (Albuquerque: University of New Mexico Press, 1988), 6.

65. Berkhofer, *Salvation and the Savage*, 152.

Chapter 2. The Missionaries' Dilemma

1. Edmund S. Morgan, *The Puritan Dilemma* (Boston: Little, Brown, 1958), xii.

2. Quoted in John M. McFerrin, *History of Methodism in Tennessee* (Nashville: Southern Methodist Publishing House, 1879), 373.

3. Cited in William G. McLoughlin, "Civil Disobedience and Evangelism among the Missionaries to the Cherokee," *Journal of Presbyterian History* 51 (Summer 1973): 12.

4. See Althea Bass, *Cherokee Messenger* (Norman: University of Oklahoma Press, 1936), 130–77.

5. The laws of Georgia specifically gave Indians only the limited rights available to freed slaves, which meant that once incorporated under Georgia's laws they would be second-class citizens.

6. See William G. McLoughlin, "Cherokees and Methodists," *Church History* 50 (March 1981): 44–63.

7. See McLoughlin, *Cherokees and Missionaries*, 255–56.

8. Trott did not actually go to prison because he agreed to leave his home and reside outside the limits of Georgia. See Edward J. Moseley, *Disciples of Christ in Georgia* (St. Louis: Bethany Press, 1954), 123–31.

9. The Baptist board did not have to face the issue because it had no mission stations in Georgia. The Sarepta Baptist Missionary Society of Georgia did employ a missionary among the Cherokees named Duncan O'Briant (or O'Bryant), who, as a citizen of Georgia, had no qualms about signing the oath. See George R. Gilmer, *Sketches of Some of the First Settlers of Upper Georgia* (New York: Appleton, 1855), 304, 344.

10. See Edwin A. Miles, "After John Marshall's Decision," *Journal of Southern History* 39 (November 1973): 520–44.

11. All of the quotations regarding this controversy among the American Board missionaries can be found in McLoughlin, "Civil Disobedience."

12. See in this regard Norman Gottwald's review of Hyam Maccoby's *The Sacred Executioner* in the *New York Times Book Review*, December 18, 1983, 8.

13. William Potter to David Greene, May 27, 1835, ABCFM Papers.

14. See William G. McLoughlin, "The Cherokee Baptist Preachers and the Great Schism of 1844–1845," *Foundations* 24 (April 1981): 137–47.

15. See William G. McLoughlin, "The Chocktaw Slave Burning," *Journal of the West* 13 (January 1974): 113–27.

16. Quoted in William G. McLoughlin, "Indian Slaveholders and Presbyterian Missionaries," *Church History* 42 (December 1973): 5.

17. For the formation of this abolition society (called "the Pins"), see Annie H. Abel, *The American Indians as Slaveholders and Secessionists* (Cleveland: A. H. Clark, 1915), and Chapter 9 in this volume.

18. Quoted in McLoughlin, "Indian Slaveholders," 24.

19. Quoted in McLoughlin, "Civil Disobedience," 13.

20. John F. Thompson to David Greene, May 25, 1831, ABCFM Papers.

Chapter 3. Two Bostonian Missionaries

1. Clifton J. Phillips, *Protestant America and the Pagan World* (Cambridge, Mass.: 1969), 3.

2. Phillips, *Protestant America*, 5. Phillips somewhat exaggerates the influence of New England Hopkinsian Calvinism when he writes, "Of the theological currents that fed American evangelicalism in this period, none was so influential as that deriving from Jonathan Edwards [as] systematized by Samuel Hopkins . . . The New England theology."

3. For early Indian policy, see Francis P. Prucha, *American Indian Policy in the Formative Years* (Cambridge, Mass.: Harvard University Press, 1962).

4. Perry Miller, *The Life of the Mind in America* (New York: Gollancz, 1965), 11.

5. Quoted in Phillips, *Protestant America*, 12.

6. Quoted in Ibid., 321.

7. Ibid., 243.

8. Bass, *Cherokee Messenger*, 196.

9. Phillips, *Protestant America*, 29. See also note 14 below.

10. Phillips, *Protestant America*, 4.

11. Robert G. Torbet, *Venture of Faith: The Story of the American Baptist Foreign Mission Society, 1814–1954* (Philadelphia: Judson Press, 1955), 19.

12. The most recent biography of Worcester is Bass, *Cherokee Messenger*.

13. For Jones, see McLoughlin, *Champions of the Cherokees*.

14. See Joseph Tracy, *History of the American Board of Commissioners for Foreign Missions* (Philadelphia, 1855). Tracy provides the names and birthplaces of all the board's missionaries.

15. See Torbet, *Venture of Faith*.

16. Robert G. Torbet, *A History of the Baptists* (Philadelphia: Judson Press, 1950), 268.

17. Winthrop S. Hudson, "Stumbling into Disorder," *Foundations* 1 (1958): 45–71.

18. Tracy, *History*, 27; Phillips, *Protestant America*, 32.

19. Phillips, *Protestant America*, 238; Torbet, *Venture of Faith*, 107–11.

20. Samuel Worcester to Cyrus Kingsbury, November 19, 1817, ABCFM Papers.

21. See McLoughlin, *Cherokees and Missionaries*, 152–55.

22. See Theda Perdue, *Slavery and the Evolution of Cherokee Society, 1540–1866* (Knoxville: University of Tennessee Press, 1979).

23. Quoted in Walker, *Torchlights*, 23.

24. Daniel Butrick to David Greene, June 21, 1852, ABCFM Papers.

25. Bass, *Cherokee Messenger*, 221.

26. Cyrus Kingsbury to Samuel Worcester, December 19, 1816, ABCFM Papers.

27. Jeremiah Evarts to Isaac Proctor, January 9, 1827, ABCFM Papers.

28. Daniel Butrick to David Greene, April 15, 1842. See also Butrick to Greene, June 21, 1842, ABCFM Papers.

29. Timothy Ranney to Selah Treat, July 30, 1857, ABCFM Papers.

30. Daniel Butrick to David Greene, April 15, 1842, ABCFM Papers.

31. Daniel Butrick to David Greene, September 11, 1842, ABCFM Papers.

32. Morey D. Rothberg, "The Effectiveness of Missionary Education among the Cherokees: The Brainerd School, 1817–1836," seminar paper, Brown University, Providence, R.I., 1972.

33. Rothberg, "Effectiveness of Missionary Education."

34. Quoted in Louis Hall to Selah B. Treat, vol. 12, 1851 (Letter 36), ABCFM Papers.

35. Walker, *Torchlights*, 140.

36. Quoted in McLoughlin, *Cherokees and Missionaries*, 141.

37. Ibid., 142.

38. Ibid.

39. Ibid., 155.

40. Quoted in McLoughlin, *Champions of the Cherokees*, 36.

41. Samuel Worcester to Jeremiah Evans, July 1, 1815, ABCFM Papers.

42. Quoted in Phillips, *Protestant America*, 65.

43. Quoted in McLoughlin, *Champions of the Cherokees*, 74.

44. Daniel Butrick to Jeremiah Evarts, November 24, 1824, ABCFM Papers.

45. Marcus Palmer, Report, February 12, 1855, ABCFM Papers.

46. For an example of a missionary of the ABCFM who aroused the wrath of the Cherokees by refusing to observe the hospitality ethic, see McLoughlin, *Cherokees and Missionaries*, 201.

47. Charles Torrey to Selah Treat, September 13, 1856, ABCFM Papers.

48. A. H. Newman, *A History of the Baptist Churches in the United States* (New York: Christian Literature Co., 1894), 379. See also Robert G. Gardner, *The Cherokees and Baptists in Georgia* (Atlanta: Georgia Baptist Historical Society, 1989).

49. George A. Schultz, *An Indian Canaan* (Norman: University of Oklahoma Press, 1972), 106–42.

50. Quoted in McLoughlin, *Cherokees and Missionaries*, 283.

51. Quoted in a letter from Ard Hoyt to Dr. Samuel Worcester, April 16, 1819, ABCFM Papers.

52. For Evarts's work, see Jeremiah Evarts, *Cherokee Removal*, ed. Francis Paul Prucha (Knoxville: University of Tennessee Press, 1981), intro.

53. For O'Briant, see McLoughlin, *Cherokees and Missionaries*, 280–82.

54. The BBFM's executive committee, McCoy said, "drank deeply of the spirit of opposition evidenced by the American Board, also in Boston." Quoted in Schultz, *An Indian Canaan*, 131.

55. Evan Jones to Lucius Bolles, April 26, 1832, ABMU Papers.

56. Ibid. For the resentment the Cherokees felt toward the Methodists for the support of the Tennessee Conference for removal, see McLoughlin, *Cherokees and Missionaries*, 292.

57. See McLoughlin, *Champions of the Cherokees*, 180.

58. Quoted in Bass, *Cherokee Messenger*, 241.

59. Samuel Worcester to Selah Treat, November 24, 1846, ABCFM Papers.

60. Samuel Worcester to Selah Treat, July 16, 1850, and January 6, 1852, ABCFM Papers.

61. McLoughlin, *Champions of the Cherokees*, 322.

62. Quoted in Ibid., 323.

63. Charles Torrey to Selah Treat, April 22, 1859, ABCFM Papers.

64. John B. Jones to Solomon Peck, February 18, 1856, ABMU Papers.

65. Walker, *Torchlights*, 299.

66. Evan Jones to Solomon Peck, March 15, 1850, ABMU Papers.

67. McLoughlin, *Ghost Dance*, 327–42.

68. Ibid., 336.

69. Ibid., 339–40.

70. Cited in Bass, *Cherokee Messenger*, 236. See also Robert T. Lewit, "Indian Missions and Antislavery Sentiment," *Mississippi Valley Historical Review* 50 (1963): 39–55.

71. McLoughlin, *Ghost Dance*, 460–61.

72. Quoted in Bass, *Cherokee Messenger*, 236.

73. Samuel Worcester to Selah Treat, June 30, 1851, and May 4, 1853, ABCFM Papers.

74. McLoughlin, *Champions of the Cherokees*, 352–62.

75. Samuel Worcester to Selah Treat, June 30, 1851, ABCFM Papers.

76. Samuel Worcester to Solomon Peck, February 20, 1856, ABMU Papers.

77. Solomon Peck to Samuel Worcester, March 26, 1856, ABMU Papers.

78. George M. Butler to George Manypenny, June 22, 1855, Record Group 75, M-234, Letters Received by the Office of Indian Affairs, reel 97, #0080. National Archives, Washington, D.C.

79. Originally called "Blue Lodges," the proslavery society later changed its name to the Knights of the Golden Circle. See Rudi Halliburton, *Red over Black* (Westport, Conn.: Greenwood Press, 1977), 119.

80. McLoughlin, *Champions of the Cherokees*, 369–70.

81. Robert J. Cowart to John B. Jones, September 7, 1860, ABMU Papers.

82. Rufus Anderson to Charles Torrey, March 21, 1860, ABCFM Papers.

83. Samuel Worcester to Selah Treat, June 6, 1849, and June 12, 1851, ABCFM Papers.

84. Samuel Worcester to Selah Treat, April 17, 1851, ABCFM Papers.

85. Samuel Worcester to David Greene, November 22, 1842, ABCFM Papers.

86. Daniel Butrick to David Greene, August 21, 1838, ABCFM Papers.

87. Hervey Upham to Solomon Peck, March 4, 1848, ABMU Papers.

88. Willard Upham to Solomon Peck, August 3, 1841, ABMU Papers.

89. Willard Upham to Solomon Peck, April 24, 1848, ABMU Papers.

90. Evan Jones to Solomon Peck, January 22, 1857, ABMU Papers.

91. McLoughlin, *Champions of the Cherokees*, 311.

92. Ibid., 309.

93. Edward Bright to Evan Jones, August 22, 1850, ABMU Papers.

94. John B. Jones to Solomon Peck, February 15, 1856, ABMU Papers.

95. Daniel Butrick to Selah Treat, February 6, 1850, ABCFM Papers.

96. Elizur Butler to Selah Treat, July 7, 1851, ABCFM Papers.

97. Willard Upham to Solomon Peck, March 16, 1843, ABMU Papers.

98. Berkhofer, *Salvation and the Savage*, 152.

99. Ibid., 10.

100. Ibid., 62.

Chapter 4. *The Reverend Evan Jones and the Cherokee*
Trail of Tears, 1838–1839

1. For a study of the first missions among the Cherokees, see McLoughlin, *Cherokees and Missionaries*.

2. For a more detailed study of the Valley Towns mission, see McLoughlin, *Champion of the Cherokees*.

3. See William G. McLoughlin, "The Murder Trial of Evan Jones," *North Carolina Historical Review* 62 (April 1985): 157–78.

4. For the Indian removal crisis, see Michael D. Green, *The Politics of Indian Removal* (Lincoln: University of Nebraska Press, 1982); Ronald Satz, *American Indian Policy in the Jacksonian Era* (Lincoln: University of Nebraska Press, 1975); Dale Van Every, *Disinherited: The Lost Birthright of the American Indian* (New York: William Morrow, 1966).

5. On the Removal party and the Treaty of New Echota, see Thurman Wilkins, *Cherokee Tragedy: The Ridge Family and the Decimation of a People* (Norman: University of Oklahoma Press, 1986).

6. For a detailed discussion of the removal process and the Trail of Tears,

not only for the Cherokees but also for the Creeks, Choctaws, Chickasaws, and Seminoles, see Grant Foreman, *Indian Removal: The Emigration of the Five Civilized Tribes of Indians* (Norman: University of Oklahoma Press, 1932). On the "sickly season" for traveling west, see p. 300. Further information on the Cherokee experiences is provided in William L. Anderson, ed., *Cherokee Removal: Before and After* (Athens: University of Georgia Press, 1991).

7. Daniel S. Butrick's journal of the events of 1836–38 can be found in the John Howard Payne Papers, Newberry Library, Chicago (hereafter, JHP Papers), vol. 9, pp. 66–75. This statement, made June 16, 1838, is on p. 75.

8. See the anonymous account (probably written by Dr. Elizur Butler) of the medical care in these camps published in the *Choctaw Intelligencer* (Doaksville, Choctaw Nation), July 4, 1850.

9. Quoted in Foreman, *Indian Removal*, 287.

10. Some of these accounts are taken from Evan Jones's journal in the ABMU Papers, and some from the *Baptist Missionary Magazine*, published in Boston, Mass. (hereafter, *BMM*).

11. Quoted in Walker, *Torchlights*, 324–28.

12. *BMM* 18:236.

13. Ibid., 19:67.

14. Ibid., 18:292.

15. Ibid., 19:39. Kaneeda and Tanenole were also very sick at this time.

16. Ibid., 18:292. Twenty-four were males, thirty-two females (one of these a white woman).

17. Daniel Butrick to David Greene, June 10, 1839, ABCFM Papers. Butrick, however, had criticized Samuel A. Worcester and Dr. Elizur Butler for going to jail in order to bring a test case against the laws of Georgia, which required all missionaries to sign an oath of allegiance to the state of Georgia. See McLoughlin, *Ghost Dance*, 432–48.

18. For Butrick's defense of his action to the Prudential Committee of the ABCFM, see his letter to Greene, December 5, 1839, ABCFM Papers.

19. Daniel Butrick to David Greene, June 10, 1839, ABCFM Papers. It is not clear whether Butrick and Jones discussed this action together or who acted on the issue first. Their churches probably voted on the matter in September or October 1838.

20. *BMM* 19:39.

21. Jones and Situagi's detachment arrived on February 2, 1839; Bushyhead's detachment arrived on February 23.

22. Evan Jones to John Ross, October 27, 1838, Letters and Documents, Grant Foreman Collection, Oklahoma Historical Society, Oklahoma City, 197.

23. Clipping in the Cherokee Collection, Tennessee State Archives, Nashville; *BMM* 19:64.

24. *BMM* 19:89.

25. Foreman estimates four thousand deaths during removal (*Indian Removal*, 312). A higher estimate can be found in Russell Thornton, "The Demography of the Trail of Tears Period: A New Estimate of Cherokee Population Losses," in Anderson, *Cherokee Removal*.

26. See Grant Foreman, ed., *A Traveler in Indian Territory* (Cedar Rapids, Iowa: Torch Press, 1930), for an account by Colonel E. A. Hitchcock of the corruption in supplying the Cherokees after their arrival.

Chapter 5. Missionaries as Cultural Brokers

1. For a full biography of Evan Jones and his son John, see McLoughlin, *Champions of the Cherokees*.

2. See McLoughlin, *Cherokees and Missionaries*, chap. 9; James Paul Pate, "The Chickamauga Cherokees," Ph.D. diss., Mississippi State University, 1969.

3. Cyrus Kingsbury to Samuel Worcester, December 19, 1816, ABCFM Papers.

4. Quoted in McLoughlin, *Champions of the Cherokees*, 323.

5. For slavery among the Cherokees, see Perdue, *Slavery and the Evolution of Cherokee Society*, and Halliburton, *Red over Black*.

6. On the Keetoowahs, see Chapters 9 and 10 below.

7. Quoted in McLoughlin, *Champions of the Cherokees*, 372.

8. Daniel F. Littlefield, Jr., *The Cherokee Freedmen* (Westport, Conn.: Greenwood Press, 1978), 78–80.

9. *Macedonian* 29 (October 1871): 40, quoted in McLoughlin, *Champions of the Cherokees*, 449.

10. Quoted in McLoughlin, *Champions of the Cherokees*, 449–52.

Chapter 6. Christianity and Racism: Cherokee Responses to the Debate over Indian Origins, 1760–1860

1. "Editor's Introduction" to the Autumn issue of *Critical Inquiry* 12 (1985): 6. See also Henry Louis Gates, Jr., ed., *Black Literature and Theory* (New York: Methuen, 1984).

2. For a discussion of the American School of Ethnography, see Stanton, *The Leopard's Spots*, and Stephen J. Gould, *The Mismeasure of Man* (New York: Norton, 1981). See also note 12 below.

3. See Reginald Horsman, *Race and Manifest Destiny* (Cambridge, Mass.: Harvard University Press, 1981).

4. See Perdue, *Slavery and the Evolution of Cherokee Society*, and Halliburton, *Red over Black*.

5. For details of Timberlake's life, see J. Ralph Randolph, *British Travelers among the Southern Indians, 1660–1763* (Norman: University of Oklahoma Press, 1972), 142–54. Discussion of the meeting with the king occurs in Henry Timberlake, *Lieut. Henry Timberlake's Memoirs, 1756–1765*, ed. Samuel Cole Williams (Marietta, Ga.: Continental Book Co., 1948), 143–44.

6. As Lee H. Huddleston notes, European discussions of the origins of Native Americans date from the sixteenth century. In 1511 Pedro Martir de Anglería suggested the possibility of a Jewish origin for them, and the Catholic missionaries Juan Suárez de Peralta and Diego Durán in 1580 expressed the same view. Huddleston points out that there was no agreement among early commentators as to whether the Ten Lost Tribes of Israel (mentioned in the thirteenth chapter of the apocryphal Fourth Book of Esdras) came across the Atlantic or Pacific, but many writers suggested that the children of Shem had dispersed eastward and were the founders of the Asian peoples. Thus the possibility that the Ten Lost Tribes went eastward and their descendants mingled with the Tartars and Scythians before crossing to the New World via some now lost land bridge was frequently considered up through the eighteenth century. Finally, Huddleston states that the first Jewish rabbi to press seriously the claim that the Ten Lost Tribes had immigrated to the New World was Manasseh ben Israel of Amsterdam in his book *The Hope of Israel (1560)*. He believed they came across the Straits of Anian and, having passed on some of their customs and rituals to peoples who came later (i.e., the Indians), were still practicing their old faith in secret places in the New World. There was no consensus as to whether Indian rituals, Indian language, or Indian physical characteristics were the best evidence for their origin. See Lee H. Huddleston, *Origins of the American Indians: European Concepts, 1492–1729* (Austin: University of Texas Press, 1969), 33–37, 128–33.

7. See Ola E. Winslow, *John Eliot, Apostle to the Indians* (Boston: Houghton Mifflin, 1968), 84–85.

8. James Adair, *History of the American Indians*, ed. Samuel Cole Williams (1775; reprint, New York: Promontory Press, 1968), vii–xxi, 3, 13–15.

9. Edward Brerewood, *Enquiries Touching the Diversity of Languages and Religions Through the Chief Parts of the World* (London, 1674), 117–18, 120.

10. John Ogilby, *America: Being the Latest and Most Accurate Description of the New World* (London, 1671), 37.

11. Benjamin Smith Barton, *New Views of the Origins of the Tribes and Nations of America* (Philadelphia, 1797), vii–xv.

12. See Huddleston, *Origins of the American Indians*, 138–40; Richard H. Popkin, "Pre-Adamism in Nineteenth Century American Thought: Speculative Biology and Racism," *Philosophia* 8 (1978–79): 205–39. For the emergence of polygenesis in the nineteenth century, see Stanton, *The Leopard's Spots;* Gould, *Mismeasure of Man;* Horsman, *Race and Manifest Destiny;* Fredrickson, *Black*

Image in the White Mind; and Robert E. Bieder, *Science Encounters the Indian, 1820–1880* (Norman: University of Oklahoma Press, 1986).

13. Perdue, *Slavery and the Evolution of Cherokee Society,* 47; Stanton, *The Leopard's Spots,* 20.

14. Bieder, *Science Encounters the Indian,* 62–65, 71–73; Reginald Horsman, *Josiah Nott of Mobile* (Baton Rouge: Louisiana State University Press, 1987).

15. See Thomas V. Peterson, *Ham and Japheth* (Metuchen, N.J.: Scarecrow Press, 1978), 42–44, 97–101.

16. *Arkansas Gazette,* November 12, 1858; the *Arkansas Gazette* identified *The Due West Telescope* as the organ of a "Reformed Church."

17. *Mississippi Baptist,* March 1, 1860.

18. Daniel S. Butrick, *Antiquities of the Cherokees* (Vinita, Indian Territory, 1884). The remnant of Butrick's research is available in the JHP Papers.

19. Brainerd Journal, June 23, 1818, ABCFM Papers.

20. See JHP Papers, 3:2.

21. Ibid., 3:57; 2:26; 1:57; 178; 4:14.

22. Ibid., 4:38; 1:7; 4:54.

23. Ibid., 1:12.

24. Ibid.

25. For early Cherokee contacts with English, Spanish, and French Christians, see James Mooney, *Myths of the Cherokees* (1900 reprint, Nashville: Charles and Randy Elder, 1982), 23–29, 36–37.

26. JHP Papers, 4:164.

27. Ibid.

28. John Ross, John Ross Papers, "Undated mss." folder, Gilcrease Museum, Tulsa, Okla.

29. See JHP Papers, 1:12. Significantly, just as the question of Indian origins arose in seventeenth-century England during a consideration of readmission of the Jews to England as part of a strategy to bring about the millennium, so could John Ross pose the importance of Jewish roots for the Cherokees in equally millennial terms during the removal crisis of 1835. Ross wrote, "Some of you [whites] have said that we were of the wanderers of that peculiar people [the Jews] whence true religion sprang. If it be so, imagine how glorious the effort to secure to those wanderers a home—and such a home as may realize the bright predictions which still exist unclaimed for the lost race of Israel. Who knows but our prayers may be the instruments to accelerate the fulfillment of that prophesy and should they prove so, how can we offer a return more exciting." John Ross, "The Cherokee Nation to the People of the United States," printed in the *Knoxville Register,* December 2, 1835, Ayer Collection, Newberry Library, Chicago. For a discussion of the significance of Jewish readmission for English millennial hopes, see Huddleston, *Origins of the American Indians,* 130–33.

30. *Latter Day Luminary* 3:213.

31. Cephas Washburn, *Reminiscences of the Indians* (Richmond, 1869), 214.

32. Ibid., 207.

33. Return J. Meigs to Benjamin Hawkins, February 13, 1805, cited in McLoughlin, *Cherokee Renascence*, 48.

34. Mooney, *Myths of the Cherokees*, 235–36, 351.

35. *American States Papers: Indian Affairs*, vols. 1 and 2, ed. Walter Lowrie, Walter S. Franklin, and Matthew St. Clair Clarke (Washington, D.C.: Gales and Seaton, 1832, 1834), 2:475–76.

36. Many of the myths in Mooney's *Myths of the Cherokees* were recorded many years earlier by Butrick, but it is important to note that the early missionary and the sophisticated anthropologist had very different views of Cherokee mythology. Butrick recorded the myths he heard as though they were quaint departures from Jewish tradition and history—a sign of the degradation and depravity of the sons of Shem. Mooney, three generations later, recorded myths trying to eliminate the Jewish or Christian interpolations as external perversions of authentic Cherokee myths (presumably the most authentic extended to the days prior to contact with whites). What we do not know is how much the Cherokees distinguished between "authentic" myths and "syncretic" myths. Many assimilated Cherokees of course rejected both after 1800. Some full-bloods probably tried to return to, or to retain, the oldest myths without European (or Christian) accretions. But probably many Cherokees made little distinction because Cherokee myths seemed to thrive best by growing, adding, and changing and not by remaining unchanged, as Mooney liked to think.

37. The best discussion of the Cherokee belief system and its emphasis upon harmony is in Hudson, *The Southeastern Indians*, 120–85.

38. For texts and discussions of several postcontact creation myths, see McLoughlin, *Ghost Dance*, 253–60. A Cherokee once informed Cephas Washburn that "black was a stigma fixed upon a man for crime; and all his descendants ever since had been born black." When the Cherokees organized their nation under a constitution in 1827, they excluded blacks from participating in the government and prohibited those with African blood from holding office. See Perdue, *Slavery and the Evolution of Cherokee Society*, 48.

39. The Cherokee myths that proclaimed that Indian men were hunters by the original design of the Great Spirit, of course, produced considerable resistance to acculturation in the years after 1794. But as game diminished and the hunters could no longer support their families by capturing hides and furs, they had no choice but to become farmers. Still, like most white frontier farmers, they taught their sons to hunt and trap in order to supplement their farm income and diet. From time to time ghost dance prophets urged the Cherokees to abandon farming and return to the old ways, but most Chero-

kees did not heed these calls. Still, they cherished their old myths, told them to their children, and continued to respect them as sources of spiritual truth and tribal identity.

40. One of the best examples of the Cherokees' finding slaveholding a sin can be found in an account of the converts of the northern Baptist missionary Evan Jones. Jones's converts lived in North Carolina prior to 1838 and were poor full-bloods who could not afford to own slaves. They argued that the effort to remove them from their homeland was a national sin, and "if Providence does not favor a nation, it cannot prosper. God cannot be pleased with slavery." Walker, *Torchlights*, 299. Cherokee slaveholders tended to be of mixed ancestry and to join the southern Methodists or southern Baptists, who taught that God had ordained slavery for the descendants of Ham.

41. McLoughlin, *Cherokees and Missionaries*, 199.

42. A New England missionary reported in 1818 that one Cherokee woman said that "there was nothing in [the Christian] religion, at least, that Indians would get to heaven without it, and that Christianity was necessary for white people only." Report of the Visiting Committee, May 29, 1818, ABCFM Papers.

43. Mooney, *Myths of the Cherokees*, 239–49. See also note 38 above.

44. See Catherine L. Albanese, "Exploring Regional Religion: A Case Study of the Cherokee," *History of Religions* 23 (May 1984): 344–71.

45. For Jews and Christians, history is the story of mankind's fall and redemption by a messiah. History therefore follows a straight path from the fall in the Garden of Eden to the Second Coming and the Day of Judgment, after which history on earth ends. Cherokee creation myths were designed to designate not the beginning of time but the origin of the cosmos and of the first man (a red man) as distinct from other animals. See Åke Hultkrantz, *Native Religions of North America* (New York: Harper & Row, 1988), 32–35.

46. The difficulty of withdrawal and a return to the ancient ways often led to a hope that the Great Spirit would intervene in worldly affairs to drive the white man back to Europe and return the game animals to the old hunting grounds. For such a ghost dance movement among the Cherokees, see McLoughlin, *Cherokee Renascence*, 168–86.

47. James A. Slover to E. L. Compere, June 26, 1861, Compere Papers, United Methodist Library, Nashville, Tenn.

48. Ironically, however, when the Cherokees were incorporated into the state of Oklahoma in 1908, they were legally designated as "white" and forbidden by law to marry blacks.

49. After 1865, as the Cherokees strove to prevent their detribalization, they sometimes returned to the comparison of their oppression to that of the Jews, but it was only as a metaphor. Chief Lewis Downing, an ordained Baptist minister, proclaimed a national fast day in 1870 and stated in a fast-day message, "Today the Cherokees lie in the hands of the government and people of

the United States as did the Jews in the hands of Ahasueris and the Persians."
Cherokee Advocate, October 22, 1870.

Chapter 7. Fractured Myths: The Cherokees' Use of Christianity

1. Mooney, *Myths of the Cherokees*, 235.
2. Mooney, *Myths of the Cherokees*, 510.
3. Axtell, *The Invasion Within*, 1.
4. Ibid., 14–15.
5. Ibid. Axtell is here citing Ian Watt and Jack Goody, "The Consequences of Literacy," *Comparative Studies in Society and History* 5 (1962–63): 304–5, 310, 344.
6. Axtell, *The Invasion Within*, 284–85.
7. Ibid.
8. Gregory Dowd, *A Spirited Resistance* (Baltimore: Johns Hopkins University Press, 1992), 15. See also Albanese, "Exploring Regional Religion," 3.
9. Sequoyah invented a method to write the Cherokee language in 1821, but most of that which survived was either political or personal or else sacred rituals kept by the medicine men.
10. See Butrick, *Cherokee Antiquities*, 2.
11. Dowd, *A Spirited Resistance*, 11.
12. Hudson, *The Southeastern Indians*, 121, 351.
13. John Phillip Reid, *A Law of Blood* (New York: New York University Press, 1970), 249; Fred Gearing, *Priests and Warriors: Social Structures of Cherokee Politics in the Eighteenth Century*, American Anthropological Memoir No. 93 (Menasha, Wis.: 1962), 31, 36; John D. Loftin, "The 'Harmony Ethic' of the Conservative Eastern Cherokees: A Religious Interpretation," *Journal of Cherokee Studies* 8 (Spring 1983): 40–43; Albanese, "Exploring Regional Religion," 358.
14. This is a Yuchi myth; see John R. Swanton, "Myths and Tales of the Southeastern Indians," Bureau of American Ethnology, *Bulletin 88* (Washington, D.C.: U.S. Government Printing Office, 1929), 85.
15. Mooney, *Myths of the Cherokees*, 239–40.
16. For a version of the Cherokee creation myth that states that the earth was formed by mud on the back of a turtle, see "The Wahnenauhi Manuscript," ed. Jack F. Kilpatrick, p. 187 in Smithsonian Institution, Bureau of American Ethnology, *Bulletin 196* (Washington, D.C.: U.S. Government Printing Office, 1966).
17. Swanton, "Myths and Tales," 84. Because this is a Yuchi myth, the first children of the Sun were said to be Yuchis. There were Yuchis (Euchees) living among the Cherokees in the early nineteenth century.
18. Hudson, *The Southeastern Indians*, 351.
19. Mooney, *Myths of the Cherokees*, 250, 252.

20. Cited in McLoughlin, *Cherokees and Missionaries*, 39.

21. Elizur Butler letter, September 13, 1826, ABCFM Papers.

22. Ibid.

23. *Cherokee Phoenix*, April 1, 1829.

24. A. W. Loomis, *Scenes in the Indian Country* (Philadelphia: Presbyterian Board of Publications, 1859), 52–54.

25. Swanton, "Myths and Tales," 74.

26. Ibid., 75.

27. Ibid., 75, note 1.

28. JHP Papers, 1:18.

29. This version of the myth appears in the *Indian Advocate*, published by the American Indian Missionary Association, October 1847; photostats of this paper made by Grant Foreman are in the Oklahoma Historical Society, Oklahoma City. For another version, see Thomas L. McKenney and James Hall, *History of the Indian Tribes of North America* (Philadelphia: 1838), 2:38–39.

30. Loomis, *Scenes*, 53.

31. See William G. McLoughlin, "A Note on African Sources of American Indian Racial Myths," *Journal of American Folklore* 89 (June–September 1976): 331–36.

32. From the English transcription of a report by Abraham Steiner and Christian de Schweinitz, October 28–December 28, 1799, of their visit to the Cherokee Nation, located in the Moravian Archives, Bethlehem, Pa.

33. Springplace Diary, Moravian Mission to the Cherokees, October 13, 1815, the statement of "an old Chief Named Elk," Moravian Archives, Winston-Salem, N.C.

34. Frans Olbrechts, "Eastern Cherokee Folktales," ed. Jack F. Kilpatrick and Anna Gritts Kilpatrick, 443, in *Bureau of American Ethnology Bulletin 196.*

35. Elizur Butler letter, September 13, 1826, ABCFM Papers.

36. Worcester, *Cherokee Phoenix*, April 1, 1829.

37. See McLoughlin, *Ghost Dance*, 274.

38. Steiner and de Schweinitz, Report, Moravian Archives, Bethlehem, Pa.

39. John Haywood, *Civil and Political History of Tennessee* (Knoxville, Tenn.: Heiskell and Brown, 1823), 246–47. Haywood obviously embroidered upon these lists.

40. H. B. Cushman, *History of the Choctaw, Chickasaw, and Natchez Indians* (Greenville, Tex.: Headlight Printing House, 1899), 206.

41. This statement is from "Undated Letter, #4" in the John Ross Papers, at the Gilcrease Institute, Tulsa, Okla. It has no address or signature, but it appears from the context to be a defense of Butrick's work and if not written to him was written to John Howard Payne.

42. Evan Jones's journal, February 2, 1829, ABMU Papers.

43. Ibid., October, n.d., 1828, ABMU Papers.

44. Mooney, *Myths of the Cherokees*, 351. Mooney took this myth from the *Cherokee Advocate*, October 26, 1844. One of the few myths that relate to how blacks reacted to the choices of vocation offered by the Great Spirit was recorded by Frans Olbrechts from the eastern Cherokees in 1927: "When people first began to live, there were Whites and Indians. Somebody [the Supreme Being] came to the people bringing a printed book. He first offered it to the Indians, but they didn't like it. Then He turned to the Whites and offered them the book. They took it. He also offered a bundle of barks and roots, which was medicine, to the White people, but they did not want it. He then turned around to where the Indians were, offered it to them and they took it. There were people who did not want either the book or the bundle, and laughed so much at both that their faces turned all black and their eyes white with laughing. Those were the black people." Olbrechts, "Eastern Cherokee Folktales," 443. The myth seems to imply that the choices made had something to do with changing the color of this group of rejecters, but whether they were Indians, whites, or some outside group is not clear. It would be of interest if the choice of vocation determined the color of the recipient rather than vice versa as in most myths of vocation.

45. Worcester, *Cherokee Phoenix*, April 1, 1829.

46. Haywood, *History of Tennessee*, 226.

47. Worcester, *Cherokee Phoenix*, April 1, 1829.

48. JHP Papers, 1:18.

49. JHP Papers, 1:7.

50. Washburn, *Reminiscences*, 203–4. See also Theda Perdue, "Southern Indians and the Cult of True Womanhood," in Walter Fraser et al., eds., *The Web of Southern Social Relations* (Athens: University of Georgia Press, 1985), 35–51.

51. Swanton, "Myths and Tales," 76.

52. Worcester, *Cherokee Phoenix*, April 1, 1829.

53. Brainerd Journal, July 26, 1818, ABCFM Papers.

54. JHP Papers, 10:38. This is contained in a long letter from William Turner to Payne written in 1817. He does not mention which of the western tribes he is speaking of, but his letter discusses the Miamis, Chippewas, Potowatomis, Iowas, Wyandots, Kickapoos, Winnebagos, and others.

55. Evan Jones to Solomon Peck, March 2, 1828, ABMU Papers.

56. Jeremiah Evarts, Memorandum, May 9, 1822, ABCFM Papers. This statement seems to imply what other Indians made explicit, namely that Indians went to a different place after death from whites. "Their most common excuse for not becoming Christians is that Christianity was designed for white people not Indians," said one missionary to the Sioux. See the letter from Rev. S. W. Pond to Dr. I. [J.] P. Evans, January 22, 1841, JHP Papers, 10:59. A Cherokee woman said that before she was converted she thought "that there

was nothing in [the Christian] religion, at least, that Indians would get to heaven without it, and the Christianity was necessary for white people only." Report of the Visiting Committee, May 19, 1818, ABCFM Papers.

57. Brainerd Journal, May 7, 1822, ABCFM Papers.

58. Springplace Diary, Moravian Mission to the Cherokees, June 1, 1824, Moravian Archives, Winston-Salem, N.C.

59. Haywood, *History of Tennessee*, 248.

60. Evan Jones, Journal, January 19, 1829, ABMU Papers.

61. Ibid., October, n.d., 1828, ABMU Papers.

62. JHP Papers, 1:6.

63. JHP Papers, 4:38; 1:7; 4:54; see also Mooney, *Myths of the Cherokees*, 261. For other versions of the Noah or deluge story, see Worcester, *Cherokee Phoenix*, April 1, 1829, and JHP Papers, 1:9–11.

64. For Jonah stories, see Mooney, *Myths of the Cherokees*, 320–21; JHP Papers, 1:7; and "The Wahnenauhi Manuscript," 187. For Tower of Babel stories, see JHP Papers, 1:9, and Worcester, *Cherokee Phoenix*, April 1, 1829.

65. Washburn, *Reminiscences*, 212–13.

66. Ibid., 215–16.

67. Ibid., 192.

68. Ibid.

69. Ibid., 195.

70. Ibid., 195, 199.

71. Ibid., 197.

72. Ibid., 215.

73. Ibid., 198.

74. Ibid.

75. Ibid., 201.

76. John Ross, "The Cherokee Nation to the People of the United States," *Knoxville Register*, December 2, 1835. Copy in the Ayer Collection, Newberry Library, Chicago.

77. Haywood, *History of Tennessee*, 226; see also JHP Papers, 7:5–7. Chief John Ross utilized the Red Sea story to indicate that the Cherokees might expect the Great Spirit's protection to his chosen people in a speech to the Cherokees in January 1830, just prior to the passage of the Indian Removal Act: "Let us not forget the circumstances related in Holy Writ of the safe passage of the children of Israel through the crystal walls of the Red Sea." JHP Papers, 1:12.

78. JHP Papers, 2:149–52.

79. Edmund Leach, *Political Systems of Highland Burma* (Boston: Beacon Press, 1954), 278.

80. Vine Deloria, Jr., *God Is Red* (New York: Dell, 1973); Raymond D. Fogelson, "Change, Persistence, and Accommodation in Cherokee Medico-Magical

Beliefs," 219–20, in William N. Fenton and John Gulick, eds., "Symposium on Cherokee and Iroquois Culture," Bureau of American Ethnology, *Bulletin 180* (Washington, D.C.: U.S. Government Printing Office, 1961).

Chapter 8. Accepting Christianity, 1839–1860

1. Evan Jones letter, October 12, 1827, ABMU Papers.
2. Evan Jones's journal, July 20, 1828, ABMU Papers. One old full-blood chief remarked to a missionary who had read to him some parts of the Bible through an interpreter: "It seems to be a good book; strange that the white people are not better after having had it for so long." Quoted in McLoughlin, *Cherokees and Missionaries*, 36.
3. Evan Jones letter, October 12, 1827, ABMU Papers.
4. See McLoughlin, *Champions of the Cherokees*, for a biography of Jones with details of his work among the Cherokees during removal.
5. See JHP Papers, 1:12.
6. *Cherokees and Missionaries*, 342–43.
7. Samuel Worcester letter, August 4, 1841, ABCFM Papers.
8. Daniel Butrick letter, March 10, 1838, ABCFM Papers.
9. See the letters of Samuel Worcester and Daniel Butrick for the years 1839 to 1845, ABCFM Papers. These measures were vetoed by John Ross because he did not want to offend the missionaries' agencies and the United States by giving the impression that the Cherokees were antimissionary or anti-Christian.
10. For a discussion of these creation myths and others, see McLoughlin, *Ghost Dance*, chap. 8.
11. Quoted in Butrick, *Cherokee Antiquities*, 2.
12. JHP Papers, 1:10.
13. See Mooney, *Myths of the Cherokees*, 242–49.
14. Butrick, *Cherokee Antiquities*, 7.
15. Evan Jones's journal, April 1, 1828, ABMU Papers.
16. Butrick, *Cherokee Antiquities*, 8.
17. Quoted in McLoughlin, *Champions of the Cherokees*, 76–77.
18. Butrick, *Cherokee Antiquities*, 2.
19. For statistical charts of estimated growth in the number of Cherokee converts in the various mission agencies, see McLoughlin, *Champions of the Cherokees*, 147 and 383. The Congregational and Moravian converts hovered around two hundred in each, the southern Methodists and northern Baptists rose to more than fifteen hundred. Southern Baptists and Mormons gained the fewest. See Daniel Butrick letter, April 15, 1842, ABCFM Papers.
20. Daniel Butrick letter, May 29, 1850, ABCFM Papers.

21. Charles Torrey letter, September 13, 1856, ABCFM Papers. Congregational missionaries commonly referred to revivalistic proselytizing as "wild fire," meaning uncontrolled. See also Daniel Butrick's letter, March 29, 1843, in which he criticizes his Congregational brethren for not adopting itinerant preaching.

22. Timothy Ranney letter, August 2, 1853, ABCFM Papers.

23. Quoted in McLoughlin, *Champions of the Cherokees*, 89. For a thorough discussion of the ceremonies and rituals of the Cherokees as well as their belief system, see Hudson, *The Southeastern Indians*.

24. William A. Potter, *My Autobiography* (Nashville: 1917), 33.

25. Elizur Butler letter, July 7, 1851, ABCFM Papers. The one full-blood minister among the Congregationalists, John Huss (who had been ordained prior to removal), "had lost his usefulness" in the eyes of the white Congregational missionaries because he was unable to prevent his daughter from leaving her husband and committing adultery with other men; he doubly sinned in their eyes by letting her live under his roof despite the wicked conduct. Samuel Worcester letter, June 6, 1849, ABCFM Papers. Daniel Butrick criticized full-blood Baptist ministers: "Our Baptist brethren do not believe as we do with regard to the covenant obligations of parents nor do they instruct their members so fully respecting the sacredness of the Holy Sabbath." As for native preachers among the Methodists, Butrick said, "Our Methodist brethren . . . leave their members to do very much as they please." Daniel Butrick letter, September 11, 1843, ABCFM Papers. When faced with their failure to discipline their church members, native ministers answered, "We do not pretend to study the heart," or "We are not able to read the human heart." That is, they declined to sit in judgment on the private conduct of others. See Edwin Teele letter, July, n.d., 1854, ABCFM Papers, and John Wickliffe letter, April 6, 1847, ABMU Papers.

26. Samuel Worcester letter, July 16, 1850, ABCFM Papers.

27. Timothy Ranney, June 12, 1850, ABCFM Papers.

28. Elizur Butler, July 17, 1851, ABCFM Papers.

29. Timothy Ranney, June 29, 1851, ABCFM Papers.

30. Cephas Washburn, November 9, 1837, ABCFM Papers. See also Samuel Worcester, September 19, 1849, ABCFM Papers.

31. Edwin Teele, June, n.d., 1854, ABCFM Papers.

32. Timothy Ranney, August 21, 1853, ABCFM Papers.

33. Elizur Butler, July 7, 1851, ABCFM Papers.

34. Timothy Ranney, August 21, 1853, ABCFM Papers.

35. Evan Jones letter, October 12, 1827, ABMU Papers.

36. Evan Jones letter, August 26, 1844. See also his letter of August 6, 1844, ABMU Papers.

37. Lewis Downing et al. in Evan Jones letter, April 6, 1847, ABMU Papers.

Much to the regret of the Methodist circuit riders, the Arkansas Methodist Conference decided not to spend any money on translations or printing the Bible in Sequoyan. However, the circuit riders sometimes used the translations made by the Congregationalists and Baptists. There was considerable controversy between the Congregational translator and printer, Samuel Worcester, and Evan Jones, the Baptist translator and printer, over the word "baptize." Jones tried to make his translation imply that baptism was by total immersion; Worcester tried to imply that baptism was by pouring or sprinkling water. For this, see McLoughlin, *Champions of the Cherokees*, 350–51.

38. Willard Upham, August 3, 1841, ABMU Papers.

39. Hervey Upham, March 4, 1848, ABMU Papers. Daniel Butrick, the Congregationalist, also believed that the Baptists' success was essentially due to their native ministers. Daniel Butrick, November 10, 1841, ABCFM Papers. For a list of the native Baptist preachers, see McLoughlin, *Champions of the Cherokees*, 146, 305.

40. Timothy Ranney, June 12, 1858, ABCFM Papers.

41. Edwin Teele, June, n.d., 1854, ABCFM Papers.

42. Daniel Butrick, May 29, 1850, ABCFM Papers.

43. "There are very few young persons in our churches and almost no young men," wrote Samuel Worcester (June 10, 1857, ABCFM Papers). It appears from general remarks that women converts outnumbered men in all denominations.

44. Evan Jones, March 26, 1849, ABMU Papers, and February 6, 1850, ABMU Papers.

45. Elizur Butler (April 26, 1845, ABCFM Papers) describes the effort to use Christian prayer in his mission church to bring rain during a bad drought. What is more, he did so deliberately to compete with the local *adonisgi* who were also performing invocations for rain. Similarly, prayers for the recovery of the sick were also competitive, or perhaps complementary, for some Cherokees.

46. Quoted in McLoughlin, *Champions of the Cherokees*, 74.

47. Ibid. He subsequently admitted this woman to his church.

48. Timothy Ranney, June 12, 1850, ABCFM Papers.

49. Jacob Hitchcock, October 13, 1842, ABCFM Papers.

50. Cited in Carolyn Foreman, "History of Tahlequah," typescript, Grant Foreman Papers, Box 59, Gilcrease Institute, Tulsa, Okla.

51. McLoughlin, *Cherokees and Missionaries*, 201–2; Charles Torrey, June 16, 1856, ABCFM Papers.

52. Daniel Butrick to Jeremiah Evarts, November 24, 1824, ABCFM Papers; Marcus Palmer Report, February 12, 1855, ABCFM Papers. Butrick with some foresight also noted at this time that the Cherokees were fast becoming two nations: "Unless peculiar caution is used, two parties will be formed which

will probably be called, though falsely, the Christian and Pagan. I say 'falsely' because objections arising from an appearance of pride and superiority cannot be said to arise from opposition to God [but rather arise from tensions of social class]." Edwin Teele noted in 1854 that this tension had dramatically increased: "There is a growing feeling of hostility between the full and mixed bloods which in a few years will probably lead to serious results" (June, n.d., 1854, ABCFM Papers).

53. See Daniel Butrick, February 6, 1850, ABCFM Papers. At this time he estimated that there were twelve hundred Baptist converts, almost all fullbloods, and two thousand Methodists, only half of whom were full-bloods.

Chapter 9. Cherokee Syncretism: The Origins of the Keetoowah Society, 1854–1861

1. Keetoowah has been spelled many ways, including Kituwha, Keetoowha, Kituwah, Ketoowa, and Ketowa. In this essay I have used the spelling Keetoowah to refer to the society formed in 1858 and Kituwah to refer to the ancient organization that antedates the arrival of Europeans in America.

2. For the last estimate, see *The Papers of Chief John Ross*, ed. Gary E. Moulton (Norman: University of Oklahoma Press, 1978), 2:596 (hereafter, *Ross Papers*). These totals usually refer to male members, but obviously their families may have sympathized with them.

3. For the last view, see Starr, *Cherokee Indians*, 479. See also pp. 140 and 258.

4. Halliburton, *Red over Black*, 118; E. E. Dale and Gaston Litton, *Cherokee Cavaliers* (Norman: University of Oklahoma Press, 1919), 225.

5. Mooney, *Myths of the Cherokees*, 225, note 47.

6. Abel, *Indians as Slaveholders*, 135. Pike made this statement in 1866. The terms "half-breed," "mixed-blood," and "full-blood," are seldom defined by those who use them. Many also note that white men who married Cherokees were often involved, usually on the side opposing the Keetoowahs.

7. Starr, *Cherokee Indians*, 479. There is no evidence that there were any Quakers among the Cherokees in the years 1855 to 1870, certainly not as agents of any mission society. Starr also fails to note the important division between the northern and southern Methodists, Baptists, and Presbyterians. Nor do most historians hazard estimates as to what proportions of the Keetoowah members were Christians by conversion, Christian congregants, and traditionalist opponents of Christianity.

8. Dale and Litton, *Cherokee Cavaliers*, 57.

9. Halliburton, *Red over Black*, 144. The critical difference between being "antislavery" and "abolitionist" in that era is seldom noted by historians; among rabid proslavery people the two were blurred, but in the northern

states and among the northern missionaries, the distinction was vital. Few ever would have called themselves "abolitionists," a term connoting Garrisonian fanatics.

10. Grace Woodward, *The Cherokees* (Norman: University of Oklahoma Press, 1963), 7–8. I have found no statement by either of the Joneses that mentions their taking any part in forming or assisting the Keetoowah Society, but that is because only their official correspondence survives. I have no doubt of their crucial role in founding and guiding it.

11. Gary E. Moulton, *John Ross, Cherokee Chief* (Athens: University of Georgia Press, 1978), 163.

12. Morris L. Wardell, *A Political History of the Cherokee Nation* (Norman: Oklahoma University Press, 1938), 120–22.

13. T. L. Ballenger, "The Keetoowahs," typescript, Ballenger Papers, Newberry Library, Chicago, 107.

14. Carolyn Foreman, "History of Tahlequah," 148.

15. Marion Starkey, *The Cherokee Nation* (New York: Knopf, 1946), 320. I have found no such philosophical statement in any Keetoowah document. I would also guess that there were no African Americans admitted to the society. Some have said that the Pin Indians helped Cherokee slaves to escape to Kansas, and that may have been true after the war began and especially when many Cherokee refugees fled to Kansas, but I have some doubt about Keetoowahs ever engaging in an Underground Railroad to Kansas prior to the war as some have suggested.

16. In this respect the Keetoowah movement may be said to resemble White Path's Rebellion in 1827 or some of the later ghost dance movements among the Plains Indians.

17. See Ballenger, "The Keetoowahs," 108.

18. Howard Q. Tyner, "The Keetoowah Society in Cherokee History," master's thesis, University of Tulsa, 1949, app. A.

19. Eula E. Fullerton, "Some Social Institutions of the Cherokees, 1820–1902," master's thesis, University of Oklahoma, 1931. The translation of the "Keetoowah Constitution" by Sam Smith is also in the Bureau of American Ethnology, Smithsonian Institution, Washington, D.C.

20. Starr, *Cherokee Indians*, 479. Starr lists Pig Redbird Smith, Budd Gritts, and Vann as the founders of the Keetoowah Society. There are some untranslated documents in the Sequoyan syllabary that seem to be records of the Keetoowah Society in the Scheppey Collection at the University of Tulsa. It is clearly inaccurate to place all "full-bloods" in one category and all "mixedbloods" and intermarried whites in another when speaking of the factional division within the Nation, the best proof of this being the Ross family and its influential relatives and friends. Nonetheless, the generalization holds in most respects, and I follow common practice in this essay.

21. See Perdue, *Slavery and the Evolution of Cherokee Society*, and Halliburton, *Red over Black*, for discussions of the growth of slavery among the Cherokees. Estimates vary, but there were probably about 4,000 black slaves in the Cherokee Nation in 1860 and perhaps 100 to 150 freed slaves. The Cherokee population at this time was about 22,000, including blacks and intermarried whites.

22. For details of the lives of Evan and John B. Jones, see McLoughlin, *Champions of the Cherokees*.

23. A copy of Ross's letter, May 5, 1855, is among the papers of Evan Jones in the American Baptist Missionary Union files of the American Baptist Historical Society, Rochester, N.Y. Hereafter, all letters from Evan or John B. Jones will be listed simply as "Jones B. Papers, ABMU," with dates.

24. Ross included this oath in his letter of May 5, 1855.

25. There were never any northern Methodist missionaries among the Cherokees. When one appeared briefly in 1849, he was mobbed and left. See Perdue, *Slavery and the Evolution of Cherokee Society*, 123.

26. For the details of this episode, see McLoughlin, *Ghost Dance*, 449–72.

27. Halliburton, *Red over Black*, 100, and Moulton, *John Ross*, 162.

28. Cited in Mooney, *Myths of the Cherokees*, 226.

29. The exact location of the church is not clear. Evan Jones said it was thirteen to fifteen miles south of Baptist Mission. This would place it in Going Snake District, but it appears to have been located earlier in Flint District.

30. Downing served in the council from 1853 to 1857 and 1859 to 1861. See Starr, *Cherokee Indians*, 262–82. He always considered himself a full-blood even though he was of mixed ancestry. For details of his long and distinguished career, see McLoughlin, *Champions of the Cherokees*, passim.

31. Slover was appointed missionary to the Cherokees by the Domestic and Indian Mission Board of the Southern Baptist Convention in 1857. See his letter from Tahlequah explaining his mission and asking for financial support in the *Mississippi Baptist* (Jackson, Miss.), September 15, 1857.

32. John B. Jones Papers, ABMU, July 12, 1858.

33. John B. Jones Papers, ABMU, May 5, 1858. John Foster had assisted Evan Jones in translating the Bible into Cherokee after his first translator, Jesse Bushyhead, died in 1844. Foster joined the southern Baptists after he was dismissed from the northern Baptists for refusing to give up slaveholding in 1852.

34. John B. Jones Papers, ABMU, July 12, 1858.

35. Ibid. Preston S. Brooks was the Congressman from South Carolina who had caned the Massachusetts antislavery senator Charles Sumner into bloody insensibility on the floor of the United States Senate in May 1856 to the great delight of many proslavery southerners.

36. John B. Jones Papers, ABMU, July 12, 1858.

37. It is possible to identify some Baptist candidates for office from the letters of Evan and John Jones and from the list of council members given in Starr, *Cherokee Indians*, 266–86. I have been able to identify three who won election in the years 1855 to 1860: Lewis Downing, Henry Davis, and Budd Gritts. Another Baptist preacher, David M. Foreman, was chief justice of the Cherokee supreme court.

38. John B. Jones Papers, ABMU, July 12, 1858.

39. For these bills before the council, see Halliburton, *Red over Black*, 100, 102; Moulton, *John Ross*, 162–63; McLoughlin, *Ghost Dance*, 464.

40. For Wilkinson's defection and John Jones's effort to stop him, see the *Western Recorder and Baptist Banner and Pioneer* (Louisville, Ky.), July 11, 1859.

41. The northern Baptists paid only $150 per year to their native Cherokee preachers.

42. John B. Jones Papers, ABMU, November 17, 1859. The loss of more than thirty Cherokees in the area of the Pea Vine Church to the southern Baptists indicates that many full-bloods were not antislavery by conviction.

43. Ibid.

44. Ibid. Davis was at this time a representative to the National Council from Delaware District. Jones did not mention the Keetoowah Society by name in this or any other letter. He too was sworn to secrecy.

45. Mooney, *Myths of the Cherokees*, 226.

46. John B. Jones Papers, ABMU, November 17, 1859. The Joneses both disowned the title "abolitionist" but called themselves "antislavery."

47. Ibid.

48. Ibid. John Jones was prepared to force Butler to employ federal troops if he wanted to remove him.

49. Ibid.

50. See app. A of Howard Tyner's thesis for this document. I have appended it to this essay for easier reference. The paragraphs of the document are numbered, and I refer to these numbers in the text.

51. Tyner's document may be a translation of the Keetoowah records in the Scheppey Collection at the University of Tulsa library. It was apparently translated from Cherokee by Levi Gritts in 1930, perhaps in connection with the Frank J. Boudinot case (the wording of this translation is the same as that in the Ballenger transcript mentioned in note 13 above). Boudinot was the attorney for one of the later Keetoowah organizations, the Keetoowah Society Incorporated.

52. The term "teachers" probably refers to northern Baptist missionaries hired by the Cherokee Nation to teach in the public schools. There were two such teachers in Going Snake District in the 1850s, Thomas Frye and Willard P. Upham. Their letters to the board indicate that they were fearful of losing their jobs to proslavery southern Methodist teachers. See McLoughlin, *Champions*

of the Cherokees, passim. The bill passed by the council and vetoed by Ross in 1855 was designed to get rid of abolitionist teachers in the public schools. Halliburton, *Red over Black,* 100.

53. Budd Gritts died in 1867. This statement was probably written in 1865 or 1866. There is another possible source of the movement suggested by Emmet Starr. He notes that Pig Redbird Smith was a person strongly devoted to sustaining Cherokee traditionalism, and he may have already organized a group called "Keetoowahs" by 1858. Gritts and the Joneses may have built their organization around this base, but it seems unlikely. It is also possible that a group called "Keetoowahs" was organized in western North Carolina in the area of the old Nation (where Evan Jones had preached) during the removal crisis in the 1830s. Starr, *Cherokee Indians,* 479.

54. Professor Raymond Fogelson has suggested that the use of the term "lodge" as the basic unit of the Keetoowah Society may reflect an effort to draw upon the continuing Cherokee concept of town organization and town house or council house. Although town organizations had been destroyed in the scattered settlements after removal, "the idea of a 'town' or 'district' as a metaphysical ideal never is fully extinguished in Cherokee thought." It is also possible that the term "lodge" was designed, Fogelson suggests, to complement the proslavery lodges and, like them, were secret. Raymond Fogelson to the author, August 12, 1986.

55. For the Cherokee creation myth about Selu and Kanati, see Mooney, *Myths of the Cherokees,* 242–49.

56. Fogelson suggests that while matriliny had greatly declined by 1858, the full-bloods probably retained their clan identity but tried to hide it from others out of fear of sorcery and witchcraft (which required clan identification of victims). Letter to the author, August 12, 1986.

57. As Halliburton notes, there was nothing in Cherokee history to make opposition to slavery a matter of conscience. Cherokees had enslaved war captives for centuries. Only the northern Baptist Christians in the Keetoowah organization held that slavery was a sin. In order to regain control of the government, the Keetoowahs had to include far more than the fifteen hundred northern Baptist church members (many of whom were women and could not vote). Probably, however, many poor Cherokees saw that the possession of slaves gave the mixed-bloods and intermarried whites an economic advantage in engrossing communal land and for that reason objected to slavery. Halliburton, *Red over Black,* 144.

58. Nothing is said here or elsewhere in the Tyner document about wearing crossed pins or any other symbol of identification. It was evidently expected at first that the members would know one another from lodge meetings. As the movement expanded, this became more difficult, and someone originated the

pins as an unobtrusive mark of identification as well as other secret gestures mentioned by MacGowan.

59. Fogelson suggests that the term "captains" derives from *ska-gus-ta,* the name used to define a war chief or the head of the cooperative work organizations called *ga-du-gi.* The term had symbolic value. Letter to the author, August 12, 1986.

60. The Tyner document contains twenty "chapters" (using Roman numerals) that are subdivided into thirty-two paragraphs numbered consecutively in Arabic numerals. Why these are not listed and numbered in their chronological order is not known, for most of the paragraphs (being resolutions or "laws") are dated. Sometimes the paragraphs are not dated, however, and my dating rests upon assumptions from the grouping of them among those that are dated and in the same "chapter." In the analysis that follows, I have taken up the "laws" in chronological order:

1858: April 15, first deliberations
      April 20, Gritts's statement of purpose (adopted by organizers)
1859: April 29, Chap. I, paragraphs 1–3 (Gritts's "constitution")
1860: March 5, Chaps. IV–V, paragraphs 12–17
      June 20, Chaps. VI–VII, paragraphs 18–19
      September 11, Chap. I, paragraphs 4–6
      September 20, Chap. III, paragraphs 7–11
      Chaps. VIII–XI, paragraphs 20–23
      December 18, Chaps. XII–XV, paragraphs 24–27
1861: March 5, Chap. XVII, paragraph 29
      March 15, Chap. XVI, paragraph 28
      July 15, Chap. XVIII, paragraph 30
1866: January 8, Chap. XIX, paragraph 31
      January 9, Chap. XX, paragraph 32

I have found no records of resolution or "laws" passed during the war years and none for 1867 to 1875. There are records for the "Re-organized" Keetoowah Society for 1876 and after, but these lie outside the scope of this essay.

61. See Starr, *Cherokee Indians,* 263, for this definition of full-blood.

62. For Cherokee scrip and warrants, see Moulton, *John Ross,* 157–59.

63. See, for example, the report of E. H. Carruth on the Keetoowahs written on July 1, 1861, and quoted in Abel, *Indians as Slaveholder,* 84–87.

64. See note 59 above and also Raymond D. Fogelson and Paul Kutsche, "Cherokee Economic Cooperatives: The Gadugi," in *Symposium on Cherokee and Iroquois Culture,* ed. William Fenton and John Gulick, Bureau of American Ethnology, *Bulletin 180,* 83–124.

Chapter 10. Political Polarization and National Unity:
The Keetoowah Society, 1860–1871

1. For Bickley's career, see Frank L. Klement, *The Copperheads in the Middle West* (Chicago: University of Chicago Press, 1960), and Frank L. Klement, *Dark Lanterns* (Baton Rouge: Louisiana State University Press, 1984).

2. John Rollin Ridge was raised in Fayetteville but murdered a man in the Cherokee Nation in 1846 and fled to California. In 1866 he became a member of the delegation of Watie's "Southern party" in Washington seeking a division of the Cherokee Nation. See James W. Parins, *John Rollin Ridge* (Lincoln: University of Nebraska Press, 1991).

3. John Ross continued to be supported as chief by those of the Cherokee Home Guard regiments that occupied Fort Gibson from 1863 to 1865, but they could hardly be said to have controlled the Nation while Watie's men waged their scorched-earth policy through it. Neither party could legitimately claim to rule in those years when Ross lived in Washington.

4. This document is in the Special Collections at Northeastern State University, Tahlequah, Okla. See also Halliburton, *Red over Black*, 119–20.

5. W. P. Adair to Stand Watie, July 17, 1860, Stand Watie Papers, Western History Collections, University of Oklahoma, Norman (hereafter, WHC.)

6. These bills are discussed in McLoughlin, *Champions of the Cherokees*, and Halliburton, *Red over Black*.

7. McLoughlin, *Champions of the Cherokees*, 337–42, 364–76.

8. Quoted in McLoughlin, *Ghost Dance*, 469.

9. Ibid.

10. Robert Cowart to John B. Jones, September 17, 1860, ABMU Papers.

11. W. P. Adair to Stand Watie, July 17, 1860, Watie Papers, WHC, and McLoughlin, *Champions of the Cherokees*, 371–72.

12. Quoted in McLoughlin, *Champions of the Cherokees*, 372.

13. Ibid., 370.

14. Ibid., 371.

15. Moulton, *John Ross*, 167–73. The neutrality proclamation was dated May 17, 1861.

16. J. P. Evans to John Ross, July 2, 1861, Papers of John Ross, Gilcrease Institute, Tulsa, Okla. (hereafter, Gilcrease).

17. W. Craig Gaines, *The Confederate Cherokees* (Baton Rouge: Louisiana State University Press, 1989), 16. For other accounts of this incident, see Perdue, *Slavery and the Evolution of Cherokee Society*, 130, and Abel, *Indians as Slaveholders*, 86.

18. *Ross Papers*, 2:477.

19. Kenny A. Franks, *Stand Watie* (Memphis: Memphis State University Press, 1979), 117.

20. Henry F. Buckner to E. L. Compere, from Tahlequah, June 20, 1861, cited in McLoughlin, *Champions of the Cherokees*, 391.

21. Ibid.

22. *Ross Papers*, 2:479.

23. Ibid., 2:481; Moulton, *John Ross*, 172–73. Some reports say only about eighteen hundred Cherokees attended this council; Ross claimed four thousand did so. See *Ross Papers*, 2:487.

24. W. P. Adair to Stand Watie, August 29, 1861, in Dale and Litton, *Cherokee Cavaliers*, 108–9.

25. Ibid.

26. *Ross Papers*, 2:483.

27. Quoted in Gaines, *The Confederate Cherokees*, 15. Albert Pike described Drew's regiment as "chiefly full-bloods and Pins." Abel, *Indians as Slaveholders*, 137.

28. *Ross Papers*, 2:488. After the war, Watie's friends admitted that "a few of Stand Watie's friends did attend the convention; they numbered between fifty and sixty, and went there armed and in a body," but they did so only "to protect themselves." See pamphlet by Elias Boudinot and W. P. Adair entitled *Reply of the Southern Delegates,* published in Washington, D.C., 1866, p. 7. A copy is located at the Gilcrease Institute, Tulsa, Okla.

29. There are no signatures on this document, but it appears to be the one referred to by Stapler. It is located in the "Unprocessed" file at WHC.

30. Several accounts tell of an effort by the Southern party to raise a Confederate flag in Tahlequah and the Pins preventing it, but it is not clear whether this occurred at the council on August 20 or in October just prior to signing the treaty. See Charles C. Royce, *The Cherokee Nation of Indians* (Chicago: Aldine, 1975), 203. See also Rachel C. Eaton, *John Ross and the Cherokee Indians* (Chicago: University of Chicago Press, 1921), 127–28. Eaton indicates that Ross was called upon to put down this confrontation, but she gives a much earlier date, April or May 1861. All accounts agree that a Confederate flag was raised in Tahlequah after the signing of the treaty.

31. Gaines, *The Confederate Cherokees*, 45–51. Gaines states that 430 out of 480 of Drew's regiment fought with Opothleyaholo; 300 of these returned to the Nation and were pardoned by Ross on December 19. Watie's regiment did not join the fight against Opothleyaholo until the end of December when Opothleyaholo's band had almost reached Kansas. For Ross's defense of the desertions, see *Communication of the Delegation of the Cherokee Nation to the President of the United States* (Washington, D.C.: Gibson Brothers, 1866), January 31, 1866, p. 11, a copy of which is at the Gilcrease Institute, Tulsa, Okla.

32. Gaines, *The Confederate Cherokees*, 102–4.

33. Moulton, *John Ross*, 175. In a pamphlet written by the Ross party delegates to the commissioner of Indian Affairs, they provided a document by one

of Weer's officers who said that Weer's invading expedition in July 1862 knew full well that "as soon as the U.S. troops advanced into the Nation the loyal Indians, including Col. Drew's regiment would join [them]." *Reply of the Delegates of the Cherokee Nation to the Pamphlet of the Commissioner of Indian Affairs* (Washington, D.C.: Gibson Brothers 1866). A copy of this is at the Gilcrease Institute, Tulsa, Okla.

34. Wardell, *Political History*, 171–74. The original records of this council are in the Oklahoma Historical Society, Oklahoma City (hereafter, OHS).

35. *Oklahoman*, August 21, 1949. Clipping in the Foreman Collection, OHS.

36. *Ross Papers*, 2:596.

37. Ibid., 2:623.

38. Wardell, *Political History*, 122. Wardell also says, "The Keetoowah Society was doubtless the nucleus of the Loyal League organized in the closing months of 1860 or early in 1861." Other writers have also claimed that the two organizations were separate and distinct although with overlapping membership. Some have also said that the Keetoowahs and the Pins were two separate organizations; see Janey B. Hendrix, *Redbird Smith and the Nighthawk Keetoowahs* (Park Hill, Okla.: Park Hill Cross Cultural Center, 1983.). Hendrix says, "Not all Keetoowahs belonged to the Pins, although probably all the Pins were Keetoowahs" (5–6). I have serious doubts about both these claims.

39. Ross delegation, *Communication of the Delegation*, January 31, 1866, 6.

40. Boudinot and Adair statement, February 1866, *Reply of the Southern Delegates*, 3–10.

41. The Southern party admitted to being a minority but exaggerated its size in this pamphlet, claiming to be eight thousand out of eighteen thousand Cherokees. Most historians place their number between five thousand and six thousand.

42. Ross delegation, *Reply of the Delegates*, 13.

43. For the Downing party, see McLoughlin, *Champions of the Cherokees*, 439–43.

44. William N. West to James M. Bell, March 1873, in Bell Papers, WHC.

45. See the Tyner document, app. A.

46. Tyner's thesis contains the laws of the "Re-organized Keetoowah Society" in 1876. Paragraph 5 of the revised laws states, "There shall be various secret lodges in various districts," and paragraph 19 refers to "an act of November 3, 1870," that is here repudiated: "We therefore withdraw that part and we go back to the act of April 29, 1859 wherein it provides it shall be a secret Keetoowah Society" (pp. 113, 115). The reason for the reorganization appears to have been the disastrous administration of William P. Ross, 1872–75, which badly divided the Nation and led to considerable bloodshed. See McLoughlin, *Champions of the Cherokees*, 466–81.

47. See the statement of Elizabeth Ross, #506 in "Pioneer History" oral interviews, typescript at OHS.

48. Starr, *Cherokee Indians*, 480, and Muriel Wright, *A Guide to the Indian Tribes of Oklahoma* (Norman: University of Oklahoma Press, 1951), 75.

Chapter 11. Fighting against Civilization:
Ghost Dance Movements in Cherokee History

1. See Anthony F. C. Wallace, "Revitalization Movements: Some Theoretical Considerations for Their Comparative Study," *American Anthropologist*, n.s., 58 (1956): 265, and Alice Beck Kehoe, *The Ghost Dance: Ethnohistory and Revitalization* (New York: Holt, Rhinehart, and Winston, 1989), 27, 123.

2. David Aberle, "A Note on the Relative Deprivation Theory As Applied to Millenarian and Other Cult Movements," in Sylvia L. Thrupp, ed., *Millennial Dreams in Action* (The Hague: Mouton, 1962), 209. See also Peter Worsley, *The Trumpet Shall Sound* (New York: Schocken Books, 1974), 239, 47, and Kehoe, *Ghost Dance*, 107.

3. Mooney, *Ghost Dance Religion*, 676–77. See also Willard W. Hill, "The Navaho Indians and the Ghost Dance of 1890," *American Anthropologist* 46 (1944): 523–27; Russell Thornton, *We Shall Live Again: The 1870 and 1890 Ghost Dance Movements as Demographic Revitalizations* (Cambridge: Cambridge University Press, 1986), 14; Kehoe, *Ghost Dance*, 110; and McLoughlin, *Ghost Dance*, 111–52.

4. See McLoughlin, *Ghost Dance*, 111–52.

5. See McLoughlin, *Cherokees and Missionaries*, 213–38.

6. Ibid., 332–33.

7. Samuel Worcester, *Cherokee Almanac* (Park Hill, Cherokee Nation: American Board of Commissioners for Foreign Missions, 1840), 20.

8. Jacob Hitchcock to David Greene, October 13, 1842, ABCFM Papers.

9. Carolyn Foreman, "History of Tahlequah."

10. Tyner, "Keetoowah Society."

11. Starr, *Cherokee Indians*, 479–87; Tyner, "Keetoowah Society."

12. Kehoe, *Ghost Dance*, 13, 7, 44–45, 47–48.

13. Thornton, *We Shall Live Again*, 7.

14. Henry F. Dobyns and Robert C. Euler, *The Ghost Dance of 1889 among the Pai Indians of Northwestern Arizona* (Prescott: Prescott College Press, 1967), 2, 19; Wallace, "Revitalization Movements," 265.

15. Wallace, "Revitalization Movements," 270–74.

16. See Wardell, *Political History*, 121; Perdue, *Slavery and the Evolution of Cherokee Society*, 129–30; Halliburton, *Red over Black*, 118–20.

17. See Moulton, *John Ross*, 191–96.

18. Wardell, *Political History*, 212.

19. Garold D. Barney, *Mormons, Indians, and the Ghost Dance Religion of 1890* (Lanham, Md.: University Press of America, 1986), 2–8.

20. Morris Wardell's history of the Cherokees accepted the accuracy of the letter but did not quote from it. See Wardell, *Political History*, 212. For the text of the letter, see William L. G. Miller to Commissioner of Indian Affairs, October 2, 1867, in Record Group 75, M-234 (Letters Received by the Office of Indian Affairs, 1824–1881), reel 101, frames 0455–58, Bureau of Indian Affairs, Washington, D.C.

21. Duane Champagne, "Social Structure, Revitalization Movements, and State Building: Social Change in Four Native American Societies," *American Sociological Review* 48 (1983): 754–63.

Index